2nd ACM Chapter International Conference on Educational Technology, Language and Technical Communication (ETLTC2020)

SHS Web of Conferences Volume 77 (2020)

Aizuwakamatsu, Japan
27 - 31 January 2020

Editor:

Debopriyo Roy

ISBN: 978-1-7138-1067-4

Printed from e-media with permission by:

Curran Associates, Inc.
57 Morehouse Lane
Red Hook, NY 12571

Some format issues inherent in the e-media version may also appear in this print version.

No changes have been made to the content of these proceedings. There may be changes to pagination and minor adjustments for aesthetics.

Printed with permission by Curran Associates, Inc. (2021)

For additional information, please contact EDP Sciences – Web of Conferences
at the address below.

EDP Sciences – Web of Conferences
17, Avenue du Hoggar
Parc d'Activité de Courtabœuf
BP 112
F-91944 Les Ulis Cedex A
France

Phone: +33 (0) 1 69 18 75 75
Fax: +33 (0) 1 69 28 84 91

contact-edps@webofconferences.org

Additional copies of this publication are available from:

Curran Associates, Inc.
57 Morehouse Lane
Red Hook, NY 12571 USA
Phone: 845-758-0400
Fax: 845-758-2633
Email: curran@proceedings.com
Web: www.proceedings.com

TABLE OF CONTENTS

Statement of Peer review

In submitting conference proceedings to *Web of Conferences*, the editors of the proceedings certify to the Publisher that

1. They adhere to its **Policy on Publishing Integrity** in order to safeguard good scientific practice in publishing.
2. All articles have been subjected to peer review administered by the proceedings editors.
3. Reviews have been conducted by expert referees, who have been requested to provide unbiased and constructive comments aimed, whenever possible, at improving the work.
4. Proceedings editors have taken all reasonable steps to ensure the quality of the materials they publish and their decision to accept or reject a paper for publication has been based only on the merits of the work and the relevance to the journal.

Title, date and place of the conference

ETLTC2020 ACM Chapter International Conference on Educational Technology, Language and Technical Communication

27-31st January 2020

Aizuwakamatsu, JAPAN

Proceedings editor(s):

Professor Dr. Debopriyo Roy

Date and editor's signature

04/27/2020

Educational Technology, Language and Technical Communication (ETLTC2020): Connecting the Dots

Debopriyo Roy
The University of Aizu, Dept. of Computer Science and Engineering, Japan

Abstract: This preface is an attempt to highlight how ETLTC2020 took an interdisciplinary approach to understand different research topics in the fields of educational technology, language and technical communication, and special topics in computer science, biomedical engineering and smart cities. This was a forum to explore how these different topics have different objectives and goals but how the researchers could collaborate and network towards more interdisciplinary research in these different areas of applied linguistics. Importantly, this conference was also an opportunity for student-student collaboration preparing them with project management and intercultural communication skills for the future workplace.

1. The Conference Focus

The ETLTC 2020 conference theme – Education Technology, Language, and Technical Communication was a collaboration between the use of technology in global education and the language that communicates such use to improve both education quality and customer satisfaction worldwide – was an opportunity to create synergy between educators and industry professionals across a wide spectrum of applications.
The conference's three cross-cutting themes were designed to help unpack the interrelations of quality education, use of technology for academic and industrial learning, and the technical communication that will help people understand the details of the use of such technology through the lenses of linguists and technical communicators, consumers of technology, customers who handle e-commerce technologies and interfaces that lead to learning; teachers including corporate trainers; education specialists, school and corporate leadership, and school and corporate governance.
ETLTC's community of educational researchers, policymakers, and practitioners increasingly recognize that educational and industrial challenges in the use of technology, language and communication are getting increasingly complex, dynamic and multidimensional. ETLTC was, therefore, an attempt to create a platform for exchange, learning, and collaboration between professionals who are working directly in the industry or in close association with it, and traditional faculty and students who work with different educational technologies in daily life. This platform also allowed the attendees to understand how to bridge the gap between what we teach in our classes, and how useful it is in real life industry (transfer skills).

2. The Fields of Research: Exploring the Topics with Opportunities for Interdisciplinary Research

Clearly, the overarching theme or question that binds educational or instructional technology, technical communication and language sciences, is how to design instructions in a way such that the design and use of language and/or the technology in combination, creates a channel, communicates a message or develop instructions for students, customers, vendors, clients etc. towards achieving a goal. When our papers for the conference talked about innovative approaches to teaching technical communication, it was mostly about the use of instructional technology or other educational software to foster technical communication pedagogy both for academic or industry [1]. Similarly, many of the language-related papers submitted for the conference focused on pronunciation research or language testing and acquisition but with the sole purpose of explaining or involving the use of an educational technology for the purpose of language learning, teaching and use in academic or commercial situations.
Educational technology or instructional technology is a systematic application and a disciplined approach to using relevant technological processes and resources in teaching with the ultimate goal of improving student performance and learning [2]. The use of technological processes and resources must be relevant to the curriculum goals and milestones, and consistent with the needs of the institution and the community at large. The need and demand to engage with technology on a daily basis both in and outside of the classroom is like never before. Technology is part of their lifestyle and the time spent with smartphones and tablets, YouTube etc. is tremendous, making learning more fun and accessible for today's students. Now, teachers are demanding it too. Technology is making the engagement with students more

diversified and time-independent, providing students with the much-needed flexibility both in terms of time and engagement patterns. Most importantly, technology is probably enriching the learning experience, and in this digital age such accessibility is becoming the new normal. However, that does not mean technology can replace teachers, and the argument is valid even with the onset of AI. Technology is there to complement human teaching, not replacing it. However, a big question to answer is does technology improve education? Some scholars will differentiate between enriching the learning experience and improving the learning itself. However, there could be strong reasoning to suggest that both experience and learning can happen simultaneously. When teachers use technology effectively, it will keep the students engaged in the learning process. Teachers need to pick the right tools for specific tasks, tests and goals. The flipped classroom model, and optimization of the blended learning format geared toward student needs could be a huge advantage, and added to that the flexible pace of learning, and collaboration in online teams should make both the learning and the experience better suited to student needs [3].

Another topic that is increasingly being researched in applied linguistics is technical communication. The academic community has been researching technical communication for a long time now, but much of that research is quite a bit independent and set apart from how technical communication is looked at, and used in the industry. Fortunately, academic research has addressed that point [4].

Technical communication in the industry is more into managing documentation processes including increased volumes, complexity and deliverables; delivering more languages to support more markets; reducing costs and shortening delivery timeframes; maintaining the highest quality, clarity and consistency to meet increased regulatory, legal and safety requirements in the 'physical' world [5]. The TC discussion in this conference shifted from the traditional research in academia and more into how digital transformation is creating challenges for traditional systems and organizational functioning to unify the customer journey. The discussion went further into exploring if there could be opportunities to re-position technical communication as a strategic activity unifying a company's conversation with the customer about products and services? The idea was to explore academia-industry relationships and partnerships and related perspectives [6].

Another interesting topic that we considered as a major theme for ETLTC2020 was the gradual shift from computer assisted language learning towards mobile assisted language learning [7], and should language teachers redefine the language context for a world in which language use is now a means to an end, where international people are using English alongside their own language in order to achieve real life purpose online. Many of the presentations in this conference also focused on different language learning, testing and administrative tools, including language learning apps, discussions on AI and big data that could have both academic, industrial and societal applications.

Moreover, as part of this conference we wanted to open up discussions on special topics in computer science, biomedical engineering and smart cities as tracks to have a more comprehensive outlook on a wide-ranging topic in a way such that a diverse multi-disciplinary approach to teaching and research could be promoted, and more ideas and approaches discussed.

Another important aspect of the ETLTC2020 was the semester-long collaboration between the students of the University of Aizu and the HSKA, Germany which is now in its second year and resulted in a collaborative project on smart cities and technical communication. The idea of the project was to promote intercultural exposure and project-based collaboration and language learning. So, this conference was designed to be a forum for networking where participants from diverse faculty with a missing link came together, and explored how they could communicate and collaborate for research and other projects in near future. Further, this conference clearly had a strong focus on student-student collaboration preparing them for collaborative professional projects in the industry by raising their project management and intercultural communication skills [8].

3. ETLTC2020 Attendance

The event was held in collaboration with the international symposium on spatial media (ISSM2020). ETLTC2020 had about 90-100 participants in total for the 5-day event. For the academic presentations and attendance, the following countries and universities were represented.

Countries Represented	Japanese Universities
• Germany (a 14-member team from academia & industry)	• Waseda Univ.
• Greece	• Kumamoto Univ.
• Hong Kong	• Nagoya Institute of Technology
• Indonesia	• University of Kitakyushu
• Ecuador	• Kochi University of Technology
• USA	• Osaka University
• Nepal	• Rikkyo University
• Mexico	
• Russia	
• Taiwan	

4. Conference Presentation

The conference included the following sessions:

Individual Paper Presentation:

Paper sessions were 90 minutes in length and included 5-6 papers, in general and included many research papers on educational technology, language, technical communication and topics in computer science.

Poster:

Poster sessions combined the graphicsdisplay of technical communication research materials with the opportunity for individualized, informal discussion of a project in research, policy and/or practice. Individual presenters set up displays in a large area with other presenters. Posters were set up to be during the final day of the conference.

Workshop:

Workshops (90 minutes long) offered a forum for discussion of a broad range of emerging and specialized topics of interest to the ETLTC community. Two workshops happened between the students of University of Aizu and HSKA, Germany. These sessions were interactive and more informal than paper sessions and involved extended discussion, group brainstorming sessions, mini-tutorials around key ideas, and proof-of-concept demonstration sessions.

5. Submission Genres and Topics

The SIX major genres for paper submission were as follows:
A. Computer Assisted Language Learning
B. Task-based Language Learning
C. Educational Technology in Academia and Industry
D. Information Design and eLearning
E. Technical Communication
F. Special Track: ICT, Design, and Planning for Smart Cities

A. Computer Assisted Language Learning

1) Language Learning Environments and CALL

- Designing and implementing contextualized technology-enhanced language learning environments
- Local versus global CALL environments
- Blended learning and hybrid courses
- E-learning systems
- Flipped classes
- Assessment & evaluation of CALL environments
- Task-based CALL in online systems
- Computer-Supported Collaborative Language Learning (CSCLL)
- Network-based language teaching (NBLT)
- Effective feedback strategies in online systems
- Productivity suites
- Project-Based Learning
- Virtual reality
- Websites for language practice
- Course Management Systems

2) Ubiquitous Language Learning

- The use of mobile technologies, such as tablets, iPads, smartphones, etc., to provide flexibility and access to language learning opportunities
- Best practices in the use of technology for learning a language anytime, anywhere, and with any device
- Methodological implications for mobile technology content development
- Developing language materials for ubiquitous learning
- Podcasting
- Apps for language learning
- Modes of delivery
- Mobile Learning and Ubiquitous Technologies

3) Intercultural Language Learning through ICT
- Telecollaboration and video-web conferencing
- Exploiting social networks for language learning
- Computer-supported collaborative language learning across frontiers
- Cross-cultural awareness through ICT
- The use of social networking technologies by language teachers and learners to share expertise, knowledge, and information
- Social networking

4) Worldwide Collaborative CALL
- Open (Linked) Data and Open Content
- MOOCs for language learning
- Harmonizing theories, research, and practice
- Free/shareware/open source technology for developing language learning materials
- Working collaboratively to disseminate and adapt innovations so that they can be used by practitioners separated by location or culture
- Growing innovation through collaborations across international institutions
- Working towards worldwide collaboration for the sharing and re-use of digital language learning materials
- Design and development of applications that cross geographical, physical, psychological, and financial boundaries
- Catalyzing international cooperation for language learning
- Open Educational Resources
- Identifying priorities of particular languages, groups and/or regions, with the aim of increasing collaboration and growth
- Facilitating wider access to multilingual quality language learning worldwide
- Growing diverse online communities of language learners/teachers

5) CALL and Multidisciplinary Approach for Targeting Learners' Needs
- From needs analysis to multidisciplinary language learning materials design
- Bridging the gap between language teachers' perspectives and new language learners' needs
- Augmented reality in second language teaching and learning
- CALL for matching learners' minds
- Learners just want to have fun: technology and games for language learning
- Game-based learning strategies in technology-enhanced language learning environments
- Gamification and virtual reality
- Language learning systems for targeting specific audiences
- Corpus-aided language learning
- Semantic Web 3.0

6) Teacher Professional Development and CALL
- Integrating CALL in initial teacher education
- Integrating CALL from k-12 to tertiary education
- Teacher training in ICT for enhancing language learning
- Developing strategies for teacher education and professional development
- CALL on a small budget
- Extra-curricular study

7) ICALL
- ICALL and ITS systems for e-learning platforms
- Natural Language Processing in language learning

8) Learner's Autonomy and CALL
- Supporting the development of language learners' autonomy
- Motivation, guidance, and accountability in language learning without the teacher present

• Self-efficacy and learner autonomy, self-regulated language learning
• Learner behavior

9) CALL Framework
• Developing theoretical frameworks, models, principles, and guidelines for the development of CALL
• Changes to the use and application of CALL terminology
• Pedagogy for developing CALL

10) CALL Research
• Current and perceived future CALL trends, gaps, and research needs
• Developing qualitative and quantitative studies (methods, techniques, tools, etc.)
• Corpora & Databases

11) Evaluation and assessment
• Assessing language learning achievements (knowledge, skills, attitudes, motivation, satisfaction)
• Criteria for evaluating the effectiveness of language learning software systems
• Assessment strategies in b-learning and e-learning environments
• Computer-based languages tests

12) CALL for Minority Languages
• Safeguarding endangered and indigenous languages through technology
• CALL for Teaching Less commonly taught languages

13) CALL and Government Priorities for Language Learning
• Evolving national and international government priorities that impact upon the overall use of CALL
• Common international language standards for curriculum and syllabus development

14) CALL Materials Design
• Listening, Speaking and Pronunciation
• Reading
• Writing
• Grammar
• Curriculum development
• Podcasting
• Video
• Sustainability of resources
• Low-cost devices
• Pedagogy for developing CALL materials

B. Task-based Language Learning
• Tasks in SLA
• Tasks in language education
• Theoretical perspectives on TBLT
• Sociocultural aspects of TBLT
• Task features, complexity, design
• TBLT methodology
• TBLT implementation and innovations
• Technology-mediated TBLT
• Tasks and the role of the learner
• The role of the teacher and TBLT-based teacher education
• TBLT in contexts
• Needs analysis in TBLT
• Task-based assessment
• Evaluating task-based instruction, materials, and programs

C. Educational Technology in Academia and Industry

1. Education in Context

- Education in the Network Society
- Educational Games
- Social Media in Education

2. Education as Professional Field

- Teacher Education
- Teachers' Professional Development
- Teachers' Workload
- Teacher Support for Grading, Time Tabling, Grading, Learning Tools, and Online Learning Software
- Teachers' learning in Communities of Practice
- Web-based Communities for Teacher Support

3. Curricular Evolution

- Problem-based Learning
- Critical Thinking Skills
- Creativity Skills
- Learning Citizenship
- Global Education with Technology
- Media Literacy / -Pedagogy
- Multicultural Education with Technology

4. Integrating Educational Technologies

- Social Media and Social Networking
- The Semantic Web 3.0
- Podcasting for Broadcasting Video Lectures
- Podcasting feedback to students
- Wiki and blogs in Higher Education
- Mobile, Virtual and Vicarious Learning
- Simulations and Modeling

5. International Higher Education

- Web-based, Mobile, Virtual Presence and Social Media to Overcome Student Mobility
- Blended Learning and Student Assessment at a Distance
- Student Mobility and Distance Education

D. Information Design and eLearning

- E-Learning Evaluation
- E-Learning Tools and Systems
- E-Learning Content Development
- Electronic Publishing Tools E-Learning
- Engaging Students with the World Digital and Global Discovery Online Virtual Universities, Classrooms, and Laboratories
- Developing and Organizational e-Learning Strategy
- Developing, Integrating, and Delivering E-Learning
- Solutions Digital Libraries for E-Learning
- Distance Education
- Distance Learning
- Methods and Procedures for the Global Classroom
- Industry-University Partnering Infrastructure of E-Learning Environments Interactive E-Learning Systems

- Knowledge Management in E-Learning
- Quality Management and Assessment in E-Learning

E. Technical Communication

- Technical Communication
- Structured authoring and information modeling
- Semantic modeling and ontology applications
- Process integration and modeling of products and information
- AI applications in technical communication
  Specific concepts of intelligent content
- Dynamic and interactive content delivery
- IoT and Industry 4.0 concepts for technical information
- Content analytics and metrics
- Search and Retrieval scenarios of technical information
- Content generation
- User-generated content
- Elimination of information silos
- Technical videos
- Augmented and virtual reality
- Mobile documentation
- Agile project management
- Cross-cultural and Global Communication
- Electronic Forums and Meetings
- Usability and Usability Testing
- Visual Communication
- Writing Processes, Thinking Processes
- Workplace Culture

F. Social Communication related to ICT, Design, Smart City and Society

- Design Thinking and Planning
- Smart Parking
- Car sharing services
- Traffic and public transport
- Clean energy
- Smart building
- Waste disposal
- Environmental protection
- Citizen participation
- Digitization of governance
- Urban planning
- Education
- Business ecosystem
- 4G LTE
- Internet Speed
- Wifi Hotspots
- Smartphone penetration
- Living standard
- Healthcare Electronics
- Smart Healthcare

6. Submission Topics & Scope

All submission types were blind refereed. The evaluators reviewed all submissions without the names of the authors and presenters.

6.1. Submission Guidelines

Papers were no more than **10 pages maximum** (including abstract, references, appendix, etc.).

Paper Length:
Full Papers: Between 6-10 pages
Short Papers: Between 3-4 pages
Extended Abstract Papers: 1-2 Pages (around 600-800 words including references)

Paper Content Type:
Full Research Paper
Tutorial
Teaching Experience
Project Experience
Software Review
Teaching or Research Position Paper

6.2. Evaluation of proposals

Proposals were blind reviewed in the EDAS system and evaluated by members of the ETLTC2020 Program Committee. Proposals were judged for their contribution to educational technology theory and application and technical communication policy, research, and/or practice, the quality of explanation pertaining to the aims of the presentation, theoretical perspectives, methods of inquiry and analysis, strength of results and conclusions, and connections to the conference theme.

- For long papers, we looked into completed research that clearly highlights how a study is conducted, the findings, the discussion of the results and its implications.
- For short papers, we looked for studies in preliminary stages, but which clearly puts a detailed framework explaining the next course of action or expected results.
- Extended Abstracts provided the opportunity for the author to share an initial work-in-progress report or an idea that could be tested through a paper and accompanying talks at the conference. An experience report is a reflection of their own industry experiences (e.g. challenges they have seen, what they tried and approaches they have taken, what worked and what didn't work).

- A Research Paper was complete with an introduction, data, and analysis of data, discussion and implications.
- A Tutorial clearly explained how software or a product (e.g., educational technology) could be used towards certain specific goals.
- Teaching Experience papers clearly highlighted the course module, how it's designed, the pedagogical strategies, classroom experience (with some data) and implications for teaching.
- The Project Experience papers clearly highlighted how the project was conceptualized, reasons for using the approach, people and resources involved, what was aimed and achieved, the learning that happened, and its overall implications.
- The Software/Hardware Review papers clearly explained the purpose of the software/hardware, the domain of application, the design of the interface, how users are expected to use it, and how it's actually used, the learning that happens, the user experience and the reliability and trustworthiness of the product in the market, and/or in the specific community of use.
- The Teaching or Research Position papers explained the idea behind an approach, whether such use or application is valid and reasonable, what are the theories backing such application, or any contrary theoretical evidence to suggest the failure of such research approach, or pedagogical strategy.

7. Publication

ETLTC2020 published an abstract proceeding with ISSN number. This proceeding included both the abstract and extended abstracts (up to 2 pages long) which were not submitted through the EDAS system. The 1st drafts or the abstracts for all the short paper (four pages long) and long paper (up to 10 pages long) submissions were peer-reviewed and submitted for publication with *SHS Web of Conferences*. However, among the list of all final short and long paper submissions, four best papers were selected, and those papers were forwarded for an additional round of review before being considered for publication in a special issue of *International Journal of Computer Assisted Language Learning and Teaching (IJCALLT)*. IJCALLT is a major journal in the field of technology assisted language learning and indexed in Scopus and other major indices.

8. The Keynote Speakers

ETLTC2020 had 11 keynote speakers from industry and academia.

Prof. Wolfgang Ziegler
Information & Content Management
The Karlsruhe University of Applied Sciences, Germany

Prof. Glenn Stockwell
Professor & Associate Dean, Dept. of Law
Waseda University, Japan

Prof. Martin Schober
Professor of Internet & Media Technology
Karlsruhe University of Applied Sciences, Germany
Prof. Gordon Bateson
E-learning Laboratory, Department of Core Studies
The Kochi University of Technology, Japan

Prof. Kiyomi Okamoto
Center for Fundamental Education
Faculty of Environmental Engineering
The University of Kitakyushu, Japan

Prof. John Blake
Center for Language Research
The University of Aizu, Japan

Prof. Satoshi Kuroda
Councilor, Chairman of the Planning Committee of Public Affairs, JTCA
Center for the Study of Co* Design
Osaka University, Japan

Prof. Ana Cristina Garcia Luna Romero
Department of Architecture
The University of Monterrey, Mexico

Mr. Christian Deschner
Siemens Healthcare GmbH
Technology & Innovation Lifecycle Excellence
Core Tool Harmonization, Germany

Dr. Sven Leukert
VP, Knowledge Management at SAP
Mannheim Area, Germany

Prof. Hiram Alejandro Cantu Campos
Director, Biomedical Engineering
Academic Program
The University of Monterrey, Mexico

9. The Organizing Committee

The organizing committee was chosen from a wide range of institutions, partner universities and from both academia and industry.

Honorary Chairs
Ryuichi Oka – Univ. of Aizu, JP
Toshiaki Miyazaki – Univ. of Aizu, JP

General Chairs
Debopriyo Roy – Univ. of Aizu, JP

PC Chairs
Debopriyo Roy – Univ. of Aizu, JP
John Blake – Univ. of Aizu, JP

PC Co-Chairs
Takako Yasuta – Fukushima Medical Univ. Japan

Special Session Chair
Gordon Bateson – Kochi Univ. of Technology, JP

Publicity Support
Wolfgang Ziegler – Karlsruhe University of Applied Sciences, Germany
Motoo Akiyama – Japan Technical Communicators Association, JP
Ana Cristina Garcia Luna Romero - University of Monterrey, Mexico
Hiram Alejandro Cantu Campos - University of Monterrey, Mexico

Publication Chair
John Blake – Univ. of Aizu, JP

Publication Advisors
Glen Stockwell - Waseda University, Japan

Local Organizing Chairs
Mohamed Hamada – Univ. of Aizu, JP
Rentaro Yoshioka – Univ. of Aizu, JP

Advisory Committee
Wolfgang Ziegler – Karlsruhe University of Applied Sciences, Germany
Thilak Hapugahage Chaminda – Lanka Nippon Biztech Institute (LNBTI), Sri Lanka
Neil Johnson – The Univ. of Sunderland, United Kingdom
Kazunori Nozawa – Ritsumeikan Univ, JP
Kiyomi Okamoto – The Univ. of Kitakyushu, JP
Bradley Irwin - Nihon University, JP
Anubhav Bhatia - VP Engineering- SAP Labs, Member-Forbes Technical Council, IEEE Senior Member
John Brine - Research Associate, Dept. of Computer Science, Univ. of Waikato, Hamilton, New Zealand

Registration Chairs
Debopriyo Roy – Univ. of Aizu, JP
John Blake – Univ. of Aizu, JP

Steering Committee
Ben Abderazek – Univ. of Aizu, JP
Michael Cohen – Univ. of Aizu, JP
Shigaku Tei – Univ. of Aizu, JP

10. Sponsors

Major Sponsors – The University of Aizu, ACM Chapter on eLearning and Technical Communication, and Karlsruhe University of Applied Sciences, Germany.
Major Partners – University of Monterrey, Mexico, and Japan Technical Communicators Association

Project Partners of the Japanese-German Academic Cooperation Project -
DOCUFY is a leading software manufacturer for multi-level documentation systems and is the first provider of Multi-Level Documentation. Besides its software products, DOCUFY also offers consulting and development services and professional support. The ISO 9001:2015 certified company is based in Bamberg and employs around 120 people. The software specialist also markets its multilingual software worldwide via a network of partners. Since 1 May 2017, DOCUFY has been a Heidelberg Group Company.
SCHEMA develops component content management and content delivery solutions for authoring departments creating product-related content. SCHEMA software supports businesses in describing complex products and in publishing and distributing content. The component content management system SCHEMA ST4 is one of the most frequently used systems for the modularised creation of documentation, package inserts, and marketing documentation. The system covers all areas of content creation in technical writing – from authoring assistance during input to the finished layout for printed catalogs. The SCHEMA Content Delivery Server provides businesses with a standard solution to automatically share intelligent information with end users.
Expert Communication Systems GmbH, a company domiciled in Haar near Munich, is the maker of the browser based XML editing system "Smart Media Creator". Thanks to modern technology and structures, SMC excels with high efficiency and usability and can be run in many areas of technical documentation and technical marketing. Sample fields of application are: Manuals / instructions, catalogs / data sheet, software documentation / online help, web content and mobile devices, e-learning or marketing media. Expert Communication Systems offers a wide range of services around the installation and application of the editing system, thereby contributing to a fast and safe ROI of projects in different dimensions.
ONTOLIS is a web-based software family for general knowledge management. Using the powers of ontologies, ONTOLIS enables you to depict all relations and coherences of your desired domain. Since ONTOLIS is highly configurable, it can easily be optimized for the customer's needs and use cases. The team behind ONTOLIS has 20 years of experience in DLM. This has left its mark: ONTOLIS offers innovative solutions for content management and delivery, which makes it the first CMDS. An essential part of this is QIRA – ONTOLIS' own language for querying, transformation and reasoning of ontology data. ONTOLIS delivers intelligence for your data.
i-views - The company intelligent views from Darmstadt, Germany was founded in 1997 is the vendor of the semantic graph database i-views and is a leading provider of semantic-based information portals. The content delivery portal iv-content is based on our core engine and brings the full power of semantic web technologies to the area of content delivery portals. iv-scontent supports a large variety of input formats for technical documents and offers a full metadata management system for the automatic and manual annotation of content. Intelligent searches, personalized access, and offline apps are further key features of the solution.

References

[1]. Woolever, K. R. (2005). Innovative approaches to teaching technical communication. *Technical Communication*, *52*(1), 73-75.
[2]. Januszewski, A., & Molenda, M. (Eds.). (2013). *Educational technology: A definition with commentary*. Routledge.
[3]. Means, B. (2010). Technology and education change: Focus on student learning. *Journal of research on technology in education*, *42*(3), 285-307.
[4]. Whiteside, A. L. (2003). The skills that technical communicators need: An investigation of technical communication graduates, managers, and curricula. *Journal of technical writing and communication*, *33*(4), 303-318.
[5]. Ballard, D. (2017). Technical Communication - A profession in transformation in the digital age or simply business as usual? LinkedIn.com (June 14). https://www.linkedin.com/pulse/technical-communication-profession-transformation-digital-ballard-1/
[6]. Bridgeford, T., & Amant, K. S. (2017). Academy-industry relationships and partnerships: Perspectives for technical communicators. Routledge.
[7]. Jarvis, H., & Achilleos, M. (2013). From Computer Assisted Language Learning (CALL) to Mobile Assisted Language Use (MALU). *Tesl-ej*, *16*(4), n4.
[8]. Roy, D., & Ziegler, W. (2019, July). Logistics and Challenges of an Intercultural Technical Communication Collaborative Project between Two Japanese and German Universities. In *2019 IEEE International Professional Communication Conference (ProComm)* (pp. 18-24). IEEE.

Solving University Course Timetabling Problem Using Multi-Depth Genetic Algorithm

Solving UCTP Using MDGA

Alfian Akbar Gozali[1,*] and *Shigeru* Fujimura[1,]

[1]Graduate School of IPS, Waseda University, Kitakyushu, Japan

Abstract. The University Course Timetabling Problem (UCTP) is a scheduling problem of assigning teaching event in certain time and room by considering the constraints of university stakeholders such as students, lecturers, and departments. The constraints could be hard (encouraged to be satisfied) or soft (better to be fulfilled). This problem becomes complicated for universities which have an immense number of students and lecturers. Moreover, several universities are implementing student sectioning which is a problem of assigning students to classes of a subject while respecting individual student requests along with additional constraints. Such implementation enables students to choose a set of preference classes first then the system will create a timetable depend on their preferences. Subsequently, student sectioning significantly increases the problem complexity. As a result, the number of search spaces grows hugely multiplied by the expansion of students, other variables, and involvement of their constraints. However, current and generic solvers failed to meet scalability requirement for student sectioning UCTP. In this paper, we introduce the Multi-Depth Genetic Algorithm (MDGA) to solve student sectioning UCTP. MDGA uses the multiple stages of GA computation including multi-level mutation and multi-depth constraint consideration. Our research shows that MDGA could produce a feasible timetable for student sectioning problem and get better results than previous works and current UCTP solver. Furthermore, our experiment also shows that MDGA could compete with other UCTP solvers albeit not the best one for the ITC-2007 benchmark dataset.

1 Introduction

The University Course Timetabling Problem (UCTP) is a scheduling problem of assigning teaching event in certain time and room by considering the constraints of university stakeholders such as students, lecturers, and departments. The constraints could be hard (encouraged to be satisfied) or soft (better to be fulfilled). Regarding its difficulty, Garey included timetabling as an NP-Hard problem [1].

Moreover, several universities such as Telkom University [2], Purdue [3], and the University of Waterloo [4] implement student sectioning. Student sectioning is a problem of assigning students to classes of a subject while respecting individual student requests along with additional constraints [5]. Therefore, the fulfillment of each students' preference is encouraged, as well.

*e-mail: alfian@tass.telkomuniversity.ac.id

In regular timetabling, we place student enrollment (the process which the students choose their classes) after the class timetable available. Oppositely, in the student sectioning, students choose a set of preference classes first then the system will create a timetable depend on their preferences. Subsequently, student sectioning significantly increases the problem complexity. As a result, the number of search spaces grows hugely multiplied by the expansion of students, other variables, and involvement of their constraints.

UCTP is a minimizing optimization problem, so the objective is to minimize all the predefined constraint violation for each of the teaching events. One of the most recently studied for UCTP is the application of genetic algorithms (GA), which are based on the theory of evolution [6], and that have proved to be efficient for problems of moderate and realistic size such as AIMGA [2], Parallel GA [7, 8], Fast Practical GA [9], Directed GA [10], and NSGA-II [11].

In GA, the most time consuming part which is in the fitness evaluation. Thus, student sectioning with large number of variables will make GA runs impractical. To implement GA as a practical solution for this problem, we need to divide the problem to be smaller problem so we could solve it, and then increase the level gradually until we reach the goal. This paper proposes Multi-Depth GA (MDGA) as a GA variation implementing such approach.

MDGA uses three levels of objective function which is differed by its complexity (depth of the problem): shallow, medium, and deep objective function. These objective functions are applied in different step of GA. Moreover, MDGA implements advanced mutation operation by combining three different local search which specifically designed for student sectioning UCTP. Finally, the combination of multi-level objective function and advanced mutation in MDGA will be a significant advantage for overcoming student sectioning UCTP.

Taken together, the primary motivation of this work is how to design MDGA for student sectioning UCTP. In detail, the main goals of this research are (1) to formalize a real-world scaling student sectioning UCTP, (2) to design MDGA to meet the problem requirements, and (3) to analyze MDGA performance in handling student sectioning UCTP.

This paper consists of five sections. We organize the remainder of this paper as follows. Section 2 talks about the student sectioning UCTP. Section 3 shows the MDGA design to meet UCTP problems. Section 4 shows how we conducted the experiments, results, and analysis. The last but not the least, Section 5 takes place as the conclusion and discussion of this work.

2 University Course Timetabling Problem

Generally, UCTP is a problem of arranging a set of teaching events (events) into a predefined packet of time and room while satisfying all constraints within the problem. Equation 1 is the formulation of a packet (q) of time (t) and room (r).

$$q = (t, r) \tag{1}$$

Time could be different from one university to another, which could be varied in weekly, daily, hourly, or even minutely. For example, a university could implement 40 minutes for a time while a certain university could have 60 minutes. Rooms are UCTP resources which could vary in capacity, facility, ownership, and specialization (for example theory and practice classroom). The notation in Table 1 is used for UCTP formulation.

An event (e) consists of a lecturer (l) who teaches a certain class (c) with a set of students (S), which is defined by following notation:

$$e = (l, c, S) \tag{2}$$

Hence, a timetable is a mapping set of all events into several or all packets. A mapping of a packet and an event is a pair (p), which is defined by following notation:

$$p = (q, e) \tag{3}$$

As referenced from previous research [2, 8], this research also used two types of constraints: the hard and soft constraints. Hard constraint (HC) is a constraint that must be satisfied. Soft constraint (SC) is better to be fulfilled to improve the quality of the timetable.

Table 1. UCTP Formulation

Indices and sets			
$p \in P$	set of pairs		
$e \in E$	set of events	e^p	event of pair p
$q \in Q$	set of packets	q^p	packet of pair p
$l \in L$	set of lecturers	l^p	lecturer of pair p
$b \in B$	set of subjects	b_c	subject of class c
$G^b \subseteq L$	set of group lecturers for subject b		
$k \in K \subseteq L$	set of special lecturers		
$r \in R$	set of rooms	r^p	room of pair p
$t \in T$	set of time	t^p	time of pair p
$c \in C$	set of classes	c^p	class of pair p
$d \in D$	set of days	d^p	day of pair p
$z \in Z$	set of all students		
$s \in S \subseteq Z$	set of students	S^p	students of pair p
Functions			
$CNTTIME(l, d, P)$	count event of l in a day		
$DATE(t)$	return the date of time t		
$CNTSTIME(z, d, P)$	count event of z in a day		
$TGAP(t, t')$	time interval of t and t'		
Parameters			
w_i	weighting of constraint i		
V_i	total violation of constraint i		
CAP_r	capacity of room r		
CAP_e^-	minimum room capacity of event e		
X_l	prohibited time of lecturer l		
$PREF_l$	preference time of lecturer l		
Constant			
LC^+	maximum lecturer event in a day		
LC^-	min time interval of two lecturer event		
CC^-	minimum class event interval in a week		
SC^+	maximum student event in a day		
GC^-	minimum group teaching event interval		

This research used five HCs and seven SCs. Where V_i is a violation count for each i constraint. Furthermore, the following equations are the mathematical models of each constraint used in this research:

HC 1. No conflict of lecturers

There is no lecturer who has been set in different room at the same time.

$$V_1 = \sum_{p \in P} \sum_{p' \in P} f_1(p, p') = 0 \tag{4}$$

$$f_1(p,p') = \begin{cases} 1, & if(l^p = l^{p'} \wedge t^p = t^{p'} \wedge p \neq p') \\ 0, & otherwise \end{cases} \tag{5}$$

HC 2. No conflict of classes
There is no packet that has been set for different event at the same time.

$$V_2 = \sum_{p \in P} \sum_{p' \in P} f_2(p,p') = 0 \tag{6}$$

$$f_2(p,p') = \begin{cases} 1, & if(q^p = q^{p'} \wedge p \neq p') \\ 0, & otherwise \end{cases} \tag{7}$$

HC 3. Any event should be scheduled in a suitable capacity room
No event that has been set in room with a less-than suitable capacity.

$$V_3 = \sum_{p \in P} f_3(p) = 0 \tag{8}$$

$$f_3(p) = \begin{cases} 1, & if(CAP^{-}_{e^p} > CAP_{r^p}) \\ 0, & otherwise \end{cases} \tag{9}$$

HC 4. Lecturers should not be scheduled within their time constraints
Lecturers such as professors, rectors, and deans should be set in their time constraints.

$$V_4 = \sum_{p \in P} f_4(p) = 0 \tag{10}$$

$$f_4(p) = \begin{cases} 1, & if(l^p \in K \wedge t^p \in X_{l^p}) \\ 0, & otherwise \end{cases} \tag{11}$$

HC 5. Some lecturers should be scheduled in their time preferences
Lecturers such as professors, rectors, and deans should be set in their preferred time.

$$V_5 = \sum_{p \in P} f_5(p) = 0 \tag{12}$$

$$f_5(p) = \begin{cases} 1, & if(l^p \in K \wedge t^p \notin PREF_{l^p}) \\ 0, & otherwise \end{cases} \tag{13}$$

SC 1. Lecturer assignment spread
The teaching event for a lecturer should be set to a maximum of LC^+ events in a day.

$$Minimize V_6 = \sum_{l \in L} \sum_{d \in D} f_6(l,d,P) \tag{14}$$

$$f_6(l,d,P) = \begin{cases} 1, & if(CNTTIME(l,d,P) > LC^+) \\ 0, & otherwise \end{cases} \tag{15}$$

SC 2. Class event spread

An event of a class should be set to a minimum of CC^- days of interval in a week. In a real-world, there is a special case which a class can be lectured in more than once a week. For example, class AR002 must be taught twice a week. Thus, it is possible to have several similar events mapped into different packet. These similar events are interchangeably, which is shown by following notation:

$$Minimize V_7 = \sum_{p \in P} \sum_{p' \in P} f_7(p, p') \tag{16}$$

$$f_7(p, p') = \begin{cases} 1, & if(DATE(t^p) - DATE(t^{p'}) \geq 0 \wedge \\ & DATE(t^p) - DATE(t^{p'}) < CC^- \wedge \\ & c^p = c^{p'} \wedge p \neq p') \\ 0, & otherwise \end{cases} \tag{17}$$

SC 3. Time constraints between different events in the same group

Group teaching is mechanism which several classes with the same subject are taught by a group of lecturer interchangeably. The time interval between two events for a group teaching should less than its minimum time constraint.

$$Minimize V_8 = \sum_{p \in P} \sum_{p' \in P} f_{11}(p, p') \tag{18}$$

$$f_8(p, p') = \begin{cases} 1, & if(b_{c^p} = b_{c^{p'}} \wedge TGAP(t^p, t^{p'}) < GC^- \wedge \\ & l^p \in G^{b_{c^p}} \wedge l^{p'} \in G^{b_{c^{p'}}}) \\ 0, & otherwise \end{cases} \tag{19}$$

SC 4. Some lecturers should be scheduled in their time preferred time

The teaching event for a lecturer should be set in their preferred time.

$$Minimize V_9 = \sum_{p \in P} f_9(p) \tag{20}$$

$$f_9(p) = \begin{cases} 1, & if(t^p \notin PREF_{l^p}) \\ 0, & otherwise \end{cases} \tag{21}$$

SC 5. Time constraints between events for a lecturer

The time interval between two events that a lecturer should not less than the minimum time constraint interval.

$$Minimize V_{10} = \sum_{p \in P} \sum_{p' \in P} f_{10}(p, p') \tag{22}$$

$$f_{10}(p, p') = \begin{cases} 1, & if(l^p = l^{p'} \wedge p \neq p' \\ & \wedge TGAP(t^p, t^{p'}) < LC^-) \\ 0, & otherwise \end{cases} \tag{23}$$

SC 6. Student assignment spread

The events of a student should be set to a maximum SC^+ events in a day

$$MinimizeV_{11} = \sum_{z \in Z} \sum_{d \in D} f_8(z, d, P) \tag{24}$$

$$f_{11}(z, d, P) = \begin{cases} 1, & if(CNTSTIME(z, d, P) > SC^+) \\ 0, & otherwise \end{cases} \tag{25}$$

SC 7. Minimize students conflict
Minimize student which has been set in different room or class meeting in same time

$$MinimizeV_{12} = \sum_{z \in Z} \sum_{p \in P} \sum_{p' \in P} V_{12}(z, p, p') \tag{26}$$

$$f_{12}(z, p, p') = \begin{cases} 1, & if(z \in s^p \wedge z \in S^{p'} \wedge \\ & t^p = t^{p'} \wedge p \neq p') \\ 0, & otherwise \end{cases} \tag{27}$$

3 MDGA for UCTP

This section explains about how we encode the chromosome, formulate the problem definition in term of objective function division, and MDGA procedure.

3.1 Encoding

We use direct chromosome as the GA encoding. Direct chromosome mimics the real-world representation, which, in this case, is the university timetabling, as shown in Fig. 1. This timetable has R rooms and timeslots, which consist of 6 days multiplied by ten shifts (7 AM to 4 PM). This direct chromosome uses enumeration encoding, so the room is encoded as 1 to R for Room 1 to Room R. In the other hand, time is encoded as 1 for 7 AM Monday, 2 for 8 AM Monday, and 60 for 4 PM Saturday. As a result, the chromosome is shown in Fig. 2 as the encoding from timetable in Fig. 1.

Fig. 2 shows that a gene block consists of five parts (time, room, lecturer, class, and students). We count the individual length is equal to the number of events (gene blocks). Furthermore, because the search space is only the packet (time and room), the other parts (lecturer, class, and students) are fixed. So, programmatically, all GA operations (mutation and crossover) are only applied to a packet.

3.2 Problem Definition

The goal of this research is solving student sectioning UCTP. However, this problem, especially with a huge number of students, is almost impossible to do. The enormous student numbers will lead to extensive-time computation due to objective function evaluations.

This condition will be more problematic because we have to guarantee that HCs are always satisfied. If we limit HCs satisfaction strictly, the possible search spaces will also be limited. As a result, we cannot produce any satisfactory solutions. Thus, in this research, we introduce HCs satisfaction in the objective function, as shown in Equation 28, with a large weighting. We call this equation as shallow objective function.

Room R

Room 2

Room 1

TIME	MON	TUE	WED	THU	FRI	SAT
7AM	AR002-NPR		AL002-AAG		AR005-TBH	
8AM	DS002-RWJ	AL002-NPR			AR002-SWN	
9AM				NC002-RVI		
10AM	DS003-RWH	PL004-BBP	HC001-HTT	PL001-AMR		
11AM						
12AM	HC001-HTT		AR002-NPR			
1PM	IM001-JDN	AR002-JPY		IM001-JDN	AL001-AAG	
2PM					AR002-JPY	
3PM			AR005-TBH			
4PM	PL001-AMR					

Figure 1. University timetabling representation

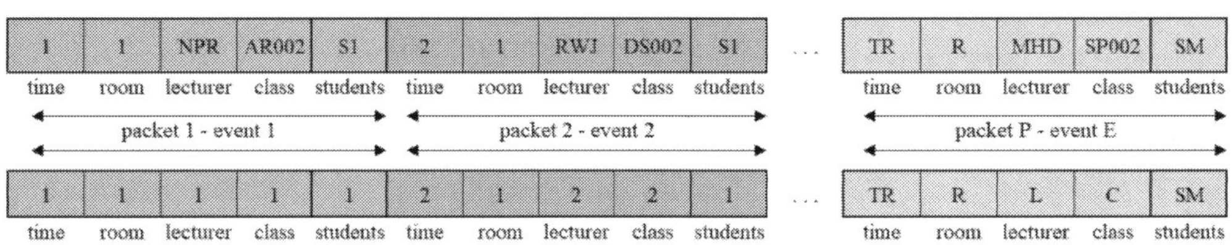

Figure 2. Directed chromosome and its encoding

$$\text{Minimize } V_{HC} = \sum_{i=1}^{5} V_i(P) \tag{28}$$

The shallow objective function focuses in maintaining HCs. The deeper objective function which are medium objective function and deep objective function focus in solving SCs and respecting the HCs as well. The medium objective function focuses in solving class-level SCs with the objective function as shown in Equation 29. The deep objective function focuses in solving student-level SCs with the objective function as shown in Equation 30.

$$\text{Minimize } V_{class} = \sum_{i=1}^{10} V_i(P) \tag{29}$$

$$\text{Minimize } V_{student} = \sum_{i=1}^{12} V_i(P) \tag{30}$$

3.3 MDGA Procedure

Basically, MDGA implements HCs satisfaction to generate initial population with greedy initialization. So, the initial population will has small number of HC violations. In other hands, the SCs satisfaction is applied in the core of GA procedure. Algorithm 1 shows that for each generation t, we perform GA steps such as elitism, selection, crossover, and mutation. Only in the first generation, we make an initial population of P by using greedy initialization with $PopSize$ as a number of individuals. For each generation, we create an empty population of P' to be the new population and save elite individuals.

We implement elitism mechanism to maintain elite individuals among the population. We put the best individual of P into P'. Furthermore, we also put the best M individuals of P into P'. So, the number of elite individuals is $1 + M$.

We use roulette wheel selection to select two individuals idv_1 and idv_2 as parents. By using a roulette wheel, we can choose the parents fairly based-on their evaluation — we crossover these selected parents with crossover probability P_c to produce offsprings then they are evaluated. In this step, we use class-level evaluation. We pick the best two individuals among parents and offsprings, to be the new parents.

We divide the mutation into two stages to solve the problem gradually. We mutate the new parents (stage 1 mutation) with mutation probability P_m to produce offsprings then they are evaluated. This stage use class-level evaluation. We pick the best two individuals among parents and offsprings, to be the new parents.

After the population size equals $PopSize$, we continue to stage 2 mutation with a mutation probability of P_m. Stage 2 mutation is the same as stage 1 mutation, albeit the evaluation. Stage 2 uses student-level evaluation for parents and offsprings. We pick the best two individuals among parents and offsprings, to be the new parents. We put the last parents into P'.

The process is repeated from selection until mutation until the number of individuals in P' equals to $PopSize$. After that, the population P' replaces P and proceed to the next generation.

3.3.1 Crossover

We use a multi-point crossover with the number of affected genes is N_c of all genes which violate constraints. The crossover follows these steps:

1. take two individuals from the selection as parents
2. select N_c of all events which violate constraint in the first parent
3. select an event of them
4. select an event randomly from the second parent which have same room capacity with selected event from first parent regardless of the violation
5. swap the selected event of first parent with second parent
6. repeat step 3-5 until all selected events from first parent are swapped

Algorithm 1 GA Procedure

Require: GA in generation t
  if $t = 1$ **then**
    Greedy Initialization population $P[PopSize]$
  end if
  $P' = \varnothing$ *//empty population*
  // elitism
  Put the best individual of P into P'
  Put the best M individuals of P into P'
  $count = 1 + M$
  while $count < PopSize$ **do**
    // selection
    Select idv_1 and idv_2 from P with roulette wheel
    // crossover
    Crossover idv_1 and idv_2 with probability P_c
    $[idv_1, idv_2]$ = best 2 individuals of parents&offsprings
    // stage 1 mutation
    Mutate idv_1 and idv_2 with probability P_m
    $[idv_1, idv_2]$ = best 2 individuals of parents&offsprings
    $count = count + 2$
  end while
  // stage 2 mutation
  Select idv_1 and idv_2 from P with roulette wheel
  Mutate idv_1 and idv_2 with probability P_m
  $[idv_1, idv_2]$ = best 2 individuals of parents&offsprings
  Put idv_1 and idv_2 into P'
  Replace P with P'

3.3.2 Mutation

We use three mutation steps to improve the probability of producing better offsprings. These three mutations are namely M1 (moving), M2 (swapping), and M3 (comparing). All mutations are always executed sequentially for each individual. The number of affected genes for mutation is N_m of all genes which violate the constraints.

- **M1 (Moving)**
  Select an event which violates the constraint. Move this event to an unused packet (see Eq. 1). The unused packet is a packet which has not been taken by an event. The target packet is selected from the list of unused packets with appropriate room capacity. M1 (Moving) is illustrated in Fig. 3.

- **M2 (Swapping)**
  Select an event which violates the constraint as the first event. Find other events which have the same subject with the first event. Select an event as a target event randomly from them. Swap the first event with the target event. If the swap decreases violations, keep the new individual, otherwise cancel the swap. M2 (Swapping) is illustrated in Fig. 4.

- **M3 (Comparing)**
  Select an event which violates the constraint. Select randomly two other events that have same room capacity regardless of the violation. Swap the violated event with the one

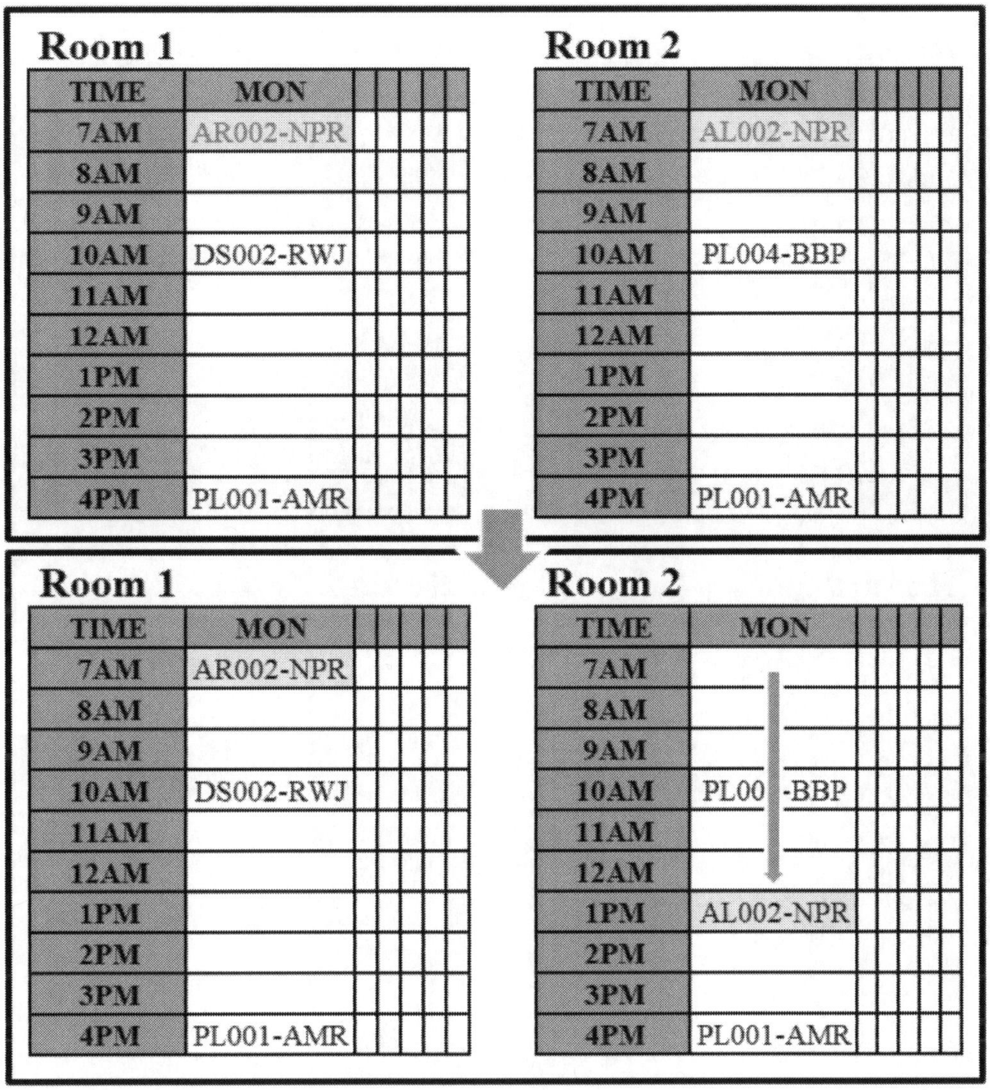

Figure 3. M1 (Moving)

which produces lower violations. If the new individual decreases violations, keep the new individual, otherwise cancel the swap. M3 (Comparing) is illustrated in Fig. 5.

4 Experimental Result

We perform the experiments to analyze MDGA performance in handling student sectioning UCTP. We also compare our proposed solution with other solvers to solve class-level UCTP benchmarks.

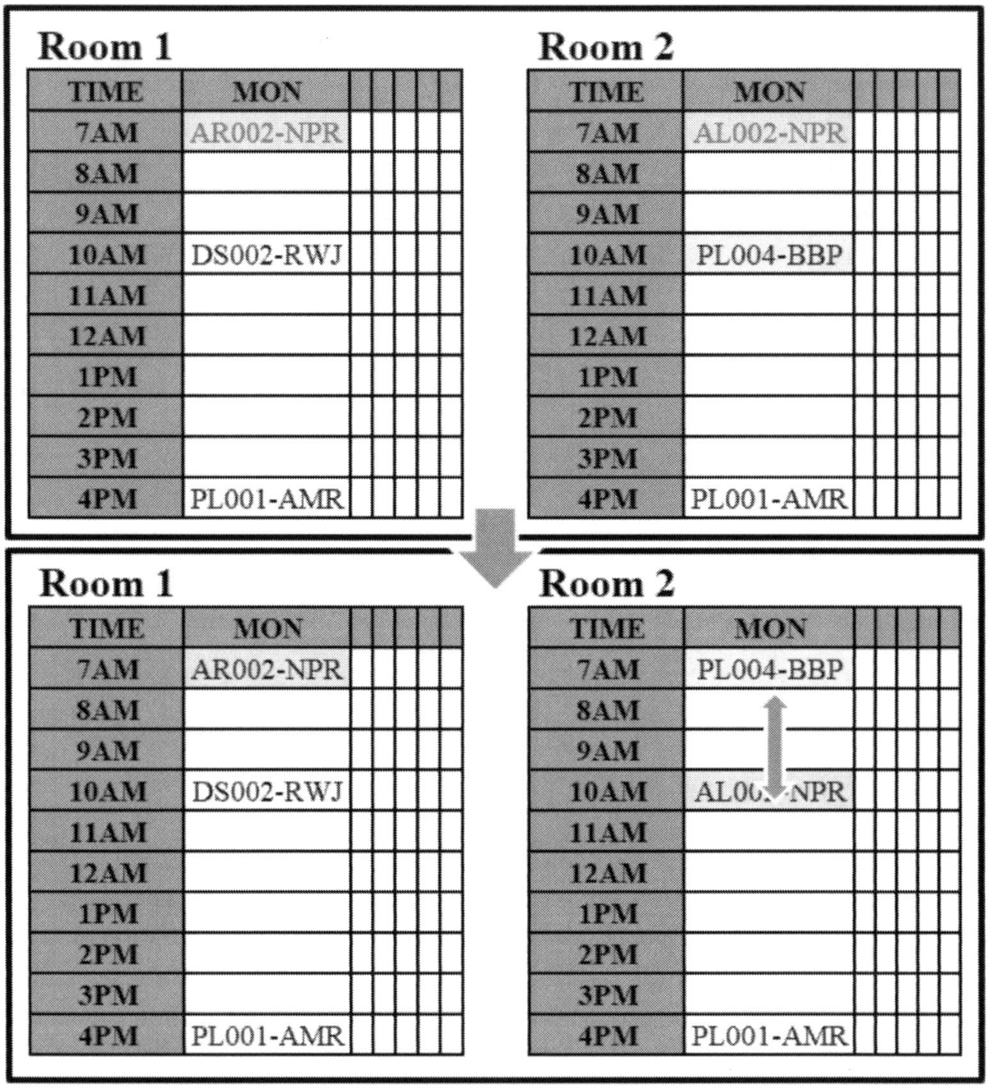

Figure 4. M2 (Swapping)

4.1 Parameter Settings

We set the weight of HCs far larger than SCs. We set the HC weight with the big number M, which $M = 1000$ programmatically. As a result, MGA will prioritize poor fitness caused by HCs. The SCs become the focus after all HCs have been satisfied. We set the penalty value of SCs as proportional to its influence. Regarding this consideration, the SCs penalty value configuration is presented in Table 2.

We set the GA parameters by considering previous research [2]. The GA parameter configurations are mutation probability $P_m = 0.1$ with number of mutated genes $N_m = 10\%$, crossover probability $P_c = 0.8$ with number of crossovered genes $N_c = 10\%$, maximum generation $MaxGen = 200$, and population size $PopSize = 30$.

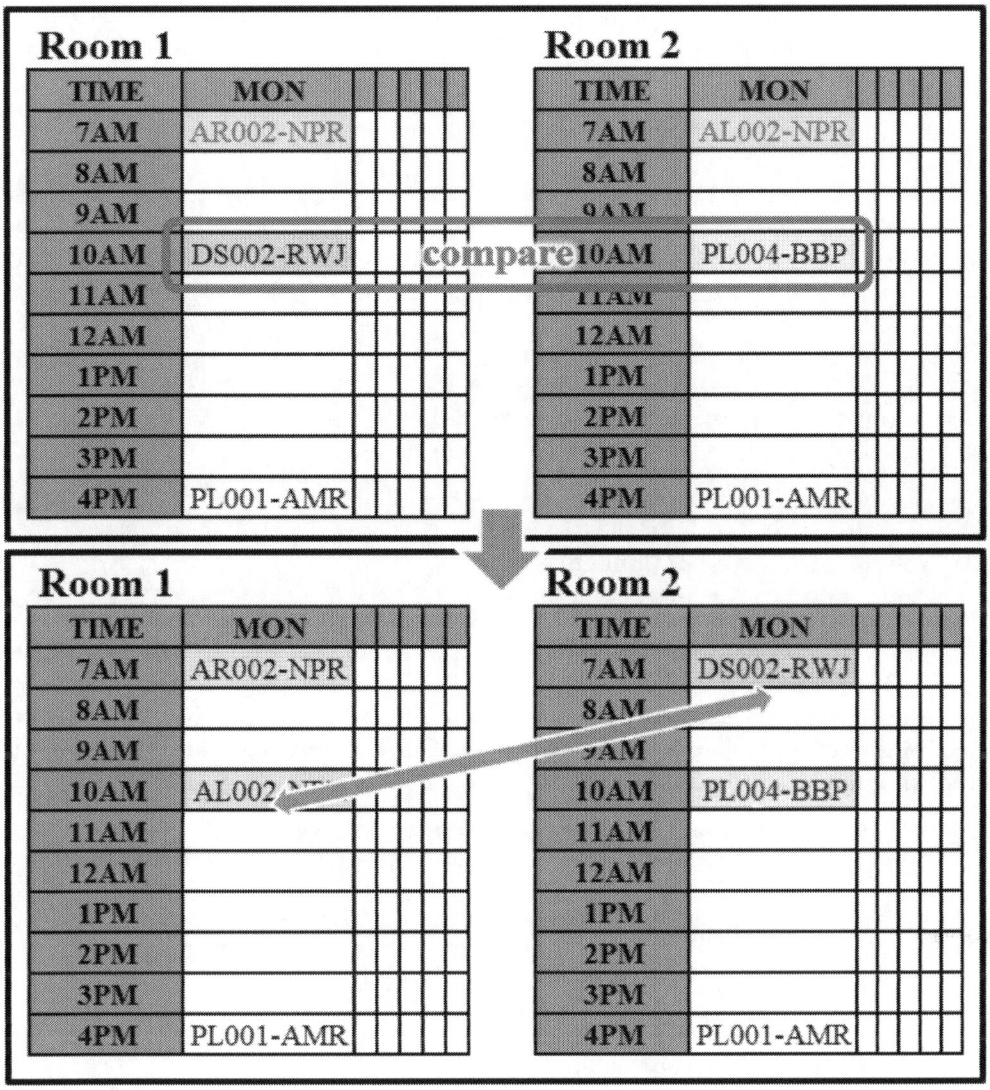

Figure 5. M3 (Comparing)

Table 2. Soft Constraint Penalty Configuration

Soft Constraint	Value
$SC1, SC2$ - high lecturer and class SCs	50
$SC3$ - group teaching SC	5
$SC4, SC5$ - low lecturer SCs	20
$SC6, SC7$ - student SCs	1

4.2 Dataset

Dataset used in this research was Telkom University odd/even semester for 2011/12 (before merging) and 2016/17 (after merging) enrollment years. To be specific, the student body at

Telkom University has increased from 6,570 students in 2011 to 23,451 in 2016. This number is a result of the merging of four universities. The detail dataset characteristics comparison is shown in Table 3.

Table 3. Telkom UCTP Characteristics

No	Attributes	2011/12	2016/17
1	Rooms	80	562
2	Classes (avg. per semester)	813	5309.25
3	Average number of meetings per class	2.75	2.62
4	Lecturers	316	1470
5	Average classes per lecturers	2.58	4.78
6	Students (avg. per semester)	6570	23451
7	Average number of classes per students	6.48	5.03

4.3 Experiment 1 - Proof of Concept

The first experiment implemented MDGA for Telkom UCTP 2011/12 as well as 2016/17 enrollment years. We observed its performance based on the best and average fitness values in 5 runs. For additional insight, we include the HC violation percentages. Table 4 shows that MDGA could yield an acceptable fitness value for 2011/12 as well as 2016/17 enrollment years. MDGA could achieve a small violation percentage timetabling, which means we can accept these results as a feasible timetable.

Table 4. MDGA Result for Telkom UCTP

Problem	Fitness		Violation %	
	Best	Average	Best	Average
2011/12	4540	4887	0.16%	0.18%
2016/17	96562	97023.43	7.36%	7.43%

4.4 Experiment 2 - Comparison Analysis

The third experiment put MDGA together with Standard Genetic Algorithm (GA) [6], Asynchronous Island Model Genetic Algorithm (AIMGA) as a previous solver for Telkom UCTP [2], and UniTime [12] as a current generic UCTP solver. The parameter configuration and chromosome structure of GA and AIMGA were the same with MDGA. The comparison details are shown in the following Table 5.

According to [12], UniTime has different constraint configuration format with Telkom UCTP. Therefore, we conducted a constraints mapping from Telkom UCTP into UniTime format (v2.3), which is explained in Table 6. Where **SAME_ROOM** means given classes must be taught in the same room, **SPREAD** means given classes have to be spread in time (overlapping of the classes in time needs to be minimized), **NHB_GTE** means given classes must have 1 hour or more in between, **NHB_LT** means given classes must have less than 6 hours from the end of first-class to the beginning of the next, and **NHB** means given classes must have exactly x hours in between the end of one and the beginning of another.

Table 5. MDGA, GA, and AIMGA Configuration Comparison

Differences	Algorithm		
	MDGA	**GA**	**AIMGA**
Chromosome encoding	direct encoding	direct encoding	direct encoding
Mutation	directed mutation	random mutation	directed mutation
Crossover	directed multi-point	random multi-point	random multi-point
Elitism	implemented	implemented	implemented
Island model	no	no	yes
GA core	three level GA	standard GA	informed GA

Table 6. Constraints Mapping from Telkom UCTP into UniTime

Telkom UCTP	UniTime
HC1	embedded in solver
HC2	embedded in solver
HC3	strictly supported in data format, SAME_ROOM
HC4	strictly supported in data format
HC5	implicitly supported in related class constraints
SC1	share same constraint with HC5
SC2	SPREAD
SC3	NHB_GTE, NHB_LT, NHB
SC4	share same constraint with HC5
SC5	NHB_GTE, NHB_LT, NHB
SC6	implicitly supported in related class constraints
SC7	embedded in solver

Table 7 shows the average of violation percentage comparison of MDGA, GA, AIMGA, and UniTime in 5 runs. The unfeasible value in UniTime cell for Telkom UCTP 2016/17 enrollment year means it could not get a result in a reasonable time (6 hours runtime limit exceeded). Besides, this table points out that MDGA could lead other algorithm results for both problems.

Table 7. MDGA Violation Percentage Comparison

Problem	MDGA	GA	AIMGA	UniTime
2011/12	1.87%	2.72%	2.39%	13.85%
2016/17	18.34%	57.34%	25.54%	unfeasible

4.5 Experiment 4 - Benchmark Analysis

This last experiment compares the MDGA performance with several UCTP solutions by using the International Timetabling Competition (ITC) 2007 benchmark datasets[13]. Table 8 shows the problem specification of this dataset. There are 24 test cases with various combination of events, rooms, features, and students. We only used the Track 3 ITC curriculum-based course timetabling. This problem is only general UCTP without student sectioning, so we must modify our algorithm to meet this requirement by the process only the Stage 1 of Directed GA (Fig. 1, Stage 1).

Table 8. Complete specification of ITC-2007 dataset

Problem	#Events	#Rooms	#Features	#Students	Max. students per event	Max. events per students
ITC-1	400	10	10	500	33	25
ITC-2	400	10	10	500	32	24
ITC-3	200	20	10	1000	98	15
ITC-4	200	20	10	1000	82	15
ITC-5	400	20	20	300	19	23
ITC-6	400	20	20	300	20	24
ITC-7	200	20	20	500	43	15
ITC-8	200	20	20	500	39	15
ITC-9	400	10	20	500	34	24
ITC-10	400	10	20	500	32	23
ITC-11	200	10	10	1000	88	15
ITC-12	200	10	10	1000	81	15
ITC-13	400	20	10	300	20	24
ITC-14	400	20	10	300	20	24
ITC-15	200	10	20	500	41	15
ITC-16	200	10	20	500	40	15
ITC-17	100	10	10	500	195	23
ITC-18	200	10	10	500	65	23
ITC-19	300	10	10	1000	55	14
ITC-20	400	10	10	1000	40	15
ITC-21	500	20	20	300	16	23
ITC-22	600	20	20	500	22	25
ITC-23	400	20	30	1000	69	24
ITC-24	400	20	30	1000	41	15

Table 9 displays the benchmark experimental result of ITC-2007 dataset. The Table values show the fewest violation result of each solutions. We compare MDGA with several current UCTP solutions, such as **CBS:** Constraint Based Solver by Muller[5], **TSA:** Tabu Search Approach by Lu&Hao[14], **CSP:** Constraint Satisfaction Problem by Atsuta[15], **TAM:** Threshold Acceptance Metaheuristic by Geiger[16], **RBT:** Repair Based TimeTable Solver by Clark[17], **ATS:** Adaptive Tabu Search by Lu&Hao[18], **HMA:** A Hybrid Metaheuristic Approach by Salwani Abdullah[19], **ITS-LS:** Incorporating Tabu Search and Local Search by Atsuta et al.[15], **GDA:** Great Deluge Algorithm with Kempe Chain by McCollum et al.[20], **ILS:** Iterative Local Search by Soria-Alcaraz et al.[21], **HGATS:** The Hybrid Approach Hybrid Genetic Algorithm and Tabu search by Jat&Yang[22], **MMA:** Mixed Metaheuristic Approach by Cambazard et al.[23], **CTI:** Combination of a General Purpose Constraint Satisfaction Solver, Tabu Search and Iterative Local Search Techniques by Atsuta et al.[24], **HA:** A Hybrid Algorithm by Chiarandini et al.[13], and **ACO:** Ant Colony Optimization algorithm in Conjunction with A Iterative Local search by Nothegger et al.[25].

These results are extracted from each paper or a review paper in UCTP by Babaei et al. [26]. Similar to the review paper, we only compare the violation numbers because, in general practice of university timetabling, the computational time is usually not the primary consideration. That is because a university is usually required to make a timetable once in a semester. So the time limit might be around a few days in the end or beginning of a semester.

Table 9 shows that MDGA could get the fewest violations for 6 of 24 test cases. This result proves MDGA could compete with other UCTP solvers albeit not the best one for the ITC-2007 benchmark dataset.

Table 9. Violation Numbers of All Solvers for ITC-2007 dataset

Problem	CBS	TSA	CSP	TAM	RBT	ATS	HMA	ITS-LS	GDA	ILS	HGATS	MMA	CTI	HA	ACO	MDGA
ITC-1	**5**	**5**	**5**	**5**	10	**5**	**5**	**5**	**5**	**5**	523	571	61	1482	15	**5**
ITC-2	51	55	50	111	111	**34**	39	50	60	48	342	993	547	1635	**0**	382
ITC-3	84	71	82	128	119	**70**	76	82	81	76	379	164	382	288	391	82
ITC-4	37	43	**35**	72	72	38	**35**	**35**	39	41	234	310	529	385	239	38
ITC-5	330	309	312	410	426	298	315	312	31	303	**0**	5	5	559	34	5
ITC-6	48	53	69	100	130	47	50	69	45	54	**0**	**0**	**0**	851	87	18
ITC-7	20	28	42	57	110	19	12	42	21	25	**0**	6	**0**	10	**0**	8
ITC-8	41	49	40	77	83	43	37	40	41	47	**0**	**0**	**0**	**0**	4	**0**
ITC-9	109	105	110	150	139	99	104	110	102	106	1102	1560	**0**	1947	**0**	**0**
ITC-10	16	4	27	71	85	16	10	9	17	23	515	2163	**0**	1741	**0**	18
ITC-11	**0**	**0**	**0**	**0**	3	**0**	**0**	**0**	**0**	**0**	246	178	548	240	547	247
ITC-12	333	343	351	442	**4.8**	320	337	351	349	324	241	146	869	475	32	242
ITC-13	66	73	68	622	113	65	61	68	43	68	**0**	**0**	**0**	675	166	**0**
ITC-14	59	57	59	90	84	52	53	59	59	53	**0**	1	**0**	804	**0**	59
ITC-15	84	71	82	128	119	69	73	82	82	74	**0**	**0**	379	**0**	**0**	**0**
ITC-16	34	39	40	81	84	38	32	40	49	42	**0**	2	91	1	41	32
ITC-17	83	91	102	124	152	80	72	102	81	81	**0**	**0**	1	5	68	81
ITC-18	83	96	68	116	110	67	77	68	79	69	**0**	**0**	**0**	3	26	**0**
ITC-19	62	65	75	107	111	59	60	75	67	65	121	1824	1862	1868	**22**	75
ITC-20	27	47	61	88	144	35	**22**	61	30	35	304	445	1215	396	2735	46
ITC-21	103	106	123	174	169	105	95	123	110	106	36	**0**	**0**	602	33	104
ITC-22	–	–	–	–	–	–	–	–	–	–	1154	29	**0**	1364	**0**	29
ITC-23	–	–	–	–	–	–	–	–	–	–	963	**238**	430	688	1275	378
ITC-24	–	–	–	–	–	–	–	–	–	–	274	**21**	720	822	30	25

5 Conclusions

This research shows that the MDGA could overcome not only Telkom UCTP 2011/12 (before merging) but also 2016/17 (after merging) enrollment year with acceptable accuracy represented by the fitness function. For both problems, this proposed approach yielded small violation percentages for all constraints. This result shows that MDGA could handle scaling UCTP well and produce a feasible timetable.

Furthermore, from the second experiment, we could conclude that MDGA shows better performance compare with previous Telkom UCTP solver and generic UCTP solver. The final experiment shows that MDGA could compete with other UCTP solvers albeit not the best one for the ITC-2007 benchmark dataset.

Finally, this research confirms that MDGA can solve the student sectioning Telkom UCTP with an acceptable result. However, further studies still need to be conducted for MDGA to the other UCTP benchmark. A more in-depth investigation for diversity preservation is also needed. Moreover, MDGA implementation in island model GA such as DM-LIMGA [27] is also encouraged.

Acknowledgments

Indonesia Endowment Fund for Education (LPDP), a scholarship from the Ministry of Finance, Republic of Indonesia, supports this work. We conduct this research while at the Graduate School of Information, Production, and Systems, Waseda University, Japan.

References

[1] M. Garey, D.S. Johnson, *Computer and Intractability* (W.H. Freeman and Company, New York, 1979)

[2] A.A. Gozali, J. Tirtawangsa, T.A. Basuki, *Asynchronous Island Model Genetic Algorithm for University Course Timetabling*, in *Proceedings of the 10th International Conference on the Practice and Theory of Automated Timetabling* (PATAT, 2014), pp. 179–187, ISBN 978-0-9929984-0-0

[3] K. Murray, T. Muller, H. Rudova, in *Practice and Theory of Automated Timetabling VI*, edited by E.K. Burke, H. Rudová (Springer Berlin Heidelberg, 2006), Number 3867 in Lecture Notes in Computer Science, pp. 189–209, ISBN 978-3-540-77344-3 978-3-540-77345-0, dOI: 10.1007/978-3-540-77345-0_13, http://link.springer.com/chapter/10.1007/978-3-540-77345-0_13

[4] M.W. Carter, *A Comprehensive Course Timetabling and Student Scheduling System at the University of Waterloo*, in *Practice and Theory of Automated Timetabling III: Third International Conference, PATAT 2000 Konstanz, Germany, August 16–18, 2000 Selected Papers*, edited by E. Burke, W. Erben (Springer Berlin Heidelberg, Berlin, Heidelberg, 2001), pp. 64–82, ISBN 978-3-540-44629-3, http://dx.doi.org/10.1007/3-540-44629-X_5

[5] T. Muller, K. Murray, Annals of Operations Research **181**, 249 (2010)

[6] D.E. Goldberg, *Genetic Algorithms in Search, Optimization and Machine Learning*, 1st edn. (Addison-Wesley Longman Publishing Co., Inc., Boston, MA, USA, 1989), ISBN 0201157675

[7] J. Abela, *A Parallel Genetic Algorithm for Solving the School Timetabling Problem*, in *Division of Information Technology, CSIRO* (Citeseer, 1991)

[8] K. Banczyk, T. Boinski, H. Krawczyk, *Parallelisation of Genetic Algorithms for Solving University Timetabling Problems*, in *International Symposium on Parallel Computing in Electrical Engineering (PARELEC'06)* (2006), pp. 325–330

[9] D. Corne, P. Ross, H.L. Fang, *Fast practical evolutionary timetabling*, in *AISB Workshop on Evolutionary Computing* (Springer, 1994), pp. 250–263

[10] Suyanto, Artificial Intelligence Soft Computing Lecture Notes of Computer Science, Springer Berlin Heidelberg **6114**, 229 (2010)

[11] F. Titel, K. Belarbi, International Journal of Electrical and Computer Engineering **7**, 2614 2626 (2017)

[12] T. Muller, *University Course Timetabling: Solver Evolution*, in *Proceedings of the 11th international conference on the Practice And Theory of Automated Timetabling, 2016* (2016)

[13] L.D. Gaspero, B.M. Mccollum, A.S. Schaerf, *The Second International Timetabling Competition (ITC-2007): Curriculum-based Course Timetabling (Track 3)*, in *Proceedings of the 1st International Workshop on Scheduling a Scheduling Competition (SSC 2007)* (2007)

[14] G. Lu, S. Areibi, *An Island-Based GA Implementation for VLSI Standard-Cell Placement*, in *Genetic and Evolutionary Computation – GECCO 2004: Genetic and Evo-*

lutionary Computation Conference, Seattle, WA, USA, June 26-30, 2004. Proceedings, Part II, edited by K. Deb (Springer Berlin Heidelberg, Berlin, Heidelberg, 2004), pp. 1138–1150, ISBN 978-3-540-24855-2, `http://dx.doi.org/10.1007/978-3-540-24855-2_123`

[15] M. Atsuta, K. Nonobe, T. Ibaraki, *ITC2007 Track 2: An Approach using general CSP solver*, in *Proceedings of the Practice and Theory of Automated Timetabling (PATAT 2008)* (2008)

[16] M.J. Geiger, Annals of Operations Research **194**, 189 (2010)

[17] M. Clark, M. Henz, B. Love, *QuikFix A Repair-based Timetable Solver*, in *Proceedings of the Practice and Theory of Automated Timetabling (PATAT 2008)* (2008)

[18] Z. Lü, J.K. Hao, European Journal of Operational Research **200**, 235 (2010)

[19] S. Abdullah, H. Turabieh, B. McCollum, P. McMullan, Journal of Heuristics **18**, 1 (2010)

[20] B. McCollum, P. McMullan, A.J. Parkes, E. Burke, S. Abdullah, *An Extended Great Deluge Approach to the Examination Timetabling Problem*, in *Proceeding of the Multidisciplinary International Scheduling Conference (MISTA) 2009* (2009)

[21] J.A. Soria-Alcaraz, E. Özcan, J. Swan, G. Kendall, J.M.C. Valadez, Appl. Soft Comput. **40**, 581 (2016)

[22] S.N. Jat, S. Yang, Journal of Scheduling **14**, 617 (2010)

[23] H. Cambazard, E. Hebrard, B. O'Sullivan, A. Papadopoulos, Annals of Operations Research **194**, 111 (2010)

[24] B. McCollum, A. Schaerf, B. Paechter, P. McMullan, R. Lewis, A.J. Parkes, L.D. Gaspero, R. Qu, E.K. Burke, INFORMS Journal on Computing **22**, 120 (2010)

[25] C. Nothegger, A. Mayer, A. Chwatal, G.R. Raidl, Annals of Operations Research **194**, 325 (2012)

[26] H. Babaei, J. Karimpour, A. Hadidi, Computers & Industrial Engineering **86**, 43 (2015)

[27] A.A. Gozali, S. Fujimura, Evolutionary Intelligence (2019)

Design and Optimization of a Deep Neural Network Architecture for Traffic Light Detection

Tomohide Fukuchi[1,*], *Mark Ogbodo* Ikechukwu, and *Abderazek* Ben Abdallah

[1]Adaptive Systems Laboratory, Graduate School of Computer Science and Engineering, The University of Aizu, Aizu-Wakamatsu, Japan

Abstract. Autonomous Driving has recently become a research trend and efficient autonomous driving system is difficult to achieve due to safety concerns, Applying traffic light recognition to autonomous driving system is one of the factors to prevent accidents that occur as a result of traffic light violation. To realize safe autonomous driving system, we propose in this work a design and optimization of a traffic light detection system based on deep neural network. We designed a lightweight convolution neural network with parameters less than 10000 and implemented in software. We achieved 98.3% inference accuracy with 2.5 fps response time. Also we optimized the input image pixel values with normalization and optimized convolution layer with pipeline on FPGA with 5% resource consumption.

1 Introduction

Recently, neural network have been applied in many fields such as farm monitoring [1], autonomous driving [2], natural image processing [3] and character recognition [4]. Traffic light detection is one of the important factors to prevent traffic accidents in advance [5].To realize safety autonomous driving system, we developed a system for traffic light detection. 11,652 [6] traffic accidents due to ignorance or violation of traffic light signals were recorded in japan in 2019. However, unrecorded traffic accidents are clearly more. Thus, traffic light detection to prevent violation of traffic light signals in advance is one of the big advantages of autonomous driving system.
Improving recognition accuracy contributes to improving safety and realizing efficient autonomous driving system. However, There are factors to consider which include the maneuverability and the power constraints of autonomous driving car environment. Thus, implementation with real time processing in compact circuit size and extremely high accuracy are necessary. Traffic light detection is also object detection, we can realize high accuracy with high speed using well known object detection algorithm such as VGG [7] base Single Shot Multibox Detector SSD [8] and You Only Look Once (Yolo) [9]. However, as we mentioned above, since this detection algorithm requires large architecture and also high power, these object detection algorithms are not suitable for traffic light detection in a power constrained autonomous driving car environment [5]. In this work, we proposed an architecture for traffic light detection. This paper contributes the design of optimized neural network for traffic light detection system both in software on CPU and hardware on FPGA. In next chapter, we introduce basic knowledge for neural network.

*Corresponding Author: Tomohide Fukuchi e-mail: m5222102@u-aizu.ac.jp

1.1 Artificial Neuron

Artificial neuron is a mathematical model of biological neuron. It abstracts the synapse connection, internal potential and neuron firing mechanism of biological neuron. Figure 1 shows a simple biological neuron model and equation (1) shows the mathematical model of the biological neuron model. Strength of synapse connection is represented by w_k, input signal by x_k, membrane potential of each axon by y_m, and final output signal y_m is obtained by multiplying Input x_k and weight w_k then the bias b is added. n is number of input.

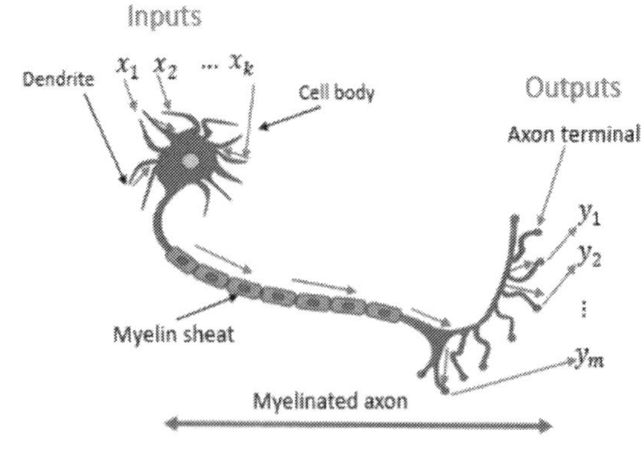

Figure 1. Biological Neuron Model

$$y_m = \sum_{k=1}^{n} x_k w_k + b \tag{1}$$

1.2 Multilayer Perceptron

Figure 2 shows an example of multilayer perceptron [5]. Multilayer perceptron has input layer, more than two hidden layer and output layer. Input image is given as one dimensional array x_k and two dimensional array weight w_k. As we mentioned previously , multiplication between input x_k and weight w_k is performed. And the product is sent to the activation function. The result from the activation function is then sent to the next layer. The activation function could be, Identity activation function , used in regression problem, sigmoid function used in binary classification problem [10], or softmax activation function used in multi class classification problem [10]. In Figure 2, final classification result is represented by probability.

1.3 Convolutional Neural Network

Convolutional neural network is one of the multi layer perceptron. Figure 3 is an example of convolutional neural network LeNet-5 [11]. Convolutional neural network consists of mainly convolution layer, pooling layer and fully connected layer.

1.3.1 Convolutional Layer

Convolution layer which we developed has three channel RGB color image for traffic light image , and background image is also given as input. There are green, yellow, red and background. In convolution layer, input image is extracted as feature using convolution filter. The output image size after it is extracted using convolution filter is given by following formula (2) and (3).

$$W_{out} = \frac{W_{in} + 2 \times padding - filter}{stride} + 1 \tag{2}$$

$$H_{out} = \frac{H_{in} + 2 \times padding - filter}{stride} + 1 \tag{3}$$

Each variable used in the formula, W_{out},H_{out}, W_{in} , H_{in}, $stride$, $padding$ and $filter$ correspond to width of output image, height of output image, row of input image , column of input image, stride size, padding size and filter size respectively. In this work, we used two convolution layer.

1.3.2 Pooling Layer

In pooling layer, row and column of image is shrinked. Pooling is robust to microscopic gap because result of pooling will be same result to small gap of image. In this work, we used max pooling layer which extract a maximum pixel value after convolution layer.

1.3.3 Fully Connected Layer

Fully Connected Layer performs flatten operation on the output from convolution layer or pooling layer is given as input. Final recognition accuracy is output as probability.

2 System Overview and Optimizations

Figure 4 [5] shows the overview of the proposed traffic light detection system. The image acquired from the camera is fed as input to the system. In region proposal phase, input image is divided into some appropriate size image blocks using slide window for image classification. In classification phase, image is classified as one of four classes; green, yellow, red and background using convolution neural network (CNN). In detection phase, traffic light Is detected using trained parameters.

2.1 pragma PIPELINE

pragma HLSPIPELINE in Figure 5, is used to increase the parallelism and calculation speed of the loops required for multiplication of weight and input values. In the case of this experiment, SDx Pipeline is used in convolutional layer.

2.2 Normalization

Normalization in Figure 6 is used to make CNN work faster. In this experiment case, training and testing image values are normalized between -1 to +1 by dividing by 255.0.

3 Evaluation

3.1 Traffic Light Detection on CPU

Table 1 shows the proposed neural network architecture for traffic light detection which performed training and detection in software , using CPU on Ubuntu 16.04. We used two convolution layers and two dropout layers. In dropout layer, connected edges to neuron are chosen randomly, then the randomly chosen weight value will be zero and trained. The number of trained weights and bias is 7884. This neural network architecture is lightweight because the number of parameter is less than 10000.It is suitable for hardware implementation in terms of hardware complexity. The inference accuracy achieved 98.3 % with the 2.5 fps response time for detection. The result of prediction accuracy is preliminarily acceptable for autonomous driving system.

3.2 Hardware Complexity

In this experiment, Zynq Ultrascale MPSoC+ FPGA is used for implementation. Figure 7 shows a demonstration of traffic light image classification on FPGA. Table 2 presents the result of evaluated hardware complexity of optimized convolutional layer using Xilinx SDx. Resource consumption of BRAM18K, DSP48E, FF and LUT are respectively 50 , 41 , 4859 and 5866. We optimized convolution layer for traffic light detection using 5% FPGA resource.

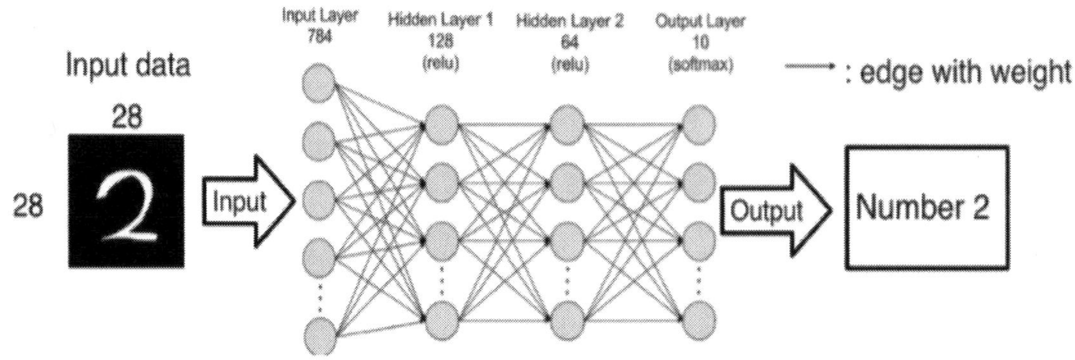

Figure 2. Multilayer Perceptron [5]

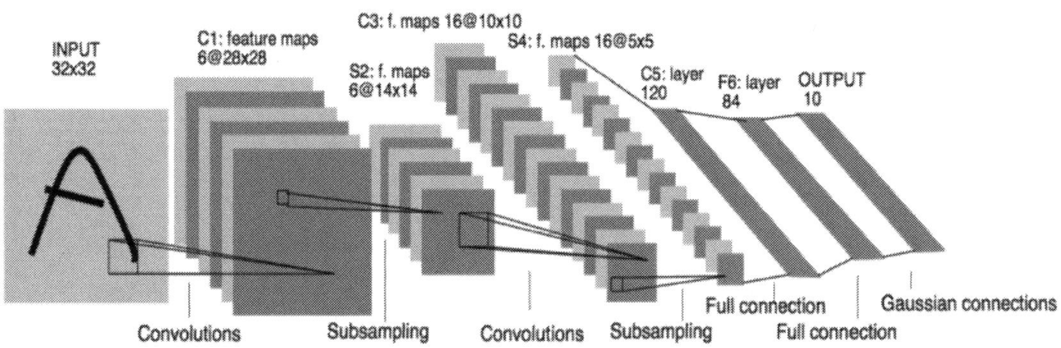

Figure 3. Convolutional Neural Network [11]

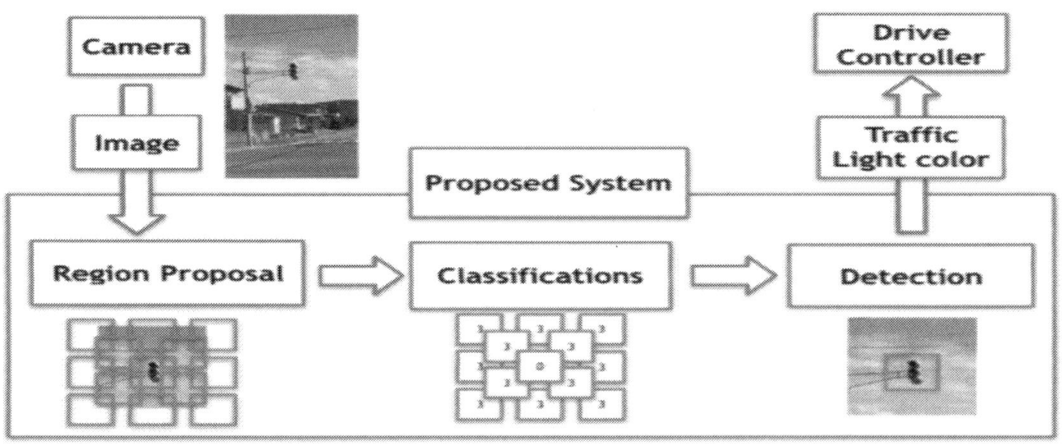

Figure 4. Proposed System Architecture for Traffic Light Detection [5]

```
for(d = 0; d < input_depth; ++d){
  offset_i = (input_width * input_height * d);
  offset_f = (filter_size * filter_size * d); // Offset of filter.
  #pragma HLS PIPELINE
  for(n = 0; n < filter_size; ++n){
    #pragma HLS UNROLL
    for(m = 0; m < filter_size; ++m){
      #pragma HLS UNROLL
      element[m] = buffer0[offset_i + ((y_start + n) *
        input_width) + (x_start + m)]
        * buffer1[offset_f + (n * filter_size) + m]; }
    // Sum of colum elements in the same row line.
    sum_srl[n] = element[0] + element[1] + element[2] +
      element[3] + element[4];}
  // Sum of multiple row lines.
  sum_mrl[d] = sum_srl[0] + sum_srl[1] + sum_srl[2] +
    sum_srl[3] + sum_srl[4];}
sum = sum_mrl[0] + sum_mrl[1] + sum_mrl[2] + sum_mrl[3] +
filter_bias;
return sum;
```

Figure 5. Convolution calculation using Xilinx SDx PIPELINE

```
cnn_layer_image[0].input_data[dst_pt] =
  (double)image->data[src_pt] / 255.0;
```

Figure 6. Input Image Normalization

Table 1. Neural Network Structure for Traffic Light Detection

Layer Name	Image Size
Input	64x64x3
Conv2d$_1$	62x62x20
MaxPooling2d$_1$	12x12x20
Conv2d$_2$	10x10x20
MaxPooling2d$_2$	3x3x20
Dropout	3x3x20
Flatten$_1$	180
Dense$_1$	20
Dropout	20
Dense$_2$	4
Activation Function	Relu
Params	7884
Accuracy (%)	98.3

Table 2. Hardware Complexity of Convolution Layers

Resource	Utilization
BRAM	50
DSP	41
FF	4859
LUT	5886

4 Conclusion and Future Works

In this work, we designed and evaluated neural network for traffic light detection with different types of activation function achieving 98.3% inference accuracy. We also implemented, optimized and evaluated the hardware complexity of the traffic light classification on FPGA using only 5% of FPGA resources. In the future, we optimize execution time per image for detection with Spiking Neural Network(SNN).

Figure 7. Setup for Demonstration of Traffic Light Image Classification on FPGA

5 Discussion

The classification accuracy is 98.3 % with ReLu activation function and 97.9% with sigmoid activation function.In Table 3, accuracy is improved 0.4% with Relu compared to sigmoid function. There is no big difference between the two result , Relu activation function is suitable for hardware implementation because it is easier to implement.

Table 3. Neural Network Structure for Traffic Light Detection

Layer Name	Image Size	Image Size
Input	64x64x3	64x64x3
$Conv2d_1$	62x62x20	62x62x20
$MaxPooling2d_1$	12x12x20	12x12x20
$Conv2d_2$	10x10x20	10x10x20
$MaxPooling2d_2$	3x3x20	3x3x20
Dropout	3x3x20	3x3x20
$Flatten_1$	180	180
$Dense_1$	20	20
Dropout	20	20
$Dense_2$	4	4
Activation Function	Relu	Sigmoid
Params	7884	7884
Accuracy (%)	98.3	97.9

References

[1] R. Murarami, Y. Okuyama, A.B. Abdallah, *Animal Recognition and Identification with Deep Convolutional Neural Networks for farm Monitoring*, in *Information Processing Society Tohoku Branch Conference, Koriyama, Japan* (Feb,10,2018)

[2] J. Kim, G. Lim, Y. Kim, B. Kim, C. Bae, *Deep learning algorithm using virtual environment data for self-driving car*, in *2019 International Conference on Artificial Intelligence in Information and Communication (ICAIIC)* (2019), pp. 444–448

[3] K. Cho, B. van Merriënboer, C. Gulcehre, D. Bahdanau, F. Bougares, H. Schwenk, Y. Bengio, *Learning Phrase Representations using RNN Encoder–Decoder for Statistical Machine Translation*, in *Proceedings of the 2014 Conference on Empirical Methods in Natural Language Processing (EMNLP)* (2014), pp. 1724–1734

[4] T.H. Vu, R. Murakami, Y. Okuyama, A.B. Abdallah, *Efficient Optimization and Hardware Acceleration of CNNs towards the Design of a Scalable Neuro inspired Architecture in Hardware*, in *2018 IEEE International Conference on Big Data and Smart Computing (BigComp)* (2018), pp. 326–332

[5] Y. Murakami, Y. Okuyama, A.B. Abdallah, *SRAM Based Neural Network System for Traffic Light Recognition in Autonomous Vehicles*, in *Information Processing Society Tohoku Branch Conference, Koriyama, Japan* (Feb. 10, 2018)

[6] *Road traffic accidents in japan* (2019), e-stat.go.jp/en/stat-search/files?page=1&layout=datalist&toukei=00130002&tstat=000001027457&cycle=7&year=20190&month=0

[7] K. Simonyan, A. Zisserman, *Very Deep Convolutional Networks for Large-Scale Image Recognition*, in *International Conference on Learning Representations* (2015), pp. 1–14, https://arxiv.org/abs/1409.1556

[8] W. Liu, D. Anguelov, D. Erhan, C. Szegedy, S. Reed, C.Y. Fu, A.C. Berg, *SSD: Single Shot MultiBox Detector*, in *Computer Vision – ECCV 2016* (2016), pp. 21–37

[9] J. Redmon, S. Divvala, R. Girshick, A. Farhadi, *You Only Look Once: Unified, Real-Time Object Detection*, in *2016 IEEE Conference on Computer Vision and Pattern Recognition (CVPR)* (2016), pp. 779–788

[10] C. Nwankpa, W. Ijomah, A. Gachagan, S. Marshall, *Activation Functions: Comparison of trends in Practice and Research for Deep Learning* (2018), pp. 1–20, http://arxiv.org/abs/1811.03378

[11] Y. Lecun, L. Bottou, Y. Bengio, P. Haffner, *Gradient-based learning applied to document recognition*, in *Proceedings of the IEEE* (1998), pp. 2278–2324

Predicting Personality Traits by Student Learning Behaviors on Blackboard Systems

Yong Zheng[1,*]

[1]Illinois Institute of Technology, Chicago, IL, USA

Abstract. Personality has been demonstrated as influential factors in technology-enhanced learning. The collection of personality is always a challenge. Human efforts are usually required in the user surveys which is the most common and popular way to collect the personality traits. Predicting personality traits, as a result, becomes one of the research directions. Some researchers consider these personality traits as labels in the classifications, while some others consider them as numeric variables in the regressions. In this paper, we made our attempt to predict the students' personality traits from their learning behaviors on the Blackboard system. More specifically, we tried both the classification and regression models, and evaluate them based on the same standards. Our initial experimental results discover the insights about these predictive models.

1 Introductions and Related Work

Recommender systems is an effective solution to alleviate the problem of information overload and assist decision making. It has also been introduced to educations as one of the technology-enhanced learning techniques. For example, recommender systems have been built to suggest books for K-12 users [1], recommend after-school programs [2], or help select appropriate course projects in class [3, 4]. In recent years, human factors, such as emotions, trust and personality, have been recognized as influential factors in the recommender systems. Particularly, the personality information has been demonstrated as influential factors in decision makings, especially in the area of educational learning. For example, Komarraju, et al. [5] identified the impact of personality on the academic achievements in GPA. Personality traits have been incorporated into traditional recommender systems [6–8], while some research distinguished user roles based on the personality traits in order to further improve the quality of group recommendations [9–11].

However, the collection of personality traits is always a challenge. One of the most popular ways is collecting personality information from user surveys. Personality can be measured by the personality traits. Several frameworks were developed to collect the personality traits. One of the most popular frameworks is the the Big Five Factor (Big5) [12] framework, in which the personality traits can be described by five dimensions [5]: *Openness* is reflected in a strong intellectual curiosity and a preference for novelty and variety. *Conscientiousness* is exemplified by being disciplined, organized, and achievement-oriented. *Extraversion* is displayed through a higher degree of sociability, assertiveness, and talkativeness. *Agreeableness* refers to being helpful, cooperative and sympathetic towards others. *Neuroticism* indicates the degree of emotional stability, impulse control, and anxiety. To collect the Big5 traits, survey is usually adopted, such as the Ten-Item Personality Inventory (TIPI) [13] questionnaire. These methods that rely on the user surveys usually require additional human efforts, not to mention that users' subjective information may not be reliable.

Predicting personality traits, as a result, becomes one of the alternative solutions. The predictions can be achieved by regressions or classifications. On one hand, the personality traits can be considered as numerical and continuous variables, so that the predictive models can be applied for predictions, in which the performance can be accessed by error-based metrics, such as mean absolute error. On the other hand, these personality traits can be treated as labels in the classification process. Ferwerda et al. demonstrate that visual and content features from Instagram pictures can be used to predict personality [14]. Kosinski et al. predicted the personality traits by using the user-likes on Facebook [15]. Chittaranjan et al. tried to infer the personality traits by from the usage data in the mobile phones (e.g., call and SMS logs) [16]. However, there are no existing research that compare the performance of these two categories of the methods. In this paper, we made our attempt to predict the students' personality traits from their learning behaviors on the Blackboard system[1] by using both classification and regression models. Our initial experimental results help discover the insights about the data and the effectiveness of the applied models.

*e-mail: yong.zheng@iit.edu

[1]https://www.blackboard.com/index.html

Table 1: Experimental Results based on the Best Methods

		Openness	Conscientiousness	Extraversion	Agreeableness	Neuroticism
MLC	Accuracy	44.2%	46.1%	35.6%	34.2%	24.4%
	RMSE	0.92	1.04	1.07	1.20	1.24
Regression	Accuracy	38.60%	38.80%	26.40%	27.10%	20.10%
	RMSE	0.84	0.98	0.94	0.99	1.00

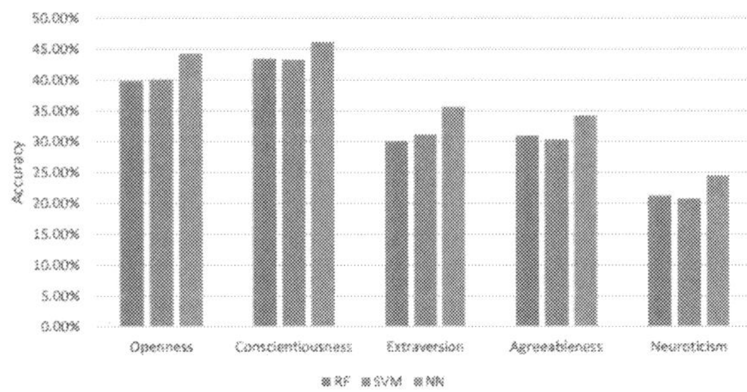

Figure 1: Accuracy Results by Different Classifiers

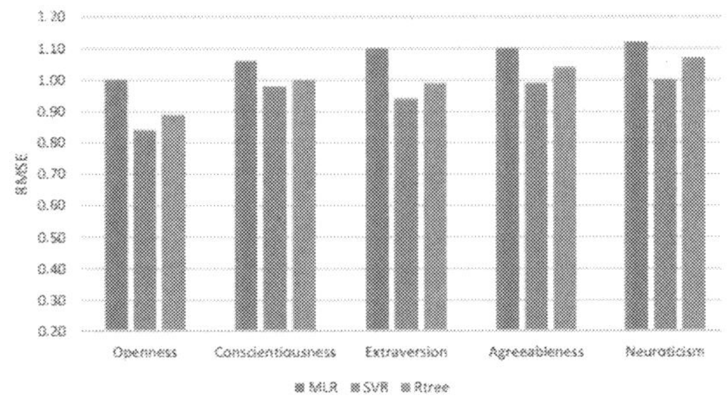

Figure 2: RMSE Results by Different Regressions

2 Data Set

We collected our own data [17] for the purpose of experiments. First of all, we assigned a questionnaire to the graduate students in which they can fill in the demographic information, including age, gender, nationality, marriage status. In addition, we represented personality traits in the Big5 framework, and collected student personality traits by using the popular TIPI questions in the questionnaire.

The demographic information are obviously not enough to predict students' personality traits. We additionally collected their learning behaviors on the Blackboard system. More specifically, instructors used Blackboard system to release assignments, and students can submit their homework to the Blackboard system. For each assignment, we are able to obtain three pieces of information – whether it is a *late* submission (i.e., binary variable), how many *attempts* were made for this assignment (i.e., numerical variable), and the *SafeAssign* score. SafeAssign is one of the components in the Blackboard system, and it compares submitted assignments against a set of academic papers or resources to identify areas of overlap between the submitted assignments and existing works. We collected the data from two courses over three semesters (i.e., 2018 Spring and Fall, and 2019 Spring semester), while there were around 10 to 11 assignments per course per semester.

We organize these three learning behavior variables (i.e., late, attempts, SafeAssign) in four blocks – by year (2018 or 2019), by semester (Fall or Spring), by year (2018 or 2019), and the overall block in which we merge all of the data associated with all assignments. For each block of the data, we calculate the descriptive statistics of the three variables for each student, including the mean, standard deviation, and skewness. It results in 63 new features, in addition to the 4 features from the demographic information. Finally, we obtained our data for experimental purpose. It contains the data for 130 students. For each student, there are 67 features in total associated with students' personality traits in five dimensions (i.e., Big5 framework). The values in the personality traits scale from 1 to 7 which describe the degree of the characteristics in the personality traits.

3 Methodologies and Results

As mentioned before, the personality traits can be treated as either categorical or numerical variables. Accordingly, we can use classification or regression models for the purpose of predictions respectively. More specifically, we can use multi-label classifications (MLC) to predict the personality traits, when we treat all of these five dimensions (i.e., personality traits in the Big5 framework) as categorical labels. In our experiment, we tried the mainstream MLC methodologies, including binary relevance [18], classification chains (CC) [19], label powerset methods [20]. CC is shown as the best multi-label classification method. We only present the results based on CC in this paper. Note that CC just defines a workflow to perform multi-label classifications. Actually we can adopt any traditional classifiers. In our experiments, we tried random forest (RF) [21], support vector machines (SVM) [22] and neural networks (NN) [23]. Alternatively, each dimension in the personality traits can be treated as a numerical variable. We tried the multiple linear regressions (MLR), support vector regressions (SVR) [24] and regression trees (RTree) [25].

Regarding the evaluations, we selected 10-fold cross validation due to the limited size of our data. In addition, we'd like to measure the performance on the same standards. More specifically, we measure the accuracy of each dimension in the personality traits when we apply MLC algorithms. Moreover, we also calculate the root mean squared error (RMSE) by converting the predicted labels as the numerical score. Accordingly, we first measure RMSE when we utilize the regression models. Afterwards, we rounded the predicted values to integers and additionally measure accuracy for each dimension. By this way, we can present the accuracy and MAE for both the classification and regression models.

We present our results in Table 1, Figure 1 and Figure 2. More specifically, we present the best results of MLC and regressions in Table 1 only. The best model for MLC is using classification chain as the MLC workflow with neural networks as the classifier. The best regression model is using support vector regressions. Table 1 only present the results based on these best models. By contrast, we compare the performance by using different classifiers and regression models in Figure 1 and 2. Figure 1 presents the classification accuracy by using three classifiers (i.e., RF, SVM and NN), while Figure 2 describes the RMSE results by using three regression models (MLR, SVR and RTree).

We can observe that the optimal performance varies from dimensions to dimensions in Table 1. The accuracies are relatively higher and the RMSE values are lower for openness and conscientiousness, while the predictions are not that well in other dimensions. In terms of the accuracy, MLC algorithms outperform the regression models, while the regression models beat the MLC in RMSE. It maybe because that the predictions by MLC have no decimals, which results in higher prediction errors in RMSE. Similarly, the rounded predicted values by the regression models also lead to accuracy loss. By using principal component analysis (PCA) [26] for feature reductions, the accuracy and RMSE can be improved a little bit in the process of MLC. Even so, there are no clear winners between the MLC and regression models. It depends on which evaluation metric (accuracy or RMSE) is selected as the key criterion.

The results in Figure 1 and 2 are much more consistent. In Figure 1, we can observe that the best classifier is neural networks. The classification results are better in all the five dimensions in comparison with the accuracies by using other classifiers. In Figure 2, we can observe that SVR is the best predictive model. However, there are no significant differences between the performance between SVR and RTree in the dimension "conscientiousness".

The prediction accuracy is relatively low, which is consistent with the existing work [16]. The major limitation in this initial experiment is the size and sparsity of the dataset. First of all, the data is very small. In addition, we only obtained student behaviors in two courses. It is not guaranteed that each student will take all of these two courses, which results in the problem of sparsity.

We can also discover more insights from the best performing models. In all of the regression models, the age groups and nationality are the two most common and influential variables. They appear in most of the regression models. Other variables, such as the ones associated with descriptive statistics are only influential in predicting selected dimensions in the personality traits, including openness and extraversion. By contrast, these descriptive statistics from the features associated with students' learning behaviors are more important in the MLC models. We can observe that PCA produced 14 components as the transformed features, while each component is a linear representation of the original features. By observing the top principle components which capture the largest variance of the data, we can observe that the weights of different descriptive statistics features are much higher than the features associated with user demographic information. However, the top influential features may vary from components to components.

4 Conclusions and Future Work

In this paper, we exploit and summarize two possible ways (i.e., classification and regression models) to predict the personality traits. Our experimental results reveal that there are no clear winners, and the best choice depends on the evaluation metrics (e.g., accuracy or prediction errors). We identify that neural network is the best classifier in the MLC task when we view personality traits as categorical variables., while support vector regression becomes the optimal regression model if we consider the personality traits as numerical variables. Both features associated with demographic information and learning behaviors are important in MLC and regression models. However, the features based on learning behaviors may be only influential in selected personality traits. We plan to collect more data, and apply more complicated predictive models (such as the deep learning techniques [27]) in our future work to further improve the predictive performance on these personality traits.

References

[1] M.S. Pera, Y.K. Ng, *What to read next?: making personalized book recommendations for K-12 users*, in *Proceedings of ACM conference on Recommender systems* (2013)

[2] R. Burke, Y. Zheng, S. Riley, *Experience Discovery: hybrid recommendation of student activities using social network data*, in *Proceedings of the 2nd International Workshop on Information Heterogeneity and Fusion in Recommender Systems* (ACM, 2011), pp. 49–52

[3] Y. Zheng, N. Ghane, M. Sabouri, *Personalized educational learning with multi-stakeholder optimizations*, in *Adjunct Publication of the 27th Conference on User Modeling, Adaptation and Personalization* (2019), pp. 283–289

[4] Y. Zheng, *Preference corrections: capturing student and instructor perceptions in educational recommendations*, Smart Learning Environments **6**, 1 (2019)

[5] M. Komarraju, S.J. Karau, R.R. Schmeck, A. Avdic, *The Big Five personality traits, learning styles, and academic achievement*, Personality and individual differences **51**, 472 (2011)

[6] R. Hu, P. Pu, *Using personality information in collaborative filtering for new users*, Recommender Systems and the Social Web **17** (2010)

[7] M. Elahi, M. Braunhofer, F. Ricci, M. Tkalcic, *Personality-based active learning for collaborative filtering recommender systems*, in *Congress of the Italian Association for Artificial Intelligence* (Springer, 2013), pp. 360–371
[8] Y. Zheng, A. Subramaniyan, *Personality-Aware Recommendations: An Empirical Study In Educations*, International Journal of Grid and Utility Computing (2020)
[9] Y. Zheng, *Identifying Dominators and Followers In Group Decision Making Based on The Personality Traits*, in *Companion Proceedings of the 23rd International on Intelligent User Interfaces: 2nd Workshop on Theory-Informed User Modeling for Tailoring and Personalizing Interfaces* (2018)
[10] Y. Zheng, *Exploring user roles in group recommendations: A learning approach*, in *Adjunct Publication of the 26th Conference on User Modeling, Adaptation and Personalization* (2018), pp. 49–52
[11] Y. Zheng, *Educational Group Recommendations with Virtual Leaders*, in *Proceeding of the 20th IEEE International Conference on Advanced Learning Technologies* (IEEE, 2020)
[12] R.R. McCrae, O.P. John, *An introduction to the five-factor model and its applications*, Journal of personality **60**, 175 (1992)
[13] S.D. Gosling, P.J. Rentfrow, W.B. Swann Jr, *A very brief measure of the Big-Five Personality Domains*, Journal of Research in Personality pp. 504–528 (2003)
[14] B. Ferwerda, M. Tkalcic, *Predicting users' personality from instagram pictures: Using visual and/or content features?*, in *Proceedings of the 26th Conference on User Modeling, Adaptation and Personalization* (2018), pp. 157–161
[15] M. Kosinski, D. Stillwell, T. Graepel, *Private traits and attributes are predictable from digital records of human behavior*, Proceedings of the National Academy of Sciences **110**, 5802 (2013)
[16] G. Chittaranjan, J. Blom, D. Gatica-Perez, *Mining large-scale smartphone data for personality studies*, Personal and Ubiquitous Computing **17**, 433 (2013)
[17] Y. Zheng, *Personality-Aware Decision Making In Educational Learning*, in *Proceedings of the 23rd International Conference on Intelligent User Interfaces Companion* (ACM, 2018)
[18] M.L. Zhang, Y.K. Li, X.Y. Liu, X. Geng, *Binary relevance for multi-label learning: an overview*, Frontiers of Computer Science **12**, 191 (2018)
[19] J. Read, B. Pfahringer, G. Holmes, E. Frank, *Classifier chains for multi-label classification*, in *Joint European Conference on Machine Learning and Knowledge Discovery in Databases* (Springer, 2009), pp. 254–269
[20] G. Tsoumakas, I. Katakis, I. Vlahavas, in *Data mining and knowledge discovery handbook* (Springer, 2009), pp. 667–685
[21] L. Breiman, *Random forests*, Machine learning **45**, 5 (2001)
[22] M.A. Hearst, S.T. Dumais, E. Osuna, J. Platt, B. Scholkopf, *Support vector machines*, IEEE Intelligent Systems and their applications **13**, 18 (1998)
[23] G.P. Zhang, *Neural networks for classification: a survey*, IEEE Transactions on Systems, Man, and Cybernetics, Part C (Applications and Reviews) **30**, 451 (2000)
[24] S.R. Gunn et al., *Support vector machines for classification and regression*, ISIS technical report **14**, 5 (1998)
[25] P. Chaudhuri, W.D. Lo, W.Y. Loh, C.C. Yang, *Generalized regression trees*, Statistica Sinica pp. 641–666 (1995)
[26] B. Schölkopf, A. Smola, K.R. Müller, *Kernel principal component analysis*, in *International conference on artificial neural networks* (Springer, 1997), pp. 583–588
[27] X. Glorot, A. Bordes, Y. Bengio, *Domain adaptation for large-scale sentiment classification: A deep learning approach*, in *Proceedings of the 28th international conference on machine learning (ICML-11)* (2011), pp. 513–520

SHS Web of Conferences 77, 01004 (2020) https://doi.org/10.1051/shsconf/20207701004
ETLTC2020

Next-Generation Programming Learning Platform: Architecture and Challenges

Yutaka Watanobe[1,*], *Chowdhury* Intisar[1,**], *Ruth* Cortez[1,***], and *Alexander* Vazhenin[1,****]

[1]Department of Computer Science and Engineering, University of Aizu

Abstract. With the rapid development of information technology, programming has become a vital skill. An online judge system can be used as a programming education platform, where the daily activities of users and judges are used to generate useful learning objects (e.g., tasks, solution codes, evaluations). Intelligent software agents can utilize such objects to create an ecosystem. To implement such an ecosystem, a generic architecture that covers the whole lifecycle of data on the platform and the functionalities of an e-learning system should take into account the particularities of the online judge system. In this paper, an architecture that implements such an ecosystem based on an online judge system is proposed. The potential benefits and research challenges are discussed.

1 Introduction

With the growing significance of technology and the ubiquitous availability of information, a number of initiatives in computer education have been promoted by various organizations. Programming has become a vital skill not only for information technology but also for industry and academia. In Japan, the Ministry of Education, Culture, Sports, Science and Technology (MEXT) has decided to make programming a compulsory subject in primary schools starting from fiscal year 2020. Many leading countries have already put great emphasis on programming education.

However, programming is a very difficult task that requires logical thinking and the ability to identify syntactical and conceptual errors. As a result, instructors must expend a lot of effort for creating tasks and evaluating and debugging code, and learners tend to become frustrated. Among educational tools for programming, online judge systems (OJSs) have become popular. An OJS refers to a web service that was originally designed for programming contests such as ACM-ICPC [1], but has become widely utilized for education since it provides reliable evaluation that reduces the workload of teachers and supports self-driven autonomous learning. An attractive feature of an OJS is that learners can repeatedly achieve success, which maintains motivation. OJSs have thus become an indispensable tool for programming education. An OJS provides a number of programming tasks at different levels and compiles and runs submitted code on its servers. Then, it determines whether the code is acceptable using strict test cases. One of the oldest major OJSs, UVa Online Judge, started providing service in 1995 [1]. A number of OJSs are currently operated by various organizations and related tools are actively researched [2].

Although learning materials have been dramatically improved, most major OJSs have shortcomings regarding their educational use. For example, black-box tests are a notable disadvantage. There is a need to improve learning efficiency, but the amount of accumulated data has grown exponentially. Fortunately, this is a great opportunity to make e-learning systems more intelligent as well as to bring research seeds not only for education but also for software engineering fields. Here, we propose an architecture for organizing an ecosystem for an educational programming platform that takes advantage of an OJS. The architecture includes the management of learning objects (LOs) [3], such as tasks, solutions, verdicts, and logs, and a judge system. Most existing e-learning tools for programming cannot be organized into such ecosystems because of their monolithic architecture or localization, which hinders data accessibility, scalability, maintainability, and reusability. Besides, monolithic architecture can be a barrier to flexibly develop user interfaces (client systems) by the third parties.

This study proposes an architecture for a programming learning platform based on the Aizu Online Judge (AOJ) [4] [2], which is one of the oldest OJSs in Japan. Although AOJ has been operated for 15 years, its original core functions and architecture have still not been fully revealed [5]. The aim of the proposed architecture is to realize a programming learning platform ecosystem where data acquisition, reuse, feedback, and research are conducted by people and intelligent software agents. To design the architecture, we first analyzed the distinctive characteristics

*e-mail: yutaka@u-aizu.ac.jp
**e-mail: d8211106@u-aizu.ac.jp
***e-mail: rpatycr@gmail.com
****e-mail: vazhenin@u-aizu.ac.jp

[1]https://icpc.baylor.edu

[2]http://judge.u-aizu.ac.jp

of an OJS, focusing on the actors and LOs. The architecture consists of six layers, which are used to obtain LOs based on a resource-oriented architecture from various perspectives. In this study, an ecosystem is proposed and its generic architecture is described. The effectiveness of the proposed ecosystem is demonstrated through a concrete implementation and initial results of research and development employing the architecture. Potential research challenges for programming education are also given. Components of the proposed architecture are related to machine learning, software engineering, user interfaces, and e-learning systems. This work thus benefits users (e.g., students and teachers) as well as researchers.

The rest of this paper is organized as follows. Section 2 discusses related work. Section 3 formulates the ecosystem and presents the characteristics of the OJS. Section 4 describes the proposed architecture, and Section 5 demonstrates its implementation. Section 6 presents the initial research results and identifies challenges. Section 7 concludes the paper.

2 Related Work

Traditional OJSs include UVa [3], SPOJ [4], and POJ [5], among others [2]. With an increasing number of problem sets from programming competitions, these OJSs continue to grow while contributing to programming education with advanced services such as integrated management interfaces (see for example [6]). A framework that considers feedback other than judge results has been proposed [7]. Jutge.org is an open online judge designed for students and instructors which integrates research and innovation such as formal verification methods, static code analysis and data-mining [8]. However, for most systems, system details are unavailable and data cannot be opened to the public because of architectural inflexibility.

Many companies hold regular programming contests. Codeforces [6], AtCoder [7] and TopCoder [8] are competition platforms with powerful and scalable judge systems that can handle a huge number of participants. They can be used for competition and human assessment and include high-quality problem sets. Although they have great potential as data resources and provide application programming interfaces (APIs) for third parties, their access policies are limited.

Systems that can be deployed in a local environment and provide functions to manage original tasks, evaluation, and grading are not only attractive, but essential for students to gain programming skills which requires deliberate practice and quality feedback [9]. CMS [9] and DOMjudge [10] are notable examples of active open-source projects for contest management that can also be applied for education. Efforts to integrate Automatic Judge to learning management system (LMS) for blended education are an attractive area, but the integration is challenging when standards are not applied, and the design of the applications are monolithic [10]. Enterprises have also released similar e-learning tools for induction courses and personal assessment. Although these closed systems provide a secure and robust environment and allow flexible task management, they are unsuitable for knowledge sharing.

In the consumer web space, some comprehensive architectures for ecosystems and data analysis have been developed [11–13]. Based on the concept of an ecosystem, many enterprises operate a data analysis system that manages data to provide additional services for end users. For example, batch and real-time data processing for Twitter [14] and the use of log data to provide additional information by a Hadoop ecosystem for LinkedIn [15] have been considered.

The concept of an ecosystem can also be applied to an e-learning system, where data is the core of services for education [16]. Massive open online courses (MOOCs) on platforms such as edX and Coursera are an attractive resource for learners and teachers. Such platforms are organized considering data processing and learning resource organization. For example, the base Open edX architecture consists of core applications (e.g., learning management systems) and client tools, which are supplemented by independently deployed applications and persistence systems. From a technical point of view, cloud computing has become a standard solution for dynamic resource allocation, virtualization, and dependable data storage.

Although a number of institutions are considering MOOC, the characteristics of data analysis in a general e-learning system are different from those for programming education, where the utilization of a trial-and-error process is much more valuable to assess the learning outcomes [17]. An example of the analysis is presented in [18], where code snapshots and modification sequence are used to discover patterns to predict students outcomes on exams. Similarly, the study in [19] focuses on understanding the variations of coding solutions to provide appropriate feedback of students learning at scale. However, to take greater advantage of these data, the systems should be able to interact under a common ecosystem.

Although many theoretical works and proposals of architectures for e-learning ecosystems have been presented [20–22], no specific architecture and a corresponding implementation for a programming learning platform have been proposed. Generally, an architecture adopted to a specific domain and specific activities can add value. With increasing demand for programming education and the potential benefits of OJSs, an architecture specifically devoted to LOs for programming education is necessary.

3 Concept of Ecosystem

The data in an e-learning system can be transformed, replicated, integrated, and shared, making them potentially

[3]https://uva.onlinejudge.org/
[4]https://www.spoj.com/
[5]http://poj.org/
[6]http://codeforces.com/
[7]https://atcoder.jp
[8]https://www.topcoder.com/
[9]https://cms-dev.github.io/
[10]https://www.domjudge.org/

reusable. Data can be used to make the system more intelligent. However, the data must be properly collected, classified, processed, and stored. Here, we review the lifecycle of data to help us design an architecture for the ecosystem. In this section, we formulate the actors and LOs in the ecosystem.

3.1 Actors

Figure 1. Concept of proposed ecosystem for programming education

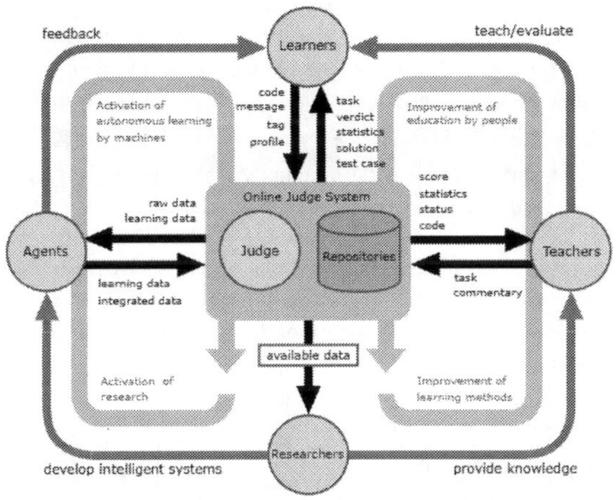

Figure 1 illustrates the concept of an ecosystem with five kinds of actor and OJS data repositories.

Learners are users (e.g., students) who want to learn programming. They search and browse problems (tasks) on the OJS and then try to solve them by coding and submitting the source code. They can also attach their own input/output data for a test submission to the judge. For clarification and discussion, they can post questions to message boards. Voting and tagging are supported. Learners receive a verdict from the judge and can view solutions offered by other uses as well as test cases (judge data) for each problem. Statistics related to problems and learners are available to users.

Teachers are users (e.g., instructors) who support learners in a classroom or group. They create and register tasks, exercises, and contests with special authorization (if needed). Comments regarding various programming languages can be also attached to a task. Teachers can observe learners' activities and solutions. They can instruct and evaluate learners based on the statistics available from the OJS.

Judge is a special software agent that receives programs from learners, makes decisions, and gives verdicts. It generates messages and status related to the decision. The judge manages the queue of submissions and handles them on back-end servers.

Agents are software agents that transform, clean, and integrate the data on an OJS. They provide intelligent feedback to learners on behalf of teachers by utilizing the learning data from the OJS. Agents are developed by researchers and deployed to facilitate development and autonomous learning.

Researchers analyze and utilize the data from the ecosystem to develop intelligent systems. They can input the research results back into the ecosystem by deploying the corresponding agents. They can also share the obtained results with teachers to improve the quality of education.

Agents and researchers can improve education by enhancing the use cases of an OJS, which conventionally involve only learners, the judge, and teachers. The advantage of the ecosystem concept is that learners can obtain feedback from a number of agents in addition to the automatic verification by the judge and instruction from teachers. Researchers can apply their algorithms to the repositories to make the system more intelligent.

3.2 Learning Objects

In this paper, we define any data generated by an actor as an LO. LOs in the ecosystem can be classified based on multidimensional perspectives, as shown in Table 1. The perspectives consider when, how, and by whom LOs were generated, activated, consumed, and processed as well as some features of the data, including data format, size, and frequency.

Notifications are chunks of real-time information broadcast to systems connected to the service. The most common notification is that from the judge for the corresponding submitted code. This notification is used to update the status of the judge queue, scoreboards, and status of other users in real time. Notifications are small but frequent.

Records are information accumulated for an activity by learners and the judge. The main objects created by learners are source code, which can be made public. The main objects created by the judge are messages regarding compilation errors, runtime errors, and program outputs as well as verdicts (Accepted, Wrong Answer, Time Limit Exceeded, Memory Limit Exceeded, etc.) with accuracy and resource usage (CPU time and memory usage). Records can also include personal profiles, trial-and-error submission history, tagging data, and discussion on message boards. Access logs for each LO (e.g., problem description and public source code) are also considered as records.

Materials are learning materials, which are generally created and registered by teachers. They include problem descriptions, images, test cases, and comments. Although access frequency is relatively low, materials can be relatively large (for example, an input file for a test case can be several tens of megabytes).

Statistics are a secondary information resource derived from records and materials. They can be used for statistical analysis and visualization related to users' performance, learning history, problem status, and verdicts from the judge. They include information for the whole system, such as overall user rankings and statistics for each language, as well as individual statistics, such as the daily effort of a learner, their weekly achievement, and ability charts.

Table 1. Classification of learning objects from multidimensional perspectives

Perspectives	Who		What (examples of learning objects)	When/How (time)	Format	Size	Freq.
	Consumer	Creator					
Notification	Learner, Teacher	Judge	verdict, messages, etc.	Push All	Object	Small	High
Record	Learner, Teacher	Learner, Judge	source code, verdict, tagging, logs, etc.	Request	Object	Med	High
Material	Learner, Teacher	Teacher	description, test cases, etc.	Request	Object	Large	Med
Statistic	Learner, Teacher	Agent	ranking, score, statistics, etc.	Request	Object	Med	Med
Feedback	Learner	Agent	hints, debugging, recommendation, etc.	Push Personal	Object	Small	Med
Archive	Researcher	Agent	set of source codes, etc.	Request	File	Huge	Low

Feedback is a chunk of real-time information provided through the intelligent system to support learning, analysis, and other activities. Examples include hints for debugging and recommended problems to be solved considering the learning path as well as other personalized tips. Note that models and the corresponding learning data are required to provide feedback.

Archive is a large chunk of data for specific purposes. It can be used for data analysis, batch processing, and data mining. Examples include a set of submitted source code, judge data, and a set of problem descriptions from a specific source. Integrated data derived from available LOs can also be archived. Although access to an archive is rare, the size of a file can be huge.

4 Architecture

According to the characteristics described in the previous section, the architecture for the ecosystem was designed. We give an overview of the requirements and then present the details.

4.1 Overview

The main functional requirement of the architecture is to cover the whole lifecycle of data in an OJS as well as to provide methods for data acquisition and management for agents and researchers. In addition, the architecture should satisfy non-functional requirements for quality of service and for scaling up through continuous development considering the following observations.

- The amount of information in OJSs will grow exponentially as OJSs become increasingly popular. Therefore, requests should be distributed to provide data with low latency in a robust environment. For example, a server with a monolithic architecture may easily be put under heavy load, affecting other services. Although request processing can be sped up using load balancing through cloud computing and physical scaling up, classification, roles, and transformation of data should be clarified considering the features of each LO for efficient management and development.
- Technologies will change. Technologies for both client side (e.g., web and UI frameworks) and server side (e.g., web servers, programming paradigms, virtualization) are continuously changing, and thus the architecture should not depend on any given technology. A promising solution is to employ a standardized interface and technology-independent data/knowledge representation.
- Requirements are becoming increasingly individualized and diverse. Therefore, the architecture should be scalable so that many applications (agents) can easily be integrated by third parties.

Figure 2 illustrates a generic architecture for the ecosystem. Data Server is used to access LOs and is connected to Client Systems and Judge Server. The main idea is that the proposed architecture is oriented around data, not views (user interfaces). The architecture is thus designed and implemented by applying concepts of resource-oriented architecture, where an application scenario is represented by a uniform resource identifier (URI). Each unique URI, with its associated parameters (keys), is a representation of an LO or a set of LOs (values for the keys). Data Server, the core part of the architecture, does not include any modules for creating views (e.g., HTML pages); instead, it provides data in a certain format (e.g., JSON and XML). The services are thus not tied to any specific operating system or programming language. Learners and teachers get and create data through client systems.

4.2 Data Server

Data Server consists of six layers for the corresponding perspectives, each of which is implemented by three modules. Controller is responsible for receiving and providing LOs as an interface between the client systems and the corresponding data. This is the entry point to get LOs or to post LOs through a URI with parameters. Repository is responsible for storing LOs as persistent data. An LO is mapped to a record in the database table, an object of a key-value store, or a file. An appropriate storage system should be employed for processing massive and structured data from various sources. Service is responsible for bridging the gap between a controller and a repository. Service can deploy transporters, as a bridge, or the judge and agents, which implement business logic for the corresponding layers.

Notification Layer is responsible for receiving information from the judge and broadcasting it to systems connected to the controller. The broadcast should be immediately and asynchronously activated when the corresponding LO becomes available. Real-time notifications make the system convenient to use. Generally, this layer does not need the repository because its role is to quickly forward information. To implement this layer, technologies

Figure 2. Proposed architecture

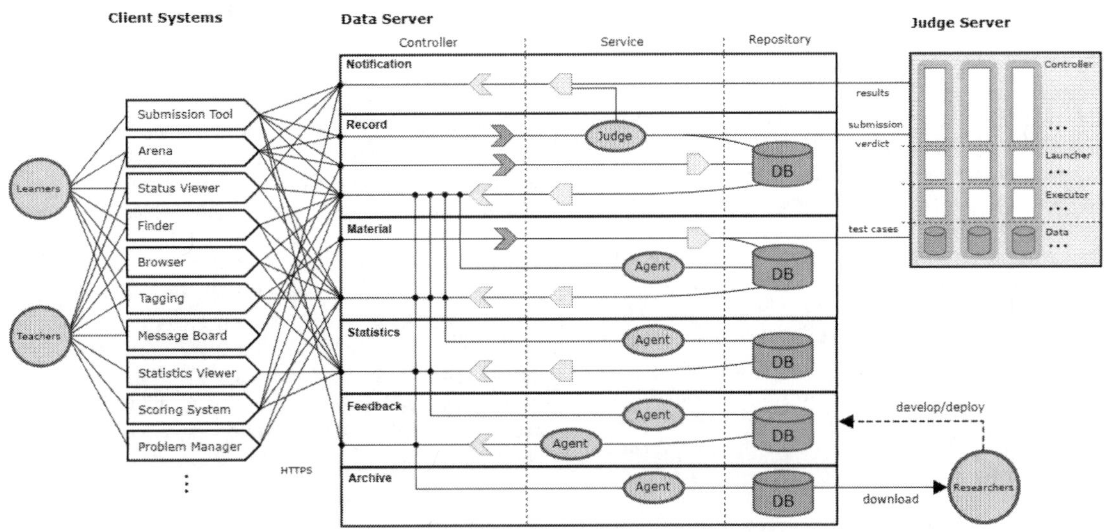

that can efficiently perform PUSH operations to a huge number of client systems at the same time should be employed.

Record Layer is responsible for processing all activities by the learner, teacher, and the judge and recording them as persistent data. It is considered as the main layer. It includes the judge and communicates with Judge Server. Activities and events from learners and Judge Server should be immediately forwarded to Notification Layer. Data should be cascaded by requests from services in the lower layers. This layer is the entry point for the main activities, so both an unstructured database for storing raw data and a structured database for CRUD (Create, Read, Update and Delete) operations should be deployed. An authentication function must be implemented for this layer so that private content can be accessed only by authorized actors.

Materials Layer is responsible for receiving available materials and forwarding and expanding them to Judge Server. The obtained data are stored in the database. Data should be cascaded by requests from services in the lower layers. Since this layer deals with relatively large data (e.g., judge data), the layer should be deployed considering scalability and latency. Materials are registered when a new LO is available from teachers. They can be obtained through request by any authorized actor.

Statistics Layer is responsible for generating and providing useful objects for analyzing data. Agents deployed on this layer regularly crawl the upper layers and create and update the analytic data as new LOs in the corresponding repositories. The frequency of crawling should be carefully specified so that it can provide the latest (not necessarily real-time) information (for example, statistics for each problem is updated every hour) without excessively loading the upper layers. An LO should be obtained through the transporter as is.

Feedback Layer is responsible for providing and broadcasting useful tips for an individual user. Agents crawl the upper layers and generate data (through a learning process, if any) for the corresponding model. The main difference compared to Statistics Layer is that another agent with business logic answers a request by utilizing the learning model (data) constructed by the crawler. The feedback should be activated when the computational results become available and delivered to the corresponding user in real time.

Archive Layer is responsible for acquiring LOs from all upper layers and providing chunks of LOs as useful archive files. Agents regularly crawl the upper layers to create an archive. For this layer, a relatively huge storage system and logging techniques are required. Content in Archive Layer could be downloaded or shared with researchers with proper authorization.

Record Layer and Materials Layer are crucial for implementing an OJS. The other layers are auxiliary layers used to make the OJS more convenient and intelligent. The six layers are loosely coupled channels that can be deployed on different hardware resources (micro services in the cloud). Required data can be transported and integrated by a cascading mechanism. The auxiliary layers are scalable and a number of systems (agents and the corresponding repositories) can be deployed on different hosts.

4.3 Judge Server

Judge Server should be isolated to allow only authorized processes to connect to it and prevent data leaks by malicious attacks and unintended operations. To improve the quality of service of judge processes as a whole, Judge Server consists of server clusters as a parallel machine, where each server can exclusively use hardware resources and execute a given program. The necessary environment (e.g., operating system, compilers, and virtual machines) should be set up for each judge server in advance. Each server should be ready to judge all problems in the corresponding OJS. All available test cases and validators from Materials Layer are replicated in each judge server. This is one of the advantages of an OJS based on the proposed architecture; all required environmental settings, data, and validators are deployed and built in advance to realize quick decisions as well as to ensure robust environments. Therefore, only connections (ports) for sending and receiving limited objects should be allowed, including 1) source code (with accompanying data) from Record Layer when the server becomes available for submission, 2) a verdict to Record Layer and Notification Layer when the judge makes a decision, and 3) a set of test cases from Materials Layer when Judge Server is deployed or data are created.

The judge in Record Layer is a core actor that receives submissions and sends them to the queue of the corresponding judge server. The role of the judge is to select a judge server for a submission depending on the language, problem ID, and other parameters, as well as to scale up by adding available hardware resources. It also makes the verdict information from Judge Server persistent data that are linked to repositories. For broadcasting, the judge sends information to Notification Layer when 1) it receives a submission from a learner and pushes it to the queue, 2) the submission is sent to Judge Server from the queue, 3) it receives the corresponding verdict after the judge has finished deciding, and 4) the verdict is made persistent.

4.4 Client Systems

Client systems that connect to Data Server through the HTTPS protocol can be developed independently. Of note, third parties can freely develop client systems using the available URIs and the data on Data Server. Any application based on a character or graphical user interface that can deal with data as an object can be considered. Generally, a client system uses LOs from a set of layers and an integrated application can be constructed with several client views. In this way, we can separate client side and server side development, and thus technological changes on the server side do not affect the client side and vice versa.

In a data-oriented architecture, the implementation of core functions for a web system is made on the client side. Functions include page generation, page transition, management of URLs, and routing mechanisms, and can be implemented in JavaScript and related frameworks, which enable the development of rich and fast front-end interfaces. Although the client side is responsible for implementing many functions, it allows a division of labor, where the front-end and the back-end can focus on a rich UI and data management, respectively.

5 Implementation

In the previous section, a generic architecture that can be implemented using various technologies was presented. In this section, a concrete implementation is demonstrated through the development of AOJ, which consists of Data Server, Judge Server, and client applications.

5.1 Overview

AOJ, developed and operated since 2005, is one of the major OJSs [2]. More than 70,000 users have been registered and almost 4 million solutions have been judged. Almost 100 contests have been held, including Online Open Contests for ACM-ICPC Asia Regionals in Japan 2014-2019. The first submission to AOJ was done in 2005 when the system was internally released. AOJ was opened to the public in 2009. Before 2018, AOJ had a monolithic architecture with Judge Server. From 2018, all services on the server side were reconstructed as Data Server and now AOJ is operated based on the proposed architecture. The user interfaces are provided through a number of client applications.

5.2 Data Server

Table 2. Frameworks and technologies used for implementation of AOJ

Layer	Frameworks	Key Technologies
Notification	Akka, Play (Scala)	WebSocket
Record	Spring Boot, MySQL	RESTful API
Material	Hybernate	
Statistics	Spring Boot, MongoDB	

Table 2 shows the key technologies used to implement AOJ for the main layers of Data Server. Each layer is deployed in a docker container on CentOS. The server for Notification Layer was developed based on the Akka toolkit [11] and its Actor model and broadcasting is realized using WebSocket. Akka provides a high-performance, robust, and scalable environment and ensures fault tolerance. Record Layer, Materials Layer, and Statistics Layer were developed based on Spring Boot [12] so that controllers can provide access to resources through a RESTful API [23]. MySQL was used for CRUD operations from repositories in Record Layer and Materials Layer. MongoDB was deployed for key-value operations to obtain objects from Statistics Layer. A total of 124 URIs, which cover most LOs required to implement an OJS, are available from the developer website [13]. Each LO obtained by a URI is represented as an object in JSON format, which can be easily and efficiently parsed in many programming languages (e.g., JavaScript and Python).

Some achievements and challenges for Feedback Layer are presented in Section 6.

In addition to the LOs available from the API, researchers can utilize archive files, presented in Table 3, from Archive Layer. For example, a set of source code from a certain range of submission IDs is available as a

[11] https://akka.io
[12] https://spring.io/projects/spring-boot
[13] http://developers.u-aizu.ac.jp

Table 3. Available archive files

Available Data	Type
source codes in specific range	files in zip directory
test cases of specific problem	files in zip directory
descriptions of all problem	files in zip directory
verdict records in specific range	csv files

zip file from the developer website. We provide not only an archive of learning materials, but also an archive of source code with submission histories, including details of verdicts (for downloading private source codes and related files, special consent for research cooperation is required). Some agents have been implemented to crawl data based on a platform similar to that of Statistics Layer. On the other hand, logging technologies such as Apache Hadoop [14] and Fluentd [15] can also be employed for data proliferation.

5.3 Judge Server

Each judge system of a Judge Server cluster is mainly realized by processes of programs written in Perl on CentOS, where all necessary software and data have been set up. In addition, the necessary security settings are performed using iptables, user management, and resource limitations.

Figure 3. Sequence diagram of a judge system

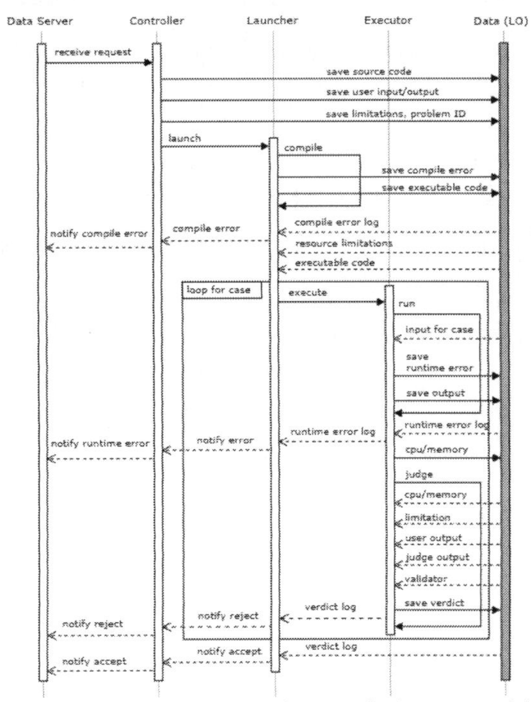

[14]https://hadoop.apache.org/
[15]https://www.fluentd.org/

The programs are mature (stable versions available for more than 10 years). Figure 3 shows a sequence diagram of a judge system, focusing on what and when LOs are generated as well as communication with Data Server. Some technical details, such as security settings for the sandbox, performance, scaling, and the deployment process, are beyond the scope of this paper. Judge Server consists of three modules, namely Controller, Launcher, and Executor. Controller waits for a request from Data Server. When it receives a request, the solution code and accompanying data, including user-defined input/output (for test submissions), problem ID (pid), language, and resource limitations, are set as data files and Launcher is activated. Following the setup, Launcher tries to compile (if needed) the source code; if this fails, it generates error messages and the process returns back to Controller and then Data Server with the message. If the launch process is successful, according to the number of test cases, the generated code is executed by Executor within the resource limitations. Executor generates a runtime signal and messages if errors occur; otherwise, it generates an output file of the program for each test case. Executor terminates the process of the user program when resource limits are exceeded. After finishing each run, Executor decides the verdict (along with CPU time and memory usage) and sends the information to Data Server. When the solution is rejected or all test cases are passed, control is returned back to Controller with a summary of the verdict.

6 Initial Results and Challenges

The proposed architecture and the implemented Data Server have enabled the development of different systems by the third parties which can contribute to both education and software engineering. The systems include the agents based on machine learning approaches as well as client systems with advanced interfaces. In this section, we present the initial results from research and development based on Data Server and possible challenges for the ecosystem.

6.1 Initial Results

6.1.1 Client Systems

The AOJ system has been migrated to the current version which consists of Data Server with a number of accompanying client applications developed by the third parties in addition to the main interface [16]. First, a problem finder and a browser were implemented as a beta version of the new AOJ interfaces [17] based on a single-page application, which is compatible with the new architecture. Other core applications include an Arena system [18], where teachers (and admin) can set exercises and contests with selected tasks and settings through the special manager. Learners can use Arena to browse, code, grade, and manage their programs. Another major product is Virtual Judge

[16]http://judge.u-aizu.ac.jp
[17]https://onlinejudge.u-aizu.ac.jp
[18]https://onlinejudge.u-aizu.ac.jp/beta/arena.html

[19], which is a virtual contest system that connects to Data Server as a part of judge system. Intelligent Coding Editor (ICE) [20] is a special interface for coding as an online compiler/editor where users can test their program with specified test cases through Data Server.

6.1.2 Detection of Errors in Source Code

One useful function is automatic error indication in source code. Error detection is one of the most important criteria to support novice programmers. In programming practice a significant amount of time is spend in formulating the logic and solution. Thus, it is important to automate the process of logic error detection so that novice programmers can learn about the mistake instantly. Although, various syntax errors can be detected reliably by current state-of-the-art compilers and integrated development environments (IDEs), the task of detecting logic (algorithmic) errors in codes is still a challenge and open research. Various approaches and solutions have been proposed in order to automate the logic error detection. Researches [24–26] approach to solve the problem by pattern analysis of accumulated compiler error messages. In addition, students debugging activities have been taken into consideration. In our research [27], we have leveraged state-of-the-art neural network such as, recurrent neural network (RNN) with long short-term memory (LSTM). This learning model was directly trained on the compiled source code of expert programmers. Thus, during the inference the trained model shows the probabilities for a given sequence of source code. Our approach also extends to static code analysis using the intermediate representation in Abstract Syntax Tree [28]. The results show that the proposed algorithms can detect logic errors in compliable code with high frequency for some specific problems. We can further analyze these approaches to best utilize them and avoid mismatches to provide more intelligent and accurate feedback. Hybrid intelligence which is focusing on strong points of these approach has also been considered [29]. We believe that Archive can be a resource for developing state-of-the-art intelligent and adaptive learning algorithms for source code analysis [30] and intelligent coding editors.

6.1.3 Recommendation of Problems and Learning Path

A learning path is an important guideline for improving education results. We previously proposed a novel RNN-based recommendation system (RC) for recommending a set of tasks (materials, programming problems) to learners considering individual learners' strengths in each category and their preferences [31]. For training the RNN-based RC, we leveraged the accumulated data of AOJ, which contains a sequence of problems previously solved by expert users. The key assumption is that the expert programmers' learning path (in the AOJ database) is an ideal guide for novice programmers. The proposed RNN trained on these data has successfully predicted the next likely problem to be solved. In practice, this work is a big challenge because the process is different from that of conventional collaborative filtering. General collaborative filtering (for example, as used by several services such as Amazon) is not applicable since the recommendation of problems is not always based on a programmer's preferences. A pedagogical sequence based on a programmer's strengths has to be maintained when recommending programming problems. This issue has been solved in the aforementioned research through the clustering of programmers based on strengths.

[19] https://vjudge.net/

[20] http://developers.u-aizu.ac.jp/ice/index

6.1.4 Estimation and Classification of Problems

For possible preprocessing of the above algorithms, we developed many intelligent expert systems to estimate the difficulties and topics of programming problems. Previously (see for example [32]), we applied fuzzy theory to derive rules that can partition programming problems into several difficulty levels. We have also taken into consideration the problem statements to predict the topics and categories associated with the problems. In one study [33], various natural language processing algorithms, such as latent Dirichlet allocation and non-negative matrix factorization, were applied for topic extraction. In addition, to make the system more adaptive and pedagogical, we have also taken into consideration the strength estimation of programmers. Neural-network-based approaches, such as the self-organizing neural network, have been applied to this problem [34]. Classification of source codes and problems based on Convolutional Neural Network (CNN) has also been performed [35]. Similar work has been conducted for other online judge systems [36]. These achievements demonstrate that personalized search, recommendation, and feedback, as well as human assessment can be improved using machine learning algorithms.

6.2 Challenges

6.2.1 Coding Support

IDEs, which support error highlighting, code completion, and refactoring, are an indispensable tool for software development. The above functions can be realized using machine learning and big data (program code). The latest technology, powered by Visual Studio IntelliCode [21], has had a great impact on software engineering. An artificial intelligence system that utilizes a number of GitHub repositories for learning provides intelligent completion functions with suggestions that consider circumstances other than conventional variable/function lists. In this context, in addition to bug detection, machine learning approaches that employ the accumulated source code in an OJS can revolutionize programming education. Of note, the data in an OJS includes not only typical mistakes by novices but also exemplary code written by talented programmers.

[21] https://visualstudio.microsoft.com/

Personalized feedback will also be possible by considering user experience. As one of our research challenges, code completion based on RNN and solutions in an OJS has been considered for programming education [38].

6.2.2 Automatic Generation of Learning Objects

The automatic generation of LOs has became an important research area for intelligent autonomous learning. We can generate secondary LOs by reusing existing LOs in the ecosystem. For example, the automatic generation of pseudocode and comments for source code is an attractive challenge (see for example [37]). For this type of generation, problem descriptions, tags, and source code can be utilized. Another idea is the automatic annotation of source code and problem descriptions to support understanding. For creating programming tasks, automatic generation of fill-in-the-blank programming problems is one of promising functions to support instructors [39]. The generation of test cases, solution code, and tasks (problem descriptions) are also big challenges. For example, automatic generation of a program code from another code which has the same function but in different programming languages, is attractive for many applications.

6.2.3 Integration of Services via Standard Protocol

The usefulness of the data goes beyond the programming platform itself because every LO can be accessed via a URI and applications can exchange data via REST, and according with the proposed architecture this task is handled by clients. In similar efforts such as MAGIC system, the integration of auto-graders at massive scale for Cloud utilize REST API [40]. As technology is evolving and adopting new standards, the clients (usually LMS, but not limited to) can also connect via Learning Tools Interoperability (LTI) standard. The LO can be seamlessly created and associated as part of the LTI client application resource. Since LTI is now widely adopted by modern LMS based on its protocol style, an OJS can become part of a larger ecosystem. CodeOcean project is an example of an auto-grader using LTI, and CodeHarbor project proposes LO organized as repository, both to reuse programming LO and integrate with other applications [41].

Based on the LTI standard, LOs and coding performance can be combined with material or study paths (in this case, in a guided environment) taken by the student on a MOOC platform such as Coursera or edX, or a LMS such as Moodle or Canvas. This would make it easier for researchers to cross reference user behaviors and interaction with specific content, the path in the OJS, the impact of their materials on coding performance. More accurate feedback could also be provided based on the data in the OJS, as each LO can be clearly identified. Other efforts integrating MOOCs and Automatic grading for improving feedback in programming are presented in [40] [42]. However, the integration and data cross-reference is still challenging due to the different architectures, and lack of ecosystem definition.

7 Concluding Remarks

An OJS can be organized into an ecosystem where learners, teachers, graders, and intelligent software agents are involved. The accumulated LOs allow effective e-learning for programming education. Such an environment gives learners significant advantages and reduces costs in terms of human resources.

In this paper, a generic architecture and the corresponding concrete implementation were presented based on the Aizu Online Judge. We demonstrated that the proposed architecture and implemented data servers have activated development of different interfaces for learning support as well as research for creating intelligent agants by the third parties. We developed some feedback systems related to bug detection, recommendation, and estimation using learning objects, which are open to the public. We also considered research challenges for the ecosystem. Although researchers can utilize data and develop their own agents, we should consider making a framework where they can easily define and deploy their actors to the cloud or the corresponding data server.

8 Acknowledgments

This work was supported by JSPS KAKENHI Grant Number 16K16174.

References

[1] Miguel A. Revilla, Shahriar Manzoor, Rujia Liu. 2008. Competitive Learning in Informatics: The UVa Online Judge Experience, *Olympiads in Informatics* 2 (2008), 131 – 148.

[2] Szymon Wasik, Maciej Antczak, Jan Badura, Artur Laskowski, Tomasz Sternal. 2018. A Survey on Online Judge Systems and Their Applications, *ACM Computing Surveys* (*CSUR*) 51, 1, Article 3 (2018).

[3] IEEE Standard for Learning Object Metadata 2002. *IEEE Std* 1484.12.1-2002, 1–40 (2002).

[4] Yutaka Watanobe. Aizu Online Judge, https://onlinejudge.u-aizu.ac.jp/

[5] Yutaka Watanobe. 2015. Development and Operation of an Online Judge System, *IPSJ Magazine* 56, 10 (2015), 998 – 1005.

[6] Luisa M. Regueras, Elena Verdu, Juan P. de Castro, Maria A. Perez, Maria J. Verdu. 2009. A Proposal of User Interface for a Distributed Asynchronous Remote Evaluation System: An Evolution of the QUESTOURnament Tool. In *Proceedings of the 9th IEEE International Conference on Advanced Learning Technologies*, 75–77.

[7] Wenju Zhou, Yigong Pan, Yinghua Zhou, Guangzhong Sun. 2018. The framework of a new online judge system for programming education, In *Proceedings of ACM Turing Celebration Conference*, 9–14.

[8] Jordi Petit, Salvador Roura, Josep Carmona, Jordi Cortadella, Jordi Duch, Omer Gimenez, Anaga

Mani, Jan Mas, Enric Rodriguez-Carbonell, Enric Rubio, Enric de San Pedro, and Divya Venkataramani. 2018. *IEEE Transactions on Learning Technologies* 11, 3 (2018).

[9] Jose Paulo Leal, Fernando Silva. 2003. Mooshak: a Web! based multi! site programming contest system, *Software-Practice & Experience* 33, 6 (2003), 567–581. https://doi.org/10.1002/spe.522

[10] Katerina Georgouli, Pedro Guerreiro. 2010. Incorporating an Automatic Judge into Blended Learning Programming Activities, Lecture Notes in Computer Science, Vol. 6483, 81–90.

[11] David G. Messerschmitt, Clemens Szyperski. 2003. *Software Ecosystem: Understanding and Indispensable Technology and Industry*, 1st ed. The MIT Press.

[12] Konstantinos Manikas, Klaus Marius Hansen. 2013. Software ecosystems - a systematic literature review, *Journal of Systems and Software* 86, 5 (2013), 1294–1306.

[13] Desamparados Blazquez, Josep Domenech. 2018. Big Data sources and methods for social and economic analyses, *Technological Forecasting and Social Change* 130, 99–113 (2018).

[14] Jimmy Lin, Dmitriy Ryaboy. 2013. Scaling big data mining infrastructure: the twitter experience, *ACM SIGKDD Explorations Newsletter* 14 (2013), 6–19.

[15] Roshan Sumbaly, Jay Kreps, Sam Shah. 2013. The big data ecosystem at linkedin, In *Proceedings of International Conference on Management of data*, 1125–1134.

[16] Qinghua Zheng, Huan He, Tian Ma, Ni Xue, Bing Li, Bo Dong. 2014. Big Log Analysis for E-Learning Ecosystem, In *Proceedings of e-Business Engineering*, 258–263.

[17] Paulo Blikstein. 2011. Using learning analytics to assess students' behavior in open-ended programming tasks, In *Proceedings of International Conference on Learning Analytics and Knowledge*, 110–116.

[18] Paulo Blikstein, Marcelo Worsley, Chris Piech, Mehran Sahami, Steven Cooper, Daphne Koller. 2014. Programming Pluralism: Using Learning Analytics to Detect Patterns in the Learning of Computer Programming, *Journal of the Learning Sciences* 23, 4 (2014), 561-599.

[19] Elena L. Glassman, Jeremy Scott, Rishabh Singh, Philip J. Guo, Robert C. Miller. 2015. OverCode: Visualizing Variation in Student Solutions to Programming Problems at Scale, *ACM Transactions on Computer-Human Interaction (TOCHI)* - Special Issue on Online Learning at Scale, 22, 2, Article 7 (2015).

[20] Bo Dong, Qinghua Zheng, Jie Yang, Haifei Li, Mu Qiao. 2009. An E-learning Ecosystem Based on Cloud Computing Infrastructure,
In *Proceedings of 9th IEEE International Conference on Advanced Learning Technologies*, 125 – 127.

[21] Lorna Uden, Ince Trisnawaty Wangsa, Ernesto Damiani. 2007. The future of E-learning: E-learning ecosystem, In *Proceedings of Inaugural IEEE-IES Digital EcoSystems and Technologies Conference*, 113 – 117.

[22] Hemant Kumar Mehta, Manohar Chandwani, Priyesh Kanungo. 2010. Towards development of a distributed e-Learning ecosystem,
In *Proceedings of International Conference on Technology for Education*, 68 – 71.

[23] Roy T. Fielding, Richard N. Taylor. 2002. Principled design of the modern Web architecture, *ACM Transactions on Internet Technology (TOIT)* 2, 2 (2002), 115–150.

[24] Fitzgerald, Sue and McCauley, Renée and Hanks, Brian and Murphy, Laurie and Simon, Beth and Zander, Carol. 2009. Debugging from the student perspective, *IEEE Transactions on Education* 53, 3 (2009), 390–396.

[25] Ahmadzadeh, Marzieh and Elliman, Dave and Higgins, Colin. 2005. An analysis of patterns of debugging among novice computer science students, *Acm sigcse bulletin* 37, 3 (2005), 84–88.

[26] Fitzgerald, Sue and Lewandowski, Gary and McCauley, Renee and Murphy, Laurie and Simon, Beth and Thomas, Lynda and Zander, Carol. 2008. Debugging: finding, fixing and flailing, a multi-institutional study of novice debuggers, *Computer Science Education* 18, 2 (2008), 93–116.

[27] Yunosuke Teshima, Yutaka Watanobe. 2018. Bug Detection based on LSTM Networks and Solution Codes, In *Proceedings of The 2018 IEEE International Conference on Systems, Man, and Cybernetics (SMC2018)*, 3531-3536.

[28] Yuto Yoshizawa, Yutaka Watanobe. 2019. Logic Error Detection System based on Structure Pattern and Error Degree, Advances in Science, *Technology and Engineering Systems Journal* 4, 5 (2019),1-15.

[29] Taku Matsumoto, Yutaka Watanobe. 2019. Hybrid intelligence for logic error detection, In *Proceedings of The 18th International Conference on Intelligent Software Methodologies, Tools, and Techniques (SOMET 2019)*, 120-131.

[30] Miltiadis Allamanis, Earl T. Barr, Premkumar Devanbu, Charles Sutton. 2018. A Survey of Machine Learning for Big Code and Naturalness, *ACM Computing Surveys* 51, 4, Article 81 (2018).

[31] Tomohiro Saito, Yutaka Watanobe. 2020. Learning Path Recommendation System for Programming Education based on Neural Networks, *International Journal of Distance Education Technologies (IJDET)* 18, 1, Article 4 (2019).

[32] Chowdhury Md Intisar, Yutaka Watanobe. 2018. Cluster Analysis to Estimate the Difficulty of Programming Problems, In *Proceedings of 3rd International Conference on Applications in Information Technology (ICAIT)*, 23–28.

[33] Chowdhury Md Intisar, Yutaka Watanobe, Manoj Poudel, Subhash Bhalla. 2019. Classification of Programming Problems based on Topic Modeling, In *Proceedings of International Conference on Infor-*

mation and Education Technology (ICIET), 275-283.

[34] Chowdhury Md Intisar, Yutaka Watanobe. 2018. Classification of Online Judge Programmers based on Rule Extraction from Self Organizing Feature Map, In *Proceedings of 9th IEEE International Conference on Awareness Science and Technology (iCAST)*, 308–313.

[35] Hiroki Ohashi, Yutaka Watanobe. 2019. Convolutional Neural Network for Classification of Source Codes, In *Proceedings of IEEE 13th International Symposium on Embedded Multicore/Manycore Systems-on-Chip (MCSoC-2019)*, 194–200.

[36] Wayne Xin Zhao, Wenhui Zhang, Yulan He, Xing Xie, Ji-Rong Wen. 2018. Automatically Learning Topics and Difficulty Levels of Problems in Online Judge Systems, *ACM Transaction on Information Systems (TOIS)* 36, 3, Article 27 (2018).

[37] Yusuke Oda, Hiroyuki Fudaba, Graham Neubig, Hideaki Hata, Sakriani Sakti, Tomoki Toda, and Satoshi Nakamura. 2015. Learning to generate pseudo-code from source code using statistical machine translation, In *Proceedings of 30th IEEE/ACM International Conference on Automated Software Engineering (ASE)*, 574–584 (2015).

[38] Kenta Terada, Yutaka Watanobe. 2019. Code Completion for Programming Education based on Recurrent Neural Network, In *Proceedings of 2019 IEEE 11th International Workshop on Computational Intelligence and Applications (IWCIA)*, 109–114.

[39] Kenta Terada, Yutaka Watanobe. 2019. Automatic Generation of Fill-in-the-Blank Programming Problems, In *Proceedings of IEEE 13th International Symposium on Embedded Multicore/Manycore Systems-on-Chip (MCSoC-2019)*, 187–193.

[40] Armando Fox, David A. Patterson, Samuel Joseph, Paul McCulloch. 2015. MAGIC: Massive Automated Grading in the Cloud, CHANGEE/WAPLA/HybridEd@EC-TEL (2015).

[41] Thomas Staubitz, Ralf Teusner, Christoph Meinel. 2017. Towards a repository for open auto-gradable programming exercises, In *Proceedings of IEEE 6th International Conference on Teaching, Assessment, and Learning for Engineering (TALE)*, 66–73 (2017).

[42] Guillaume Derval, Anthony Gego, Pierre Reinbold, Benjamin Frantzen and Peter Van Roy. 2015. Automatic grading of programming exercises in a MOOC using the INGInious platform, In *Proceedings of European MOOC Stakeholder Summit 2015*, 86–91.

Cross-Platform Mobile CALL Environment for Pronunciation Teaching and Learning

Andrei Kuznetsov[1,*], *Anton* Lamtev[2,**], *Iurii* Lezhenin[2,***], *Artem* Zhuikov[2], *Mikhail* Maltsev[2] and *Elena* Boitsova[2] and *Natalia* Bogach[2], and *Evgeny* Pyshkin[3,****]

[1]JetBrains s.r.o.
[2]St.-Petersburg Polytechnic University, Russia
[3]University of Aizu

Abstract. Mobile technologies promote computer-assisted language learning (CALL) while mobile applications, being learner-oriented by design, provide a powerful founding to build individual self-paced environments for language study. Mobile CALL (MALL) tools are able to offer new educational contexts and fix, at least, partially, the problems of previous generations of CALL software. Nonetheless, mobile technologies alone are not able to respond to CALL challenges without cooperation and interaction with language theory and pedagogy. To facilitate and formalize this interaction several criteria sets for CALL software has been worked out in recent years. That is why an approach based on using mobile devices is a natural way to transfer the learning process from teaching-centered classroom to a process, which is oriented to individual learners and groups of learners with better emphasis on supporting individual learning styles, user collaboration and different teaching strategies. Pronunciation teaching technology in one of areas, where the automated speech processing algorithms and corresponding software meet the problems of practical phonology. Computer-assisted prosody teaching (CAPT), a sub-domain of CALL, is a relatively new topic of interest for computer scientists and software developers. Present-day advancement of mobile CAPT tools is supported by evolutionary processes in the theory of language learning and teaching. This paper explores language–technology relations using a case of StudyIntonation – a cross-platform multi-functional mobile CAPT tool based on a digital processing core for speech processing, visualization and estimation developed by the authors. We particularly address the problems of developing CAPT evaluation frameworks. To define the problematic points of the project and understand the directions for future work, we discuss an approach to formalized evaluation using a set of CAPT-specific criteria drawing attention to such evaluation factors as general descriptive information, instructional purposes, functionality, usability, and presentation.

1 Introduction

Mobile technologies for language study have gained much attention in recent years for their potential benefits for teachers and learners. Computer assisted language learning (CALL) tools developed for mobile devices (MALL) have strongly promoted their popularity due to the ability to foster a stress-free and self-paced learning environment, virtually unlimited input, and rich multimodal feedback [1].

In context of pronunciation training, an immediate and diverse feedback is especially beneficial. A wide scope of pronunciation teaching technologies and software aggregate speech processing algorithms and apply them in pronunciation pedagogy and assessment. Speech production patterns used to be detected by special instruments (e.g., CSL) or acoustic software (e.g., PRAAT) [2]. Speech science has been largely integrated into identifying various pronunciation features and favors either research or teaching (e.g., [3], [4]). The inventory of CALL tools to support learners through the use of a variety of multimodal feedback possibilities including sound, graphics, video, animation, spectral and pitch displays [5] becomes much more flexible and rich when implemented on a mobile platform.

Computer-assisted prosody teaching (CAPT), a subdomain of CALL, is a relatively new topic of interest for computer scientists and software developers. Automatic speech recognition (ASR) used pronunciation instruction is an important technology making a measurable impact on CALL by enabling the identification of particular parameters of the learner's output [6]. In turn, the advancement of mobile CAPT is supported by evolutionary processes in the theory of language teaching. Research on the role pronunciation plays for the overall language competency (e.g., [7], [8]) and points out the emergence of a number of shifts in instructional focus. The focus is moving from teacher-oriented to learner-oriented classrooms; the advancement of communicative and pragmatic goals of teaching over the abstract language learning [9] favors

*e-mail: andrei.kuznetsov@jetbrains.com
**e-mail: antonlamtev@gmail.com
***e-mail: lezhenin@kspt.icc.spbstu.ru
****e-mail: pyshe@u-aizu.ac.jp

the appearance of more concern about pronunciation. Pronunciation training is no longer considered a minor field; it is understood as one of the principle pivot points of successful communication [10].

By their design paradigm, mobile solutions support and encourage user personalizing and collaboration. That is why an approach based on using mobile devices is a natural way to transfer the learning process from teaching-centered classrooms to a process oriented to both individual learners and groups of learners with better emphasis on supporting individual learning styles and strategies. Moreover, mobile language learning tools can provide a private and flexible environment for self-study. The latter issue is particularly important for pronunciation learning, which is not mere acquisition of a new different phonological system, but mastering a complex cognitive skill of an individual [10].

Being in a rich, informal, contextual, and ubiquitous learning environment, in which it is possible for students to control their learning and receive diverse multimodal authentic input with tailored instructive feedback is highly motivating [11]. Students raise their awareness to improve pronunciation, become more conscious about their faculty of language and acquire a better understanding of many phonological features of a foreign language [1]. With mobile approach, learners gain a larger opportunity to act as active co-creators in cognition-driven process of pronunciation training.

In [12], the authors argue that the tool's availability is the primary factor of technology usability. Hubbard [13] names the foremost CALL principles to follow as access, authenticity, interaction and feedback. Unfortunately, even scientifically sound and engaging CAPT products often have a long way to everyday L2 pedagogy, while direct interaction with learners is the primary practical task of CAPT tools. Mobile CAPT tools can bridge this gap, making the instructional products more handy, available and intuitive to use. But so far, mobile CAPT software has not occupied its due place in teaching practice among other computer-based instructional products. The reasons of it might be attributed to three different sources: personal attitude of teachers and learners; developmental and algorithmic issues; lack of common evaluation guidelines.

In [14], Bitner et al. name eight areas of important consideration to form teachers' positive attitude to integrate technology into the curriculum. Even being inserted in teaching practice, CALL software might be used quite differently from what developers and teachers intended [15]. Human–computer interaction tracking research has shown that there is much individual learner variability in interaction with CALL programs [16], [17], [18], [19]. Kim [20] even reports that from the college EFL learner's perception, MALL are a sort of "subway-time study". Subsequently, the expectations of MALL content, style, and design are different from the concept of effective MALL in the literature and even far distant from effective CALL. Still an intrinsic learner motivation may origin from the possibilities that technology can offer. According to multiple evidence ([21], [22], [23]), the major drawback of existing CALL systems, and CAPT systems in particular, is a lack of guidelines how to employ technology to make courseware.

Although formal criteria, containing development agenda and benchmark sets, have been worked out to evaluate CALL, they are largely based on general software evaluation frameworks (e.g., [24], [25], [13]) and does not mainly address prosody but other language aspects such as computer assisted learning of vocabulary or grammar. While the frameworks for CALL evaluation are far from being inconsistent, none of them explicitly describe workflows for conducting evaluations or, moreover, articulate any guidelines for CAPT software development [26].

CAPT evaluation frameworks have been created only in very recent years. In [27] a checklist of criteria for CAPT software, websites, and mobile apps is proposed; a question-based instrument in [5] evaluates to what extent the software programs teach pronunciation in accordance with the principles of the communicative approach [28]. Having accumulated the previous background in CALL evaluation, these instruments concisely and explicitly inform CAPT developers about the expectations and priorities of CAPT target audience.

Based on the recent new release of StudyIntonation CAPT software [29], [30], [31], in this paper we discus the results of its screening [32] against the criteria from [27], in order to evaluate StudyIntonation functionality and disclose the limitations of its design.

2 Method

StudyIntonation software was conceived as a free open-source mobile application to provide language learners with the visuals of phrasal intonation [29]. Its availability for teachers and learners was discussed in [30]. StudyIntonation approach suggests the collaboration between teachers and native speakers in co-creation of the learning content and supposes various learning scenarios with respect to the learning style of a student.

StudyIntonation workflow (Figure 1) implements all the stages of prosody processing, beginning from pitch detection and approximation up to pitch visualization and pitch estimation. The system incorporates the modules for pitch detection and pitch approximation enabling processing both the model (native speaker) and the record (learner) pitch patterns, as well as for displaying the pitch curves in the client application. The module for pitch estimation is necessary for providing a primary feedback to learners. It can also be used for formalization of pitch similarity evaluation.

Our previous efforts led us to the implementation of a prototype for StudyIntonation developed for Android OS. The similar functionality was later implemented for Apple iOS as an independent application. The efforts towards more similarity of both versions resulted in the latest version which is a cross-platform CAPT environment that works identically under Android and Apple iOS. Both StudyIntonation implementations share the same digital signal processing core and can be used for both university education and self-training. As StudyIntonation has now evolved into a full-fledged mobile CAPT, cross-platform

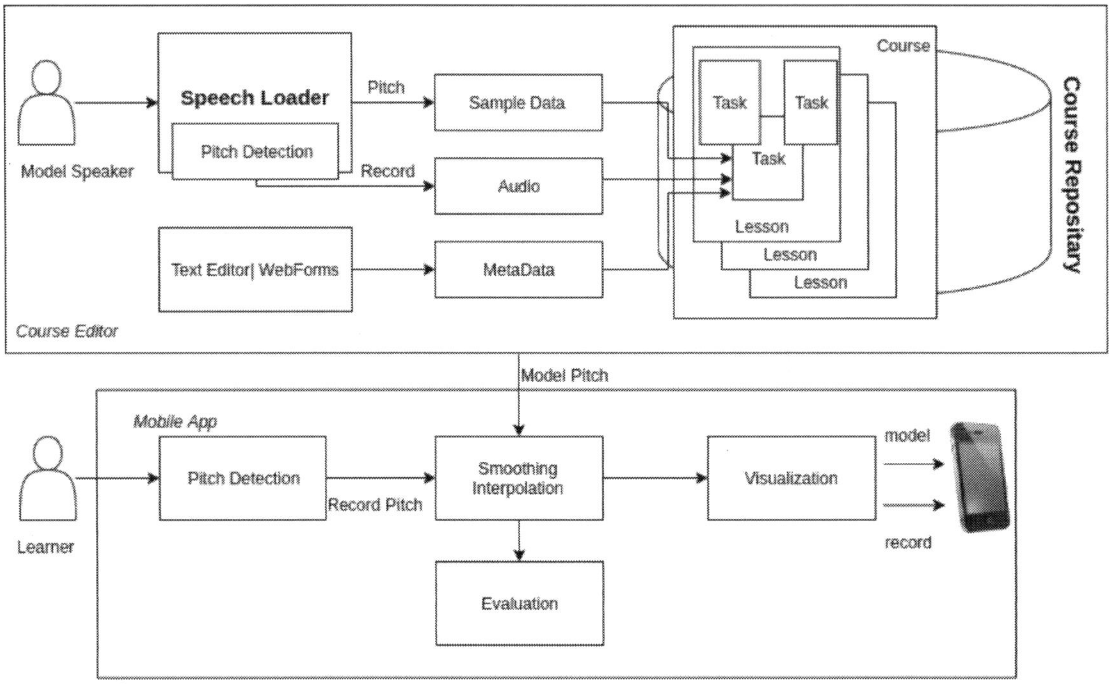

Figure 1. StudyIntonation Workflow

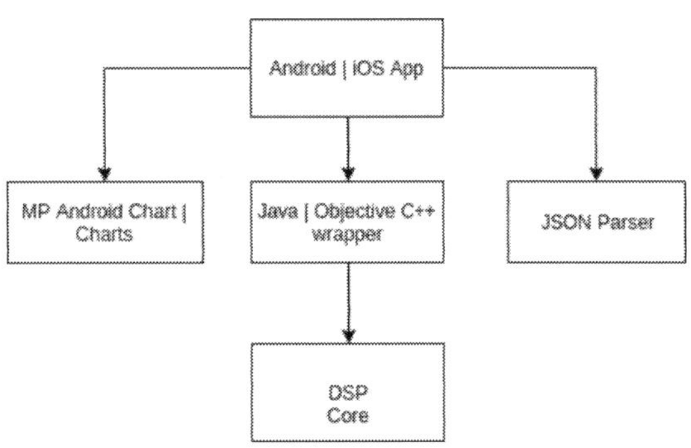

Figure 2. Cross-platform functionality support

and multi-functional, it needs to be validated with respect to the latest formal methods of CAPT tools evaluation, e.g., [27] to understand its soundness for linguistics and pedagogy.

3 Cross-Platform Implementation and DSP Core Assessment

Cross-platform implementation (Figure 2) does not change the workflow. Cross-platform functionality was mostly achieved through the choice of the development instruments and libraries existing for both target operating systems. For example, pitch graphics is processed and rendered by MP Android Chart and iOS Charts, the similar approach was used for the other functional components (such as json parsers, etc.).

In contrast to the the first prototype [29] where Java TarsosDSP was used for signal processing components, for the latest release, the DSPCore was rewritten in C++, thus, both applications share the same DSPCore library for pitch processing, and the pitches look identically (Figures 3, 4). This library is incorporated into Android and iOS applications through Java and Objective C++ wrappers respectively.

For fundamental frequency processing (signal interpolation, resampling, low-pass filtering), DSPCore uses a number of third-party components from Essentia open library of tools for audio data. The project leverages the ability to build Essentia library with a direct indication to the set of algorithms used. In this case, the algorithms not engaged into pitch processing are not included in the output file. Thus, the final output file of the DSPCore library has smaller size and weaker external library dependencies compared to the full assembly.

The DSPCore library API includes the following important functions. The function *bool loadAudioFile()* reads audio data from the specified file; *bool detectPitch()* calculates the fundamental frequency vector by using YIN algorithm; *bool smoothPitch()* is responsible for making the pitch signal more uniform; *float dtw()* implements the DTW time sequence comparison.

DSPCore has the following external dependencies: *fftw3f* for calculating the Fourier transform (FFT), and

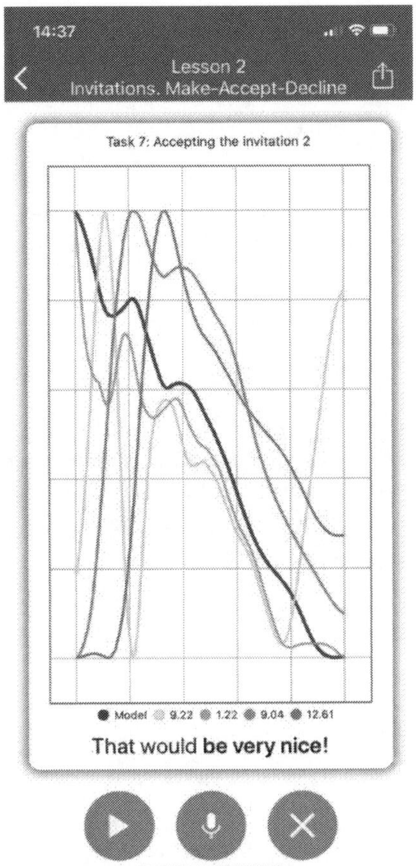

Figure 3. Application Appearance under Apple iOS (task interface)

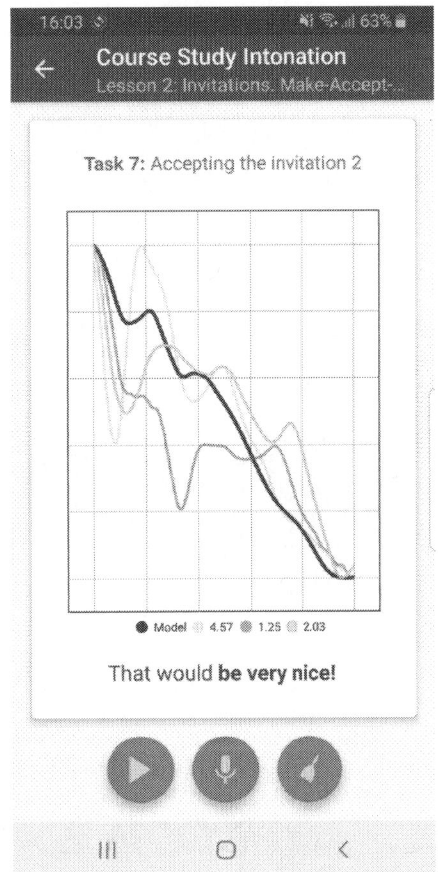

Figure 4. Application Appearance under Android OS task interface

samplerate for converting the sampling audio data frequencies.

To read audio data from a file, *ffmpeg* libraries are used; *avcodec* library implements audio codecs; *avformat* library implements streaming protocols, container formats, as well as basic input/output operations; *avutil* library implements some auxiliary functions; *avresample* library is used for audio mixing and resampling.

To test the DSPCore function, we used the prosodically labelled corpus IviE. Intonation contours in audio recordings of IViE speech stimuli were loaded into PRAAT and DSPcore. For each IViE record bearing the tones indicated in tone markup (H*, L+H*, L%, 0%, etc.), the corresponding tone movements were observed in both programs.

4 Criteria Evaluation and Discussion

Searching for a thorough professional analysis of the software product, we assess the proposed architecture as per criteria set introduced in [27], which are focusing attention on the characteristics that need to be considered when evaluating CAPT software. This set of criteria is particularly helpful because it draws attention to the factors that might be otherwise ignored. Therefore, it enables getting quick CAPT functionality summary and setting the goals for future development.

Henrichsen [27] organized the criteria in five sections: (A) general descriptive information, (B) instructional purpose(s) and activities, (C) functionality and usability, (D) instructional factors, and (E) presentation. The tables 1,2 contain the results of how StudyIntonation underwent the estimation with respect to this set of criteria.

C, D, and E contain aggregate quantitative measures, which are obtained through each of the items in sections C, D, and E rated according to the scale: -2 -1 0 1 2 (strongly disagree, disagree, no opinion, agree, strongly agree, NA=Does not apply, CT=Cannot tell (insufficient data)) (table 2).

In functionality and usability test (section C) StudyIntonation has got 14 points of 20 which were assigned for every positive answer. 6 points were subtracted since there is no operational "Help" for users (except the initial tutorial) nor a possibility to contact the creators (the terms

Section.Parameter	Value
A.Platform	iOS, Android
A.Language	British English
A.Instruction Language	English, Russian, German
A.Cost	Free
A.Target Audience	Any
A.Level of language	Any
B.Primary Objective	Intonation learning
B.Secondary Objective	Tone movement practice
B.Aspects of Pronunciation Addressed	Suprasegmentals
B. Activities	Listen, record, repeat
B.Feedback and Record Keeping	Instant, visual

Table 1. CAPT evaluation criteria. Parts A, B

Section	Score
C.Functionality and usability	14/20
D.Instructional factors	35/42
E.User interface and presentation	13/16

Table 2. CAPT evaluation criteria. Parts C, D, E

from [27] are used hereafter to name the features of the product under evaluation).

With respect to instructional factors (section D) StudyIntonation has got 35 out of 42 points. Positions where points were subtracted are related to our hesitation about the adequacy of pitch visualization and the feedback quality (-2 points in total). Multi-speaker mode, the choice of pronunciation features to work on and assignment diversity still requires further efforts (it resulted in -5 points). Just like for the acquisition of sounds, especially, of native language, multiple-talker models seem to be particularly efficient to improve perception of novel contrasts as the inherent variability allows for induction of general phonetic categories [33].

The score 13 (out of 16) was given in section E for user interface and presentation quality. 3 deduction points are due to the difficulty of user interface aesthetics and usability validation. 2 points were deduced because of the current inability to play audio at different speed.

5 Conclusion

Prosody models and tonal pattern classification are beneficial for both language education and research purposes, including speech processing an annotation algorithms based on the hypothesis that the informative parts of speech are usually prosodically highlighted by a speaker and have discernible characteristics [34]. That is why our approach addresses three target groups of users (namely, language learners, language teachers, as well as the researchers working in the domains of ASR and language phonology). The approach connects four basic ideas:

1. Harnessing multimodality in language learning (e.g., perception of interactive audio-visual channels) enforced by multimedia features of mobile devices;
2. Supporting different learning styles of students (e.g., visual, auditory and kinesthetic);
3. Advancing signal and speech processing, visualization and estimation algorithms to enhance technology-driven education and research;
4. Developing mobile tools leveraging rich existing experience of portable device users.

Our research continues the works (see, for example, the extensive studies [35],[36]) on developing approaches to extending audio perception by using visual perception channels represented as pitch graphs demonstrated to learners. Intelligent CALL using ASR algorithms becomes one of key innovations in language learning requiring more personalized and flexible tools for perceptual training [37]. However, it is important to mention that the CAPT tool usability factors are of equal importance as technical features (such as intelligent pitch processing techniques, ASR, pitch visualization, etc.).

Though there are important features, which are still missing in the current version of StudyIntonation (such as playback at different speed, speech context representation, more interactive feedback display), we may conclude that the evaluation frameworks (similar to one demonstrated in this paper), create an important environment for further collaboration between technical society and language teachers. Such a collaboration is one of ultimate priorities of present-day human centered technology and education development.

References

[1] M.C. Pennington, P. Rogerson-Revell, in *English Pronunciation Teaching and Research* (Springer, 2019), pp. 235–286

[2] O. Kang, *Relative impact of pronunciation features on ratings of non-native speakers' oral proficiency*, in *Proceedings of the 4th Pronunciation in Second Language Learning and Teaching Conference* (2012), pp. 10–15

[3] H. Obari, H. Kojima, S. Itahashi, Glasgow, 10-13 July 2013 Papers p. 245 (2013)
[4] H. Obari, H. Kojima, *The Effect of Blended and Flipped Lessons on L2 Learning Using Mobile Technologies*, in *E-Learn: World Conference on E-Learning in Corporate, Government, Healthcare, and Higher Education* (Association for the Advancement of Computing in Education (AACE), 2015), pp. 449–454
[5] C.G.d.F.M. Martins, J.M. Levis, V.A.M.C. Borges, Ilha do Desterro **69**, 141 (2016)
[6] E.M. Golonka, A.R. Bowles, V.M. Frank, D.L. Richardson, S. Freynik, Computer assisted language learning **27**, 70 (2014)
[7] T.M. Derwing, M.J. Munro, TESOL quarterly **39**, 379 (2005)
[8] J. Jenkins, Annual review of applied linguistics **24**, 109 (2004)
[9] J. Morley, TESOL quarterly **25**, 481 (1991)
[10] P. Trofimovich, *Interactive alignment: Implications for the teaching and learning of second language pronunciation*, in *Proceedings of the 4th Pronunciation in Second Language Learning and Teaching Conference* (2012), pp. 1–9
[11] H. Obari, S. Lambacher, *Successful EFL teaching using mobile technologies in a flipped classroom*, in *Critical CALL–Proceedings of the 2015 EUROCALL Conference, Padova, Italy* (Research-publishing. net, 2015), pp. 433–438
[12] D. Chun, R. Kern, B. Smith, The Modern Language Journal **100**, 64 (2016)
[13] P. Hubbard, Language Teacher Education and Technology: Approaches and Practices p. 153 (2017)
[14] N. Bitner, J. Bitner, Journal of technology and teacher education **10**, 95 (2002)
[15] J.T. Pujolă, ReCALL **14**, 235 (2002)
[16] D.M. Chun, CALICO Journal **30**, 256 (2013)
[17] D.M. Chun, J.S. Payne, System **32**, 481 (2004)
[18] J. Collentine, Language Learning & Technology **3**, 44 (2000)
[19] T. Heift, M. Schulze, *Errors and intelligence in computer-assisted language learning: Parsers and pedagogues* (Routledge, 2007)
[20] H. Kim, Glasgow, 10-13 July 2013 Papers **138** (2013)
[21] C. Chapelle, Language Learning & Technology **1**, 19 (1997)
[22] J.F. Jones, ELT Journal **55**, 360 (2001)
[23] M.C. Pennington, Computer Assisted Language Learning **12**, 427 (1999)
[24] C.A. Chapelle et al., *Computer applications in second language acquisition* (Cambridge University Press, 2001)
[25] J. Leakey, An integrated approach to effectiveness research in CALL. Bern: Peter Lang (2011)
[26] B.L. McMurry, D.D. Williams, P.J. Rich, K.J. Hartshorn, TESL-EJ **20**, n2 (2016)
[27] L. Henrichsen, *A System for Analyzing and Evaluating Computer-Assisted Second-Language Pronunciation-Teaching Websites and Mobile Apps*, in *Society for Information Technology & Teacher Education International Conference* (Association for the Advancement of Computing in Education (AACE), 2019), pp. 709–714
[28] M. Celce-Murcia, D.M. Brinton, J.M. Goodwin, *Teaching pronunciation hardback with audio CDs (2): A course book and reference guide* (Cambridge University Press, 2010)
[29] Y. Lezhenin, A. Lamtev, V. Dyachkov, E. Boitsova, K. Vylegzhanina, N. Bogach, *Study intonation: Mobile environment for prosody teaching*, in *2017 3rd IEEE International Conference on Cybernetics (CYBCONF)* (IEEE, 2017), pp. 1–2
[30] E. Boitsova, E. Pyshkin, Y. Takako, N. Bogach, I. Lezhenin, A. Lamtev, V. Diachkov, *StudyIntonation courseware kit for EFL prosody teaching*, in *Proc. 9th International Conference on Speech Prosody 2018* (2018), pp. 413–417
[31] N. Bogach, *Languages and cognition: towards new CALL*, in *Proceedings of the 3rd International Conference on Applications in Information Technology* (ACM, 2018), pp. 6–8
[32] T.M. Derwing, M.J. Munro, *Pronunciation fundamentals: Evidence-based perspectives for L2 teaching and research*, Vol. 42 (John Benjamins Publishing Company, 2015)
[33] A. Neri, C. Cucchiarini, H. Strik, L. Boves, Computer assisted language learning **15**, 441 (2002)
[34] A. Batliner, B. Möbius, in *The integration of phonetic knowledge in speech technology* (Springer, 2005), pp. 21–44
[35] E. Estebas-Vilaplana, Linguistica **57**, 73 (2017)
[36] C. Cucchiarini, H. Strik, in *Smart Technologies: Breakthroughs in Research and Practice* (IGI Global, 2018), pp. 367–389
[37] M. Qian, E. Chukharev-Hudilainen, J. Levis, Language Learning & Technology **22**, 69 (2018)

A failure mode and effects analysis of pragmatic errors in learner e-mails

Allan Nicholas[1*] and *John* Blake[1]

[1]Center for Language Research, University of Aizu, Aizu-Wakamatsu, Japan.

Abstract. E-mailing in the English is an important mode of communication for Japanese learners of computer science both during and after their studies. A key element of effective e-mail communication relates to pragmatic competence—understanding the relationship between social context and language choices and accordingly adapting one's language in an appropriate manner. Despite this importance, there have been few learner e-mail corpora annotated for pragmatic errors. As part of a larger ongoing study developing online tools for assessing and developing learners' e-mail writing ability, a failure mode and effects analysis was conducted on a learner corpus of e-mails, manually tagged for pragmatic errors. Tagged errors were ascribed a value between 1-5 in terms of severity, detectability and frequency, with most sever errors assigned a score of 5. Weighted priority scores were calculated, allowing for errors to be prioritized in terms of importance. Preliminary results indicate severe errors are associated with failing to address the face needs of the e-mail recipient, violating pragmatic norms, with potential negative consequences in terms of relationship maintenance. Results allow for the creation of a job queue for the software developer, and usefully inform teaching priorities in the language classroom.

1 Introduction

E-mailing in the English L2 is a key mode of communication for Japanese students in higher education institutions, due to the need to communicate effectively with non-Japanese faculty members [1]. While alternative modes are becoming increasingly common in the workplace, such as Slack [2], e-mail remains a common communication tool in academia [3] [4] and important for receiving timely feedback from faculty [5]. Furthermore, e-mail remains a frequently used tool in many workplaces; with an increasing need to operate in global networked environments and teams, the ability to communicate effectively via e-mail in future potential workplace contexts is an important skill.

Broadly, errors within e-mail texts may be grammatical-syntactical, factual, or pragmatic in nature. All three categories of error may have an adverse impact on the recipients' perceptions of the e-mail sender. Grammatical and factual errors can be relatively easily agreed upon, identified and addressed by educators. However, the relationship between context and language — the pragmatic aspect of e-mail communication is more challenging, due to the role of subjectivity and awareness of L2 pragmatic norms.

As part of a larger ongoing study of learner e-mails and pragmatic competence, this current study investigates the application of a failure mode and effects analysis of pragmatic errors in a learner corpus of e-mail text data, evaluating the severity, detectability and frequency of errors. Implications for software development and classroom practice are discussed.

2 Background

2.1 Pragmatics and pragmatic errors

Pragmatics is "the societally necessary and consciously interactive dimension of the study of language" [6, p.315]. Pragmatics is an aspect of communicative competence addressing the complex relationship between our language choices and the social scenarios in which we interact with others. Failure to attend to the pragmatic norms of an L2 interaction can lead to negative social consequences for the learner [7], and/or perceptions of "rudeness" [4].

While the identification of pragmatic failure is, to an extent, a subjective endeavour, and the need to avoid overly prescriptive approaches to pragmatics classroom instruction important [7] [8], the potential negative consequences of pragmatic failure point to a clear need to raise learner awareness in this area [4]. Studies typically employ native English users to evaluate L2 learner e-mail texts [5] and assess faculty perceptions of students' e-mail communications [3] [4] [5] [9].

2.2 Learner corpora and pragmatic annotation

Use of corpora allows for a systematic approach to identifying patterns, common features or errors in large

* Corresponding author: anich@u-aizu.ac.jp

collections of text data. Corpora have been used for a wide variety of purposes, with the majority employed in the identification of features in the formal aspects of language use, such as grammatical patterns and lexis. Pragmatic annotation of corpora is less common [10] [11], often focusing on oral communication and speech acts, such as requesting, apologizing or thanking in telephone conversations [12].

While a number of corpora have annotated for learner errors, these have been non-pragmatic (the Cambridge Learner Corpus; the Longman Learner's Corpus). Automatically annotating pragmatic features or errors has proved difficult, due to a lack of information regarding patterns of such features or errors [13]. Few corpora, therefore, have annotated for pragmatic errors, due to the time and resource-intensive nature of manually annotating large amounts of text data.

2.3 Learner e-mail and pragmatic errors

E-mails received by university faculty from students vary greatly in terms of appropriacy. Figure 1 shows an illustrative example of a learner e-mail to university faculty at a Japanese higher education institution.

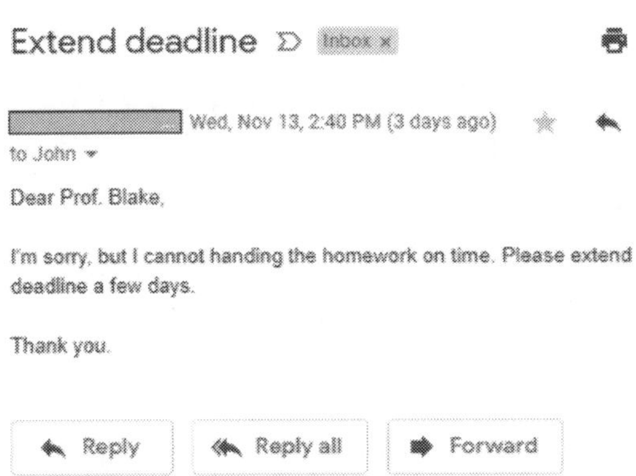

Fig. 1. Screenshot of email with sender details redacted

3 Method

3.1 Corpus specifications

The target users were undergraduate students at a computer science university in Japan, aged 18-21 years. The institution has identified e-mailing in the English L2 as a key task students should be able to perform [1], due to approximately 40% of faculty members being non-native Japanese.

Request-based e-mails were chosen as the target e-mail type, due to their prevalence in e-mail communications [4] [5] and their inherently face-threatening nature [14]. Learners of English as a Foreign Language (EFL) have been found to struggle with constructing pragmatically appropriate e-mail requests [5] [9], indicating a clear need for learners in this regard.

Target e-mail scenarios were primarily those in an academic context. However, to explore learners' abilities to adapt their e-mail writing to a variety of contexts, private social communications and e-mails to business persons outside of academia were also identified as useful task types. Rather than collect authentic e-mail data, for this study, e-mail texts were elicited via in-classroom tasks. This allowed for control of the contextual variables *power* (P; akin to relative social status between interlocutors), *distance* (D; how well the interlocutors know each other) and *imposition* (R; how potentially troublesome the request may be to the receiver), identified by [14].

3.2 Corpus creation

To create task scenarios for data elicitation, an exemplar generation questionnaire was administered to a sample of the student population (*n=108*), eliciting examples of situations in which they had needed to make a request in their daily lives, with a particular interest in academic scenarios. A count of the results was carried out, with scenarios ranked in terms of frequency. The most frequent scenarios were then used as templates for task creation, with additional scenarios added to ensure a variety of social contexts and challenges for students. The task items were then drafted, before being moderated by expert English users to ensure the tasks elicited the target (requesting), the economy of the task language, and that appropriate task responses could only be obtained through knowledge of L2 pragmatic norms. In addition, moderators were asked to evaluate the values P, D and R for each task scenario, to ensure they matched the P, D and R values assigned by the researchers. For each variable, two values could be assigned, as shown in Table 1.

Table 1. Contextual variables Power, Distance and Imposition (adapted from [15])

P	Meaning	D	Meaning	R	Meaning
+	Receiver has a higher rank, title or social position. E.g. president, supervisor	+	Sender and receiver do not know, or identify with, each other.	+	Great expenditure of goods or energy by the receiver to carry out the request.
-	Receiver has a lower rank or social position. E.g. salesperson serving a customer.	-	Sender or receiver know, or identify with, each other.	-	Small expenditure or energy by the receiver to carry out the request.

Following these steps, four e-mail tasks were selected for administration to students (*n=426*). The tasks were chosen based on their differing combination of P, D and R values, with students needing to adapt their language choices accordingly in order to write pragmatically appropriate texts. Table 2 shows the four task scenarios administered, and their assigned values. Tasks were administered to the participants in both the L1 and the L2 to ensure understanding, with responses required in the English L2.

Tasks were administered in the classroom using Google Forms. A total of 1,474 e-mail texts were elicited, across the four task scenarios.

Table 2. Administered task scenarios and assigned contextual values.

Task Scenario	P	D	R
You are organizing a university event in which local businesses' products are showcased to the public. To help fund the event, you are contacting local business people to ask for financial donations. Email Mr. Smith- a local business owner in Aizu-Wakamatsu- to ask for a financial donation. You do not know Mr. Smith.	+	+	+
You have a close friend who is an international student at university. You want to practice your English conversation skill next week, so you email him/her asking if they can spend five minutes of their time talking with you in English.	-	-	-
You need to go to Sendai for an academic conference next week, but the train there is too expensive. You email your friend (who has a car) asking them to drive you there. It takes about three hours to drive from your home to Sendai by car. Your friend will be busy next week, so this will be inconvenient for him/her.	-	-	+
You must submit a document to the local government office in Aizu-Wakamatsu proving that you are a student at the University of Aizu. Email the manager of the Student Affairs Office at the university asking them to provide you with the document you need.	+	+	-

3.3 Tagset and schema creation

The initial tagset was adapted from the Cross-Cultural Study of Speech Act Realization Patterns (CCSARP) framework [16], developed to identify features of speech acts in conversation, and used in adapted form by [5] to analyze learner e-mail texts. An inter-annotator reliability check was carried out, in which the tagset was further developed and adapted to suit the needs of non-expert annotators who may be unfamiliar with academic-oriented pragmatics tagsets, and to reflect the way we typically read an e-mail text, from opening to closing. An excerpt from the tagset that annotates use is given below.

H2A The marker "please"
H2B consultative devices ("would you mind" "do you think")
H2C Subjectivisers ("I'm afraid" "I wonder")
H2D Downtoners ("possibly" perhaps" "just")
H2E Hedges ("a bit" "a little" "sort of")
H2F Cajolers ("You know" " You see…")
H2G Appealers ("will you…Prof. Johnson?")

In the annotation label H indicates that this annotation relates to the sentence that contains the main request (head request). The annotations focus on content that should have been included. This type of annotation is problematic as the annotator has to judge what should be present but is not. An extract of the annotation schemata is shown in Figure 2.

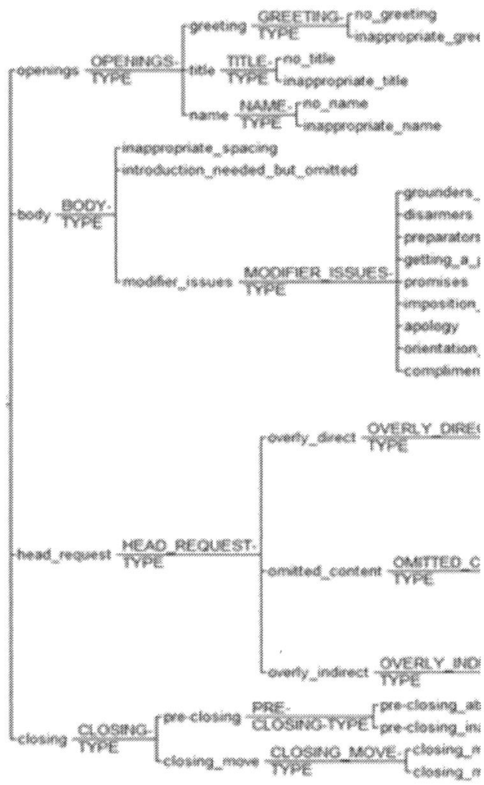

Fig. 2. Annotation schemata

4 Failure mode effects analysis

4.1 Introduction to FMEA

Failure Mode Effects Analysis (FMEA) is a quality management process to investigate points of failure and evaluate the effects of failure [17]. In this project, FMEA analysis is applied to pragmatic errors, and so the severity, frequency and detectability are evaluated.

The sum of three values of severity (S), detectability (D) and frequency (F) gives a priority score for an error. Each score category is multiplied by a coefficient to create a weighted priority score (WP), as shown in equation (1). The weighted priority provides a mechanism to take into account the relative importance of each category.

https://doi.org/10.1051/shsconf/20207702001

$$\alpha S \cdot \beta D \cdot \gamma F = WP \quad (1)$$

where:

S= severity — α=coefficienct of severity
D= detectability — β=coefficient of detectabilty
F= frequency — γ=coefficient of frequency
WP= weighted priority

To conduct the FMEA, annotated errors were extracted from the corpus and collated into an error bank. Each error was ascribed a value of between 1 and 5 for the three criteria of severity, detectability and frequency. The coefficients of each criterion were initially set at 1, meaning that the range of weighted priority score was from 0 to125.

4.2 Severity

Severity was judged by the researchers based on the perceived effect on the reader of the email. Errors judged to be more likely to create negativity in the recipient were judged as more severe. Errors that were judged as severe received a score of 5 while non-serious errors received 1.

4.3 Detectability

Detectability was judged by a software developer who based the value on the difficulty of automatically identifying the error with precision [18]. Precision is calculated by dividing the number of true positive results by the sum of the number of true and false positive results as shown in Equation (2).

$$P = \frac{TP}{TP+FP} \quad (2)$$

where:

P = precision
TP = number of true positive results
FP = number of false positive results

False positive results are those that are detected incorrectly while false negative results are those that should have been detected but were not. In short, the more likely the occurrence of false positive and false negative results, the lower the precision score and the lower the detectability score. The detectability score correlates with the precision score but also takes account of the difficulty in creating the expression to match the error. In this category, a score of 5 means that the error is easy to automatically identify.

4.4 Frequency

The frequency of each error type was counted in the pilot corpus of 50 email texts. The likelihood of the same error type occurring in the full corpus was estimated. A score of 5 was awarded for errors that were frequent and 1 for errors that occurred rarely.

As an illustrative example, professors frequently receive requests to extend the deadline for assignments from their students. Should an email begin with "I want you to extend the deadline," it would be unlikely to put the professor in a favorable mood. In this example, the student failed to employ strategies to soften the request, such as providing a reason. In this example, the key problematic phrase is "I want you". When an FMEA analysis is applied to this pragmatic error, the resultant values can be tabulated as shown in Table 3.

Table 3: Example FMEA score for pragmatic error

Error type	S	D	F	WP*
I want you	4	5	3	60

* The coefficient weighting is set at 1

5 Results

The expected main outcome was achieved. The job queue for the software developer can be created by sorting the pragmatic errors in descending order by weighted priority. The software developer needs to write the program to automatically match the errors using rule-based parsing. The cost-benefit of the task decreases as the weighted priority decreases, and so this is an effective way to maximize productivity.

Preliminary results from the pilot study (see Table 4) show that errors allocated the highest scores in severity failed to address the face needs of the e-mail recipient by, for example, failing to include the recipient's title in the opening, or the sender's name in the closing. Pragmatic failure relating to the head act are also categorized as high in severity, with a lack of internal modifiers or use of 'want' or 'need' statements being perceived as overly direct. This lack of adherence to pragmatic conventions has the potential to lead to difficulties in the sender-receiver relationship.

Among the most frequent errors, many also scored highly for detectability. Examples of these include a lack of the recipient's name in the opening or a lack of a closing salutation. On the other hand, other frequent errors, such as a lack of external modifiers in the email body, scored lower for detectability. Errors that received the highest scores for detectability leaned towards the lexical side of the lexical-grammatical cline.

Grammatical errors tended to receive medium scores for detectability while functional errors were considered the most difficult due to the complexity of the form-function relationship. Reader intuition is needed to deduce the intended function. This implies that there is a degree of subjectivity and that two readers with differing world knowledge and expectations can interpret the same language form in different ways.

The lack of a one-to-one correlation between form and function makes automatic detection considerably more difficult. A particularly difficult error to detect is the lack of presence of an expected item. Errors of omission vary in detectability depending on whether the words omitted could be considered a closed or open set. Closed sets comprise of a fixed number of items and so can be stored as lists in a detection system, while this is not possible for open sets. For example, the omission of the term 'please' is simple to detect; however, this does not take into account whether a writer used the slightly archaic 'kindly' instead. The difficulty is exacerbated when there are multiple functional exponents that can be used. Checking the presence or absence of language features using a computer script is therefore a non-trivial task.

Currently, the frequency of error types in the full corpus is estimated based on the count in the pilot study. The errors in the full corpus will be tallied using a tailormade script once the corpus is fully annotated.

Table 4. FMEA scores for pragmatic errors, ranked for severity

Error type	S	D	F	Tally	WP*
No recipient name	5	5	5	28	125
Imperative used	5	4	3	15	60
No title	5	5	2	11	50
Head act- 'want' statement	5	5	2	10	50
No closing salutation /name	4	5	5	36	100
No greeting	4	5	3	14	60
No self-introduction when needed	4	4	2	5	32
No self-introduction because no name in closing	4	4	2	4	32
Head act- 'would like' statement	4	5	1	2	20
Head act- 'need' statement	4	5	1	1	20
No pre-closing	3	3	5	37	45
No or insufficient external modifiers	3	1	5	25	15
Head act- 'would/ could /can'	3	5	2	13	30
Greeting- 'nice to meet…'	3	5	1	2	15
Inappropriate closing	3	5	1	2	15
Inappropriate pre-closing	3	5	1	1	15
Body runs on from greeting	2	5	4	24	40
Greeting- 'hello'	2	5	3	17	30
Head act- performative	2	5	2	4	20
Opening- inappropriate name, office	2	4	1	1	8
No or insufficient internal modifiers	1	2	4	19	8
Greeting- 'dear my friend'	1	5	1	2	5
Greeting- given name	1	5	1	1	5

6 Discussion

Our findings provide useful insights into the types of pragmatic failure in learners' email texts, their frequency, perceived severity, and the potential detectability of such failure types by software. Such instances of failing to adhere to pragmatic norms may potentially lead to perceptions of impoliteness by the recipient of an e-mail text. This is in line with research on the perceptions of grammatical versus pragmatic errors in the business community showing that pragmatic errors in politeness by non-native users of English were more troublesome than grammatical errors [19].

Preliminary findings from this initial pilot study are in line with studies in other contexts [5] that found students' failure to attend to the recipients' face needs, such as employing overly direct requesting strategies, or failing to modify a request with an appropriate e-mail opening or closing, can lead to perceptions of 'rudeness' by the receiver of an email text. It is these errors- ones that most baldly fail to reflect the degree of imposition of a request- that rate highest in severity in the FMEA analysis.

7 Conclusion

This current study describes the process of creating a corpus of English L2 learner e-mails, annotated for pragmatic failure, and a subsequent FMEA analysis of pragmatic errors, evaluating severity, detectability and frequency. This analysis allows the researchers to create a job queue for programming of future error-detecting tools, and provides useful insight into how learners' pragmatic errors are perceived by e-mail recipients.

Results of the pilot study and FMEA analysis also provide useful information not only for the software programmer, but also for classroom practice. Priority weighting scores for error types provide guidance for teachers working under classroom time constraints, who wish to address learners' needs for developing pragmatic competence in their e-mail writing.

Acknowledgments

This research is supported by a JSPS KAKENHI (Grants-in-aid for Scientific Research), Grant Number 19K00826, "Developing a diagnostic language assessment of Japanese EFL learners' English language e-mail writing."

References

[1] E. Kaneko, M. Park, I. Wilson, Y. Heo, D. Roy, T. Yasuta, A. Nicholas, J. Blake, *English curriculum innovation for computer science majors in the Japanese EFL context: From needs to tasks,* in Proceedings of IEEE International Professional Communication Conference (ProComm), Toronto, ON, pp.84-89 (2018)

[2] C. Durscheid, C. Frehner, *Email communication,* in S. Herring, D. Stein, T. Virtanen (eds.) Handbook of Pragmatics of Computer-Mediated Communication. De Gruyter Mouton, Berlin, pp.35-52 (2013)

[3] C. Felix-Brasdefer, *Email openings and closings: pragmalinguistic and gender variation in learner-instructor cyber consultations.* in E.A. Soler and M. Safont-Jorda (eds.), Discourse and Language Learning Across L2 Instructional Settings. Brill Academic Publishers, Amsterdam/New York (2012)

[4] M. Savic, J. Prag, **124,** 52-72 (2018)

[5] M. Economidou-Kogetsidis, J. Prag. **43**, 13, 3193-3215 (2011)

[6] J. Mey, Pragmatics: An Introduction. Blackwell, Oxford (1993)

[7] V. LoCastro, Pragmatics for language educators: A sociolinguistic perspective, Routledge (2013)

[8] N. Ishihara, A. Cohen, Teaching and Learning Pragmatics: Where Language and Culture Meet. Longman, London (2010)

[9] S. Biesenbach-Lucas, Lang. Learn. Tech. **11**, 2, 59-81 (2007)

[10] C. Maynard, S. Leicher, *Pragmatic annotation of an academic spoken purposes*, in E. Fitzpatrick (ed.), Corpus linguistics beyond the word: Corpus research from phrase to discourse, Rodopi, Amsterdam (2007)

[11] J. Kallen, J. Kirk, SPICE-Ireland: A User's Guide. Clo Ollscoil na Banriona, Belfast (2012)

[12] G. Leech, M. Weisser, in *Generic speech act annotation for task-orientated dialogues'*, in D. Archer, P. Rayson, A. Wilson, and A. McCenery (eds.), Proceedings of Corpus Linguistics, 28-31 March 2003, Lancaster University, United Kingdom, pp.441-446 (2003)

[13] Y. Tono, *Learner Corpora: Design, development and applications.* in D. Archer, P. Rayson, A. Wilson, and A. McCenery (eds.), Proceedings of Corpus Linguistics 28-31 March 2003, Lancaster University, United Kingdom, pp.800-809 (2003)

[14] P. Brown, S. Levinson, Politeness: Some Universals in Language Use, Cambridge University Press, Cambridge (1987)

[15] T. Hudson, E. Detmer, J.D Brown, Developing Prototypic Measures of Cross-Cultural Pragmatics, University of Hawai'i Press, Honolulu (1995)

[16] S. Blum-Kulka, E. Olshtain, App. Ling. **5**, 3, 196-213 (1984)

[17] D.H. Stamatis, Failure mode and effect analysis: FMEA from theory to execution. ASQ Quality press (2003)

[18] D. Olson, D. Dursun, Advanced data mining techniques, Springer Science & Business Media (2008)

[19] J. Wolfe, N. Shanmugaraj, J. Sipe., Bus. Prof. Comm. Quart. **79**, 4, 397-415 (2016)

Analyzing the Communicative Efficacy of a Soft CLIL Focused Project-based Language Learning EFL Course on Smart Homes

Debopriyo Roy, Peter Kudry and Kagome Naya

The University of Aizu, Dept. of Computer Science and Engineering, Japan

Abstract: The rampant urbanization across the world is forcing city planners to be more innovative and creative with technology in how limited resources and amenities are used. Smart homes (SH) technology is one such use. Until now, this has not been a subject for study in the language curriculum, and more so, not as part of the EFL curriculum. This paper discussed a model project-based language learning (PBLL) coursework on SH offered as part of foreign language coursework in a computer science university in Japan in collaboration with a German technical university. This course is aimed at developing students' ability for information comprehension, data analysis, note-taking, summarization, speaking, video design, technical presentations, and poster design, all in English. The paper is a case study on how to make such technical writing/communication courses interesting and engaging for students who see the technology side of a smart city design context but do not necessarily see through the human side of the urban design and usability. This paper is aimed at helping language practitioners offer language courses using a soft-CLIL model that focuses on design thinking, urban planning, language acquisition, and project management all as a package in the pedagogical design, as is often necessary for industrial projects. The idea is to help language practitioners offer coursework that has societal relevance and transfer skills in-built, and is just not focused on language elements in isolation, but develops project management and communication skills as well.

1. Introduction

CLIL (Content Language Integrated Learning) refers to situations where subjects or topics are taught through a foreign language with the dual-focused aim to teaching both the content and the simultaneous learning of the language (Marsh, 1994). SOFT CLIL is a situation where some language learning is taught with the content, while HARD CLIL is one where language and content are both taught at the same time. As part of this paper, we discussed a SOFT CLIL teaching situation combining a separate graduate and undergraduate course teaching students to handle a technical communication-based SH project with collaboration between the two different undergrad-graduate student groups, with foreign student groups collaborating as overseas partners. With this framework, the course took a project-based language learning (PBLL) approach within a SOFT CLIL framework. Research in CLIL incorporating PBLL is almost non-existent. This paper highlights one such project which focused on content, group coordination, time management, data management, technical documentation and technical presentation skills as part of overall English communication and project management skills development.

As part of this project, three undergraduate student groups from a third year EFL elective course on information management in a Japanese computer science university effectively collaborated to read, understand, and deliver audio-video presentations, graphics-based projects and text reports on short SH projects on SH technology and business, using different information management and advertising software and templates. These short two weeks long assignments during the coursework were handled and completed with two graduate students acting as mentors for undergraduate student groups, and then the completed projects were turned over to German graduate student partners from a German university who took the content and then designed ontology and XML metadata for component content management and delivery structures as part of their advanced technical communication coursework. For this entire exercise, the German graduate students communicated with the Japanese graduate students for project-level understanding of the content. The entire package of content on SH (written by graduate and undergraduate Japanese university students in the course) was delivered to the German students, with effective communication and back-and-forth information exchange happening along the way. Each undergraduate team had a team leader and the leader coordinated with the graduate student mentor, and the mentor in turn communicated with the German student groups. The undergrad team leaders were in charge of managing their group content, making sure the graduate mentors received it and understood it; the graduate mentors had to write their own reports (as part of their own graduate course on SH) making sure the Germans understood the SH projects (the graduate assignments largely depended on the undergraduate projects), and ensuring smooth communication with their German graduate student partner groups.

Corresponding author: droy@u-aizu.ac.jp

This entire process happened over a two-months window leading up to an international ACM conference where all the Japanese and German students came face to face and made project presentations. The above collaborative coursework structure on SH suggest that this is not merely a SOFT CLIL course using standard CLIL-teaching tools; but one which depended a whole lot on project management skills, and intercultural communication at different levels. Language acquisition was expected to happen through diverse collaborative reading, writing, video design, and communication activities.

The next section discussed the value of CLIL, and PBLL, and how the SH technology and business context provides an appropriate platform to contextualize an international project in a PBLL-based SOFT CLIL context. That will help us answer the following research question:

- How could we design groupwork and collaboration within a SOFT CLIL-PBLL framework? How did the graduate-undergraduate-foreign collaborators combine towards handling this international project, and does it provide preliminary indication that some amount of cultural awareness, exposure, experience of project handling, communication, and technical communication skills developed?
- How was SH used as an effective project topic towards building project management skills?

The above two questions were answered through comments documented by the two graduate students who collaborated with the three undergraduate student groups (11 students) and the German student groups (10 students). We explored the above research questions in light of the communication between the graduate students and the undergraduate groups enrolled in the elective English course at the Japanese university, the suggestions made by these graduate student mentors and how they were accepted, initial impressions about group communication and project management skills etc.

2. Review of the Literature

Foreign language teaching in a STEM context, ideally should consider the fact that CLIL provides a definitely unique, advantageous and effective pedagogical structure based on the Coyle's 4Cs framework which situates CLIL to be complex and context-sensitive, is based on the general parameters in CLIL such as cognition, culture, content and communication and acknowledges that any CLIL structure should incorporate a specific combination of the parameters above based on needs analysis, and that language as a learning tool operates in three ways: OF-FOR-THROUGH (Coyle, 2007; 2008). Another important consideration in EFL teaching is to identify EAP and ESP pedagogy that are compatible with the CLIL ideology and framework. Such planning will generally incorporate feedback and contribution from the content matter experts as well helping to optimize the CLIL teaching framework (Uemura et al., 2019). Research has effectively shown that there is a significant improvement in EFL students' writing skills with CLIL pedagogy, and that students show positive attitude towards the implementation of CLIL in teaching and learning process (Kusmayadi and Suryana, 2017). CLIL is becoming more prevalent in the Japanese educational system and is increasingly seen as an answer to Japan's English language deficiencies. Research data on students' perceptions of the soft CLIL approach at a Japanese junior high school suggest that overall the students have a positive sentiment towards the soft CLIL lessons. The most challenging thing students reported was understanding the native English teachers and English instruction. It's important that native English teachers pay careful attention to their English usage in classes and that teachers and administrators try to find an optimum balance of soft CLIL lessons that complement the institutional needs of the school (Mahoney, 2019). CLIL coursework has been seen to be using many different tools including graphic organizers, hands-on, multimedia, interviews, videos, demonstrations, debates, games, storytelling, flash cards, labeling, visual aids, diagrams, role-plays etc. Specific software use includes Flickr.com, wordpress.com, Bitstripsforschools.com, projectnoah.org iOS/Android App, creately.com, vine.co, tumblr.com, emojiscience.com, piktochart.com, social bookmarking and curation, educlipper.net, virtual fieldtrips (Google.com/cultureinstitute), makerspaces, 3D printing and coding etc.

2.1. Project based Language Learning

PBL is defined as "an instructional approach that contextualizes learning by presenting learners with problems to solve or products to develop" (Moss & Van Duzer, 1998). Project-based instruction for language learning is a valuable way to promote the simultaneous acquisition of language, content, and skills, provided that students in academic ESL classes can see the value of learning through projects, which has not always been the case (Beckett and Slater, 2005). PBLL can play a key role in language teaching and what this implies for teachers and learners. PBLL not only allows for a practical and meaningful approach to teaching and assessing language learning; it also promotes effective learning strategies and critical thinking skills (Dooly, 2013). A typical PBLL context could also be analyzed for its efficacy with learner reflections of project work through Activity Theory, where tool-mediated activity is understood as the central unit of analysis for human interaction (Gibbes and Carson, 2014). Research on EFL teaching has aptly demonstrated that in reality, studying English does not necessarily focus on syntactic accuracy or competency in grammar usage. Instead, giving opportunities to students to use as much English as students can in real life contexts should be critically considered, especially for those students who have limited chances not only to be exposed to native English speakers, but also the opportunity to use English in their real-life settings. PBL is consistent with this English teaching and learning need. It's now important to explain how SH is an appropriate topic to explore for CS majors, both from CLIL and PBLL purposes.

2.2. The Context of Smart Homes: A Case Study

A "smart home" can be defined as a residence equipped with computing and information technology which anticipates and responds to the needs of the occupants, working to promote their comfort, convenience, security and entertainment through the management of technology within the home and connections to the world beyond (Aldrich, 2003). This course is important for CS majors for the following reasons:

(1) It's an opportunity to read about and understand important SH technologies as a digital ecosystem that are otherwise, not covered and taught as part of regular computer science courses.
(2) It's an opportunity to read about and investigate how the society perceives the relevance of such technology, and how should it be advertised as a regular feature, making everyday life easier?
(3) It's an opportunity to investigate the SH business both in Asia and Europe, and this knowledge was used to better communicate with the German partners as part of the coursework.
(4) It's an opportunity to learn about information design and technical writing using some of the standard SOFT CLIL tools, such as brainstorming tools, graphic organizers, storytelling, video design etc.

3. The Coursework and Methodology

The course was offered as a 3rd year undergraduate elective with the title *Technical Writing for IT Business*, in combination with a graduate elective course with the title *Technical Writing for Software Engineering*. Both were essentially technical writing courses offered for CS majors and with SH as the central theme revolving around a SOFT CLIL-PBLL pedagogical approach. Since the course topic was focused centrally on SH, the weekly assignments for both the courses were designed such that the graduate assignments to a certain extent depended on the undergraduate assignments; and also, it opened up an opportunity for the undergraduate teams to be mentored by the graduate mentors as and when needed. It's also important to note that none of the students had any course experience on SH related topics; and no English course that included SOFT CLIL and PBLL as a continuum. Both the graduate and undergraduate courses were launched under the same course pocket in *Schoology* (learning management system) with three central content theme folders, namely (A) Introduction to SH Concepts (B) SH Business Worldwide (C) Advertising SH to Citizens and New Customers.

The folder (A) included short online readings and videos on the introduction to SH concept (including how it works in daily life) and primary technologies used in the market including Amazon Echo, Google Home and Siri. This folder also included a major journal article on the end user perceptions for SH technology. The folder (B) included a short reading on opportunities and challenges in the Japanese SH market, the value of the European SH market, and potential and opportunities in the Asian SH market. Folder (C) included a template on analyzing advertisements, reading on how to target users of SH products with Facebook Ads, and SH video documentaries highlighting different SH technologies on use in real life.

The major technical communication themes from the language learning perspective were as follows: (A) technical writing essentials such as technical reading, documentation, brainstorming tools etc. (B) technical presentations (C) analyzing advertisements and commercials and (D) technical collaboration using *TeamViewer, Slack* and *Google Docs*. The SH course was organized as a one-quarter (7 weeks) course including the ACM conference where both the German and the Japanese university groups who collaborated throughout the length of the course came together for joint workshops and presentations of their respective topics, with SH as the central theme. From the Japanese side, the undergraduate course had three groups with the first group having 4 members, the second group 3 members and the third group 4 members (11 students in total). The undergraduate class had 10 Japanese students and 1 Vietnamese student. All the 3 groups completed the same set of assignments. They were mentored and partnered with two graduate students at the Japanese university on SH. The graduate class had one European student and one Japanese student, both with superior English proficiency. The three undergraduate Japanese groups completed the same bi-weekly assignments separately, but they were overseen and mentored by the graduate students, who also collaborated for their own graduate assignment. The graduate course assignments were similar to the undergraduate ones, but much more intense, investigative with higher level requirements for technical report writing and information design and analysis. The 5 German groups (2 members each with 5 groups totaling 10 students) were part of an advanced technical communication and content management course being taught at HSKA, Germany focusing on ontology creation, XML metadata creation, content management and delivery portals.

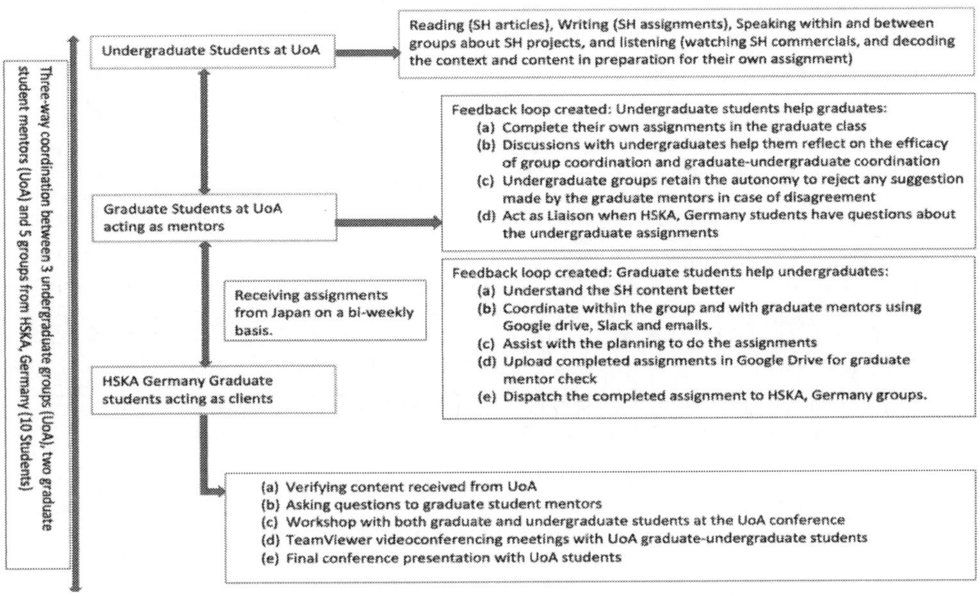

Figure 1. The 3-way Collaboration Schema for Content Comprehension and Exchange

Figure 1 shows the planned collaboration and flow of activities between the undergraduates, graduates and the HSKA, Germany students.

Table 1 provided a layout of the weekly assignments that would help us understand how the SH course was laid out, and how it helped students with English communication skills and group coordination opportunities. The table shows the range of guidelines provided, and the nature of questions that led students to investigate the course notes intensely, and reflect on it when answering assignments.

Table 2 provided an outline of the expected tasks/activities and communication requirements for each assignment.

Table 1. The SH Course Layout

Assignments	Major Tasks
Week # 1: Introduction to Smart Homes	**Undergraduate**: Summarization of Ideas: Key idea of SH, Major technologies of SH, Importance of having SH, Advertising SH, Examples of SH technology advertised in media, Designing SH t-shirt. **Graduate:** Design Newsletter with lucidpress.com - Robust explanation of why society needs SH technologies, Using Sketchup to draw an illustration of how smart phones are used for SH technology? Evidence of how SH improves lifestyles, will SH business be successful worldwide, how can media help us advertise SH technologies, critique SH technology video commercial.
2nd & 3rd Week: Introduce Two Different SMART HOME Technologies	**Undergraduate:** • Select two technologies/products that you believe are unique and could be appealing to common citizens. • Design an extensive ***Sketch-boarding & Mind Meister*** **Mind Map (2 SEPARATE MAPS)** explaining your group's plan for designing an ADOBE SPARK movie, introducing Technology/Product1 and Technology/Product 2. • *Design a short 20-25 Scene Advertising Presentation with* ***Adobe Spark*** *explaining how the above technologies work in SMART HOMES* and make a video commercial for an established company in the field, demonstrating a movie that appeals to the common people. **Write a 200-words REPORT explaining:** (A) How you have planned and designed the Adobe Spark movie on SH technology using Mind Meister and Sketch boarding software? (B) Why did you choose the following two technologies/products? Why did you find it interesting and appealing for common people?

	Graduate: **PART A:** A. How do you think a tool such as Mind Meister and Sketchboarding could help commercial designers plan documentary movies or commercials to conceptualize the concept of smart homes? Is it an effective tool? Give an example of what will be part of your concept map using these tools for a topic such as "commercializing smart homes"? **PART B:** Read the Article marked as "Graduate SH" from this folder. Now, explain the concepts in the article in a coherent way using Mind Meister and Sketchboarding. We must be able to see the interrelationship between the ideas and concepts and execution of the plan. You can draw multiple concept maps based on how the ideas are connected and what makes sense from the perspective of a person trying to understand the concepts for both functionalities and the structure of the devices/products. **PART C:** B. How do you think a tool such as Adobe Spark could help citizens conceptualize the concept of SH? Is it an effective tool? **Mentoring:** B1. Use the work done by the undergrad students to demonstrate what technically qualifies as a good or bad idea? Critique the work done by undergrads and show how to turn the concept into something really marketable. WRITE A 200-WORDS REPORT ON THE MENTORING EXPERIENCE, INCLUDING THE PRODUCT, WORKING WITH IDEAS IN THE GROUP, EXECUTION ISSUES, ETC.
4th & 5th Week: Smart Home Technology: An Exploration of End-User Perceptions	**Undergraduate:** ***Study the links and articles from the folder "Smart Home Business - Worldwide".*** • Design an infographic **(VENNGAGE)** representing the research of the SH technology business and its use in Japan, and in Asia, in general versus North America/Europe. • https://venngage.com; https://www.canva.com • Design a 5-slide presentation summarizing the information from the link in your own words. Save it as a .mov file with your voiceover. Upload the .mov file on YouTube and submit the YouTube link. • Use **IHMC Concept Mapping** software to outline the major concepts of the article "Technologies for an aging society" as a network of ideas that are connected to each other in different ways. https://cmapcloud.ihmc.us/ • Now, prepare a 5-slide presentation summarizing the information from the link in your own words. Save it as a SlideShare link. • Study the two software: **pipefy** and **smartcitizen.** ***Pipefy*** could be used for community architects, city planners, etc. very successfully. ***Smartcitizen*** could be used for community awareness. • Now study these websites closely, and explain how are these two websites related to community awareness and planning of SH. Explain your detailed understanding in 75-80 words. https://smartcitizen.me/; https://www.pipefy.com/ **Graduate:** • Write a 300-words explanatory report of how media design with tools such as Canva, Venngage, IHMC Cloud, etc. could help as media documents to advertise and explain the benefits of SH TECHNOLOGY. • Write one paragraph for each software (after studying the software features and what it allows customers to do with free and paid versions). • What is the role played by this workflow management software towards designing the idea of a smart city by architect planners? : https://www.pipefy.com (75 words) • What is the role played by the following citizens' website: https://smartcitizen.me (75 words)? • Use the undergraduate course examples of different media use (including, **pipefy** and **smartcitizen**) to interview 3 ordinary citizens from Aizuwakamatsu who are NOT students at the University of Aizu. Please interview in a way to find out how much the idea of SH technology fits their lifestyle. Prepare list of 10 questions to know about their lifestyle, exposure to technology, willingness to embrace new technology, learning about system, etc.
6th & 7th Week: ACM Presentation	**Undergraduate:** Presentation on topics covered above **Graduate:** • Explain the concept of *Ontology in a SH application context;* • Explain the concepts of the *Component Content Management System (CCMS)* and *CDP and how it could be used in an SH documentation context* • Explain the role of Ontology for SH planning contexts? • Conclusion Statement about SH

Table 2. Outline of Expected Activities and Communication Requirements for Assignments

Assignment	Expected Tasks and Communication
Week # 1	A. Study the concepts related to SH – Reading extensively in English B. Free writing practice – Writing longer paragraphs explaining the concepts and ideas C. Newsletter design (graduate class) – Technical design
Week # 2 & 3	A. Extensive reading and selecting SH technology & market analysis B. Information design exercise with Canva, Mind Meister, Sketchboarding and Adobe Spark C. Communicate with graduate student mentors and get feedback, revision based on feedback D. Divide the task among group members; timely completion E. Response in Slack and TeamViewer F. Group leaders in charge of communicating the progress with mentors
Week 4 & 5	A. Information design exercise with Venngage B. Analytical reasoning exercise with IHMC Cloud concept mapping C. Technical presentation design D. Analytical reasoning with community websites E. Technical report authoring (graduate) F. Feedback loop with graduate student mentors and German groups
Week 6 & 7	A. Technical presentations design in consultation with graduate mentors B. Reading advanced journal article on SH C. Ontology creation (graduate) D. Coordination with German students in conference workshops on SH E. International conference presentations

3.1. Data Collection

When the graduate students acted as mentors for the undergraduate students, it also allowed the two graduate students to reflect on the overall assignments as and how those were completed during each stage of each assignment. The two graduate students collaborated with their undergraduate student groups, gave them advise and suggestions on how to complete the assignment, what the content meant and how they were supposed to approach it when answering. Because of the lack of English language proficiency for most of the undergraduate students (significant lack of English-speaking ability), the above-mentioned range of advice and suggestions were important and needed. For each assignment, several class sessions were spent where graduate student mentors took over the class (instead of the instructor), advised and helped the undergraduate students design and write the assignments. In more cases than not, the graduate students were shown the final bi-weekly assignments by the three undergrad teams before posting it in Schoology and sending it over to the German groups.

Some of the graduate class assignments during the 6th and 7th weeks were independent of the undergraduate class assignments, and were based on the reading and understanding of advanced journal articles on SH. This paper documented the suggestions made by graduate students toward organizing the undergraduate assignments on SH, which in turn was used to answer their own graduate assignments, highlighting content comprehension, the collaboration, where the range of activities definitely lacked timely content delivery to the German students, and how the content was organized for assignment completion.

4. Findings

The findings section included comments made by the two graduate student mentors about how the content was organized for the undergraduate assignments; how the assignments could have been better answered, the actual and expected collaboration between the graduate student mentors and the undergraduate groups, and the collaboration with the German groups.

Project Orientation: We have learned in this course to mimic a project on the theme of SH with undergraduate students as project members, collaborating German students as clients and we as project managers. As project managers, we were (a) responsible for managing the relationships between all parties /groups concerned, (b) keep track of the work in progress of members, (c) adjusting the amount of work done, (d) exchanging information with clients, and (e) managing delivery times and quality required and expected by clients for such intercultural project collaboration. The results obtained from the quarter-long (2 months) project were presented at an ACM international conference by project members (undergraduates) and project managers (2 graduate mentors) in collaboration with the German partner groups. This conference was held at the Japanese university being discussed here.

4.1. Overall outlook on the SH content

4.1.1. 5 Major Topics and the Value of Information Management in Smart Home Market

The Week 2 and 3 assignments outlined the differences between the SH markets in Europe and Asia. The undergraduate students did create an SH infographic with major differences between these two. However, the work lacked comprehensive research on the relevant topics.

Suggestions for improvement (Communication with undergraduate groups): Specific differences between the markets were not outlined and there was no explicit statement about the value of information management. Therefore, one topic could outline, for example, the "SH feature demand" differences between Germany and Japan which could then be related to information management. Another point that could have been described in this topic is to reason why the feature sets are different - i.e. many houses lack central heating system due to the fault probabilities caused by earthquakes, while a house without central heating system in Europe is unimaginable. Other topics could talk about the openness of the public towards implementing such technologies in their daily lives. Of course, this is subjective to every person / household but as it can be seen later with the interviews done by the graduate students, there might be differences in customer perceptions about potential use of SH technology, even within Europe itself. Hence, this section could be differentiated into 4 major topics:

- Differences between European and Asian market for SH
- Relate previous section to information management
- Extend the information management segment with description of openness of public towards adopting smart technologies
- Relate the openness to expandability of both markets in the future

Internal notes for the section above:

- *Split the topics into two groups (EU vs Asia) to highlight the importance of the Value of Information Management in the SH Market*
- *Another reason to split them is because of different demands of "features" between the SHs in EU and Japan,*
- *Identify the 5 major issues / topics for this chapter from the posters that the undergrads made.*

4.1.2. How SH as a topic was used to discuss communications and information management?

We collaborated with undergraduate student groups as a member of this project. First of all, we gained basic knowledge about SH that we treated as the major theme. Also, as a project, we tried to get the members to know each other both within the scope of class sessions, and through email and Slack communication. Next, after learning about the SH overview, we learned about the various technologies that make it possible. The undergraduate students learnt the use of mind maps and sketch boards for organizing SH advertising content, and learnt how to convey new knowledge to others in a way that is easy for people to understand; and how the end user perceives the SH concept. We investigated whether the undergraduates did understand the context of mind map/sketchboarding use, and created the poster as a report. We helped them more with the schematization of the plan for the mind/concept maps, and less help was needed on the use of the software. We also consulted the undergraduates on how to plan the *Adobe Spark* movie by designing and planning the different topics, characters/objects and sections in the movie. The results of the entire project were compiled into one presentation and presented at the ACM conference, during the final week of the course. The project managers (grad student mentors) took over the work done by the undergraduate members, and further developed on the idea with advanced information and content management with genres such as ontology and content management and delivery portals (studied at the very basic level), and the final results were presented at the conference by us (the graduate students), as a presentation different from the undergraduate groups.

4.1.3. Data Collection Process

The planning for the final technical report (authored by us - the two graduate students) highlighted the importance of the information that includes a short description of the materials that were provided to us exclusively later on in the course, and a short description of what was expected from the undergraduates for each assignment cluster. A great example of an exclusive reading material provided to the graduate class was the journal article on *apartment block transformation for elderly people*. Subsequently, the report planning also asked for describing the information processing - for example guidance of the undergraduates by graduate students, and how the data output from the undergraduate class was used as input to write graduate class technical reports. This way it will be shown that the data collection was done by 2 different internal factions (undergrads and grads separately) and then shared with an external entity, the HSKA, Germany students, where the information was refined and adjusted to the needs of their (HSKA) study. Therefore, it's important to describe the internal teamwork at UoA and the collaboration with HSKA.

Internal notes before writing the section above:

- *Actual communication between the groups - making sure that they know about events, classes ... we had Slack ... we sent repeated e-mails as and when needed to make sure the groups are working on the assignment and keeping track of the time... we had Google drive where we supervised the ongoing process.*

- *Delivery of the solutions from the grads and undergrads to the HSKA and material organization on the Google drive.*

4.1.4. Findings from Interview / Undergraduate Student Assignments

In order to understand how commercials for SH should be designed, we (the graduate students) had to do an audience analysis of the different markets to try and understand end user perceptions (this interview was NOT done in collaboration with the undergraduate class). That helped us develop preliminary understanding of the extent to which the design of the Adobe Spark movie, and the poster would be well received by users of SH technology the world over. Reflecting on our own work in the graduate class, this audience analysis interview section should contain differences between the European and Japanese interviewees. It could be outlined that even though the interviewees from Europe were from different countries and belong to two every different age groups, some opinions were similar. However, the willingness of implementation and perception of usefulness of SH technologies were completely different. What was even more surprising was that the person with a software engineering background was less open towards ownership of an SH than the interviewee from the clothing industry. The segment about undergraduate student assignment on designing advertising videos could very well be related to the interviews recorded later on. The information design assignment (with Adobe Spark, Canva, Mind Maps, etc.) could very well be a follow-up of the interview assignment for seamless topic transition. On a separate note, undergraduates should definitely be asked about reporting short descriptions of the skills they learned by doing this activity. For example, during the data collection process, students were provided with articles / websites about the different SH technologies which were then processed and the information was transformed into an advertising video.

Internal notes before writing the section above:

- *Outline the differences between the interviewees from Eastern / Central and Northern Europe and also write about the possible perception of technology between different age groups.*
- *Outline the overall perception of SH technologies for the Japanese interviews*
- *Then relate those differences and opinions stated in the reports to the market descriptions*
- *Describe that the undergraduate approach to the information design assignments (mind maps, sketchboarding, IHMC cloud map etc.) were according to the guidelines that could be practically used in the process of making real documentation / advertisement and then were verified by the grads.*

4.1.5. Discussions / Implications of this study for technical communication and project-based learning?

We assumed undergraduates to be project members and German students to be project clients for this course. As a buffer during that time, it was important to sample the client's needs and accurately communicate it to the members. In addition to managing the progress of the members, the situation was communicated to the client, and detailed adjustments were made. By establishing a client, we were able to conduct a simulation experiment closer to the actual project.

4.1.6. Limitations of the Study / Future Study

The limitations of this study were that the undergraduate students were not taught proper project management skills (as it was not the course focus) and the undergraduate students could not implement their assignment solutions in real life. Therefore, the success rate of some advertisements they created was a pure estimation. And for the graduate students (us), the course did an evaluation of the project management skills rather implicitly, by seeing progress within the project and perceivable clarity of next milestone among the undergraduate students. In the future, during such a project, the point for greatest importance should be the communication between respective teams and their group members. It has been proven that sometimes, the communication between all interested parties was insufficient. Therefore, in the future, there should be "ice breaking" sessions at the beginning so the team members will be comfortable in each other's presence. Also, communication exercises and training between the teams are highly recommended especially for the sake of the assignment solution quality. This recommendation is due to the observed quality difference between teams, where the members knew each other, as opposed to ones where the team composed of strangers.

Internal notes before writing the section above:

- *The project management has not been taught per say, rather practically implemented than theoretically explained.*
- *In the future, we have to focus on communication as it is the most essential part of any collaboration.*
    - *An example of the above point could be a comparison between the groups that have had different quality levels. For example, the group #1 was a good example because the group members were familiar with each other and they generally knew what to do, and if they were not sure, they were not afraid to ask questions.*

4.1.7. Conclusion

In this course, I learned how to run and manage projects using the theme of SH. As a result, undergraduates learned about the subject, how to share it with members, and how to efficiently communicate the learned knowledge with people, using various media such as posters and videos. Graduate students learned how to manage project members and outcomes, communicate with clients, and organize and better understand things. These results were presented to participants through the conference. The resulting final international conference was a great opportunity to highlight the work done, and also reflect on what could have been better managed – and this was done with joint workshops with the undergraduates, graduate students from UoA and HSKA, Germany. These joint workshops happened during the conference week, in advance of the final conference presentation. This allowed all parties concerned to smoothen the differences in understanding, and clarify how each group thought about their respective projects, and what it meant. It was an opportunity for the HSKA groups to ask us questions and then incorporate the content as part of their own projects. We often went back and forth clarifying the content and it's representation by the Germans in their ontology and metadata

.

Figures 2a and **2b** highlighted the two interfaces - *TeamViewer* and *Slack* used extensively during most parts of the course.

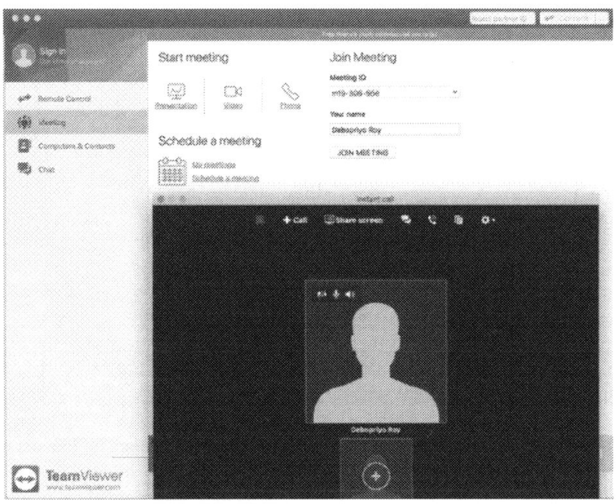

TeamViewer Tasks for the Japanese Groups (as completed)

1. Set up the TeamViewer "Ice-breaking" meeting with the German groups
2. Undergraduate students - self-introduction in English during the meeting with the Germans (in-class practice ahead of the meeting)
3. Graduate students - self-introduction in English during the meeting with the Germans
4. Short project explanation by each undergraduate team leader in English (in-class practice ahead of the meeting)
5. Answering questions in English as asked by the Germans about the project – assisted by the graduate student mentors
6. Communication about the next set of meetings and the expected timeline for project stage completion.

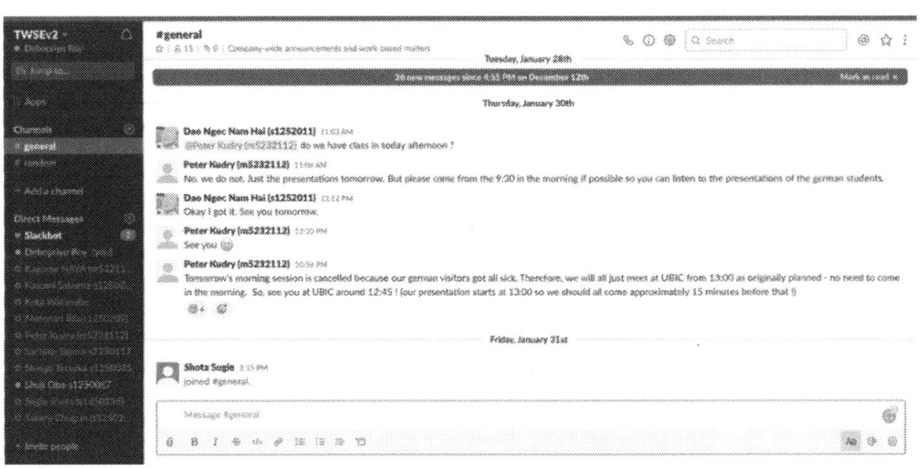

Figure 2a and 2b: TeamViewer (Japan and Germany Teams) and Slack Workspace (Undergrad and Grad Teams in Japan)

4.2. Comments on the coordination between graduate-undergraduate teams

(Week 1): *The initial coordination in preparation for writing of this newsletter was done when we discussed various points of the undergraduate equivalent of this assignment. For example, one example is steering the undergraduate groups towards correct content selection and representation, and correcting some of their grammar. Then the draft of the answers, alongside other materials posted on Schoology and from the internet was included in the draft of the final assignment # 1 response written by the undergrad groups, which was then read by both graduates and constructed into the final graduate newsletter file that was handed in.*

Week 2 and 3: *The mentoring experience during the completion of the week two and three undergraduate assignments was, from the side of the graduate students, not completely satisfactory. The timeline of these assignments has spanned the Christmas/winter vacation which resulted in poor communication between the students and mentors. For this reason, even though the students were questioned during the holidays, there has not been a significant collaboration between these parties while the assignments were worked on. Rather, the students were questioned about their experience post-deadline and therefore, this section had a rather retrospective feel to it. The overall feeling was that the respective groups were able to evenly distribute the workload among the members of each group. Furthermore, there have not been any disputes over which part should have been done by which student. Most of the group members' decisions were based on either their experience and how well they can utilize their already known skills, or the lack of their experience and how they can lower their skill deficit. Two out of three groups have experienced scheduling difficulties as their hand-ins were turned in later than the prescribed deadline, therefore there was much room for improvement in regards to time management. Time management has been proven to be difficult as when the students were asked if they had more time to complete their assignments, what would they do? A general answer to this question was that they would work on certain parts longer, elevating the quality of their work. The quality of work has also been reviewed by the mentors, particularly, the short videos created in Adobe Spark. If the students decided to include narration in these videos, this was the aspect which showed the lowest quality. In this case, it was not the quality of the videos themselves or quality of the audio recording, it was the English pronunciation which has been, even for bilingual English speakers, difficult to understand. Even though there have been occasional hiccups in quality, planning or execution of this set of assignments, students themselves were satisfied with the work they have submitted. When it comes to the evaluation of the mentors, there have been no complaints, nor request for increased engagement in their work. The amount of mentoring seemed appropriate to them; however, the mentors were left feeling slightly left out and requested higher engagement in communication from their side. This will be in the form of more frequent status updates and immediate access to their workspaces on Google Drive.*

4.3. Note-taking by Graduate Students during Mentoring Activities

1. *Talk to the representatives of the three groups and make notes about their impression of how the work was done, are they happy with it, why did they not communicate with us etc.*
2. *Tell them strictly that we want to know, and to use the SLACK account we created so that we can follow their work as and when it's updated.*
3. *Tell them to always post the google doc folder link whenever they create it and start working on the assignment. We also want to be able to check the progress ourselves. So, whenever they create a repository for the latest assignment, they have to make the topic of their group channel a link to the google doc folder.*
4. *Write three paragraphs (one for each group) where we describe our interactions, their work, content strength, group coordination and also critique the overall quality of their work.*
5. *Tell the students that we are not TA's, but our results depend on their results too, so we are on the same boat.*
6. *Get all of the hand-ins from the groups and reply to the e-mail from the German student coordinators.*

5. Limitations of the Course and Future Directions

This paper provided an opportunity to explore how the group coordination took place, and the types of assignments handled that led to development of group communication and project management skills. It's obvious from the reports by the graduate students that the undergraduates did not directly deal with the German students and the communication followed in most cases, through the graduate student mentors. However, direct communication ensued between the graduate student mentors and the undergraduates. A large part of the problem as observed by the course instructor was the lack of confidence in speaking English by the Japanese undergraduate students, and that resulted in deliberate attempt to avoid direct intercultural exposure on the part of the Japanese students. Things were better as the graduate students were confident individuals and they mediated the conversations during video conferencing and when the German student groups visited in the Japanese university campus. I think, in future, at least for this course, we will need to pay closer attention to the points raised by the graduate student mentors, including have extended ice-breaking sessions which might include informal and casual meetings before immersing into course-related activities. More videoconferencing sessions with German students would be ideal as well. It's evident from the report above that in more cases, the undergraduates could handle the assignments on their own, and sometimes resisted graduate mentoring, but the larger problem was the avoidance or lack of interest in intercultural communication. Future versions of this course could also consider making the undergraduate students visit local stores and engage in direct client communication and explore the extent to which SH technologies are sold in the local market, including interviewing store managers to understand the local SH market. This approach could then act as a prelude or preparation for direct intercultural engagement with the foreign students. However, an important administrative question would be the extent to which this would be possible in a 7-weeks teaching duration.

References

Aldrich, F. K. (2003). Smart homes: past, present and future. In *Inside the smart home* (pp. 17-39). Springer, London.

Beckett, G. H., & Slater, T. (2018). Project-Based Learning and Technology. *The TESOL encyclopedia of English language teaching*, 1-7.

Coyle, D.: 2007, Content and language integrated learning: Towar ds a connected research agenda for CLIL pedagogies, The International Journal of Bilingual Education and Bilingualism 10:5, 543--562.

Coyle, D.: 2008, CLIL: A pedagogical approach from the European perspective, in N. Van Deusen-Scholl & N. Hornberger. (eds.), Encyclopedia of Language and Education, Volume 4: Second and Foreign Language Education (2nd ed.), (97--111). Springer, New York.

Dooly, M. (2013). Promoting competency-based language teaching through project-based language learning. In *Competency-based language teaching in higher education* (pp. 77-91). Springer, Dordrecht.

Gibbes, M., & Carson, L. (2014). Project-based language learning: an activity theory analysis. *Innovation in language learning and teaching*, *8*(2), 171-189.

Kusmayadi, Y., & Suryana, Y. (2017). Improving students' factual report writing skill by using content and language integrated learning (CLIL) method. *Indonesian EFL Journal*, *3*(1), 21-3.

MAHONEY, J. (2019). Student perceptions of soft CLiL lessons in a Japanese junior high school. *自然・人間・社会= Nature-people-society, Science and the humanities: 関東学院大学経済学部・経営学部総合学術論叢*, (66), 13-28.

Marsh, D. (1994). Bilingual Education & Content and Language Integrated Learning. International Association for Cross-cultural Communication, Language Teaching in the Member States of the European Union (Lingua) University of Sorbonne. Paris.

Moss, D., & Van Duzer, C. (1998). Project-Based Learning for Adult English Language Learners. ERIC Digest.

Uemura, T., Gilmour, G. J., & Costa, L. F. (2019). Testing the Water: Implementing a Soft CLIL Approach for Future Global Engineers at a Japanese University. In *Content and Language Integrated Learning in Spanish and Japanese Contexts* (pp. 175-201). Palgrave Macmillan, Cham.

About the authors

Professor Debopriyo Roy is a full professor of technical communication and computer assisted language learning at the Center for Language Research, Dept. of Computer Science and Engineering at the University of Aizu.

Mr. Peter Kudry is a graduate student at the Dept. of Computer Science and Engineering at the University of Aizu.

Miss. Kagome Naya is a graduate student at the Dept. of Computer Science and Engineering at the University of Aizu.

Improving Japanese English pronunciation with speech recognition and feedback system

Kanta Igarashi[1,*] and *Ian* Wilson[1,**]

[1]CLR Phonetics Lab, University of Aizu, Tsuruga, Ikki-machi, Aizuwakamatsu, Fukushima-ken, Japan

Abstract. For Japanese people, communicating with English speakers from abroad has become more common because of internationalization, and there are many people who want to improve their English-speaking skills. However, there are few environments where we can speak English outside of the classroom, so Japanese students rarely have a chance to study English pronunciation. Even if students do have a chance to take an English pronunciation class, teachers do not have enough time to individually teach each student pronunciation in a big class. Because of that, computers and smartphones may be one good type of tool to solve this problem. In this research, we develop a web-based application to help Japanese learners with their English pronunciation.

1 Introduction

According to Dizon [1], intelligent assistants such as Siri or Alexa, which use speech recognition, could be helpful tools for language learners, especially Japanese second-language (L2) English learners, who usually do not have many opportunities to use English outside of the classroom. Daniels and Iwago [2] have compared Siri to Google Speech Recognition (GSR) and found that GSR is more accurate for transcribing Japanese undergraduates' L2 English speech. However, although intelligent assistants can recognize speech, they do not advise users about their pronunciation. So, the current research is focused on creating a web-based feedback system that would be helpful for language learners. The feedback system advises users from the point of view of articulation and correctness based on typical errors in real test results that we collected. In this research, the web application with feedback system to evaluate users' English pronunciation uses Mozilla Developer Network (MDN)'s Web Speech API [3]. In order to make the range of possible feedback more manageable, the words and phrases used for this web application are limited. They are chosen from the "Wolf Story" [4], a phonetic passage adapted from an Aesop fable, because of the wide range of English phonemes and different combinations of phonemes. It is easy for teachers and students to access the system, because the web application is hosted on the University of Aizu's CLR Phonetics Lab website at http://clrlab1.u-aizu.ac.jp/acoustics.html.

2 Speech Recognition Interface

There are many speech recognition applications, so it is possible to choose an interface according to one's individual requirements. For example, Google Speech Recognition (GSR), IBM Cloud, Siri, Alexa, and Speech Recognition API (MDN) are all popular. As previously stated, GSR is better for L2 English learners than Siri and Alexa. So, we compared GSR, IBM, and MDN's API. Table 1 shows a list of these APIs' advantages and disadvantages.

Table 1. Comparison of three APIs for speech recognition (GSR = Google Speech Recognition; IBM = IBM Cloud; MDN = Mozilla Developer Network's Web Speech API)

	Advantages	Disadvantages
GSR	•High accuracy	• Need account, many source files, must pay according to use
IBM		• Need account, must pay according to use
MDN	• Need only Javascript • Free	•Accuracy is lower •Only works with Chrome

3 Method

The web application created in this research consists of HTML, CSS and JavaScript. First, the HTML and CSS functions are "recognition start button", "sample mp3 files control", etc. Javascript controls the speech recognition and feedback system. The Web Speech API is an interface that Mozilla Developer Network (MDN) provides and this API can recognize any language. In this web application, we selected American English as the language setting because much of the English education in Japanese primary and secondary schools seems to focus on American English. In addition, the application needs users to install and use Google Chrome because MDN's Web Speech API works on Google Chrome only (this API does not work on iOS).

*e-mail: s1240221@u-aizu.ac.jp
**e-mail: wilson@u-aizu.ac.jp

4 Web Application Details

This web application uses Web Speech API [3]. A part of the web application is shown in Figure 1. The application includes a feedback system and a lecture page. The feedback system must give advice to users, so we created an advice dataset corresponding to words from test participants that were commonly misunderstood by the speech recognition system. In case the recognized word is not in the dataset, the feedback given is very general ("please try again and speak more clearly").

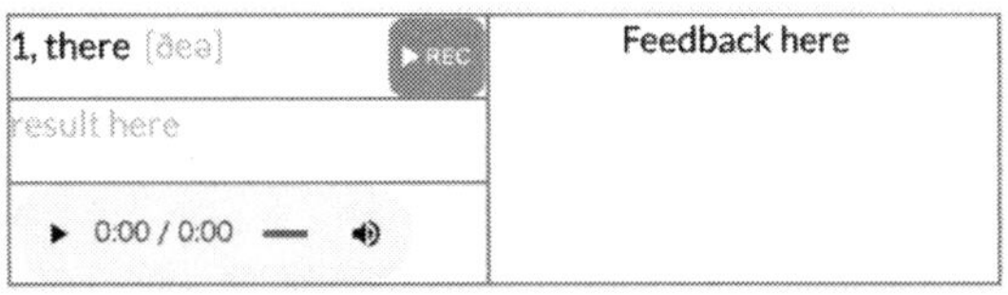

Figure 1. Part of the "word practice" page of the resultant web application

The lecture section of the application contains three pages. First, an explanation of what the International Phonetic Alphabet (IPA) is. Second and third, lessons teaching how to pronounce vowels and consonants, respectively. For each type of sound, static MRI images of articulators producing the sounds can be seen. Although this study's purpose is a complete web application with feedback system, we also made a lecture page to help with the study of English pronunciation.This application is mainly for Japanese L2 English learners, so the lecture page is written in Japanese. According to Ono [5], the way of effective pronunciation teaching is that the student repeats the teacher's English pronunciation and the teacher explains, in words and illustrations, how to pronounce.

4.1 Feedback System

The web application can return advice for a word from a list of common errors by Japanese speakers. Figures 2, 3, and 4 show examples of feedback. In case the recognized word is not in the list, the application returns common advice. For example, if the word is missing "th" sound, the application returns appropriate advice such as "Put your tongue tip between your teeth to make "th" sound."

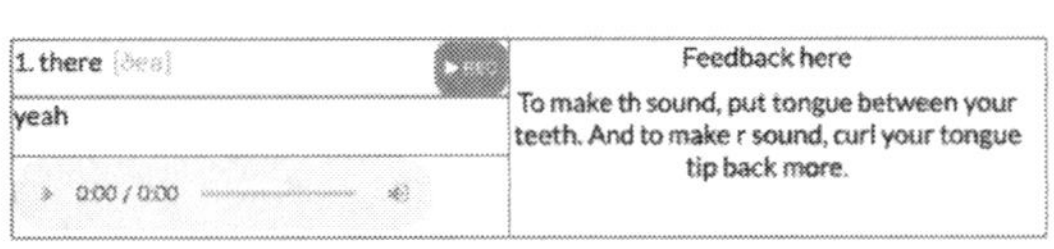

Figure 2. Example showing feedback given to the user for "th" sound

4.1.1 Common Pronunciation Errors

There are many common errors that Japanese speakers make when speaking English as a second language. Table 2 and Figure 5 show the consonants and vowels, respectively, that exist in Japanese and English. In Table 2, consonants only used in English are shown in blue and consonants only used in Japanese are shown in red. Also, consonants used in both English and Japanese are shown in black. Common pronunciation errors by Japanese speakers of English usually occur in vowels and consonants that are not found in Japanese (i.e., the ones shown in blue). In Figure 5, the vowels underlined in pink are those found in North American English but not in Japanese.

Figure 3. Example showing feedback given to the user for a vowel sound

Figure 4. Example showing feedback given to the user for "f" sound

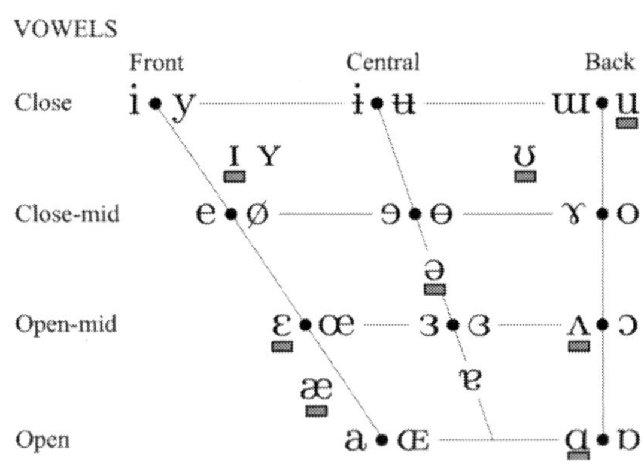

Figure 5. International Phonetic Alphabet chart of vowels showing (underlined in pink) English vowels not found in Japanese

4.1.2 Data Collection

In order to build a feedback system, we collected real examples of the Web Speech API's transcriptions of Japanese speakers' English utterances. In order to collect test samples, we created a website that recognizes users pronunciation and sends data by email to us. Participants were mainly students of the University of Aizu. Anyone could access the website easily because it is hosted on the University of Aizu's CLR Phonetics Lab website at http://clrlab1.u-aizu.ac.jp/acoustics.html. The data collected can be seen in Table 3. The target word is shown

Table 2. International Phonetic Alphabet chart of consonants showing differences between English and Japanese. Red phonemes are found only in Japanese, blue ones are found only in English, and black ones are found in both languages

	Bilabial	Labiodental	Dental	Alveolar	Postalveolar	Palatal	Velar	Glottal
Plosive	p b			t d			k g	
Nasal	m			n			ŋ	
Trill								
Tap or Flap				ɾ				
Fricative	ɸ	f v	θ ð	s z	ʃ ʒ			h
Lateral fricative								
Approximant	w			ɹ		j		
Lateral approximant				l				
Affricate				ts dz	tʃ dʒ			

in the left column, and for each participant (A–M) the resultant transcription by MDN's Web Speech API is shown. The number of mismatches ("errors") between target word and transcription can be seen in the bottom row. Note that even for the native speaker (participant L), the system indicated an error for two words: *threaten* and *fool*.

4.2 Lecture Page

In the lecture page, learners are taught how to pronounce English vowels and consonants with MRI pictures. Figure 6 shows the top page of the web application. This webpage has four tabs. In "About IPA", "Vowels" and "Consonants" pages, it explains how to read the IPA chart and how to make vowel and consonant sounds. In the "Word Practice" page, users can practice pronunciation and get feedback. I referred to [6] in making the "Vowels" and " Consonants" pages.

5 Source Code Description

5.1 HTML Source Code

The following is HTML source code. This code is for showing what is found in Figure 1.

```
<div class="box_2">
 <div class="practice-place">
  <div class="example">
   <div class="practice-right">1, there
    <span class="ipaDiv">[]</span>
   </div>
   <button  class="rec-btn"id="p1">
   <i class="fas fa-play"> REC</i></button>
  </div>
  <div class="resultDiv" id="practice-result1">
   result here</div>
  <div class="btn-box">
  <div class="audio-btn">
  <audio src="there.mp3" controls>
  </div>
 </div>
</div>
```

The above code is for the left side of Figure 1. This display example word and REC button in example class, recognized word place in resultDiv class and example sound in audio.

```
 <div class="feedback-place">
  <div class="fb-title">Feedback here</div>
  <div id="fb1"class="feedback-here"></div>
 </div>
</div>
```

The above section of code is for the right side of Figure 1.

5.2 Javascript Source Code

The following is part of the Javascript source code.

```
var misThere =[
  ["yeah","To make th sound, ..."],
  ["sarah","You are confusing ..."],
  ["date","Put your tongue ..."],
  ["dale","You confuse d sound ...."],
  ["zelle","You confuse z ...."]
];
```

This is part of arrays for making advice list.

```
 startBtn[0].onclick = () => {
  recognition[0].start();
}
recognition[0].onresult = (event) => {
  clickFunc(0,event);
}
```

When the REC button is clicked, the speech recognition function is called and starts. Also, each button has a number to identify it.

```
var clickFunc = function(clickNum,event){
  finalTranscript='';
  let interimTranscript = '';
  for (let i = event.resultIndex;
  i < event.results.length; i++) {
    let transcript = event.results[i][0].
                        transcript;
    if (event.results[i].isFinal) {
      finalTranscript += transcript;
    } else {
      interimTranscript = transcript;
    }
  }
  resultDiv[clickNum].style.color = '#000000';
  resultDiv[clickNum].innerHTML = finalTranscript
  + interimTranscript;
  feedbackDiv[clickNum].innerHTML =
                      checkFunc(clickNum);
}
```

The clickFunc code above is for displaying the results of recognition and feedback.

Table 3. Results of MDN Web Speech API speech recognition for 13 participants including one native speaker

	Participants (A–M)												
sample	A	B	C	D	E	F	G	H	I	J	K	L (native)	M
there	there	yeah	yeah	there	sarah	date	there	there	dale	zelle	sarah	there	there
poor	cooler	frac		poor	poor poor	poor	pearl	cool	cool	hua	torah	poor	poor
flocks	flat	frock	trunks	crocs	lyrics	clocks	trucks	rocks	crooks	clocks	frocks	phlox	phlox
dark	dark	DAC	dak	dark	doc	doc	dirk	dark	dog	dogs	dark	dark	dogs
plan	brown	put on		prawn	rap	brown	plum	put on	brown		prom	plan	slime
run	noun	land		run	long	ren	long	la	wrong	wrong	wrong	run	wrong
village	ferrets	Dodge	petr cech	greenwich	spirits	we teach	pH	pH	spinach	philles	village	village	village
little	little	retina	little	little	critter	I don't	little	later	little	little	little	little	beetle
fun	song	fan	front	fun	fang	phone	farm	farm	farm		phone	fun	bomb
third	todd	turn	sad	third	salt	surd	third	sade	sad	surag	shirt	third	todd
wolf	hello	all right			lowe's	oops	bro	both	wolf	waltz	earth	wolf	wall
threaten	threatened	Toyota	threatened	threatened	samaritan	threatened	creighton	slaton	sheraton		veteran	threatened	310
sheep	sheep	sweet	seep	sheep	seat	see	sheep	sheep	seep		sheep	sheep	sheep
louder	louder	ladder	ladder	louder	browser	rhoda	louder	yoda	louder	louder	louder	louder	louder
exactly	exactly	exactly	exactly	exactly	echoes act 3	duck tree	exactly	exactly	you can suck 3	exactly	exactly	exactly	exactly
who	who	who	2	who	who	TRUE	who	food	who	crew	who	who	who
bother	bother	brother	bozeman	brother	weather	butter	bother	buzzer	father	squirrel sound	bouncer	bother	bother
fool	who	woo	food	full	food	coup	whole food	food	who	who	tune	cool	pool
cousins	cousins	cousin	cousins	cousins	cousins	consonance	cousin	cozy	cousins		cousin	cousins	cousin
fist	quit	quest	tryst	fist	fist	fixed	first	feast	fist	wrist	cost	fist	best
# OF ERRORS	11	18	13	5	16	19	12	16	14	12	13	2	11

Figure 6. The Vowels page of the web application

```
var checkFunc = function(clickNum){
  var result=resultDiv[clickNum].innerHTML;
  var advice="";
  var listFlag = 0;
  result = result.toLowerCase();
  if(result.indexOf(sample[clickNum]) != -1)
  return 'correct!';
```

The checkFunc code above makes and returns advice according to recognized word. If the recognized word is not collected, go to branch of switch.

```
  switch (clickNum) {

    case 0:
    for(let i = 0;i<misThere.length;i++)
    {
     if(result.indexOf(misThere[i][0]) != -1)
     {
        advice = misThere[i][1];
        listFlag = 1;
      }
    }
```

If the recognized word is not in the advice list, return common advice against the word.

```
    if(listFlag == 0){
      if(result.indexOf("th") == -1){
        advice+=commonAdvice["th"];
      }
      if(result.indexOf("r") == -1){
        advice+=commonAdvice["r"];
      }
    }
```

```
    break;

    case 1:
    .......
```

6 Future Work

We believe that this web application should be developed further, because the feedback system in the web application is based on too little result data. In the future, we must collect more recognized word data and improve the feedback system.

References

[1] G. Dizon, Computer Assisted Language Learning **29**, 1249 (2016)

[2] P. Daniels, K. Iwago, JALTCALL Journal **13**, 229 (2017)

[3] Mozilla Developer Network, *Web Speech API*, `https://developer.mozilla.org/ja/docs/Web/API/Web_Speech_API`

[4] D. Deterding, Journal of the International Phonetic Association **36**, 187 (2006)

[5] K. Ono, J. Fac. Edu. Saga Univ **17**, 57 (2012)

[6] A. Nogita, Japan Association of Foreign Language Education bulletin **21**, 1 (2018)

 https://doi.org/10.1051/shsconf/20207702004

Using deep learning to classify English native pronunciation level from acoustic information

Aozora Kobayashi[1,*] and *Ian* Wilson[1,**]

[1]CLR Phonetics Lab, University of Aizu, Tsuruga, Ikki-machi, Aizuwakamatsu, Fukushima-ken, Japan

Abstract. The main purpose of this research is to test the use of deep learning for automatically classifying an English learner's pronunciation proficiency, a step in the construction of a system that supports second language learners. Our deep learning dataset consists of 28 speakers – ranging in proficiency from native to beginner non-native – reading the same 216-word English story. In the supervised deep learning training process, we first label the English proficiency level of the data, but this is a complicated task because there are a number of different ways to determine someone's speech proficiency. In this research, we focus on three elements: foreign accent, speech fluency (as measured by total number of pauses, total length of pauses, and speed of speech) and pronunciation (as measured by speech intelligibility). We use Long Short-Term Memory (LSTM) layers for deep learning, train a computer on differently labeled data, test a computer on separate data, and present the results. Features used from audio data are calculated by Mel-Frequency Cepstrum Coefficients (MFCCs) and pitch. We try several combinations of parameters for deep learning to find out what settings are best for our database. We also try changing the labeling method, changing the length of each audio sample, and changing the method of cross-validation. As a result, we conclude that labeling by speech fluency instead of by speech intelligibility tends to get better deep learning test accuracy.

1 Introduction

1.1 Motivation and goal

English is an important tool for communication in an increasingly global society, and many non-native speakers study English-as-a-Foreign-Language (EFL). However, it is sometimes difficult for second language (L2) speakers to perceive and produce pronunciation differences between other speakers (including natives) and themselves. Although this is not necessarily a problem for communication, such differences often do result in communication breakdown.

Japanese English learners have common tendencies in their English pronunciation errors [1]. For instance, Japanese learners of English tend to mistake the pronunciation of the high back lax vowel /ʊ/ because it is not an underlying phoneme in Japanese words. So, a minimal pair such as "fool" and "full" may sound the same to them. Moreover, in general, L2 speakers' speed of speech is slower than native speakers, because they are overly careful when speaking in English. In this way, there are many English pronunciation differences between native speakers and non-native speakers, some of which lead to communication problems.

Based on this situation, the ultimate goal of our research is constructing a system that supports pronunciation study for EFL learners. A system that can give feedback about differences between L2 speakers' and native speakers' English pronunciation would be a valuable pedagogical tool. Aside from pedagogical purposes, such a system might be useful for forensic phonetics and security, when people need to make positive identifications of speakers. To construct such a system, it is helpful to automatically detect errors in speech and judge the level of English pronunciation (see [2] for a good overview).

However, categorizing a speaker's pronunciation proficiency is not a straightforward task. To categorize speakers, the problem is determining what factors cause people to think "This speech sounds like a native speaker" or "Person A sounds more proficient than person B". Ratings of language proficiency can be measured in many different ways [3], [4], [5].

As a step towards making a pedagogical system as described above, we first use deep learning for categorizing non-native speakers' English speaking proficiency. Deep learning is a type of machine learning that uses deep neural networks (DNNs). One of the merits of using deep learning is that a machine can choose the salient features from many features in the data. To investigate speaking proficiency of L2 speakers, this method seems more appropriate than general machine learning because speech has so many features, and proficiency has so many indicators. Therefore, we chose deep learning for the main method in this research.

Moreover, to get a large enough training dataset for use with deep learning, we used (and added to) an existing database in our lab. There are 4 types of data in our

*e-mail: m5221101@u-aizu.ac.jp
**e-mail: wilson@u-aizu.ac.jp

database: audio data, ultrasound tongue video data, side-view face video data, and front-view face video data [6]. In this paper, we focus on only the audio data.

1.2 Deep learning

As mentioned above, deep learning is a type of machine learning that uses DNNs. A deep neural network (DNN) is an artificial neural network with multiple layers between the input and output layers. The type of neural network that we choose is important. For example, Convolutional Neural Network (CNN) is suitable for image data, and Recurrent Neural Network (RNN) is better than CNN for data with a time series [7].

In our research, Long Short-Term Memory (LSTM) is most frequent. LSTM is one type of RNN architecture. A common LSTM unit is composed of a *cell*, an *input gate*, an *output gate*, and a *forget gate*. The cell remembers values over arbitrary time intervals and the gates control the information flow into and out of the cell. Thus, an LSTM network is very suitable for classification and prediction with time-series data.

In machine learning, the method the computer uses to learn during training is important, specifically unsupervised learning or supervised learning. Unsupervised learning means using a training dataset without pre-existing labels – the computer determines categories on its own – whereas supervised learning means using a training dataset with pre-existing user-defined labels [7].

In the case of labeling for training deep learning models, one factor that could affect results is label noise – the problem of not being able to clearly label some of the data or the problem of a lack of agreement between experts on a given label [8]. If one trains DNNs on noisy labeled data, overfitting can occur, which lowers the effectiveness of the deep learning [9]. In the past, some researchers tried to make DNNs that overcome strong label noise [10] and estimate probabilities of label noise.

In past research, many researchers have tried to automatically recognize pronunciation differences between native speakers and non-native speakers by using a variety of ways (for an overview, see [2]). One example is using tongue trajectories of ultrasound tongue images [11]. In that research, a cosine convolution filter was used to extract features from ultrasound tongue images. Native and non-native speakers' tongue motion was compared and pronunciation errors could be automatically detected, especially for /k/, /ʃ/, and /r/.

Other deep learning research has used not only audio speech data, but also ultrasound image data [12] and the combination of the two. In that research, the authors compared (1) the accuracy of deep RNN by using only audio data to (2) the accuracy of using both audio and point-tracked tongue information. They found that using features of both types of data can get higher accuracy for deep learning than using features of only one data type.

2 Database for deep learning

2.1 Participants

We used data from a total of 28 participants in this study – 23 who were from a preexisting database [6] and an additional 5 participants whose data we collected in exactly the same way as in the past. The former 23 were used in Trials 1 & 2, and the entire 28 were used in Trials 3 & 4. Table 1 shows information about the participants: their sound (WAV) file identification number(s) for internal use, age, gender, and English proficiency (TOEIC) score, if available. The 5 participants who were added after Trials 1 & 2 have an asterisk after the participant number.

Table 1: Participant list (ordered by TOEIC score)

Participant #	WAV file #	Age	Gender	TOEIC score
1	618	32	M	990[1]
2	621	33	F	965
3*	635, 636	28	M	960[2]
4	619	30	F	920
5	617	—	F	910
6	622	60	F	900[3]
7	616	49	F	900[3]
8*	632, 633	44	M	900[3]
9*	639, 640	21	F	810
10*	637, 638	22	M	765
11	620	32	F	685
12	598	23	M	650
13	597	24	M	600
14*	641, 642	19	M	595
15	603	20	M	560
16	605	24	M	510
17	599	23	M	450
18	612	24	M	440
19	613	20	M	425
20	604	24	M	400
21	606	24	M	400
22	610	19	M	400
23	600	19	M	395
24	607	19	M	375
25	609	18	F	375
26	602	23	M	350
27	615	23	M	350
28	608	21	M	225

* participant added after Trials 1 & 2
[1] actually native speaker (USA)
[2] converted from TOEFL iBT=98
[3] converted from Eiken Level 1

2.2 Data collection

2.2.1 Apparatus

The apparatus used to collect data can be seen in Figure 1 and is described in detail in [6]. Participants sat on a chair in front of a laptop that displayed stimuli using Powerpoint slides. Ultrasound tongue image video was mixed with audio and exported to an iMac computer. Participants needed to wear a helmet holding the probe of the ultrasound machine to prevent the probe from shifting relative to the skull during speech. We recorded participants' speech at a 48,000 Hz sampling rate, using a DPA 4080 cardioid lapel microphone and a Korg MR-1000 recorder. Speakers repeated the same stimuli passage twice, because we recorded ultrasound movies in two separate planes: mid-sagittal and coronal.

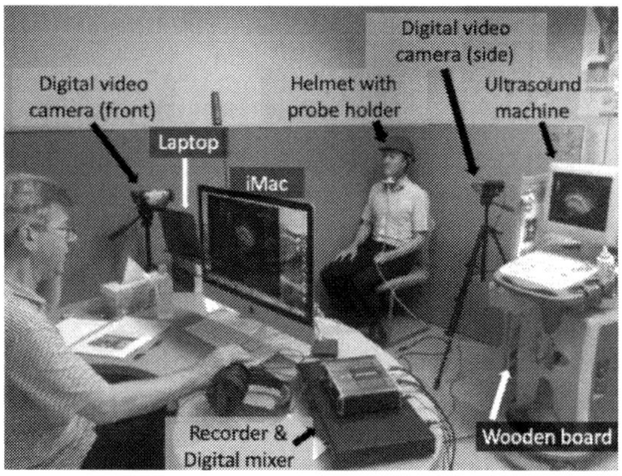

Figure 1: Data collection apparatus in the CLR Phonetics Lab

2.2.2 *Stimuli*

As English stimuli, we used a version of the famous Aesop fable "The Boy Who Cried Wolf" [13]. The sentences below show the whole 216-word Wolf Passage. Note that this stimuli has at least three clear instances of each of the English monophthong vowels, most of the diphthongs and consonants, and even some minimal pair words such as "fist"/"feast" and "raising"/"racing". There are 134 unique words in the passage, in a great range of phonetic environments.

> There was once a poor shepherd boy who used to watch his flocks in the fields next to a dark forest near the foot of a mountain. One hot afternoon, he thought up a good plan to get some company for himself and also have a little fun. Raising his fist in the air, he ran down to the village shouting "Wolf, Wolf". As soon as they heard him, the villagers all rushed from their homes, full of concern for his safety, and two of his cousins even stayed with him for a short while. This gave the boy so much pleasure that a few days later he tried exactly the same trick again, and once more he was successful. However, not long after, a wolf that had just escaped from the zoo was looking for a change from its usual diet of chicken and duck. So, overcoming its fear of being shot, it actually did come out from the forest and began to threaten the sheep. Racing down to the village, the boy of course cried out even louder than before. Unfortunately, as all the villagers were convinced that he was trying to fool them a third time, they told him, "Go away and don't bother us again". And so the wolf had a feast.

2.3 Data cleaning

When training a computer on a dataset for deep learning, it is important to have as clear a signal as possible – whether it is audio, visual, or other. Since participants sometimes made whole-word mistakes in their pronunciation of the stimuli, and since the signal intensity was not consistent across participants, we had to clean the data before deep learning. We used Praat software [14] to carry out the following steps for data cleaning: (1) extracted the required part of the English stimuli, (2) scaled intensity to a new average of 70 dB, (3) converted audio from stereo to mono, and (4) downsampled audio sampling rate from 48,000 Hz to 24,000 Hz. In step 2, the root-mean-square amplitude of the sound will come to lie 70 dB above the assumed auditory threshold of 0.00002 Pa.

2.4 Data labeling

As mentioned in Section 1.2, before using the supervised learning type of deep learning, we needed to label the data. The problem is that there are so many ways to categorize participants into English native speech levels: foreign accent, pronunciation intelligibility, fluency, grammar, vocabulary, pragmatics, etc. To measure fluency, past researchers have used speech rate in words per minute (WPM) [15] and number and length of pauses [16]. Measurement of speech intelligibility is often done by having listeners transcribe spoken speech and seeing how many words they get correct [17].

When determining the final labels in the supervised deep learning training process, we decided to try defining labels using different factors such as perceived foreign accent, fluency, and intelligibility. These different labeling methods will be described in more detail in Section 3.

3 Deep learning data analysis and results

3.1 Trial 1: Two-second audio segments

In this trial, we used audio data from 23 participants. Before extracting features from the data, we separated the audio into many 2-second files because the length of the original sound files were too long to process in computer memory. We allocated 1139 files (about 80%) for training and 310 files (about 20%) for testing. As for features, we used 13-dimensional Mel-Frequency Cepstrum Coefficients (MFCCs) and pitch (fundamental frequency (f0)). MFCCs are coefficients that collectively make up the Mel-frequency cepstrum. To calculate both MFCCs and f0, we used the MATLAB function "HelperComputePitchAndMFCC" [18]. After calculating MFCCs and f0 features, we normalized the features to be from -1 to 1. Adding the pitch feature to the MFCCs, the resultant input data was 14-dimensional vectors.

We categorized the 23 participants' data into groups, labeling based on judgements of degree of nativeness obtained from 8 native or near-native EFL professors at the University of Aizu. At first, we made a questionnaire using a Google form, a free tool provided by Google. Professors listened to each person's first two sentences from the Wolf Passage. The order of the files was randomized. After listening to an audio sound file from a given speaker, they rated the speaker's English pronunciation level on a scale from 1 to 7, where 7 meant that it sounds like an English native speaker and 1 meant that it sounds like a very poor non-native English speaker. After collecting all results, we calculated an average level for each speaker and divided the 23 participants (speakers) into 5 levels.

After that, the machine trained on the labeled data and output the test results. Settings for this trial and all the others are shown in Table 2. Optimizer is the algorithm for operating parameters from input layer to output layer. Initial learning rate is the step size in optimization for weight adjusting. The size of MiniBatch is the number for choosing training data randomly. If we set MiniBatch size to be 25, training data is split into 25 sets randomly. Epochs means the number of times that the machine trained on the whole training dataset. The purpose of L2 regularization is to prevent overfitting, which is a failure to fit additional data to the training data or to predict future observations reliably. The activation function is a function that is included in the optimization step.

After training the computer on 80% of the sound files, we used the remaining 20% to test how well the computer could learn to classify the sound files into proficiency levels. The test results for Trial 1 are shown in Figure 2. The row labels in this figure are the actual given labels of the test data, and the column labels are ones calculated by the neural network. So for example, in the top-left cell of the table, 6159 samples of Level 1 (labeled as the lowest proficiency from the professors' judgments) were accurately classified as Level 1 by the computer. In the top-right cell of the table, 848 samples of Level 1 were inaccurately classified as Level 5 (the highest proficiency) by the DNN. In the line above the 25 cells, accuracy can be seen to be 25.246% – only about 5% better than random chance, which would be 20%. In an attempt to obtain a higher accuracy, we decided to use different lengths of audio segments in Trial 2.

3.2 Trial 2: One-second and 0.1-second audio segments

In the previous deep learning trial, audio files were divided into many 2-second samples for deep learning. However, past researchers have used other lengths of samples [12]. Therefore, in Trial 2, we used three different sample lengths for the audio files, to discover what sample length could achieve the best test accuracy for our data.

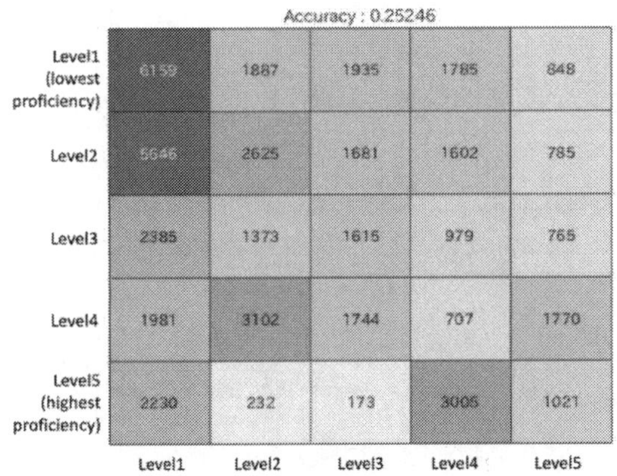

Figure 2: Test results and accuracy in Trial 1. Row labels are the actual given labels of the test data, and column labels are ones calculated by the DNN

The three sample lengths were 100 milliseconds, 1 second, and 2 seconds. Table 3 shows the number of files used in training and testing for each sample length. In Trial 2, the labeling method, the features that were used and the amount of data were the same as in Trial 1. Because of the increase in the number of sound files, we had to decrease the setting for maximum number of epochs, otherwise the training portion would have taken much too long (i.e., many days of processing).

The results showing the highest test accuracy for each of the three sample lengths are shown in Figure 3. As can be seen, the test accuracy of 100-millisecond sample lengths (25.9%) was slightly higher than the other two sample lengths. Therefore, in Trials 3 and 4, we used 100-millisecond sample audio data for deep learning.

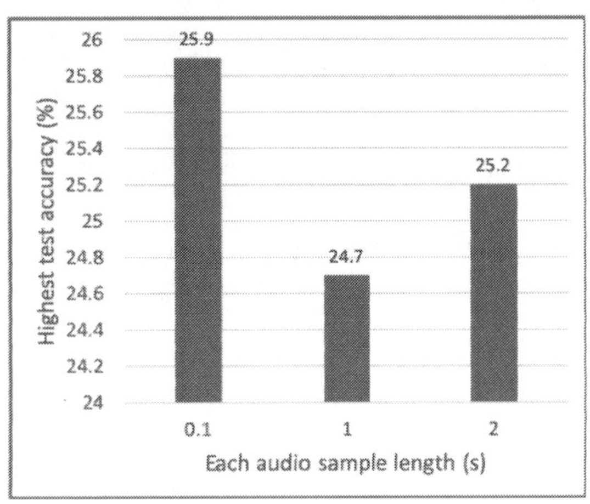

Figure 3: Highest test accuracy obtained for each sample time length in Trial 2

Table 2: Participants, stimuli segments, labeling, and deep learning parameters used in Trials 1–4

Parameter	Trial 1	Trial 2	Trials 3 & 4
# of participants	23	23	28
Audio segment length (s)	2	2, 1, 0.1	0.1
Labeling	Nativeness	Nativeness	Fluency & intelligibility
Optimizer	Momentum (SGD)	Momentum (SGD)	Momentum (SGD)
Initial learning rate	0.01	0.01	0.1
MiniBatch size	25	25	64
Max epochs	70	30	30
L2 regularization	0.00001	0.00001	0.0001
Classification output activation	Softmax	Softmax	Softmax

Table 3: The number of training and testing files for each sample length in Trial 2

Sample length (s)	Total # of training wav files	Total # of testing wav files
0.1	22922	6249
1.0	2279	621
2.0	1139	310

3.3 Trial 3: More participants and a variety of labeling methods

In Trials 1 and 2, two problems existed in our database: (1) not enough high-proficiency speakers meant that our database was unbalanced, and (2) subjective judgments caused excessive noise in the labeling of data. For these reasons, after adding five new higher-proficiency speakers' audio data, in Trial 3 we compared results of different labeling methods (the labeling used for categorizing English pronunciation proficiency level). The labeling methods in Trials 3 and 4 are as follows: (1) number of pauses in the whole speech, (2) total length of pauses in the whole speech, (3) speed of speech as measured by WPM, and (4) labeling of data by intelligibility calculations obtained from a native speaker transcription task in Amazon Mechanical Turk (AMT).

3.3.1 Labeling data by acoustic fluency information (Trials 3 & 4)

Fluency of speech is one factor in judging someone's L2 pronunciation. In this research, we calculated and labeled fluency using three methods: (1) total number of pauses in the whole speech, (2) total length of pauses in the whole speech, and (3) speed of speech in WPM. In the first two methods, a pause was defined as ≥400 ms, following [19].

In this way, we divided the 28 participants into 4 levels. We changed the number of levels from 5 in the first two trials to 4 here because 4 is a divisor of 28, so each of our groups could have an equal number of participants. Unbalanced group numbers in Trials 1 and 2 were unavoidable, but could have negatively affected deep learning results. Table 4 shows proficiency group labeling for total number of pauses, total length of pauses, and speed of speech in WPM. Figure 4 shows the same data as Table 4, but plotted for each individual participant.

3.3.2 Labeling data by intelligibility scores from Amazon Mechanical Turk (Trials 3 & 4)

Another way of objectively labeling the data was using the AMT system to get many listeners' intelligibility scores. AMT is one of the services offered by Amazon Web Services. AMT is a social marketplace for tasks that require talented human intelligence. AMT is useful for L2 speech judgements by crowdsourcing, because we can easily decide the requirements of participants [20]. To evaluate intelligibility, we used a dictation test [21], which is used to determine how many words listeners are able to correctly identify in the speakers' speech. For judging this factor, we used AMT because of the potential for a greater number of available participants. We set a requirement that AMT participants be native English speakers resident in the USA.

We used HTML for making the survey page and based it on past research [22]. Overall, there were 56 randomly-chosen questions for each AMT worker – two sound files from each of the 28 participants – plus one practice question with a native English speaker's audio file. At first, we divided the wolf-passage stimuli into 56 short phrases. Table 5 shows all the phrases. Second, we made mp3 files of all 56 phrases from each participant in the database. After that, we pseudo-randomized the order such that the first half (28 questions) for a given worker were randomly selected from phrases 1 to 28, with each phrase being a different speaker. The second half (28 questions) for a given worker were randomly selected from phrases 29 to 56, again with each phrase being a different speaker. Doing this enabled us to make sure that AMT workers listened to each database participant twice in this survey and each AMT worker heard phrases and participants in a random order. A flowchart of how we sorted pseudo-randomly is shown in Figure 5. Workers could listen to each of the 56 audio files up to two times and had to type exactly what they heard each participant say.

After making the HTML file, we registered our questionnaire in AMT as a requester, and we set it to close in 10 days. As a qualification of our questionnaire, we required that the workers' (listeners') locations be within

Table 4: Proficiency group labeling, for Trials 3 & 4, for all participants by each of three measurements of fluency (total # of pauses, total length of pauses, speed in words/minute) and one measurement of pronunciation (% intelligibility calculated from 54 native listeners' transcriptions)

Proficiency Ranking (high to low)	Proficiency Group label	Partic. #	Total # of pauses	Partic. #	Total length of pauses (s)	Partic. #	Speed (WPM)	Partic. #	Word intelligibility from AMT (%)
1		7	12	1	23.2	10	156.9	8	93.5
2	↑	1	17	15	23.2	1	152.4	7	92.2
3		15	19	12	23.5	7	134.5	4	89.6
4	4	6	19	10	23.8	3	127.8	1	89.4
5		10	19	6	27.0	8	125.4	5	89.0
6	↓	4	20	5	28.5	11	125.3	12	85.7
7		8	20	7	28.5	15	124.3	15	85.5
8		12	21	11	29.5	6	115.2	6	84.3
9	↑	5	21	2	31.1	26	111.3	14	83.1
10		2	21	13	31.1	4	110.9	3	81.3
11	3	11	23	8	31.2	12	109.6	11	78.3
12		9	26	18	31.3	5	108.1	26	76.8
13	↓	13	28	26	33.9	16	107.3	27	76.3
14		26	28	3	35.3	13	105.1	10	72.2
15		3	29	22	35.3	23	103.7	17	72.1
16	↑	16	32	16	37.0	9	103.3	13	72.0
17		18	32	27	37.8	18	102.1	2	70.2
18	2	14	32	17	39.1	22	101.0	9	68.6
19		25	33	4	39.6	21	99.8	18	66.8
20	↓	27	33	25	40.5	17	99.2	24	64.4
21		23	34	9	45.0	27	95.1	16	64.1
22		22	35	24	45.8	2	94.2	22	64.1
23	↑	24	36	23	48.2	24	92.9	21	62.9
24		19	37	19	49.5	25	90.3	19	62.4
25	1	17	39	21	53.1	19	87.8	28	58.4
26		21	41	20	60.3	14	87.8	20	55.7
27	↓	20	46	14	62.5	20	84.9	23	54.5
28		28	79	28	96.9	28	64.0	25	36.4

the USA, because most English learning systems in Japan are based on American English, and the location is easy to set that way in AMT. We also set the qualification that workers must be master-level workers to raise the probability that we got only dedicated workers. Master level is an Amazon-defined level meaning that workers have received a very high percentage of positive feedback from requesters in the past. In 10 days, we could get answers from 55 workers. Looking at the answers, one worker's results were considered unreliable, because that worker completely mis-transcribed the native English speaker's clear pronunciation, which we had added as a practice part in the questionnaire. Therefore, we used the remaining 54 workers' answers to determine the group labeling. After checking answers, we paid 2 dollars to each worker, except for the worker who we judged to be unreliable.

Based on 54 workers' answers, we calculated the score of each participant speaker. We evaluated speakers by comparing the workers' typed results and the correct answer for each word. For measuring intelligibility, whole-word identification rather than phoneme identification is important, so we scored intelligibility based on the number of correct whole words. Then for each speaker, we calculated their AMT accuracy by dividing the number of workers' correct answer words by the total number of words in the phrases. After that, we divided the speakers into 4 equal groups based on the results, labeling them from level 1 (low proficiency) to level 4 (high proficiency). The final proficiency labels according to AMT workers' transcriptions are shown in Table 4, and Figure 4 shows the same data as Table 4, but plotted for each individual participant.

We then compared test accuracies for each labeling method, in order to find the best way to label for classifying English pronunciation levels. The numbers of files per label is shown in Table 6. The deep learning training network layers were: input > LSTM > dropout > fully connected > softmax > classification. The test accuracy results for each labeling method are shown in Figure 6. As can be seen, when data was labeled by elements of speech fluency (total number of pauses, total length of pauses and WPM) it got better test accuracy than when data was labeled by AMT intelligibility.

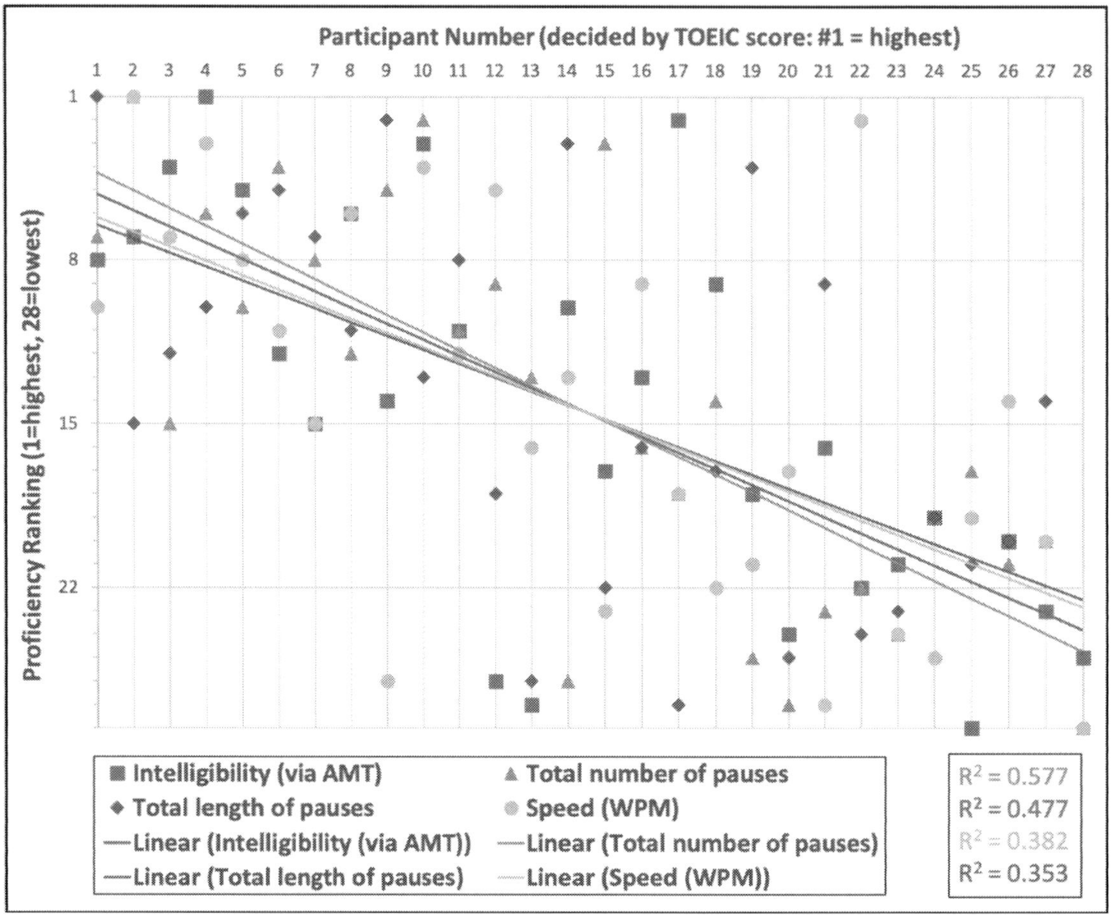

Figure 4: Proficiency ranking of all 28 speakers by each measurement method

3.4 Trial 4: Deep learning with 3-fold cross validation and flexible accuracy definition

In Trial 4, we changed only two things from Trial 3. The first one is 3-fold cross validation. Before this trial, test results were not stable because there was a possibility that features in the training data were unbalanced. To avoid this variability, we adopted the system of 3-fold cross validation in Trial 4. Cross validation is performing multiple rounds of cross-validation using different partitions and then averaging the results over all the rounds.

The second change is changing the definition of test accuracy. In the previous definition, we specified that only test data that were labeled by the computer at exactly the same proficiency level as were labeled by us were accurate. However, in this way, data labeled as even only one level out of position (e.g., proficiency group 3 participants being categorized as group 2 or 4) were considered to be hard errors (i.e., accuracy = 0) and this was not helping the computer to learn the categories as quickly and accurately. Therefore, in a new, more flexible definition of test accuracy, we set data labeled as only 1 level out of position to be soft errors ("almost correct"), and we gave those accuracies a value of 0.5 points instead of 0 points. Through this change, we could get much higher accuracy here than in our previous deep learning trials.

Figure 7 shows the highest test accuracy results for each labeling method in Trial 4. Because of the flexibility in the definition of test accuracy, almost all test accuracies are higher than in Trial 3. Labeling proficiency by total number of pauses led to the highest test accuracy (47.7%) in deep learning Trial 4.

4 Discussion

4.1 Labeling data

Usually when using supervised deep learning, training sets can be unambiguously labelled. For example, if training a computer to recognize animal images, the training data contains images of cats, dogs, elephants, etc. that are clearly labelled as such. These labels are often called the "ground truth". However, in some machine learning cases in the medical field for example, different experts diagnose (i.e., label) the same patient's problem in different ways [23]. Likewise, in our research, it is difficult to

Table 5: The 56 selected phrases from the Wolf Passage used in the AMT intelligibility test in Trials 3 & 4

No.	Phrase	No.	Phrase
1	There was once	29	that a few days later
2	poor shepherd boy	30	he tried exactly
3	who used to watch	31	the same trick again
4	his flocks	32	and once more
5	in the fields	33	he was successful
6	next to a dark forest	34	However, not long after
7	near the foot of a mountain	35	a wolf that had just escaped
8	One hot afternoon	36	from the zoo
9	he thought up a good plan	37	was looking for a change
10	to get some company	38	usual diet of chicken and duck
11	for himself	39	overcoming
12	have a little fun	40	its fear of being shot
13	Raising his fist	41	it actually did come out
14	in the air	42	from the forest
15	he ran down	43	and began to threaten the sheep
16	to the village	44	Racing down to the village
17	shouting Wolf Wolf	45	the boy of course cried out
18	As soon as	46	even louder than before
19	they heard him	47	Unfortunately
20	the villagers	48	as all the villagers
21	rushed from their homes	49	were convinced that
22	full of concern	50	he was trying to fool them
23	for his safety	51	a third time
24	and two of his cousins	52	they told him
25	even stayed with him	53	Go away
26	for a short while	54	don't bother us again
27	This gave the boy	55	And so the wolf
28	so much pleasure	56	had a feast

Table 6: Number of training and testing files for each label in Trial 3

Label	Total # of training wav files	Total # of testing wav files
Total # of pauses	29833	4943
Total length of pauses	30311	4465
WPM	29822	4954
AMT	29611	5165

establish the ground truth about someone's language proficiency, because there are so many ways of measuring it and each way may give different results.

In our research, we decided to have five levels of proficiency in Trials 1 and 2, and four levels of proficiency in Trials 3 and 4. Each level was a different label for deep learning. In Trials 1 and 2, we had expert listeners judge the nativeness of our speakers on a 7-point scale. However, this method has a problem: since the expert listeners were listening to whole sentences, they had suprasegmental information like stress and intonation, which were not available to the AMT workers, who were only judging very short phrases. It is not clear what points the expert listeners were judging nativeness on. Hence, we decided to use an objective measure – fluency indicators found in the acoustic signal.

In Trials 3 and 4, we used four methods of measuring speaking proficiency: total number of pauses, total length of pauses, words per minute, and subjective judgements by AMT participants. As seen in Figure 4, the proficiency ranking of any given participant varies somewhat depending on the labeling method, indicating that a ground truth is difficult to establish. For example, participant #1, who has the highest TOEIC score, is also ranked #1 in total length of pauses, but is ranked #7 in total number of pauses, #8 in intelligibility, and #10 in speed of speech. It may be that a combination of measurements would be a better way of labeling the proficiency of participants for the purpose of training a DNN.

In Figure 4, the straight lines are linear estimates of the rankings for each label. The R^2 values in the key under the plot show the strength of correlation between each proficiency ranking method and the TOEIC ranking of the participants. Note that the total number of pauses in the read speech for each participant correlates most strongly with their TOEIC scores (R^2=0.577). The TOEIC scores are from the Listening and Reading test and did not include Speaking or Writing, so this strong correlation makes sense. It is interesting that this same measure

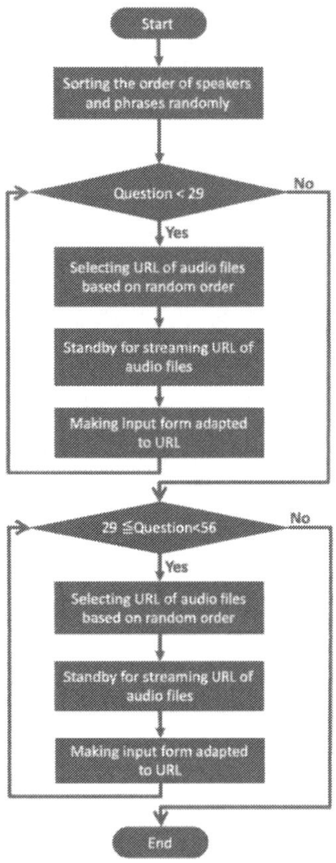

Figure 5: Flowchart of algorithm used in the HTML file for pseudo-randomization of phrases in the AMT intelligibility transcription task. This was used in Trials 3 & 4.

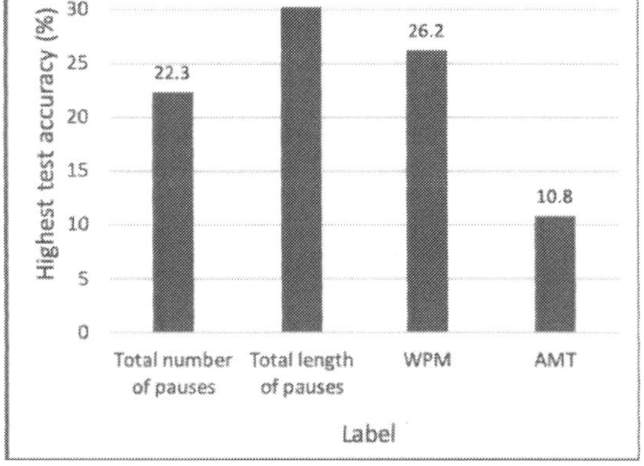

Figure 6: Deep learning highest test accuracies by labeling method in Trial 3

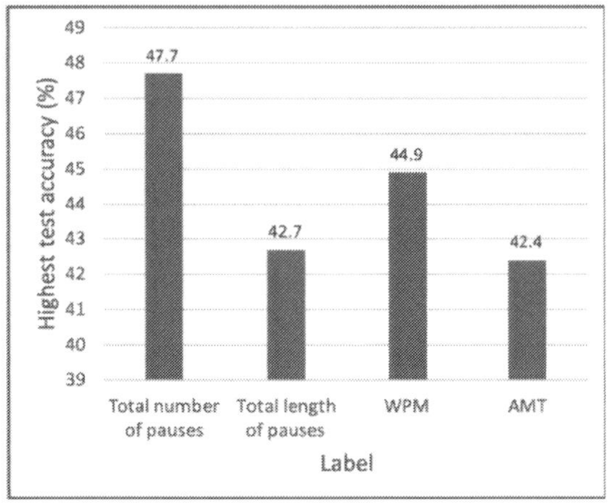

Figure 7: Deep learning highest test accuracies by labeling method in Trial 4 – with flexible definition of test accuracy

(total number of pauses) is the one that gave the highest test accuracy in the final deep learning trial (Trial 4).

As seen in the results of both Trials 3 and 4, when labeling by AMT, deep learning test accuracy was the lowest among the four ways of labeling. From these results, we can say that when a machine classifies English proficiency level from audio data, it appears to be easier for the machine to learn from speech fluency labels than from speech intelligibility measures. One reason for this phenomenon is probably due to label noise. Labeling by speech fluency (number of pauses, total length of pauses, WPM) avoids label noise because labels are calculated using objective scientific measurements. However, when labeling intelligibility, even though the calculations themselves are done objectively, the correct/incorrect transcriptions are entirely based on the subjective listening task of the AMT workers. This may have affected the accuracy of deep learning. Therefore, in the case of our audio database, the neural network can learn features more easily when data is labeled by speech fluency – specifically by the total number of pauses in the read speech of a speaker.

As a whole, the deep learning accuracy tended to be low in this study. We believe that there may be two possible reasons for this problem: overfitting in the training process and an insufficient amount of training data. Overfitting means that the production of an analysis corresponds too closely or exactly to a particular set of data, and may therefore fail to fit additional data or predict future observations reliably. Thus, if we prevent overfitting and also add more audio files, we may get better accuracy and would be able to use this DNN algorithm in a future system.

5 Conclusions and future work

In our research, we tested deep learning classification of speech proficiency while using several ways of labeling degree of proficiency from the data. In the case of the

https://doi.org/10.1051/shsconf/20207702004

labeling method, we could show it is easier for neural networks to learn elements of speech fluency rather than speech intelligibility. However, we trained and tested data by deep learning using only a fairly small database. In future work, we should test our neural network with an unknown database. Based on testing with unknown data, we could make a better system in the future.

Moreover, we labeled our data in several ways: total number of pauses, total length of pauses, WPM, and speech intelligibility from AMT. Although each of these points are important for those who are English native speakers, it does not necessarily mean that any given one of them can determine one's proficiency. If proficiency was simply decided by a single objective measurement, it would be easy for a machine to rank proficiency. However, proficiency is most probably dependent on various objective factors, and not necessarily in an equal way. In future work, it is necessary to combine various types of labeling, with each one weighted in various ways, to determine the best result of deep learning.

References

[1] B. Smith, Polyglossia **23**, 199 (2012)

[2] S. Greenberg, Acoustics Today **14**, 19 (2018)

[3] M.J. Munro, T.M. Derwing, Language and Speech **38**, 289 (1995)

[4] K. Saito, P. Trofimovich, T. Isaacs, Applied Linguistics **38**, 439 (2017)

[5] N.H. De Jong, Language Assessment Quarterly **15**, 237 (2018)

[6] Y. Iguro, Master's thesis, University of Aizu (2018)

[7] Y. Saito, *Zero kara tsukuru Deep Learning [Making deep learning from 0]* (O'Reilly Japan, Inc., Tokyo, 2016)

[8] B. Frénay, M. Verleysen, IEEE Transactions on Neural Networks and Learning Systems **25**, 845 (2014)

[9] J. Li, Y. Wong, Q. Zhao, M.S. Kankanhalli, 2019 IEEE/CVF Conference on Computer Vision and Pattern Recognition (CVPR) (2019)

[10] G. Patrini, A. Rozza, A. Krishna Menon, R. Nock, L. Qu, *Making deep neural networks robust to label noise: A loss correction approach*, in *Proceedings of the IEEE Conference on Computer Vision and Pattern Recognition* (2017), pp. 1944–1952

[11] S. Moriya, Y. Yaguchi, I. Wilson, *Ultrasound tongue image denoising for comparison of first and second language speakers' tongue trajectories* (2016), poster presented at the 5th Joint Meeting of the ASA and ASJ

[12] J. Yu, K. Markov, T. Matsui, IEEE/ACM Transactions on Audio, Speech and Language Processing (TASLP) **27**, 742 (2019)

[13] D. Deterding, Journal of the International Phonetic Association **36**, 187 (2006)

[14] P. Boersma, http://www. praat. org/ (2020)

[15] B.F. Freed, N. Segalowitz, D.P. Dewey, Studies in Second Language Acquisition **26**, 275 (2004)

[16] N. Iwashita, A. Brown, T. McNamara, S. O'Hagan, Applied Linguistics **29**, 24 (2008)

[17] T.M. Derwing, M.J. Munro, Studies in Second Language Acquisition **19**, 1 (1997)

[18] Mathworks, *Speaker identification using pitch and MFCC*, https://jp.mathworks.com/help/audio/examples/speaker-identification-using-pitch-and-mfcc.html

[19] T. Isaacs, P. Trofimovich, Studies in Second Language Acquisition **34**, 475 (2012)

[20] C. Nagle, Journal of Second Language Pronunciation **5**, 294 (2019)

[21] K. Yamato, The Journal of Foreign Language Education and Media (LET) Kansai Branch Methodology Research Group (2011)

[22] Y. Sekiguchi, *The effect of speech speed and word frequency on native listeners' comprehension of L2 speakers* (2016), Undergraduate thesis, University of Aizu

[23] H. Valizadegan, Q. Nguyen, M. Hauskrecht, Journal of Biomedical Informatics **46**, 1125 (2013)

Web application to convert English into helpful characters for pronunciation learners

Keita Nakatsuka[1,*], *Akitsugu* Nogita[1,**], and *Ian* Wilson[1,***]

[1]CLR Phonetics Lab, University of Aizu, Tsuruga, Ikki-machi, Aizuwakamatsu, Fukushima-ken, Japan

Abstract. The International Phonetic Alphabet (IPA) is the most commonly used set of phonetic symbols but it can be difficult to understand and too abstract for non-phoneticians, such as English learners and foreign language educators. One of the factors that makes it difficult for English learners is the number of vowels used in English. In previous research, this problem was solved by proposing a condensed list of 13 English vowels and 24 consonants that are logically organized for North American English, and by assigning a new phonetic symbol font called *Sound Spelling* to these phonemes. However, there are currently no English texts that have *Sound Spelling* to show learners this easy way to pronounce and it is difficult for non-phoneticians to write transcriptions right away, because materials using those symbols are lacking for English learners. In this research, we developed a web application, now publicly available, that converts input English into *Sound Spelling* quickly and accurately to solve this problem.

1 Introduction

Our research is the development of an application that helps to improve the pronunciation of English learners by using a new phonetic symbol system called *Sound Spelling*, which is used instead of the International Phonetic Alphabet (IPA) [1]. In previous research, Ueda and Otsuka [2] showed that there are substantial differences in how different companies (dictionary publishers, etc.) handle pronunciation guidance items, and it is pointed out that the textbook used has a great influence on the learner. Nogita [3] showed that the list of phonetic symbols in IPA notation in English-Japanese dictionaries and pronunciation materials, especially the list of vowel symbols, contains a surplus and also dialect differences, resulting in a number of symbols far more than the actual number of phonemes in one dialect. Since it is difficult for an English language learner to grasp the whole picture of pronunciation, Nogita proposed a condensed list of 13 English vowels and 24 consonants that are logically organized for North American English – especially Canadian English. Also, a phonetic symbol font system called *Sound Spelling*, which is based on English speaking Children's phonics and spelling books, was assigned to these phonemes. This *Sound Spelling* is useful because non-phoneticians only have to learn a 13-character sound set to talk with accurate pronunciation that native speakers can understand when focusing only on vowels. However, there are currently no English texts that have *Sound Spelling* to show learners this easy way to pronounce and to give examples to teachers for creating practice materials. It is difficult for non-phoneticians to write transcriptions right away in a timely manner, because materials using those symbols are lacking for English learners. Our research is to develop a publicly available web application that converts input English into *Sound Spelling* quickly and accurately to solve this problem. Eventually, we aim to incorporate *Sound Spelling* into actual English teaching and learning through the web application.

*e-mail: s1240213@u-aizu.ac.jp
**e-mail: anogita@u-aizu.ac.jp
***e-mail: wilson@u-aizu.ac.jp

2 Some phonetic symbol sets for English

2.1 International Phonetic Alphabet

The International Phonetic Alphabet (IPA) is the most commonly used set of phonetic symbols. However, it can be difficult to understand and too abstract for non-phoneticians, such as English learners and educators. It is especially tough for people who are learning English for the first time. One of the factors that makes it difficult is the number of vowels used in English. For example, the list of phonetic symbols in IPA notation in English-Japanese dictionaries and some pronunciation materials in authorized textbooks, especially the list of vowel symbols, contains a great surplus and is subject to dialect differences, making the total number of symbols far more than the actual number of phonemes in one dialect.

2.2 ARPAbet

ARPAbet [4] is a phonetic symbol set developed by Advanced Research Projects Agency (ARPA) as a part of their Speech Understanding Research project in the 1970s.

It represents phonemes and allophones of General American English with distinct sequences of ASCII characters. ARPAbet has been used in several speech synthesizers, and it is also used in the Carnegie Mellon University (CMU) Pronouncing Dictionary [5].

2.3 Sound Spelling

Sound Spelling is a phonetic symbol set developed by Nogita [3] by organizing pronunciation-based spellings used in English speaking children's phonics and spelling books for the purpose of establishing instruction to grasp the overall picture of the English pronunciation system. It consists of a condensed set of 13 English vowels and 24 consonants that are logically organized for North American (especially Canadian) English. This *Sound Spelling* set is useful because non-phoneticians only have to learn a 13-character vowel set to talk with accurate pronunciation that native listeners can understand when focusing only on vowels.

The correspondence between each of these three phonetic notations (i.e., IPA, ARPAbet, and *Sound Spelling*) can be seen in Table 1 for 13 vowels and 24 consonants.

Table 1. Correspondence between IPA, ARPAbet and *Sound Spelling* for 13 vowels and 24 consonants in various sample words

13 Vowels	IPA	ARPAbet	*Sound Spelling*
hate	eɪ	EY	ā
Pete	i	IY	ē
site	aɪ	AY	ī
note	oʊ	OW	ō
cute	u	UW	o͞o
hat	æ	AE	ă
pet	ɛ|e	EH	ĕ
sit	ɪ	IH	ĭ
not	ɔ|ɑ	AO or AA	ŏ
cut	ʌ|ə	AH or AX	ŭ
coin	ɔɪ	OY	oy
loud	aʊ	AW	ow
book	ʊ	UH	o͝o
24 Consonants	**IPA**	**ARPAbet**	***Sound Spelling***
buy	b	B	b
pie	p	P	p
die	d	D	d
tie	t	T	t
vie	v	V	v
fight	f	F	f
guy	g	G	g
kite	k	K	k
high	h	HH or H	h
joy	dʒ	JH	j
China	tʃ	CH	ch
lie	l	L	l
my	m	M	m
nigh	n	N	n
rye/turn	ɹ/ɹ̩	R	r/ur
zoo	z	Z	z
sigh	s	S	s
wise	w	W	w
yacht	j	Y	y
pleasure	ʒ	ZH	zh
shy	ʃ	SH	sh
they	ð	DH	dh
thigh	θ	TH	th
sing	ŋ	NX or NG	ng

3 Method

To achieve the goals of this research, a database had to be created first. The database has all English words in *Sound Spelling* form. Then a webpage could be created that calls the database when the user inputs English text.

3.1 Database creation

3.1.1 CMU pronouncing dictionary

To create a database, we first needed a dictionary with one-to-one correspondence between English words and pronunciation. In this research, we downloaded the dictionary *cmudict-0.7b.txt*, distributed by Carnegie Mellon University (CMU) under the BSD license, from the CMU webpage [5] and used it as the source of the database. The dictionary has more than 134,000 items of data and covers all common words. *Sound Spelling* is a phonetic symbol set logically organized for North American English, and the CMU dictionary is also made for North American English. The dictionary is well managed and expanded. For these reasons, we considered it appropriate to use this dictionary. A sample of the format of the data from file *cmudict-0.7b.txt* can be seen in Figure 1.

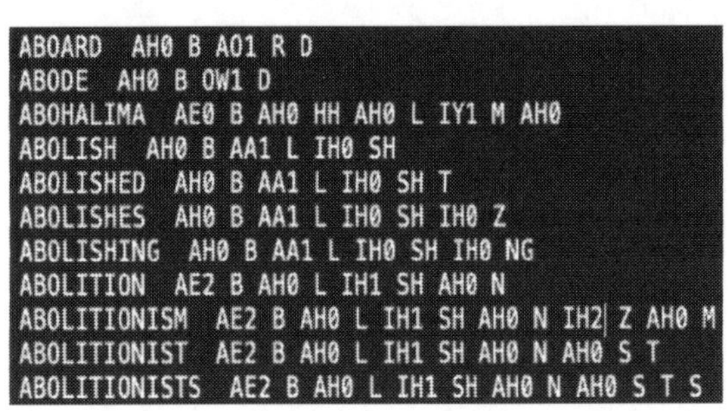
```
ABOARD  AH0 B AO1 R D
ABODE  AH0 B OW1 D
ABOHALIMA  AE0 B AH0 HH AH0 L IY1 M AH0
ABOLISH  AH0 B AA1 L IH0 SH
ABOLISHED  AH0 B AA1 L IH0 SH T
ABOLISHES  AH0 B AA1 L IH0 SH IH0 Z
ABOLISHING  AH0 B AA1 L IH0 SH IH0 NG
ABOLITION  AE2 B AH0 L IH1 SH AH0 N
ABOLITIONISM  AE2 B AH0 L IH1 SH AH0 N IH2 Z AH0 M
ABOLITIONIST  AE2 B AH0 L IH1 SH AH0 N AH0 S T
ABOLITIONISTS  AE2 B AH0 L IH1 SH AH0 N AH0 S T S
```

Figure 1. Sample format of CMU's Pronouncing Dictionary file *cmudict-0.7b.txt*

3.1.2 Conversion from ARPAbet to Sound Spelling

Since *cmudict-0.7b.txt* has phonetic symbols in ARPAbet, *Sound Spelling* is not immediately available. So we must convert the phonetic symbols to be expressed in *Sound Spelling*. However, since *cmudict-0.7b.txt* has more than 134,000 entries, it would be very tedious to change every single word in the database. Instead, we created a PHP program that instantly converts ARPAbet notation into *Sound Spelling* notation.

In creating the PHP program, a helpful program was an MIT-licensed program [6] to convert *cmudict-0.7b.txt* from ARPAbet to IPA. We improved it and created a new program to convert *cmudict-0.7b.txt* from ARPAbet to *Sound Spelling*. A flowchart of the program is shown in Figure 2.

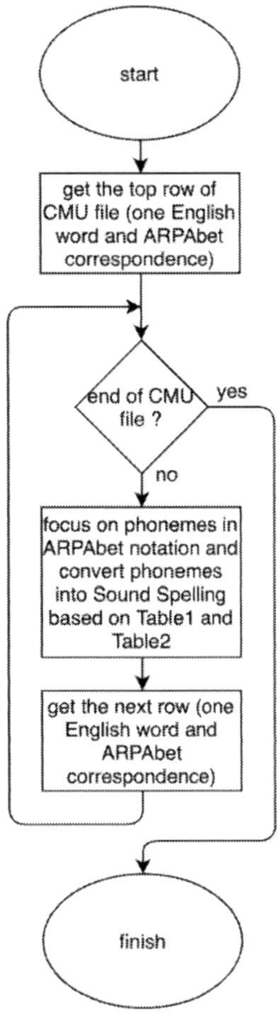

Figure 2. Flowchart of the PHP program that converts ARPAbet to *Sound Spelling*

First, we will examine the *cmudict-0.7b.txt* lines from top to bottom. There is an English word and ARPAbet in one line, and the English word and ARPAbet are separated by two single-byte spaces. Next, we pay attention to ARPAbet and make sure that the ARPAbet is not empty. Then, we split the ARPAbet into phonemes. We look at the phonemes one by one. If phonemes exist, they are converted into *Sound Spelling* according to correspondence Table 1. When all ARPAbet phonemes have been converted into *Sound Spelling*, we write the English words and *Sound Spelling* into a new .txt file. We repeat this sequence until the last line of *cmudict-0.7b.txt*.

3.1.3 Addition of syllabification and syllable stress functions

Being able to convert ARPAbet to *Sound Spelling* is helpful, but it does not show syllable and stress information that are important for pronunciation. Therefore, a program was created to add this information.

The first step in adding syllable and stress information is to add syllable information. This is because, according to phonetics, one syllable is made up of consonant(s) + vowel + consonant(s) (CVC), and the stress varies from syllable to syllable. Any consonants before the CVC vowel are called the *onset*, and any consonants after the vowel are called the *coda* of the syllable. There are various ways to divide English pronunciation into syllables using a program, but this time we divided it into syllables according to the complex branching coda rules shown in one phonetics textbook [7]. They are rules stating that there are about 60 different onsets and they consist of at most three consonants. A flowchart for that is shown in Figure 3.

First, the English word in the *Sound Spelling* notation is divided on the right side of each vowel, and each segment is stored in an array. Next, we check whether the last segment contains a vowel. If the last segment does not contain a vowel, then that segment is regarded as the last syllable coda and it does not continue to the loop. Then, from the second segment from the beginning of the array, we determine if each segment has one onset out of about 60. If so, we add a hyphen to the left of each onset to separate them into syllables using a loop. Adding stress information involves simply adding into each of the syllables a primary stress symbol with upper case letters and optional secondary stress information using only upper case letters (with no symbol).

For example, the English word *captain* is *KAE1PTAX0N* in ARPAbet notation in the CMU Pronouncing Dictionary. The letters in that ARPAbet notation are converted to kă1ptŭn in the *Sound Spelling* notation (with the number 0 removed). Then, that word is divided on the right side of each vowel to create k*ă1 pt*ŭ *n*, and each segment is stored in an array. Next, we check whether the last segment contains a vowel. The last segment *n* does not contain a vowel, so that segment is regarded as the last syllable's coda and is attached to the second last segment, giving k*ă1 ptŭn*. Then, from the second segment from the beginning of the array *ptŭn*, we determine if each segment has one onset out of about 60 allowable ones. The array *ptŭn* has one onset *t* out of the 60, so we add a hyphen to the left of onset *t* to separate it into syllables k*ă1p-tŭn*. Finally, the primary stress level indicated in ARPAbet (by the number *1*) is shown by converting that syllable to upper case letters with a stress symbol, giving the final '*KĂP-tŭn*. For words with a secondary stress level indicated by the number 2 in ARPAbet, upper case letters are used with no stress symbol.

https://doi.org/10.1051/shsconf/20207702005

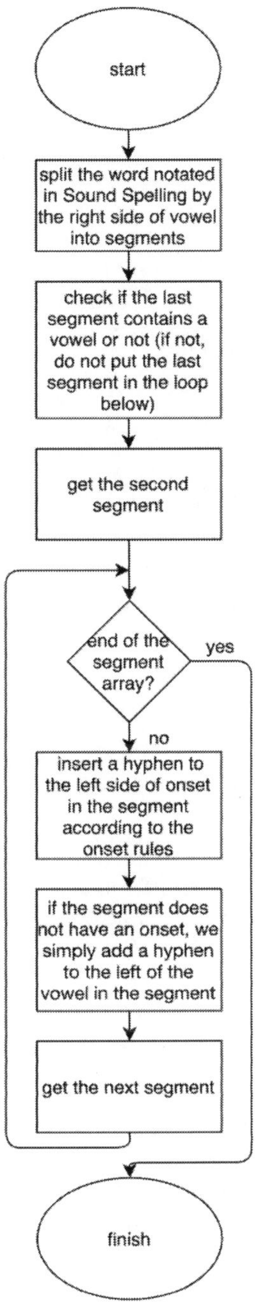

Figure 3. Flowchart of the syllabification program

3.1.4 Registration of .txt file into MySQL database

The next step in the database creation was to register the text file into a MySQL database. To do that, various preparations were made first. We started MySQL and executed the following with MySQL statements: First, we created one database and one table. Next, we created four fields in the table. The *id* field stores the primary key. The *english* field stores English words. The *ss* field stores *Sound Spelling* corresponding to English words. The *modified* field stores the date and time when the data was registered.

After those preparations, we imported the created .txt file into the table using the following MySQL statement:

LOAD DATA INFILE '~ /filename.txt' INTO TABLE 'table name' fields terminated by '\t' (english,ss);

3.2 Webpage creation

The webpage that was created in this research is made up of multiple files: HTML, PHP (ver. 7.3.7), CSS (ver. 3), and Javascript. First, the HTML file is used to explain the purpose of the research and about *Sound Spelling*. We prepared HTML files written in English and Japanese to support users accessing the website in either language. Next, the PHP file is used to add the ability to convert English to *Sound Spelling* on the webpage. We also prepared PHP files written in English and Japanese. With these PHP files, the webpage can access the database, which contains about 134,000 pairs of English words and *Sound Spelling*. In a PHP file, one can additionally write by HTML. So, when creating the page that converts English to *Sound Spelling*, we use one PHP file to access the database with the description of PHP and obtain the necessary data, and display on the screen with the description of additional HTML. Then, CSS files and Javascript files are used to determine the design of the webpage. Bootstrap 3 is also used. To maintain consistency, the webpage design was made in the same style as that of the Center for Language Research Phonetics Laboratory at the University of Aizu [8].

4 Resultant webpage

The resultant webpage is shown in Figure 4 and it is publicly available at http://clrlab1.u-aizu.ac.jp/convert_e.php. It shows results that were converted to *Sound Spelling* for all vowels and consonants of General American English using typical words (e.g., off, father, bee, ... yes, way) User-inserted English text is moved to the bottom of the screen and *Sound Spelling* corresponding to that is then displayed in the center [9].

5 Challenges and future work

A functioning website to convert English into *Sound Spelling* was created. However, various challenges were encountered. When syllable stress was to be expressed, the primary stress was planned to be in bold and upper case letters, and the secondary stress was to be simply in upper case letters, but it was difficult to express bold characters from PHP. As before, the primary stress symbol (') is tentatively attached. A second challenge is that there are words with different pronunciations and meanings, such as "read" and "increase", even with the same spelling. In future work on this webpage, it would be helpful to solve these problems.

Figure 4. Screenshot of the actual working webpage [9]

References

[1] G.K. Pullum, W.A. Ladusaw, *Phonetic Symbol Guide* (The University of Chicago Press, 1996)
[2] H. Ueda, T. Otsuka, Bulletin of Osaka Jogakuin University **7**, 15 (2011)
[3] A. Nogita, Studies on Foreign Languages and Cultures XXVIII (Kokushikan University) **28**, 30 (2018)
[4] J.E. Shoup, *"Phonological Aspects of Speech Recognition" in Trends in Speech Recognition* (Englewood Cliffs: Prentice Hall, 1980), pp. 125–138
[5] Carnegie Mellon University, *The CMU Pronouncing Dictionary*, http://www.speech.cs.cmu.edu/cgi-bin/cmudict
[6] W.E. dos Santos, *Arpabet-to-IPA*, https://github.com/wwesantos/arpabet-to-ipa
[7] Y. Hattori, *Phonetics* (Asakura Publisher, 2012)
[8] *The CLR Phonetics Lab*, http://clrlab1.u-aizu.ac.jp
[9] *Website to convert English into Sound Spelling*, http://clrlab1.u-aizu.ac.jp/soundspelling_e.html

Ontologies and use case based planning of content delivery

Daniela Burkhardt[1*] and *Stefanie* Clesle[1**]

[1]Karlsruhe University of Applied Sciences, Faculty of Information Management and Media, 76133 Karlsruhe, Germany

Abstract. This papers objective was the development of an ontology-based Content Delivery Portal (CDP) in combination with use cases. The aim was to find out how to enrich content in general through an ontology and to investigate the added value of ontologies. In particular, it has been researched how content can be delivered in CDP via an ontological context. The focus of the research team was on the knowledge builder of the ontology system manufacturer *i-views* for modelling the ontology and embedding content. Furthermore, the research team planned a CDP and implemented the model in the CDP *i-views content*. To accomplish this, use cases for users in the context of smart homes were developed to derive which information users want and when and how to grant access to the desired content. The implementation in the CDP was fully based on the ontology which was developed over the course of the project. Although the research team presumes that part of the implementation could have been realised with metadata from a CMS, the ontology can be used to provide context information that goes beyond the metadata that is traditionally assigned to individual topics in a CMS.

1 Introduction

The volume and complexity of products has risen sharply in recent years – also as a result of industrial digitalization and globalization. Traditional print manuals are often no longer sufficient to reflect the complexity of products and product variants. Users also consume products now differently than before and have increased expectations of companies in terms of information procurement [1].

In order to create and manage this increasingly large amount of information, there are different ways of content management and delivery to support both users and companies with this process.

The aim of the hereby presented paper was to research intelligent information in the context of smart homes with a focus on exploring the value that ontologies could add in connection with content delivery.

In the following report, the research team gives an overview of the main results and aspects of ontologies and use cased based planning of content delivery.

The authors of this paper worked with the content management system Smart Media Creator, provided by Expert Communication Systems GmbH, with the ontology software i-views knowledge builder and with the content delivery portal i-views content, provided by intelligent views GmbH.

2 How to plan a CDP based on ontology

2.1 Definitions

First, important terms from the field of intelligent information are explained for better comprehensibility.

2.1.1 Content management systems

A content management system (CMS) is a tool for technical editors to create, manage and publish content. When writing technical documents, technical editors are constantly faced with the challenges of handling multiple content variants, writing in multiple languages and publishing to multiple media. To tackle these challenges, topic-oriented documentation, standardization, single sourcing and the use of metadata are employed as basic principles.

Content is divided into topics (also called "modules"). A topic is a self-contained information unit that can be reused in multiple contexts. Modules are created as XML files according to a defined information model, typically in the form of a DTD (document type definition) or XSD (XML schema definition). Further methods can be applied to achieve standardized content. [2, p. 379ff]. It is crucial to prevent a copy-paste workflow, but rather to reuse individual modules. This allows to trace them back to their single source, thus eliminating duplicates. [2, p. 293].

In a CMS, modules are annotated with metadata. This includes metadata that comes from content lifecycle,

* Daniela Burkhardt: buda1031@hs-karlsruhe.de; daniela.burkhardt1991@gmail.com
** Stefanie Clesle: clst1012@hs-karlsruhe.de; stefanie.clesle@gmail.com

which is often generated automatically by the software, and descriptive metadata that comes from the organization's individual metadata concept. An often used concept for metadata is the PI-Classification, where classification considers intrinsic and extrinsic metadata, both product-related and information-related. Further metadata can be used to enable efficient variant management and automation processes. [2, p. 362ff]

2.1.2 Content delivery portals

In recent years, content delivery portals (CDP) have gained popularity in technical communication. Before CDP, technical information was aggregated and published from CMS and delivered as a static document to users.

In contrast to this procedure, CDP give users access to modular content that can be retrieved and detached from the document structure it might be embedded into. Other information types, like the metadata, can be provided as well. Users can retrieve content via structured search using facets and filters, classic document structures, text search, automated retrieval mechanisms, or by means of a mixture of the above. CDPs are usually web-based and offer access by various end devices. [3, p. 49]

2.1.3 Ontologies

An ontology describes and represents a field of knowledge by defining concepts and the relationships among them. In order to make the knowledge that is represented by the ontology machine-readable, ontology languages are used, such as RDF or OWL. [4]

Software manufacturers that offer tools for modelling an ontology don't always use consistent terminology, hence in the following report, definitions for the terminology used by i-views are given which will be applied throughout this paper [5, 6]:

- **Semantic network** (also called "domain"): The semantic network contains knowledge of a part of the world. Objects within the semantic network are modelled within the context of the corresponding area of knowledge.
- **Instance** (also called "object", "individual") and **type** (also called "class", "concept"): Instances are classified into types; types can therefore be more abstract. An instance inherits properties of its corresponding type. In i-views, types can contain subtypes, building a hierarchy based on *is a subtype of* relations.
- **Relation** and **relation type** (also called "relationship"): Relations are classified into relation types. The relation types defines how a relation can be used, the relation itself is the manifestation of a relation type that expresses the relation between instances or types.
- **Attribute** and **attribute type**: Attributes are classified into attribute types. Attributes express properties of other objects in the ontology.

2.2 Key steps

The research team identified the key steps shown in Fig. 1 to plan a CDP based on an ontology in combination with use cases. These steps do not need to be executed in a chronological order but can instead overlap and influence each other.

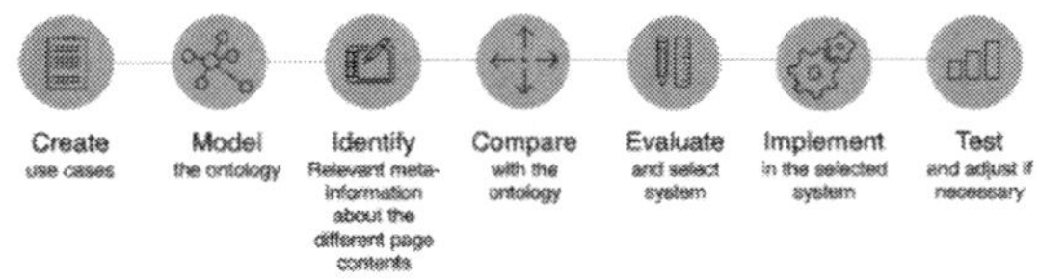

Fig. 1. Overview over the key steps of CDP planning.

2.2.1 Create use cases

The possibilities for building an ontology and a CDP are virtually unlimited. In order to identify what is relevant for users, use cases should be defined at the beginning of a project. [1]

A use case is a tool to describe how users will perform within the functionality of a system that already exists or that is being planned. Therefore the interaction between the actor and the system has to be documented for each use case as a sequence of different steps. The added value consists in reducing the costs and complexity of planning and maintaining the system. Furthermore use cases are also a source for identifying requirements and typical scenarios. [7]

Initially it was determined that the research team would not approach the project component-oriented. Instead, the research team wanted to provide information that enable users to explore the topic of smart homes in general and to link together knowledge.

The modelled use cases had to be constantly adapted and checked throughout the entire project. A tabular form for the best possible development of use cases is recommended. See the following Table 1 for an elaborated example of a use case:

Table 1. Example of use case planning.

Use case	**How can I save energy in the kitchen?** **Anne cooks every day. She needs a lot of energy. She wants to know if there are some smart home devices, which could help her to save energy and costs in the kitchen.**
Situation (actor, knowledge level, implementation scale)	· private person · knowledge level (in terms of smart home technologies): beginner
Intent	· uses a lot of energy in the kitchen; accordingly, wants so save energy
Output	· devices that fulfil the purpose energy efficiency and/or cost efficiency · general description of the corresponding devices
Input	· purpose: energy efficiency; cost efficiency

	· room: kitchen
Scenario	1. User opens CDP. 2. CDP shows facets. 3. User choses facet "kitchen". 4. CDP filters content. 5. User choses facet "energy efficiency" and "cost efficiency". 6. CDP filters content. 7. User choses facet "general description".

2.2.2 *Model the ontology*

In this step, the necessary information is modelled in the ontology. System designers can now create suited types for the instances and model the instances accordingly. Instances can inherit information from the according type and if the system allows it, types can be structured in supertypes and subtypes. Attributes can be an option to record information for types or instances. To create an information network, relations are created that connect either a type to a type or an instance to an instance. Mixtures should be avoided. Depending on the software, developers can define which types a relation can connect and restrict the model, e. g. the number of a certain relation for a certain type. [5]

The content that will be provided to users is embedded into the ontology. This could be realised via an automated import or via manual processes. For more information on this, refer to the article "Approaches for deployment and access of content in delivery portals" (Rauffman and Wolf) in this volume. Relations are used to connect the modules' respective information units to the types and instances of the ontology. For more information on ontology modelling, refer to the article "Ontology based modelling for content delivery systems" (Bürkel and Padeken) in this volume.

It should be pointed out that the ontology must not cover all possible aspects of a domain. In this project, the research teams experienced that it is, in fact, likely to represent "too much" information in the model, including aspects that are not necessary later on. Over the course of the project, the research team reduced and summarized the ontology multiple times, discarding elements that were not required in the use cases. It is highly recommended to refer to the use cases repeatedly during this step.

The following statement applies as a guidance principle: the model must enable the recipient (or a computer) to "read" the ontology, so that the recipient (or a computer) can deduce the information that is required in the use case.

In this project for example, for the use case *How can I save energy in the kitchen*, the model must represent the statement: "A smart refrigerator serves the purpose energy efficiency". To model this information in an ontology, the type *purpose* with its instance *energy efficiency* is required, along with the type *smart home device* with its instance *refrigerator*. The two instances are connected by a relation that can be evaluated in both directions *serves* resp. *is fulfilled by*.

2.2.3 *Identify relevant meta-information*

In the next step, system designers identify the meta-information that should be provided in the CDP in different pages and decide how it will be presented.
Helpful key questions during this step are:

- What information can help users access the information they need?
- What context information do users need?

Metadata to help users accessing the required information can be suited to implement as facets or quick access options. Typically, this is information that users know and can therefore enter or select whilst using the CDP.

Metadata that provides context can be suited to implement as visible meta-information for a topic, document or information object. Since the goal of this project was to enable users to explore the topic of smart homes in general and to link together knowledge, the meta-information displayed for a specific topic enables users to put the topic into context and also serve as a starting point to access more related content. Depending on the system, a section of the ontology can be displayed to users either as text or interactive graph display.

In this project, the research team decided to present quick access links for expected input, such as the purpose or the specific smart home device. To allow users to narrow down the hit list, metadata should be presented as facets. When reading a specific topic, the document structure of the source document should be provided, along with descriptive metadata such as the smart home device or the location of the device.

It was also decided to explore more applications of the ontology and enhance the user experience. For this, synonyms are maintained as attributes in the ontology and are considered in search mechanisms. Furthermore, the metadata presented with the content of a specific topic is linked to a visualization of a section of the ontology. Users can start browsing the ontology, getting an insight of the knowledge network and accessing related topics. The research team also planned an interactive search with drop-down-lists to cover typical user intents that should be presented on the start page of the CDP.

2.2.4 *Compare with the ontology*

After having a clear idea on what will be presented in the CDP, the requirements are compared with the ontology. The purpose of this step is to ensure that the ontology as data basis is complete and efficient for the application in the CDP. System designers check whether the requested information can be derived from the model or if the model needs to be adjusted, e. g. specified to get more precise results. They should also consider if the ontology allows an efficient retrieval of the information or if it can be simplified for easier implementation.

Over the course of the project, the research team introduced a relation as supertype of the three relations *is located at area*, *is located at item* and *is located at environment*. The subtypes were required to indicate the exact location of the device, but it made queries more complex when all subtypes were meant to be included in the query results. By using the superordinate relation in the hierarchy, the research team was able to define queries more easily and efficiently.

2.2.5 Evaluate and select system

Content delivery systems are extremely costly and vary greatly in their function. In order to select the system most suitable for the individual needs of the respective company, an evaluation should be carried out, which requires a software requirements specification software requirements specification. The decisions made in previous steps result in requirements that need to be met by the system. [8]

The research group used the ontology system i-views knowledge builder and the CDP i-views content. Since the systems had already been selected at the beginning of this project, this step has not been executed.

2.2.6 Implement

After the software has been selected and set up, the implementation can begin. In this step, content and ontology are implemented in the CDP as planned in previous steps.

Depending on the software being used, this can require data transformations via XML and XSLT [9, p.26ff]. The ontology system and the CDP that were used by the research group have the advantage that both systems are interrelated and thus do not require special data transformations. However, a thorough understanding of the functionality as well as the modelled ontology are required.

In both cases, system designers might want to get support from developers during this step. Detailed information on the implementation in this project is given in Chapter 3.

2.2.7 Test

The implementation should be tested before it is released, preferably by a person that is part of the target group. All functionalities should be tested as well as the user experience. Special focus is given to the question of whether the use cases can be fulfilled. Test results should be documented and evaluated to decide whether adjustments are necessary.

Due to the limited time and resources in this project, this step has not been executed.

3 Implementation using software

3.1 Introduction i-views

i-views (intelligent views GmbH) is a company based in Darmstadt, Germany, that manufactures software. Their software solutions enable customers to use semantic technologies to manage data and link it, building knowledge networks. [10]

3.2 Software architecture

As a tool to develop ontologies, i-views offers the i-views knowledge builder. Developers can work with tree structures as well as a graph editor.

The content delivery portal is called i-views content that is based on the data modelled in i-views knowledge builder. Hence, it is not only a CDP that is able to integrate ontologies, but is fully based on ontologies.

As an interface between the two, i-views offers the built-in tool ViewConfig-Mapper (VCM). All panels that are visible in the CDP represent an object in the VCM and can be edited in terms of graphic display, content and functionality. It is not necessary to write code to do so, since the VCM offers a GUI for the developer. The possibility to create queries with an in-built editor should be emphasized here. These queries allow developers to search the knowledge network and evaluate it according to individual requirements. For more advanced actions, extensions with JavaScript can be used. [5, 6]

3.3 Implementation of i-views content

The start page of the CDP offers a search bar within which users can search for keywords. Per default, it is a full-text search mechanism. The research team enriched the full-text search mechanism by the use of synonyms that are maintained in the ontology. In addition, there are also pre-searched questions below to assist users even more effectively with specific use-case-based questions. As described in chapter 2.2.3, these were planned to be implemented as interactive search phrases with drop-down-options, but due to the current state of the technology, this would have required some development effort that could not be realized within the given time frame. Instead, a more simple variation has been implemented.

Via clicking a button on the start page, users get to the overview page of the CDP. Here, one has various quick access options. Based on the use cases, the research team implemented quick access tiles for expected input, such as a specific smart home device and a specific purpose. Also, basic introductions are provided, along with user-defined bookmarks.

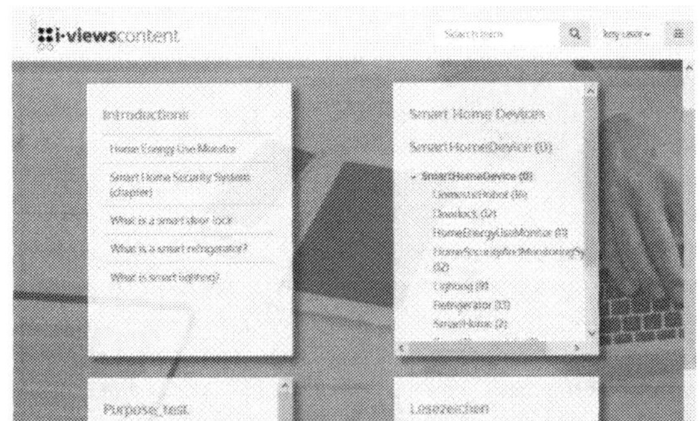

Fig. 2. Overview page of i-views content

The respective search can be narrowed down further by using the provided facets. Topics that match the search parameters are listed with the title, a text excerpt, the document and chapter they are contained in, the topic version and language. In this project, only one language and no different versions were maintained, but the research team considers this metadata helpful in a real scenario. When viewing a topic, the document structure is provided, from which users can click through all topics available in the respective document. The content of the selected topic is shown together with meta-information, providing context (see Fig. 6).

If users then select one of the facets, they can browse through the ontology. Users can display the connected knowledge network in a graph view or as a list and by selecting different relations, they can identify connections and thus get contextual information.

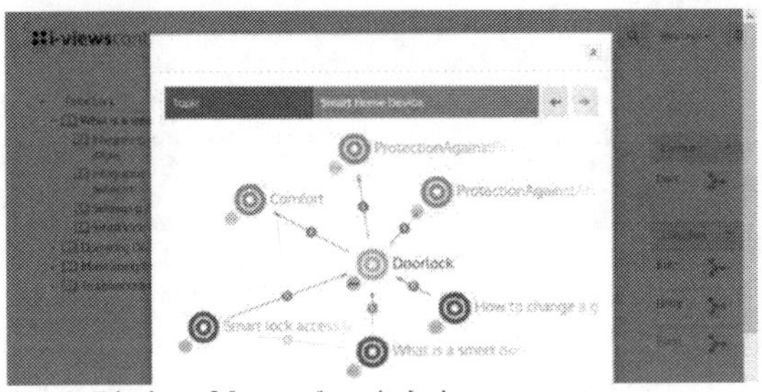

Fig. 3. Display of the ontology in i-views content

3.4 Show case applying VCM

As described in chapter 3.2, the VCM is used to transform the ontology of the knowledge builder into i-views content. In the following report, a concrete example is presented to illustrate how this works.

According to the use cases in this project, users might be interested in the location of a smart home device. In the knowledge network, the instances of the type smart home device have a relation to instances of the type location resp. its subtypes. The information that needs to be modelled includes, for example, the statements "The smart device smoke detector is located in the bedroom / entry / hall" and "The smart device doorlock is located at a door, which is located at the entry / balcony / parking lot". Their representation is shown in Fig. 4.

Within the CDP, the location of a device will be presented as context information when the user is currently viewing a topic about said device. To implement this into the CDP, the corresponding object in the VCM needs to be edited, as displayed in Fig. 5. i-views content offers a plug-in to easily identify the object. [5]

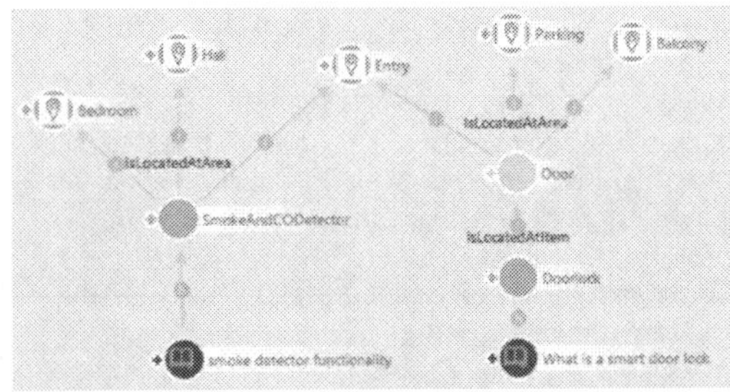

Fig. 4. Relevant section of the ontology

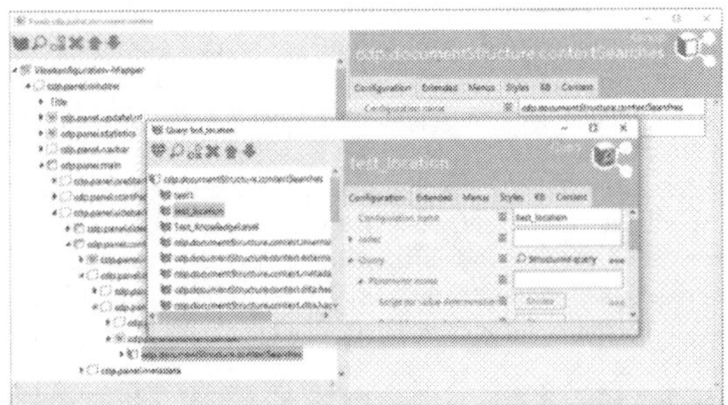

Fig. 5. Relevant object in VCM

A structured query can be defined within the VCM that evaluates the ontology. In this case, the query must cover two different logics. A: A device is located in an area; query will return the area. B: A device is located at an item, the item is located in an area; query will return the area. The query shown in Fig. 7 meets these demands.

The result in the CDP is shown in Fig. 6. All context panels, facets, quick access panels etc. are defined in this manner. In principle, the software i-views can be used to create queries of any complexity that evaluate the ontology.

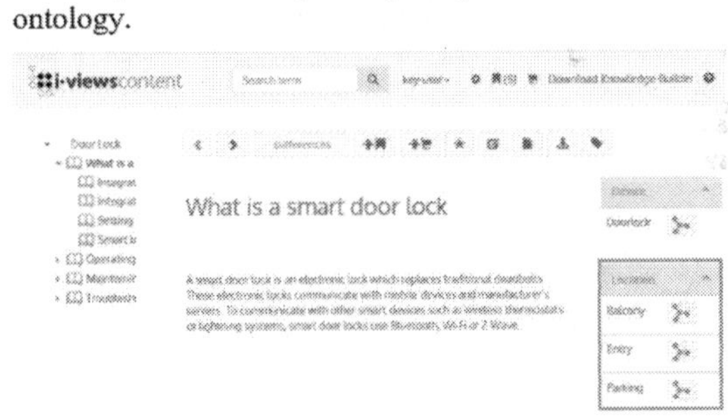

Fig. 6. Topic with context information location

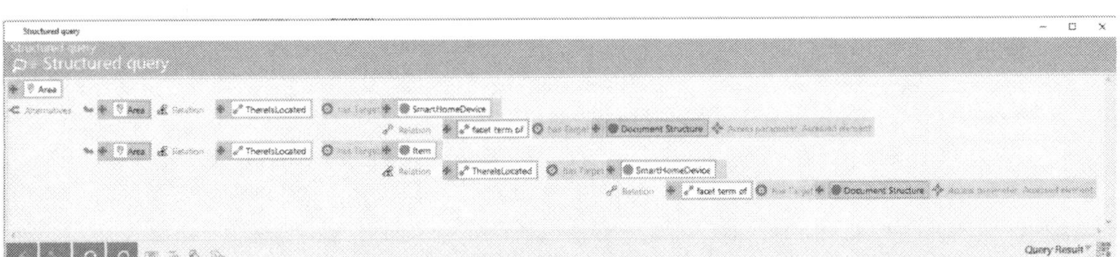

Fig. 7. Structured query in VCM

4 Discussion and conclusion

We have shown the key steps for planning a CDP based on an ontology and use cases. The process of this must be seen as iterative and we want to encourage system designers to check and adapt their decisions throughout the project.

Using ontologies for planning and implementing a CDP offers many possibilities.

It enables system designers to provide different retrieval mechanisms that are far more individual and specific than static documents. Users benefit from modular content and annotated metadata that is presented within the CDP. In this project, the metadata from the CMS could not be imported in the used software due to technical reasons, so the CDP was fully based on the developed ontology. Although we presume that part of the implementation could have been realised with metadata from a CMS, the possibilities of using an ontology go beyond the metadata that is traditionally assigned to individual modules in a CMS. In the ontology itself, developers are not restricted to hierarchical metadata, which is usually the case in a CMS. Relations specifically created for the requested use cases allow to represent connections that are far more complex. While tracing the ontology e. g. by using queries, system designers can benefit from evaluating indirect relations, so implicit knowledge can be gleaned.

Furthermore, the knowledge network itself can be presented to users and, depending on the system being used, allow them to navigate through the ontology, thus recognizing the correlations and connections and easily accessing related information. The CDP obtains an explorative character and supports users to familiarise themselves with a subject autonomously.

Due to the current status of the technology, data cannot be exchanged smoothly between different systems. The lack of cross-tool-standardization led to additional manual effort, which would presumably be eliminated in future versions. The research team estimates that software manufacturers will implement standards such as iiRDS (intelligent information Request and Delivery Standard) developed by the *tekom working group information 4.0* to address this challenge [11].

We would like to express our gratitude to the International Office at Karlsruhe University of Applied Sciences, the University of Aizu, the Faculty of Information Management and Media, and the Master's program of Communication and Media Management at Karlsruhe University of Applied Sciences for the generous financial support that made this project and exchange possible. Furthermore, we would like to thank Prof. Dr. Roy for organizing and coordinating the ACM Chapter Conference. We would also like to thank the Intelligent Views GmbH for providing their software for us to work with, and especially Dr. Steinacker for helping them to tackle technical questions about the knowledge builder and CDP. Last but not least, we would like to thank Mrs. Newcomb Wölfle for her constructive criticism and for proofreading this paper.

[1] W. Ziegler, H. Beier: *Content delivery portals: The future of modular content.* In: tcworld e-magazine 02/2015 (2015) Retrieved January 19, 2020 from http://www.tcworld.info/e-magazine/content-strategies/article/content-delivery-portals-the-future-of-modular-content/

[2] P. Drewer, W. Ziegler: *Technische Dokumentation: Übersetzungsgerechte Texterstellung* und *Content-Management.* 2nd Edition. Vogel, Würzburg, Germany. (2014)

[3] W. Ziegler: *Drivers of Digital Information Services: Intelligent Information Architectures in Technical Communication*. In: ACM Chapter Proceedings on Educational Technology, Language & Technical Communication, Volume 1 (2019)

[4] W3C: *W3C* Semantic *Web Frequently Asked Questions.* (2009) Retrieved February 13, 2020 from https://www.w3.org/2001/sw/SW-FAQ

[5] intelligent views gmbh: *i-views 5.2.* (n.d) Retrieved January 10, 2020 from http://documentation.i-views.com/manual/5.2/a97dbe1b-5931-499d-8dde-034a6a6fe106

[6] intelligent views gmbh: *Einführung in die Modellierung.* (n.d.) Training document

[7] Usability.gov: *Use Cases* (n.d.) Retrieved March 5, 2020 from https://www.usability.gov/how-to-and-tools/methods/use-cases.html

[8] IEEE: *830-1984 – IEEE Guide for Software Requirements Specifications* (02/10, 1984) Retrieved March 4, 2020 from https://ieeexplore.ieee.org/document/278253

[9] K. Hanczaryk: *XML Content Transformation and Import Interfaces for Content Delivery Portals*. In: ACM Chapter Proceedings on Educational Technology, Language & Technical Communication, Volume 1 (2019)

[10] intelligent views gmbh: *About us.* (n.d.) Retrieved March 2,2020 from https://i-views.com/en/about-us/

[11] tekom e.V.: What Is iiRDS, Exactly? A Short Introduction (n.d.) Retrieved March 10, 2020 from https://iirds.org/iirds-a-short-introduction/

Enhanced model-based engineering for centrally managed configuration management in product lifecycle management

Christian Deschner[1*]

[1] Siemens Healthcare GmbH, 91058 Erlangen, Germany

Abstract. In times products gain in complexity and variety whereby release and development cycles become even shorter, consistent and systematic variant management is essential not only for technical communication but also for the very most processes in PLM. Therefore, system engineering and system configuration themselves must be leading for a centrally managed, reliable variant management for all PLM processes. We depict how enhanced model-based system engineering approach based on product and product component models can be the enabler for variant management in all PLM processes by specific, explicitly deduced views in different stages of the entire Product Lifecycle.

1 Introduction

In the very beginning of industrial car manufacturing, Henry Ford allegedly said, customers can buy the famous T-model in "any color so long as it is black". This statement clearly depicts how variant management was handled in former times, where cars have been pure pieces of hardware, assembled within factory as a monolithic good.

Since then, modern products have become more and more complex and diverse. Vertical range of manufacturing has decreased, and software has become even more important.

This – still ongoing – process makes modern products more and more complex and built-up from numerous single sub-components manufactured, engineered and integrated asynchronously widespread all over the world.

Therefore, integrating all sub-components and its information to real, sellable products is one of the most challenging aspects in modern product lifecycle management processes. In order to manage this challenge systematically, all relevant product engineering and configuration information is systematically accessible at each stage just in time.

2 Multilevel component-based system engineering

In times of IoT, increasing individualization, and even shorter development cycles, products and product lifecycle management (PLM) processes and correspondingly all product integration and product information integration processes are changing.

Smart and high-tech products nowadays consist of hardware and software. Modern medical devices like CT scanners, smart home solutions and modern cars are a symbiosis of hardware and software.

Both, hardware and software very often are also no monolithic components, but are assemblies consisting of different subcomponents with independent lifecycles.

Building up products means, that different assemblies, assembly groups, accessories, software libraries and applications are integrated, combined and configured bottom up in multiple stages as multilevel assemblies.

In terms of software, a commercial or open source operating system is used and maybe configured for individual purposes. Different third-party software and/or self-developed applications are to be run on the operating system, integrated and configured specifically. The same holds true for hardware, where different assemblies and parts are to be combined. Gearboxes, motors and chassis of cars as well as gantries, housings, power supplies and patient tables of Computed Tomography (CT) scanners.

At the latest when hardware and software components are integrated, there will be a clash of domain cultures. More traditional hardware development setups meet agile software development approaches with different tools and processes. Nevertheless, both worlds can't be treated as isolated domains, since there are functional dependencies between different subcomponents and groups. A patient table of CT scanner can be controlled by software from the workstation or a tablet, as well as by hardware like joysticks or buttons.

Depending on product types, portfolio definitions and strategies, these multilevel assemblies might not be sellable products, but platforms for product families or mass customization and define large numbers of valid product configurations. In mathematical terms, the assemblies can be conceived as complex formulas with given value sets defining logical solution sets. That

* Email: christian.deschner@siemens-healthineers.com

means, a specific product can be derived from the overarching product platform or family by defining specific configuration settings and selections for all relevant parameter and options. Since any configuration setting and selection may affect different subcomponents (assembly groups, software features etc.) within the entire assembly, all relevant dependencies, parameters, options and constraints within and/or between subcomponents must be well defined and systematically evaluable.

2.1 Model based system engineering and model driven software development

A well-established methodology in hardware engineering is the "Model Based System Engineering" (MBSE) approach which is defined as follows:

> *Model Based System Engineering (MBSE) is "the formalized application of modeling to support system requirements, design, analysis, verification and validation activities beginning in the conceptual design phase and continuing throughout development and later life cycle phases" [1].*

Typically, with this approach, all technical constraints and within one hardware assembly are systematically created during the engineering process.

For similar methodology for software development, is the "Model Driven Software Development" (MDSD) approach. MDSD is designed to automatedly create software by using standardized modelling languages, code generators and interpreters.

If only MBSE and MDSD are applied consistently, all technical constraints, dependencies, configuration items and interfaces will be well defined for resulting engineering artifacts and product subcomponents.

Even if these engineering methodologies are internally applied for all subcomponents, there is a gap for the multilevel assembly scenario. Whereas in software engineering, APIs usually are well documented, MBSE mostly focusses to the inner structure of the engineering artifact only, but not systematically to its usage or configuration within other, higher level artifacts.

Consequently, the missing links for systematic, multilevel product engineering are:

- Hardware API documentation standards and interfaces in MBSE
- Compatibility of these standards with to software API standards
- Enhancements in software API standards for hardware related settings and constraints
- Standardized and precise set of meta information

By closing these gaps, all engineering and configuration artifacts created asynchronously and independently can be integrated to consistent and comprehensive models. This enhanced Model Based System Engineering approach bridges bottom-up system development and top-down product and variant configuration.

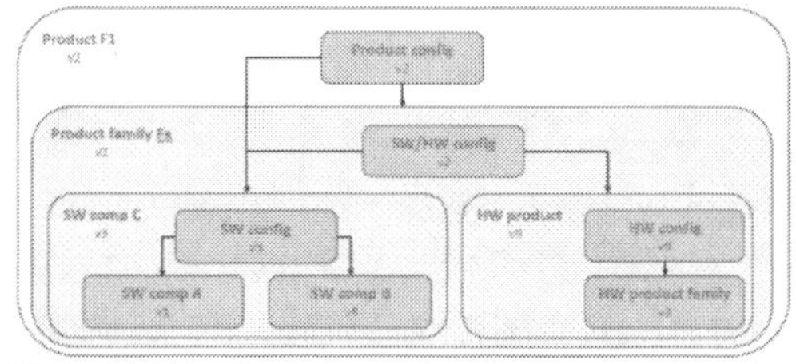

Fig.1. Multi-level component-based system and product assembly

2.2 Benefits of enhanced model-based system engineering

In agile and short-term development setups, product and product information integration is one of the most challenging tasks in many process steps. New components and updates must be systematically integrated just-in-time, including a reliable and comprehensive impact and risk analysis for the entire system.

Any change in system or product configuration may have impact in different aspects all over entire product related processes. It's not only about technical constraints between different components and subsequent updates and changes. Replacement only one small component in a hardware assembly might have strong impact due to embargo regulations. Replacing or updating an open source software component might result in obligations to disclose sensitive data and knowledge.

These examples show, how much different information, data and constraints need to be integrated into entire "Digital Twin" models of complex products and systems. Well defined and documented data structures and appropriate tools are necessary to handle this complex setup and to make any kind of relevant data and information generally accessible.

3 Unique models and specific views

The resulting complex and big data structures with multidimensional dependencies, properties result in big ontologies as single access points to any kind of engineering related information. These data structures must be unique and as exact as possible within its scope.

As a bold and simple postulate, the model shall be trusted as the truth.

In mass customization or product family setups, concrete product configurations and/or variants are created by filter mechanisms and configuration settings applied to a master model for product family models. Resulting product models are real subsets of the basic master model with a reduced scope but with the same information and data space.

3.1 Specifically configured product models

To preserve the information space and to ensure completeness and correctness of the resulting product instance models, configuration settings must be applied to the master model in multiple steps by following a from inside (in model engineering settings) to outside (outer configuration setting from higher levels) and bottom-up approach.

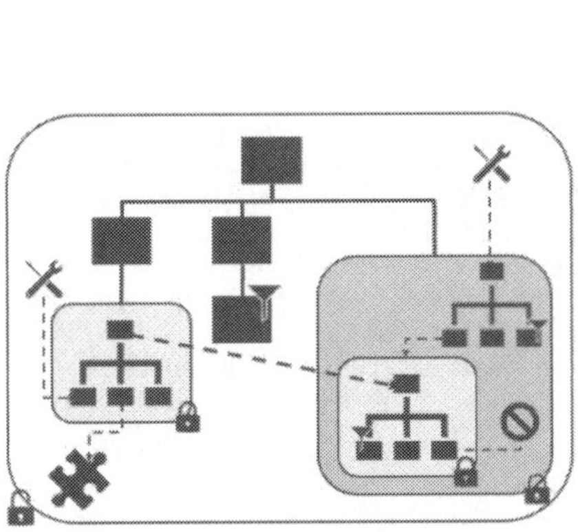

Fig. 2. Deriving a specific product model from a product family model in a multi-level engineering setup.

The process how to create a product variant from product family (master) can be described as follows:

1. Resolve engineering settings per model
   a. Remove "filtered out by validity element" elements
   b. Remove elements by essentially depending "dead" relations (relation types) after step 1.a.
2. Resolve configuration settings bottom up (component to model)
   a. Remove "deactivated by config" elements
   b. Remove elements by essentially depending "dead" cross model relations (relation types) after step 2.a.

3 Specific views based on unique models

Based on engineering models, specific views for specific purposes and sub-processes can be extracted. These views are specific aspects to the entire system and reduces the complexity to the minimum for a given purpose.

In contrast to the uniqueness and absolutely correctness of the model, specific views can't be declared neither as unique nor as absolutely correct but need to be stable and sufficient for its designated purpose. Views are of reduced complexity and carry only a subset of the entire information from the base model. Whereas systems models result in an ontology-based data structure, views most likely will end up in more simple taxonomies.

From a processing point of view, it's very important, that underlying qualitative and quantitative constraints and considerations for the specific purposes can be well defined and implemented in a ruleset on how to automatically derive the respective view in a suitable data format. Examples for such specific views and formats are system test plans to be imported to a given test management system, publication structures imported to Content Management Systems and bills of material for SCM tools.

Systematically created views based on stable rulesets applied to specific system models and revisions, complexity can be removed from specific sub-processes, scalability for entire product engineering process can be increased.

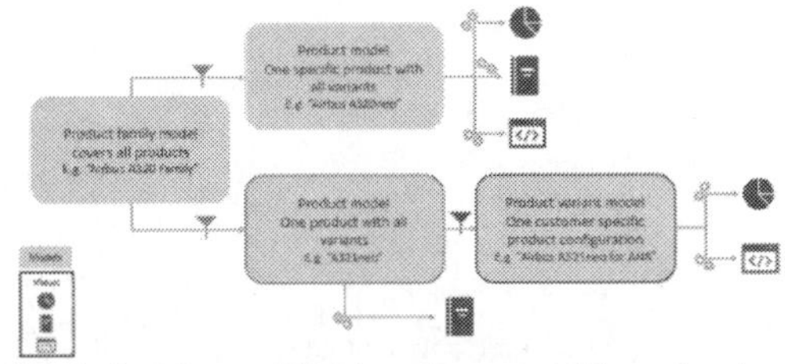

Fig. 3. Deriving specific views from a specific product in a multi-level engineering setup

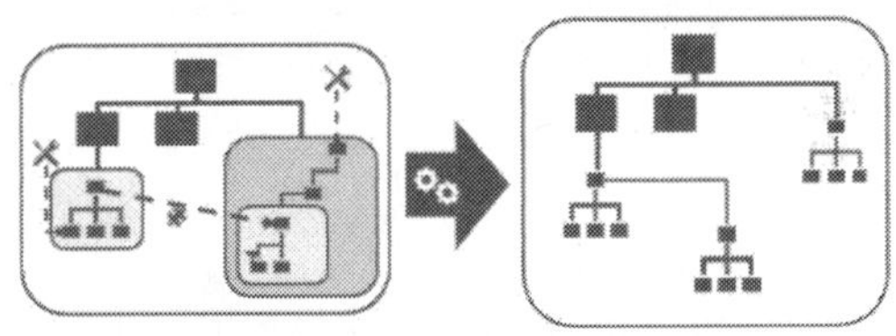

Fig. 4. Deriving a specific view (taxonomy) from a product model (ontology)

Creating specific views from a model also requires a fixed proceeding to ensure well-formed, self-contained and valid output.

The transformation process how to create views from models can be described as follows:

1. Transforming an Ontology Model to a View
   From a defined root element...
   a. Removing elements to be ignored
   b. Removing relations to be ignored
   c. Removing (resulting) dead-end relations
   d. Removing resulting free elements/sub models
   e. Rule based resolving of remaining relations by precedence
2. Transforming Taxonomy to target format
   a. Sorting and nesting structure by explicit criteria
   b. Transformation to specific target format

Whereas this process holds true for all views, rulesets and transformations must be defined for each view specifically depending on purpose and further processing.

Ruleset must contain specific definitions and constraints for the different processing steps.

Rules and constraints for steps 1.a to 1.d:

Ignore elements by

- type
- values
- type and property values

Ignore relations by

- type
- left/right element
- type and left/right element

Rules and constraints for step 1.e:

Precedence of relation type to be processed in a defined a sequence

Rules for relations to be defined by

- type
- left/right element
- type and left/right element

and to be processed like

- Ignore/remove
- Resolving/transformation to parent/child structure
- Multiply to left to right
- Multiply right to left
- Move left to right
- Move right to left

Transformations for steps 2.x:

Rules for rearranging the view (nesting sequencing, moving elements)

Data transformation for specific data format (e.g. XSL)

4 Summary

In this article, the challenges of widespread, agile and component based system and product engineering and its consequences to system integration and configuration are discussed.

To enable different process steps within the entire Product Lifecycle to follow short-term and agile development processes and diverse product portfolios, all relevant engineering and configuration information of all engineering artifacts must be accessible and integrated within all stages of a multilevel system engineering setup.

Subsequently, this article describes how modern development approaches like Model Based System Engineering (hardware) and Model Driven Software Development (software) can be integrated, and therefore be the basis for closing the gap between component-based engineering information and multilevel system and product integration and configuration.

Next to this basic concept, basic considerations to unique component and system models are described, and how specific views are delimited.

Finally, basic rules and constraints necessary for ensuring validity and completeness of specific product, product variants and custom configurations are figured out.

References

1. INCOSE, *Systems Engineering Vision (2020), INCOSE-TP-2004 (September 2007)*
2. Deschner, Ziegler, *Informationsmanagement und Ontologien – entwicklungsnahe Produkt-dokumentation in der Medizintechnik, tcworld conference Stuttgart 2018 (November 2018)*

Interdisciplinary Project Approach at the Analysis of Urban Happiness

Developing, managing and displaying interdisciplinary content with the outlook on designing smart cities from a humanistic approach

Ana Cristina García-Luna Romero[1], *Alessa Fleischer*[2]

[1] Universidad de Monterrey, Monterrey, Mexico
[2] University of Applied Sciences, Karlsruhe, Germany

Abstract. The following paper illuminates the process of interdisciplinary teamwork alongside a real project at the University de Monterrey. Connecting the faculties of architecture and medicine as well as integrating participants of the University of Applied Sciences in Karlsruhe, Germany, the project is aiming to get a new view on the connection of urban happiness, architecture and corresponding systems and processes in the human body. It combines philosophical research to define the term urban happiness as well as practical analysis of the city of Monterrey resulting in different problem cases for citizens nowadays. These problems were then used to draw a line to similar systems and cases which can be found in the human body and to see, how the human bodies way of solving problems can help architecture and especially the development of smart cities in the future – because keeping a focus on the human side will be an important part of realizing smarter cities. The paper is also focusing on the process of teamwork itself. It shows the necessary steps from initiating the project to organizing teams and communication up to the process of communicating and displaying the acquired knowledge.

1 Interdisciplinary projects

Working in teams can have a great benefit on the outcome of a project as well as playing a huge role in the personal development of each team member. Another possibility reveals itself by working in interdisciplinary teams.

The following chapter will give an introduction into the term of interdisciplinary work, the project work at the University of Monterrey, showing why it was initiated as well as its goals and the methods used. This lays the foundation for the subsequent chapters who will dive deeper into the actual process of the interdisciplinary teamwork at UDEM.

1.1 Definition of interdisciplinary work

The term interdisciplinary can be described by "involving two or more academic, scientific, or artistic disciplines" [1] and shows the potential that can unfold when people with a different background knowledge work together on solving specific issues. Repko and Szostak define interdisciplinary work as a "process of answering a question, solving a problem, or addressing a topic that is too broad or complex to be dealt with adequately by a single discipline, and draws on the disciplines with the goal of integrating their insights to construct a more comprehensive understanding." [2]

These definitions also underline the fact that interdisciplinary projects require a lot of planning communication throughout the process to be a success.

1.2 Introduction into the project

Project work has always been a big part of every field of study at the UDEM, even though the project mentioned in this paper has been one of the first to be developed in this manner.

The project was initiated in early 2019 and set for the fall semester of 2019. The goal was to connect the architectural approach on human life in cities and the quality of life in cities with the human life itself and to give solutions for future developments.

It was set to find parallels in each structure and to show how the city can benefit from the way the human body solves problems within those structures, further explanations are in chapter 1.2. The approach on the project was changed and modified according to research results throughout the process, which will be explained in chapter 2.3.

Apart from the main goal, the project had the aim to dive deeper into the possibility of having different faculties as well as students and professors to work together on one topic. It was also hoped that the project could only be the first step in a series of related projects, more on that will be evaluated in chapter 2.4.

Next to students and professors from the faculties of architecture and human sciences it was also the first project to offer a space for a student from the Karlsruhe University of Applied Sciences to be involved in a research stay and contribute to the project as well as further developing its topics in upcoming projects.

Therefore, it was also a multilingual project with meetings and documentation to be held either in Spanish or English.

1.3 Overview on objectives and schedules

The projects main objective was defined as the following:

"Interdisciplinary approach of conceptual and practical type to establish parallelisms between aspects of health sciences, especially medicine, and aspects of architecture, especially urbanism within the framework of the 50th anniversary UDEM." [3]

To narrow down the main objective further objectives were defined as well, initially consisting of the following:

"Present common concepts, apparently independent, that apply in both disciplines or scientific areas.

ii. Find similarities between urban grouping patterns and cell grouping patterns, according to functions and environment.

iii. Find elements of design and aesthetics in the previous groupings.

iv. Find common patterns in proper functioning and dysfunction as well as when such patterns are broken in both sciences.

v. Organize, classify and process the information in a layout that allows the visualization of the project from a digital platform" [3]

At first, the title was set as *bioarchitecture* but then later changed into *La fenomenología de la felicidad urbana: proyecto transdisciplinario* [4] to better incorporate the aspect of urban happiness and also to better separate the project from the original meaning of the term "bioarchitecture" which is rather "a blending of art/architecture and biomimetics/bioinspiration, and [...] bioinspired design" [5] rather than the approach of urban happiness and its human correlation that the project was aiming at.

The three main goals in the project for the semester of 2019 turned out to be the following:

- The publication of the important extracts of the research findings in an exhibition in the Museo de Arte Contemporary in Monterrey.
- The creation of a book with ISBN containing the entire and its results, to be published in 2020.
- The creation of a book as intellectual property containing a manual to recreate the process of the project.

The official kick-off was scheduled for mid-August 2019 so that all the participants had started the new semester and were able to participate. The rest of the timeframe was adjusted accordingly and modified if necessary. The following graphic shows the main milestones of the project.

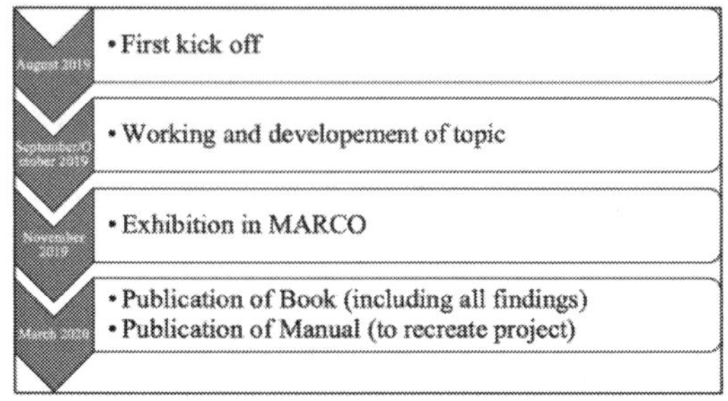

Fig. 1. Broad time frame of the project

1.4 Defining and creating urban happiness

There is no single source of truth when it comes to the term urban happiness. Different approaches see different key factors in what is being needed to make the residents of a city satisfied with their life.

Montgomery states that the initial creation of urban happiness "has nothing to do with buildings or roads or trees or bicycles. The first step is to agree on what matters for wellbeing." [6]. His model on creating urban happiness encompasses subjective wellbeing, psychological wellbeing and the healthy live years spent in a city [6]. He also admits, that "various elements of wellbeing contribute to this ideal condition" [6].

Each person has their own view on what is needed to make the life in a city worth living. The projects interdisciplinary approach provided views from multiple fields of study and nations of this world. It aimed to show how all of these views could be merged into one definition and how this definition could be the base of further research and the solution to future problems.

The elements that form urban happiness as approached in the project will be evaluated in chapter 3.1, more input on how the project's research and definition of urban happiness can be used in the actual development of (smart) cities is given in chapter 3.3.

1.5 Methodology of the project

The research throughout the process was mainly based on qualitative factors, taking a phenomenological approach into account. Since the goal was to develop a qualitative analysis, quantitative methods were not as useful and therefore not in focus.

The project could mainly be divided into three parts:

- Philosophical Approach
- Practical Approach
- Human Science Approach

The existing knowledge was analysed and worked through in a content analysis, for example getting familiar with the theories of E. Dussel and C. Alexander and developing the wheel of happiness out of those theories.

The observation of the city and the connection to the human side through the medical approach was a thematic analysis, working bottom-up to develop problem cases, more explanation on that in chapter 3.1,

https://doi.org/10.1051/shsconf/20207703003

and later on working top-down to derive solutions and directions for the cities in the future.

Figure 2 shows the main three approaches in the project and the necessary steps that were taken in them. It visualizes how the different views blend together and how the process forms a full circle, meaning that the entire project can be redone using the information that was gathered in the previous rounds.

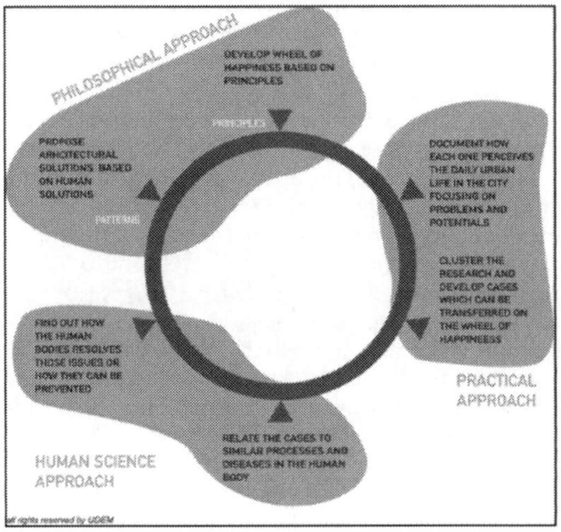

Fig. 2. The blending of different approaches

2 Structuring the work of interdisciplinary teams

To ensure that the project would actually be able to fulfil its goals and objectives and that everyone was able to give his best input possible, it was necessary to continuously monitor the current process, react to problems and to propose new solutions.

The following chapter will deal with the way the project work was structured and the research findings were documented and shared. It also shows how this knowledge can be preserved and shared with future students to expand the project and be the base for future and ideas and further developments.

2.1 Structure, research and communication

After a first kick off was set it was important, especially in the first weeks, to keep a tight connection between the team members to ensure that they would all have a common understanding of the roadmap.

At first, all the schedules of the team members were collected, and weekly meeting times were set so that every team member had the possibility to plan ahead and be present in the meeting. The first meetings were the base to build clusters (research areas and goals) in the project and set the team structures so that everyone knew in which cluster he was responsible and to whom he had to report to.

It was important that from every faculty there was a team leader to keep track of the process as well as people being sorted into the clusters where their knowledge would benefit the progress the most.

To share any kind of information and to document the knowledge that was developed throughout the project a Google Drive folder was set up and all the relevant participants were invited to share.

It also contained protocols (and sometimes audio recordings if important participants were missing and needed the possibility to listen to the meeting) of each meeting so that the outcomes were documented to prevent further discrepancies.

Throughout the project, different roadmaps were set up to document the necessary To-Dos and steps in each phase of the project. The initial roadmap started out on a weekly base but was later on enriched by a daily layout so that meetings and tasks for each individual person could be documented.

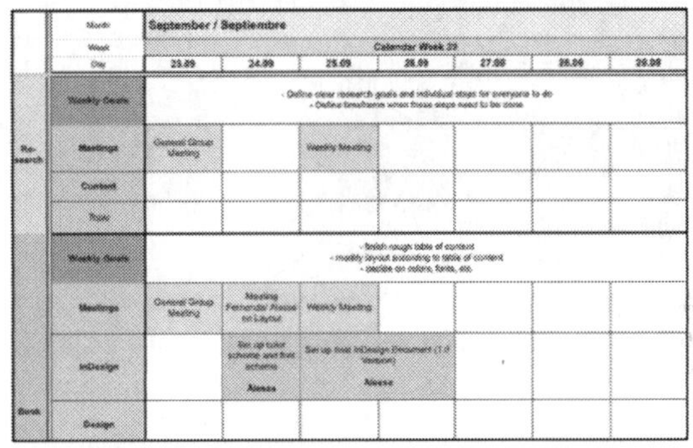

Fig. 2. Part of the September roadmap

Keeping track of all the tasks through roadmaps was especially important since all of the team members were also part of other projects and had their daily job routine, more on that will be evaluated in chapter 2.3.

2.2 Documentation and presentation of content

Throughout the project, a lot of content was created and documented which needed to be taken care of. The most important fact to keep in mind with the interdisciplinary work was that with the book and the exhibition it had a very broad target audience with different levels of background knowledge and understanding. Therefore, the content needed to be presented in a way that every viewer would understand the facts, the facts were correct in each way of depth of the content and that no viewer would be bored because the level of depth was not aligned with his level of background knowledge.

It was also important to keep in mind that a lot of different content from different approaches needed to be present in a uniform way to underline the fact that the project was an interdisciplinary work but still had one fixed goal that everyone was working towards to.

Since the main place for all information was Google Drive most of the documentation in the first phase was done in either Google Sheets or Google Docs. These documents allowed all the participants to view the produced content, add comments and to make changes in one place. It also brought the possibility to create folders to especially include external feedback from participants that weren't supposed to view the rest of the content.

As the goal of the project was defined in showing the results in an exhibition as well as a book it was clear that next to textual content there was also a lot of graphical content to be produced. Since this is especially time-consuming, all of the graphics started out as hand-made sketches that were evaluated in meetings with all group members and then created with the help of software from the Adobe Suite (Illustrator, InDesign, Photoshop).

The following graphic shows such a process during the development of the wheel of happiness, going from first sketches to the final approved version a couple of weeks later.

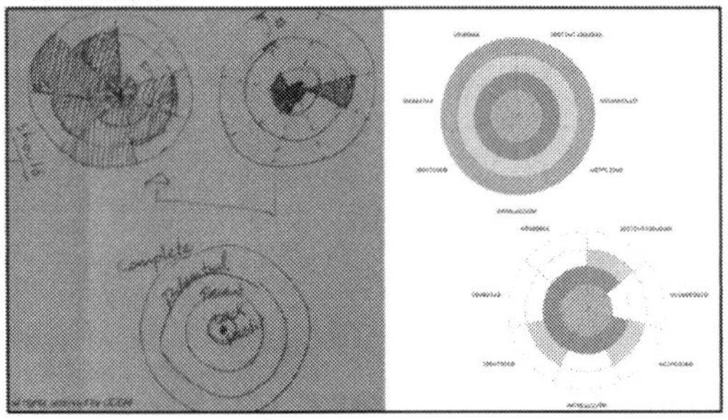

Fig. 2. First sketch and final version of a graphic

Another reason to put a special focus on the graphics was the fact that they allowed to explain the complex structures and processes of the project in a much faster way. If presented in a correct manner, humans can perceive information in a graphical form much faster than in textual form [7] which was especially important for the parts that were to be presented in the exhibition.

2.3 Prioritizing and changing perspectives

Throughout the project there were certain shifts in the process or the targeted goals which were necessary to keep the project a going and which also brought up possibilities for new, thematically connected projects in the future, building upon the research that was already made.

In the first scope, as already mentioned in chapter 1.3, one of the objectives was the development of a digital platform to share the knowledge and to enable people to share their own experiences.

During the first weeks of the project, it got clear that at this point the development of such a platform was not useful as on one hand there was no capacity and skills available to do so and also that the structure of the content that was supposed to be shared wasn't validated yet as the content wasn't even created in the project itself. In order to not spend too much time on an objective that wasn't going to work out at this point, the objective was moved to the next semester with the possibility to be a future project or thesis that would be connected to the project.

Being flexible throughout the process and adapting to the current situation was very important and helped in putting the focus on things was were going well and therefore being able to reach the objectives

2.4 Dealing with difficulties and deriving learnings for future projects

In working with people from different faculties and even people with different native languages, naturally, some problems appeared that this subchapter is taking into focus.

One of the main problems was the availability of all the participants. Finding dates and time slots, where all the participants where available, was a problem that was present throughout the entire process. It shows the importance of planning with everyone's availability in an early stage, e.g. through collecting all schedules and setting weekly meetings throughout the first weeks. Meetings cannot be as productive as planned, especially when expert knowledge from one side of the interdisciplinary approach is not available. This also shows that it's important to integrate at least two people from each field of study so that the absence of one person can be compensated through another. Setting up a clear list of participants and their responsibilities also helps all of the members of the team to know who to turn to as well as helping the team leaders to plan ahead with the resources.

Another difficulty that needed to be overcome in everyday communication was the language barrier, as most of the meetings were held in Spanish, which led to some misunderstandings when it came to topics that required more background knowledge, especially meetings dealing with medical content.

In this case, it was always helpful to take a short time after the meeting, break down the main points (and document them in the protocol) and making sure that everyone had the same understanding on the outcome.

Generally, one of the first things in the project work should be the decision on one main language which every one of the participants should at least be able to understand up to a certain level so that meetings can be held without having to translate throughout the process. English should also be a requirement for all the participants taking a bigger part in the project, also because next to meetings a lot of documentation online, that was needed for deeper research, is in English.

A single source of truth in documentation can only help the participants if it is continuously updated and managed. At certain points throughout the project, some of the documents were in danger of becoming obsolete because they were not taken care of. In this case, it is the responsibility of the team leader to decide whether this means that they were simply not relevant to the project anymore and could be archived but also to keep reminding the other project members to keep the documentation updated. Creating a WhatsApp group or providing a different way of fast communication was very helpful to send reminders as these messages were read much faster than emails.

2.5 Connection with future projects

As already mentioned, some of the objectives, like the data-sharing platform, were moved from being realized right away to being realized in the future so they could further expand the research on the project.

Some other projects, like the re-creation of the entire process in different cities, were already planned as an extension for the next semesters. The recreation in other cities shows enormous potential and could take place in any other city of the world, benefiting each city on an individual scale but also being able to compare the cities to each other.

Documenting these possibilities for further projects right away and sharing them with other people in advance helps in planning the resources for the next projects and ensures that they will actually be put into action.

One possibility to connect the research with other topics will be explained in the following chapter

3 Impact of Research on the development of smart cities

The following chapter will get a closer focus on the actual content that was created throughout the project and shows how to even expand the idea of interdisciplinary work further in connecting the research with another topics – in this case the topic of smart cities.

3.1 Results of the projects

After a semester of interdisciplinary team work the project had a lot of different results to show off, which can be grouped into three different parts.

The first part covers the philosophical research, working with the theories of E. Dussel [8] and C. Alexander [9] to create twenty principles that build the base for human live and needs in their city – their desires to live and their approach on urban happiness, as it was already introduced in chapter 1.4. Throughout the research, the principles were grouped into similar clusters, thus creating a Wheel of Happiness which can be used to apply the concepts to each own surroundings and to measure the quality of live in the city. The Wheel of Happiness contains the following seven parts:

- Sustainability
- Development
- Mobility
- Interaction
- Identification
- Wellbeing
- Beauty

The second part draws the first connection to the human body and looks into three different systems (circulatory, neurological, immunological) and their connections to cities on a larger scale.

The third part applies the Wheel of Happiness to the city of Monterrey itself, analyzing different problem cases that each of the participants encounter in their everyday way to university and also drawing the connection to similar problems in the human body. It derives solutions from the way the human body solves those problems and applies them back to the urban side.

3.2 The term smart cities

To show how the field of Smart Cities can benefit from the research it is important to define the term itself and show its importance for the future development of urban life.

In general, the term Smart City encompasses "the new urban environment, one that's designed for performance through information and communication technologies (ICTs) and other forms of physical capital." [10]. Applying smart technologies to all areas of urban life can "have the unprecedented ability to not only describe [...] cities in granular detail but to also discover new, creative ways to design and maintain [...] cities in the most sustainable, innovative, and efficient way possible." [10]. This shows, that smart cities have the ability to measure and improve their residences lives, an approach also followed in the interdisciplinary project work. Andrews states that smart cities could have a great positive aspect on a lot of areas:

"Public safety: Smart applications could reduce urban fatalities by 8 to 10 percent.

Time and convenience: Cities can use smart technologies to cut commuting times by 15 to 20 percent giving workers back two to four full days every year.

Health: Cities could use smart technologies to reduce their health burden by 8 to 15 percent, and in the developing world could make significant strides through data-driven public health interventions.

Environment: Cities can use a range of smart applications to cut emissions by 10 to 15 percent, save 25 to 80 litres of water per person each day, reduce un-recycled solid waste by 30 to 130 kg per person annually, and reduce the negative health effects from air pollution by 8 to 15 percent." [11]

At this point the importance and relevance of smart cities has just begun to develop, which makes it even more important to already understand the term and help cities to grow into future smart cities.

3.3 Connecting Smart Cities with the outcomes of the project

In his article "Unleash the (Smart City) Power within" Hwang states that for a smart city to fully develop and increase the quality of live, it is important to "define the result desired and the purpose and need first before there's a pressing problem to be solved" [12]. This aligns with the development of the Wheel of Happiness defining the needs of all inhabitants of the city, Smart City or not. The Bottom-Up and following Top-Down-approach already mentioned in chapter 1.4 containing the analysis of each on Monterrey's problems and the connection with the Wheel of Happiness shows exactly what kind of areas of the city need further development and what parts of the clusters (like security or sanity) need improvement before the problems get too overpowering. Connecting these situations with the human body, its diseases and its solutions can help in finding a way to prevent problems from emerging in the future and if they do appear it can show ways on how to handle them.

 https://doi.org/10.1051/shsconf/20207703003

There is another reason to connect the Smart Cities with the human being itself. Barkho states an important thing to keep in mind when developing Smart Cities: "While historical cities may take years or even decades to develop, their existing populations give them an advantage over glitzier new smart cities, forgoing the need to recruit "residents." [13]. If the Smart Cities do not focus on the aspect of the human will to live and the human expectations on living in a city, such as the project work does in its philosophical research, humans will not feel the will and urge to live in such a city. In this case keeping the principles and the Wheel of Happiness in mind is a key factor in ensuring a good quality of live and a growing population within the city.

3.4 Future outlook on development

The connections made in the previous chapter show the value that the research can bring for the development of Smart Cities. Especially the possibility of bringing the project into other cities, mentioned in chapter 2.5, could greatly benefit because in this way every other city could also take the research and findings and integrate them into its way of working towards a Smarter City. The importance is also underlined by the fact that the development of sustainable cities and communities was chosen as one of the main objectives for a sustainable future by the United Nations [14].

4 Conclusion

Summing up all the findings it can be said, that interdisciplinary project works can bring a great benefit to every aspect of life. Not only they help in the personal development of each of their team member, they also bring new input to their related universities as well as giving the opportunities to develop many new research projects out of their result. The described project even takes a step further and shows how the correlation of urban happiness and biology can not only help the inhabitants of a city to analyze and define problems and strengths of their own city but also to see how their own body and its complex processes and structures can be used to improve the everyday life of each inhabitant and even play a role in the future development of the Smart Cities in which, next to the technology, the human factor should still play the most prominent role for all actions in development that will be taken.

5 ACKNOWLEDGMENTS

At first, a big thank you to Mrs. Ana Cristina García Luna Romero for initializing such an interesting project and for supporting all of the members through every step.

As well, a thank you to all the other members of the projects for their support, their time and their hard work to reach the projects's goals.

And thanks Prof. Dr. Debopriyo Roy from the University of Aizu, Japan for giving the opportunities to participate in the conference and for the participants of the project to submit their research.

References

1. Merriam Webster - Definition of interdisciplinary. Retrieved November 04, 2019 from https://www.merriam-webster.com/dictionary/interdisciplinary. (2019)
2. Repko, A. / Szostak, R. *Interdisciplinary Research: Process and Theory*. Third Edition. SAGE Publications INC, Thousand Oaks (2017)
3. García-Luna Romero, A. *Art project of Bio architecture*. UDEM, Monterrey, 2-3. (2019)
4. García-Luna Romero, A. / Alvarez Moreno, A. *Plan de Investigación – Proyecto Transdisciplinario*. UDEM, Monterrey, 2. (2019)
5. Ripley, R. / Bhushan, B. *Bioarchitecture: bioinspired art and architecture—a perspective.* In *Philosophical Transactions of the Royal Society A: Mathematical, Physical and Engineering Sciences.* Retrieved November 05, 2019 from https://doi.org/10.1098/rsta.2016.0192, 374. (2016)
6. Montgomery, C. *A Recipe for Urban Happiness.* Revtrieved January 14, 2020 from https://medium.com/happy-cities/happiness-framework-ead6430997ca (2019)
7. Eisenberg, H. *Humans process visual data better.* Retrieved November 05, 2019 from http://www.t-sciences.com/news/humans-process-visual-data-better. (2014)
8. Dussel, E. *20 tesis de política.* SIGLO XXI Editores, Madrid. (2006)
9. Alexander, C. / Ishikawa, S. / Silverstein, M. *A pattern language.* Oxford City Press, Oxford. (1977)
10. Stimmel, Carol L. *Building Smart Cities: Analytics, ICT, and Design Thinking.* CRC Press, Boca Raton. **4-7** (2015)
11. Andrews, J. *How Smart City initiatives can improve quality-of-life indicators by 10-30%: report.* Retrieved November 06, 2019 from https://news.itu.int/smart-cities-improve-quality-of-life-says-mckinsey/. (2018)
12. Hwang, B. *Unleash the (Smart City) Power within.* Retrieved November 06, 2019 from https://medium.com/predict/unleash-the-smart-city-power-within-ae22f477e9c9 (2018)
13. Barkho, G. *Good Smart Cities Actually Need People to Live in Them.* Retrieved November 06, 2019 from https://medium.com/new-york-magazine/good-smart-cities-actually-need-people-to-live-in-them-3ef2e62cd6d1 (2018)
14. United Nations. *Objetivos de desarollo sustenible.* Retrieved November 08, 2019 from https://www.un.org/sustainabledevelopment/es/objetivos-de-desarrollo-sostenible/ (2017)

Ontology-based modelling for content delivery systems

Lena Mareike Padeken[1*] and *Annika Johanna* Bürkel[1**]

[1]Karlsruhe University of Applied Sciences, Faculty of Information Management and Media, 76133 Karlsruhe, Germany

Abstract. Instead of managing metadata in a content management system (CMS) for content delivery, this research uses an ontology to make use of augmented intelligence. Hence, the retrieval of specific information in a content delivery system (CDS) is provided by a concise metadata concept. Ontology-based metadata concepts can have advantages in comparison to taxonomy-based metadata concepts because of the possibilities they offer to display linked information. The creation of an ontology depends on the vendor's system, the vendor's approach and most importantly the particular use case. Due to the ontology modelling, a data transformation for an external CDS is needed. When working with different vendors, requirements and considerations need to be discussed because the outcome can add value to user experience. The goal of this research is to identify the advantages of an ontology system over metadata management in a CMS. These advantages can be extracted by opportunities offered by the ontology modelling and by the transformation process.

1 Introduction

An easy accessed and customized retrieval of information is highly demanded in times of information 4.0 and intelligent information. Users do not want to be overwhelmed by too much information; they need the right information at the right time. Due to changes in user behaviour and technologies, content delivery systems (CDS) are used to enable web access to information depending on specific use cases [1, 2]. In most cases, content management systems (CMS) are used to manage modular content and the corresponding metadata. These metadata can also be used to retrieve content modules in a CDS. Another way to provide information for a CDS is using a knowledge network like an ontology. Ontologies are more reality-oriented as they not only represent the hierarchical structure of metadata but also realise cross-linked relationships between elements of different levels. For the ontology modelling process, it is key to make observations about potential use cases. This helps specifying the user's needs and simultaneously gain understanding about the needed search and filter options.

To deploy information in a CDS, vendors' either must own a CDS or need to carry out a transformation process to import content into a CDS [2]. Running one's own transformation process offers the chance of balancing the content and context deployment for a CDS. Possible advantages can be found by analysing the ontology output file and the requirements for the data import into an external CDS. This way, content, context and facets can be adjusted for an ideal user experience.

2 Context of research

This paper resulted out of a collaboration between students from the master's program at Karlsruhe University of Applied Sciences, Germany, and students from University of Aizu, Japan. As part of the course *XML-Based Information and Content Management* by Professor Wolfgang Ziegler, these students developed an ontology as a metadata model for content delivery on the subject of *Smart Home Technologies*. This knowledge network helps to retrieve intelligent information on a CDS. Therefore, a transformation from the data given in the ontology to the external CDS was needed.

In order to carry out this research, the students from Karlsruhe got access to the ontology system i-views Knowledge Builder and the content delivery system DOCUFY TopicPilot. Thus, this research mainly refers to the above-mentioned vendors' options and functions.

3 Theoretical overview

3.1 Importance of metadata

Metadata are additional information to describe, manage and identify objects such as modules in a CMS. Additionally, metadata are also used to aggregate product or context specific output in a CDS. In fact, cross-linked metadata allow a complex and automated aggregation of information. Therefore, metadata are the basis of intelligent content management and content delivery [3]. This intelligence manifests in the extraction of specific information through facets in content delivery systems and in the automation of product documentation [4].

*Lena Mareike Padeken: pale1014@hs-karlsruhe.de
**Annika Johanna Bürkel: buan1024@hs-karlsruhe.de

https://doi.org/10.1051/shsconf/20207703004

3.2 Ontologies as a concept of organising metadata

Metadata can be organised in a hierarchal system like a taxonomy. It describes a two-dimensional visualisation of elements containing classes and subclasses in a parent-child relationship. But when it comes to relationships between subclasses of the same or different class, a taxonomy reaches its limits. An ontology, in contrast, is extended with relations between elements on different levels. If the same underlying ontology is used, information of different origins can be combined in a common output medium [5]. Also, the usage of an ontology simplifies the search process in a content delivery scenario. Through the linking of contextual relevant information, a more precise search result can be displayed. Furthermore, facets can be managed in an ontology and adapted in a content delivery solution.

Ontologies are already widely used in the area of knowledge management and several other areas. The next step then would be to apply the benefits of ontologies to technical communication. However, the concepts of ontologies are relatively new in this field. But the demands of contextual linked information in search scenarios of content delivery systems are growing. In content management as well as content delivery systems, metadata models can be extended using an ontology and thus creating a more intelligent content. The benefits of ontologies are the following: Due to the usage of formal language to describe them, they are machine readable and therefore a basis of machine learning and artificial intelligence [6]. For technical communication this means that new opportunities can be created for knowledge sharing and displaying contents.

Yet, there is neither standardised methodology in ontology engineering nor a standard language to document ontology modelling. However, the two most common modelling languages used are RDF (Resource Description Framework) and OWL (Web Ontology Language).

3.3 Importance of content, context and facets

Deploying information to users is often defined by too much content and too few context [7]. Considering a CDS, topics can be displayed individually by running a search, selecting facets or as hierarchical structures like table of contents or directories. Hierarchical structures often imply a document-oriented CDS approach. This document-oriented approach is for example used by the CDS of SCHEMA [2]. In contrast, the CDS TopicPilot of DOCUFY uses a topic-oriented approach, but also displays (hierarchical and non-hierarchical) directories next to each topic. Providing hierarchical structures can result in too much content for users because they contain non-relevant information, whereas topics without references create not enough context. The later explained transformation process introduces an approach to enrich information deployment by using the connection between an ontology and a CDS (see chapter 7).

3.4 Thematic classification into the project

In this research project, the ontology marks the intermediate step between content creation management and content delivery (Fig. 1). For content creation and management, the modular-based content management system Smart Media Creator (SMC) was used. Different content modules about the topic *Smart Home Technologies* were collated. The aim of this project was to enrich the content we created in the CMS with the metadata from the ontology system to display user specific information in an external CDS.

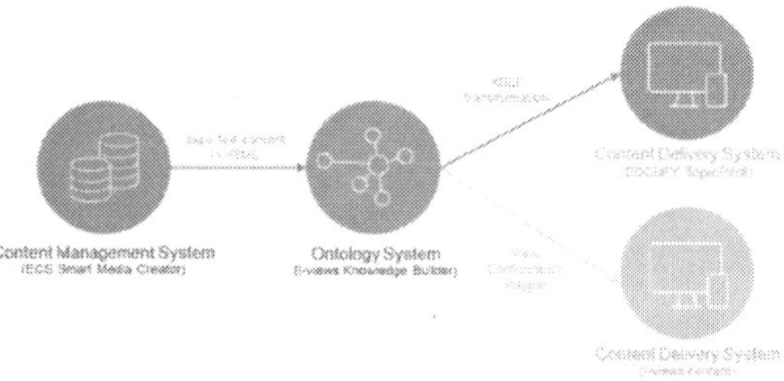

Fig. 1. Correlation of the software systems.

For this research, the data from the ontology system was used to feed an external CDS. Reasons for using an external system are that company owned CDS are often aligned to their own company language and company philosophy including their approach. This leads to a one-way thinking which channels processes in one direction and results in lost and missed chances of identifying and using better alternatives. In this research, we figure out possibilities, chances and advantages by using an ontology with linkage to an external CDS. It is our goal to find out how individually we can feed a CDS by following the requirements.

4 Ontology modelling with the i-views Knowledge Builder

4.1 General introduction in i-views

Intelligent views GmbH (i-views) is a German company founded in 1997 that is specialised in providing semantic technologies [8]. Part of the i-views solution is the Knowledge Builder which allows the modelling of metadata in the form of a knowledge network. The i-views Knowledge Builder allows the creation, editing and graphical visualisation of metadata and their relations in an ontology. Users can work in the textual and in the graphical interface (see Fig. 2). Both options offer different aspects and overviews. Also, contents from various CMS can be integrated via common standards and cross-linked to related elements in the ontology. The corresponding CDS 'i-viewscontent' allows to display the imported content which is directly linked to the metadata from the ontology system. For more information about the i-views internal delivery system, see "Ontologies and use case based planning of content delivery" (Burkhardt and Clesle) in this volume. Logical queries help retrieving use case specific information in the knowledge network as well as in the i-views content delivery solution. These queries can be realised as facets, guiding the user through possibilities of content search. Also, these facets from the ontology system can be reused for facet creation in an external CDS (for more information, see chapter 6.3.3).

Within the scope of the course, the i-views Knowledge Builder was chosen as the main tool to model the ontology. To understand further approaches in the ontology creation process, a short introduction into the internal terminology of the Knowledge Builder is given. A knowledge network in the Knowledge Builder consists of four main elements. 'Types of Objects' (Types) describes the superior area an object belongs to [9]. In the area of Smart Home Technologies, the Type 'PhysicalObject' can have multiple objects, for example 'SmartHomeDevice' and 'ControlDevice'. These hierarchical relations are reflexive. The lowest element in such a hierarchy is called 'Instance' (or special object), it classifies the most specified object of a chain of objects. These instances can be connected through a 'Relationship'. Relationships can have different validities and therefore be valid for selected instances of objects [8].

4.2 Use case oriented ontology modelling

Due to simplicity, the following process description is shown in chronological order. In the practical realisation of this project, the different steps depended on one another and resulted in retroactive changes and adaptions.

As a preparatory step, we collected content about the topic *Smart Home Technologies* in the CMS Smart Media Creator, which served as the basis for the actual ontology modelling. At this point, we were supported by the students from Aizu University, Japan, that collected and prepared topics about Smart Home Technologies and provided them for us. Then, the topics were exported without metadata in HTML-format and manually transformed to be imported into the i-views Knowledge Builder.

To get a more precise metadata concept and on this basis a purposeful outcome, different use cases must be taken into consideration in advance. We collected information about the user's knowledge level, their intends, the user's input and the displayed content output as well as the information search scenario. The created use cases mainly focus on gaining first insight and general information about the topic Smart Home Technologies from non-specialists.

For more details about the use cases created for the ontology modelling in the Knowledge Builder refer to the article "Ontologies and use case based planning of content delivery" (Burkhardt and Clesle) in this volume. In this paper, we use one use case as an example to outline the functionalities of the modelling software i-views Knowledge Builder.

The next step marks the creation of 'Objects', their 'Instances' and their connection through 'Relationships'. Therefore, the first approach is a hierarchical organisation of 'Objects'. These parent-child relationships are called 'is object of' and 'has object' and are automatically drawn when creating objects in a hierarchical order. For example, the object 'SmartHomeDevice' has the instance 'HomeSecurityAndMonitoringSystem'. Furthermore, additional relationships can be created to connect instances of the same or different objects. To continue with the example, the instance 'HomeSecurityAndMonitoringSystem' is connected by the relationship 'Serves' to the instances 'Comfort', 'ProtectionAgainstAttacks', 'ProtectionAgainstFire' and 'ProtectionAgainstWaterDamage' of the object 'Purpose', which are represented by the red elements in the graphic below.

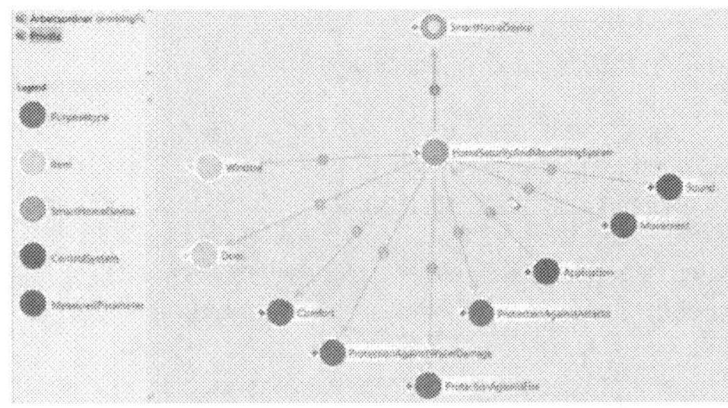

Fig. 2. Graph editor view in the i-views Knowledge Builder.

After modelling the metadata concept, the exported content modules from the CMS have to be implemented into the ontology. Therefore, the i-views Knowledge Builder offers a section called 'Chapter' to upload HTML-content. At the time of this research, an iiRDS-export has not been possible yet, therefore the content modules had to be inserted manually. Every module from the CMS was implemented as a 'Chapter'-element which could then be connected to the objects and instances of the ontology via the relationship 'has facet term'. Every chapter could then be connected to the corresponding metadata and in this way enable a three-dimensional metadata concept.

5 Process for the data import into the content delivery system

The process of providing information in a CDS by using a CMS is the same as providing information by using an ontology. In a heterogeneous system landscape [2], the information of a CMS or an ontology needs to be imported by a content package with the use of an own transformation. The only difference between a CMS and an ontology during this process is the export file format. The CMS export file is usually provided in an xml-format while the ontology export file usually is provided in a descriptive language format. This leads to different adjustments of the transformation process and to different possibilities of utilising the ontology output data. To transform the content of the export file, XSLT is used to generate files for the content package. Content packages are needed to create content in a CDS.

6 Content delivery system planning

The transformation process depends on many considerations and needs to be adjusted to the given conditions. An example for difficulties while planning is that the ontology system i-views Knowledge Builder describes the content in a book-oriented way and the CDS TopicPilot displays the content in a topic-oriented way [2]. Therefore, the export data and the import data for the CDS need to be analysed closely. Furthermore, the possibilities of maintaining content, context and the resulting facets in a balanced way will be discussed.

6.1 Structure of the ontology output

The significant components of the output file for the transformation can be divided into four parts. These parts are responsible for satisfying the content package requirements (see 6.2.2). The first part describes the book structure by *document roots*. *Document roots* are the main chapters inside a book and include *containing chapters* which are described individually in the second part as *chapters*. These *chapters* can have facet-like elements which are attached to a *chapter* as a *facet term*. The content of each *chapter* is described in the third part in hidden HTML (HTML displayed by entities). The fourth part contains the definition of each *facet term*.

6.2 Components of DOCUFY TopicPilot

6.2.1 Displaying content

The CDS TopicPilot of DOCUFY GmbH offers three general ways of finding information in the CDS [10]. The content is displayed in topics which can be accessed by searching for specific keywords, filtering metadata and navigating through related topics inside a *Publication*.

When *searching* for specific content by using the search field, the CDS TopicPilot offers keywords for matching and completing the written letters. The CDS TopicPilot searches through topics, trees and metadata [10]. *Facets* are used to filter content in a CDS and to give an orientation to users to find information according to a specific topic and its related information [1]. This enriches the searching process. Directories are placed next to each topic to enhance the *navigation* process between connected topics. All connected topics belong to the same content package and are also displayed inside a *Publication* container (*tree*) on top of the CDS [2, 10].

6.2.2 Requirements for data import

To import data into a CDS, vendors have different approaches (e. g. document-oriented or topic-oriented) and requirements because there is no standardised structure or content for a content package [2]. Adding content to the CDS TopicPilot is realised by uploading content packages in ZIP-format. These content packages consist of (1) files for the content (topic), (2) a filter hierarchy (facet-data), (3) a reference structure of the topics (tree), (4) a media folder which contains all media files and (5) a manifest file (MANIFEST.MF) for declaring the version of the manifest itself and the DYXML-version. DYXML is a mark-up language and was developed by DOCUFY based on XHTML.

6.3 Usage of content, context and facets

The structure of the ontology output file and the requirements of the content package for the CDS give an insight to the chances that can enrich content deployment by adjusting the data transformation. These chances are discussed considering possible implementations of content, context and resulting facets.

6.3.1 Content

Since the CDS TopicPilot is topic-oriented, there is no high risk of having too much content. Each topic content is attached to a chapter in the ontology output file. The additional directory shown in the CDS is built by the tree file in the CDS TopicPilot and is based on all topics displayed in the CDS. It is mandatory to upload a tree file, which on the other hand makes it difficult to implement major changes in the directory representation.

6.3.2 Context

The ontology output file provides nested structures between chapters and facets as well as relations between facets. Nested structures can add context information by static linking in the CDS TopicPilot to generate links between topics. Relations between chapters can also add context information because most *chapters* contain *facet term* elements. These *facet terms* have relations between each other, which can be used for dynamic linking in the CDS TopicPilot. Dynamic links provide shorter access to information by a direct facet link.

6.3.3 Facets

Facet term elements are also of great importance to the facet structure in the CDS TopicPilot because the export file of the ontology does not provide a facet structure itself. The book structure of the ontology output file offers a structure consisting of *document roots* and *containing chapters*. These *document roots* and *containing chapters* may have defined facets which are declared within an own superordinate local name (namespace) at the end of the document. This rough structure already includes a facet structure based on the document structure itself and based on the facets of the *document roots* and *containing chapters*. Using facets based on the document structure is undesirable for a CDS because these facets would be displayed as a table of contents. Therefore, the facet structure should resemble the structure of the attached *facet terms* of the *chapters*. Allocated facets for the *document roots* cannot be used, because these *document roots* do not include any HTML. Thus, only facets for *chapters* will be used. Using the superordinate local names, the facet structure will have a maximum of two hierarchical levels. Following this structure, relations between *chapters* are used because the superordinate local names also define relations between every instance.

6.3.4 *Final considerations for the transformation process*

Taking all discussed considerations into account, two key points can be concluded:

- The ability to filter more than two hierarchy levels is restricted.
- Given relationships can be used for filtering and adding context information.

These key points play a major role for the whole transformation process and determine the focus on the topic files for the context and the facet-data file for the facets. This conclusion also gives a first impression of the advantages of using an ontology for content delivery.

7 Transformation process

The students from the University of Aizu provided their content in PDF documents. In TopicPilot, a PDF document can be uploaded in the media folder and be referenced as an <embed> element inside a topic. During the transformation process, we transformed the ontology output file for the topics, the tree and the facet file. The use case for the transformation process is a user searching for information about the smart home device 'Home Security and Monitoring System'.

7.1 Metadata deployment of topic file and tree file

Topic and tree files are written in DYXML2-format, which means that these files generate XML-documents within a DYXML namespace and are displayed as HTML in the CDS [2, 11]. Topics and trees deliver metadata information to the CDS. This information is written in a <head> element. All metadata information given in Fig. 3 is mandatory, except for the <fingerprint> element.

```
<title>Functionality of a Smart Alarm System</title>
<doctype>Topic</doctype>
<id>15765913326571111111111111111111</id>
<version>1</version>
<fingerprint>00000000000000000000000000000001</fingerprint>
<lastupdate>2019-12-12T15:23:46.242+02:00</lastupdate>
```

Fig. 3. Metadata information of a topic file.

Information of the <title> element is used for search results in the CDS TopicPilot and displayed in a *Topic* preview, trees are displayed in a *Publication* preview. The distinction is made according to the <doctype> element by defining either Topic or Publication for the document type. Inside the <head> element, primary keys are used which consist of ID, version, language and language variant [10]. Primary keys are used to define topics and trees in a non-ambiguous way. The ID needs to have 32 hexadecimal digits and can be generated as shown in the upper part of Fig. 4 [10].

```
<xsl:variable name="ShortNumber">
    <xsl:value-of select="substring(replace(./krdf:frameID, '_', ''), 3, 14)"/>
</xsl:variable>
<xsl:variable name="Number">
    <xsl:value-of select='format-number($ShortNumber, "#1111111111111111111")'/>
</xsl:variable>
```

Fig. 4. XSLT snippet for generating the ID.

The *krdf:frameID* inside the output file has variable lengths and non-hexadecimal digits, which is why the substring and replace function were used in XSLT. The format-number function adds necessary digits.

7.2 Topic file

7.2.1 *Content information*

The <body> element specifies the content of a topic and has a similar structure as an HTML-document. This is helpful because the ontology content output is also written in HTML. Even though DYXML has a strict structure, customers can use *data-type* attributes to customise the content. It is crucial to have good knowledge of the DYXML2-documentation because the topic file will only be uploaded if there is no mistake in code. The content of each topic can be extended by adding context information and making use of the relations inside an ontology. Topics can also comprise external elements like PDFs (with corresponding MIME types) by using an <embed> element [11].

7.2.2 *Context enrichment*

Context information can only be added in the content part of the topic file because of the restrictions in DYXML2; therefore, it can only be displayed inside a topic. For each topic, static and dynamic links can be created depending on the use case and the users' needs. This additional information can be added by using the relations between chapters and facets (*facet terms*) visible in the output file of the ontology. In general, static links are set between chapters or sections of chapters and dynamic links to a specific facet. This implies that static links have exactly one target, whereas dynamic links can have more than one target. Static links are built based on *chapters* having the same *facet terms* and by comparing their *labels*. If *labels* contain two or more equal words, a link is generated which relates to another *chapter*. Dynamic links are based on the facets inside a *document root*, containing all *chapters* that are relevant for the use case. This means that each topic is linked to other facets included in the *document root*. These facets can lead users to different topics and give a deeper insight.

7.3 Tree file

To specify the content, the tree file uses a <root> element instead of a <body> element, implying that no topic content itself will be shown. The tree file uses <node>

elements to link and nest given topics into a reference structure. It contains an *ID* attribute which is used for internal representation [2, 10]. Inside the <node> element, <topicref> elements refer to a specific topic using the *href* attribute. Based on the given structure of the ontology output file, the tree structure will not be nested because only *chapters* will be used (see chapter 6.3.3).

7.4 Facet file

The facet file consists of nested metadata attached as facet definitions in the first part of the document and of references between the defined facets and the assigned topics in the second part of the document [2]. Topics reference to facets with the lowest hierarchical level. Not all topics need to have a facet and not all facets need to be referenced by a topic which is why only referenced facets and topics will be displayed in the CDS [10]. The structure of the ontology output file for the facet structure is a combination of the facet terms of the relevant chapters and the relations between the facet terms. Each facet is assigned to one of four <facet-tree> elements because each type attribute of a <facet-tree> represents one of the four basic classes of the PI-Class® method (https://www.i4icm.de/en/research-transfer/pi-classification/).

8 Outlook

This research paper only shows the realisation of one content delivery solution based on an ontology. The data transformation, however, can be adjusted for multiple CDS and the ontology can be used as a model for different content inputs. Due to the concrete specifications of the knowledge network, content elements are machine readable, which enables the usage of this content according to artificial intelligence.

9 Conclusion

This research has shown that ontologies do not only grant advantages in contrast to a CMS but also offer transformation processes for the data import into a CDS that lead to unforeseen advantages. Ontologies as knowledge networks use relationships to set logical references between elements and use relations in more than one context. These relationships were used for the transformation process and were able to enrich context information for users by offering static and dynamic linking inside topics. The filtering of the facet file is restricted because of the considerations regarding the adoption of the given book structure. Since a book structure is not helpful in enriching the information deployment, an ontology sets clear restrictions of how to be able to use context information. This has the advantage that users do not have too many options when searching for information, helping them to find information with as little effort and little time as possible. Considering this aspect and the representation of content inside a CDS, the possibility of not being stuck to a document or book structure is given within this research. Further research on using even deeper relations inside an ontology is recommended to enrich the user experience even more.

We would like to give thanks to all the institutions which rendered our journey to Japan possible and helped with the realisation of this project. We therefore thank the International Office, the Faculty of Information Management and Media, the AStA Studierendenschaft HsKA, the Master's program Communication and Media Management for financial support, Dominik Kremer from DOCUFY GmbH and Achim Steinacker from intelligent views GmbH for great collaboration and insightful discussions. Especially, we would like to thank Prof. Dr. Ziegler of Karlsruhe University of Applied Sciences, Germany, and Prof. Dr. Roy of University of Aizu, Japan, for organising the exchange between the countries and for managing the whole project.

References

1. A. Ahmadpour and A. Wilhelm, *From Information Modeling of Technical Content to Intelligent Delivery*, in ACM Chapter Proceedings on Educational Technology, Language & Technical Communication, ACM 2019, pp. 3–9 (2019)
2. K.-B. Hanczaryk, *XML Content Transformation and Import Interfaces for Content Delivery Portals*, in ACM Chapter Proceedings on Educational Technology, Language & Technical Communication, ACM 2019, pp. 25–34 (2019)
3. W. Ziegler, *Intelligente Informationen*. in Schriften zur Technischen Kommunikation, Volume 22, pp. 51-53 (2017)
4. W. Ziegler, *Basic Concepts Which Support the Management and Delivery of Intelligent Content*, In Frontier, Official Journal of Japan Technical Communicators Association JTCA, p. 89 (2017)
5. N. F. Noy and D. L. McGuinness, *Ontology Development 101: A Guide to Creating Your First Ontology*, Stanford University, Stanford, CA, https://protege.stanford.edu/publications/ontology_development/ontology101-noy-mcguinness.html (n.d.)
6. D. Gaševic, D. Djuric, and V. Devedžic, *Model Driven Architecture and Ontology Development*, Springer Verlag, Berlin, Heidelberg, p. 46 (2009)
7. W. Ziegler, *Delivery zwischen Kontext und Content*, in technische kommunikation, 41(6), pp. 58–61 (2019)
8. intelligent views GmbH, *About us*, https://i-views.com/en/about-us/ (2019)
9. intelligent views GmbH, *i-views 5.3*, http://documentation.i-views.com/manual/5.3/86cc538a-370b-4899-b711-191aca85bdff#4aa2898f-2bf5-4cdc-b41a-aebd09b6c56a-chapter (n.d.)
10. DOCUFY GmbH, *TopicPilot 3.5 – Importspezifikationen*, pp. 8–12, 17, 20 [unpublished] (2019)
11. DOCUFY GmbH, *Spezifikation – DYXML2*, pp. 22, 104 [unpublished] (2018)

Approaches for deployment and access of content in delivery portals

Theresa Rauffmann[1*] and *Monika* Wolf[1**]

[1]Karlsruhe University of Applied Sciences, Faculty of Information Management and Media, 76133 Karlsruhe, Germany

Abstract. In the field of Technical Communication the focus has always been on supporting users in their search for information in a way that is appropriate for the target group. Products are becoming more and more complex, current standards require manufacturers to provide up-to-date Technical Documentation and digitalization is advancing rapidly. Content Delivery Portals offer new possibilities to provide information in a timely and user-friendly manner. They make it possible to provide the user with web-based, target-group specific information through navigation with facets and presents a new possible use of search engines in Technical Documentation. This paper deals with different possibilities on how content can be deployed and accessed for the user. The approaches are implemented in tools that are already on the market to illustrate the possibilities of deployment and access on real-life circumstances. In addition, an outlook is given on what the conceptual implementation of microDocs might look like.

1 Introduction

Search engines are ever-present in our everyday life. The most used search engines providing us with various information are Google, Yahoo!, bing, Baidu and YANDEX RU [1]. They present search results when the user, for example, searches for a restaurant nearby, for specific products or simply to retrieve general information of just about anything.

In our research we dealt with search engines in a very specific field. Companies try to use enterprise search systems to provide users with the necessary information needed for their situation in the shortest time possible. We investigated two approaches to provide content for the user, tested the possibilities of filtering and elaborated on both of the approaches by means of two different Content Delivery Portals.

2 Theoretical Overview

Although already widely known within the field of Technical Communication, this paper will give a short overview on the methods of generating Technical Documentation, especially on those used for the academic project of Karlsruhe University of Applied Sciences and the University of Aizu in context of Content Delivery Portals and ontology usage. In order to do so, it is important to explain the definition of the terms topics and documents with which technical writers work while generating Technical Documentation and the reasons why some technical writers prefer one method over the other. Furthermore, the usage of metadata and its relevance will be clarified, especially relating to this research.

For our research topic we wanted to find out if it is more practicable to work with single topic files or with whole documents. To accomplish this, we worked with different systems and different types of filters. The initial question was: How can we best engineer our content for the user accessing it in a Content Delivery Portal?

2.1 Topic

In the field of Technical Communication a topic is defined as content that is self-contained and can be understood without further context. Overall, there is a rule that just one thought should be integrated in one topic, so that the content is clear and easily understandable and the user does not get overwhelmed with too much information he does not need at that time [2].

2.1.1 Topics and metadata

To define a topic unambiguously, metadata is needed. With clearly defined metadata, a specific topic can be retrieved and differentiated from other, similar topics. There are different concepts for attaching metadata to a topic. In the academic project of Karlsruhe University of Applied Sciences and University of Aizu, the PI-Concept which was developed by Prof. Dr. Wolfgang Ziegler was used for the metadata. This concept consists of different types of metadata. On one hand, there is metadata that describes the product and on the other hand there is metadata that describes the type of information given. Furthermore, the PI-Concept differentiates between intrinsic and extrinsic metadata [3]. Intrinsic metadata describes the product or the information itself and explains what it is, so for example, the product is the smart home device "smart bulb" and the information type is a task. Extrinsic metadata describes, where the product or the information is used, for example, a specific cable is

*Theresa Rauffmann: rath1019@hs-karlsruhe.de
**Monika Wolf: womo1012@hs-karlsruhe.de

used in the smart home device "smart bulb" and the information is used in an installation manual.

2.2 Document

Often, it is not enough just to view a single topic to help the user deal with his problem. For example, if the user wants to know how to install the app for controlling the smart home device "home energy use monitor", he may need further information about the app, the registration for the app or maybe he needs to know how he can connect his smartphone to wifi to download the app. For some topics, it is insufficient to just show the user this specific topic, but he needs further information from other similar topics to fulfill the steps he wants to do with his product.

One approach to solve this problem is by working with full documents. In the field of Technical Writing it has long time been the standard and often still is to think of documents as a whole that consists of different topics in a logical order. Documents are structured by different concepts, for example, the table of contents at the beginning gives a first overview as to where the user can find certain information. But there are other approaches for the user to navigate as well, like glossaries or cross-references in printed document and hyperlinks in Online- or PDF-documents. The benefit of a document is that you have full context and all of the information that is needed for one special product to be found in one place. There should be no questions without answers left after reading the whole documentation. But that is just a theoretical view on how a user can use Technical Documentation. In real-life nearly no one reads an entire document of Technical Documentation for a certain product. He simply searches for the information piece or topic he needs and possibly uses other topics to get some more context. Therefore, sometimes a single topic isn't enough because the user needs more context, but a whole document is often too much.

2.3 Evaluation of topics vs document

In every-day life both approaches – giving user information with single topics or in a whole document – have their reason for existence. Everything depends on how much content the technical writer has already gathered. If there is no Technical Documentation readily available, many technical writers work with a top-down-approach where they generate single topics based on rules and use them in a Content Delivery Portal. If there is already some published Technical Documentation the technical writers often already thought in whole documents and normally just works ahead with this bottom-up-approach [4].

3 Implementation of the research topic in a real project

For the project between the students of Karlsruhe University of Applied Sciences and the University of Aizu, the topic "Smart Home" was defined, which is why the content in the following chapters will be related to this topic.

For the research, the software Smart Media Creator, developed by Expert Communication Systems, was used as a Component Content Management System (CCMS) to create the content, metadata and facets in. In the course of the project, content was implemented into the CCMS and provided with metadata oriented on the PI-Concept, which builds the basis for this research. Additionally, two Content Delivery Portals were used into which the content and facets were imported to see the output. The two portals are i-views content, which is the Content Delivery Portal developed by the company intelligent views gmbh and Schema Content Delivery Server, short SchemaCDS, developed by Schema gmbh.

3.1 Export of content and facets in the Component Content Management System

To export content and facets into the Component Content Management System Smart Media Creator, so-called "books" are packed. To clarify the difference between a book for the export of content and a book for the export of facets in this project, the terms "content book" and "facet book" are used. To export content, a "content book" is created and the modules containing the metadata are referenced. Metadata must also be assigned to the "content book" itself, as to be able to filter for the book later in the Content Delivery Portal. To export facets, a "facet book" is created and metadata is arranged in a structure that should show up later as facets in the CDP.

3.2 Implementation of the approaches for deployment of content

For the approach of deploying documents, "content books" were created in the CCMS that included all topics that belong to a certain smart home device and metadata were assigned to that book. On the other hand, for the approach of deploying single topics, a "content book" was created for each topic and all the metadata were assigned to that book that the topic itself contained. On the Figures 1 and 2 the outcome is displayed. The single topic book has a lot more metadata assigned than the document book, because the content of the book can be specifically classified.

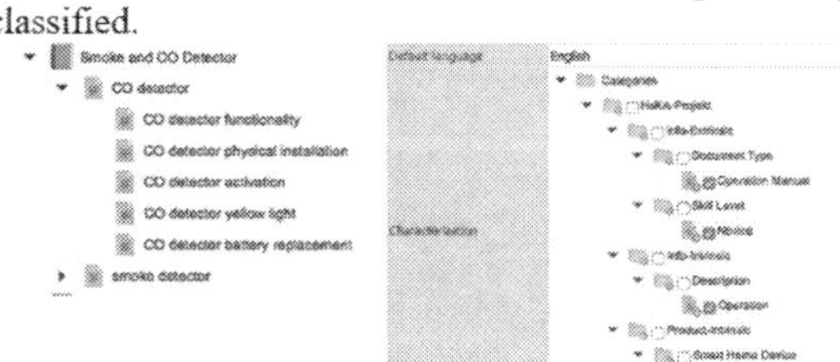

Fig. 1. "content book" and metadata for the approach of deploying documents

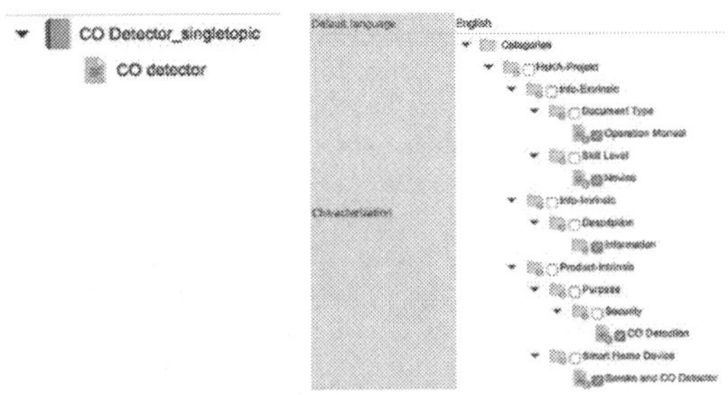

Fig. 2. "content book" and metadata for the approach of deploying single topics

3.3 Implementation of the approach for access of content

For the access, a "facet book" was created in the CCMS. The structure for these facets was not designed to comply with the PI-Concept, but to fit the user behaviour looking up information and to name the facets self-explanatory.

This decision is based on the consideration that a user is not familiar with the terms and the logic of the PI-Concept. This means, for example, that he would rather search for a facet that is called "Installation" and maybe then filters for a "description" or a "task" about the installation than to search for a facet that is called "Information-intrinsic".

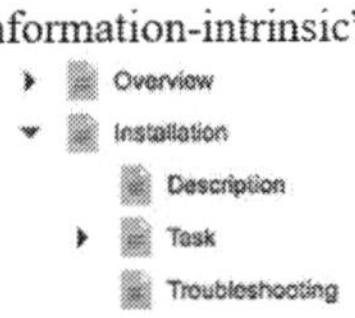

Fig. 3. "facet book" for the approach of access of content

3.4 Evaluation of the approaches for deployment and access of content in Content Delivery Portals

3.4.1 Import of the content and the facets into i-views content

For the research the intelligent views gmbh provided the Graph knowledgebuilder where the ontology was created by a group of students and the functions of the CDP could be configured. The settings made for the CDP in the Graph knowledgebuilder are displayed immediately in the CDP. For more information about the ontology and functions in the Graph knowledgebuilder see: Ontologies and use cases based planning of content delivery.

In the Graph knowledgebuilder it is intended to import content and metadata with the iiRDS format. To do this, the imported metadata must have exactly the same name as the ontology objects in order to automatically link the content with the Knowledge Network.

Because the CCMS that was used in this project couldn't provide the content with iiRDS, the workaround was to create single Chapter-Instances in the i-views Graph knowledgebuilder for each topic and add the plain HTML-Code of the content.

Using this workaround, it was not possible to import the metadata that were already assigned to the content in the CCMS or to import the "facet book". To still get a filter option in the i-views CDP, a relation to the ontology had to be set manually.

Since there was only the opportunity to import the HTML-Code for every single topic manually, there were already single topics created. For the documents the same procedure had to be applied but in the end, the single Chapter-Instances had to be interlaced to get a "document".

3.4.2 Output of the approaches in i-views CDP

Since the transfer of metadata and facets from the CCMS to i-views was not possible due to the different exchange formats, the differences between the approach of deploying a document and single topics cannot be specifically identified. However, the general possibilities of searching in the CDP can be mentioned:

In the CDP the user has to type in the search field of the starting page a keyword to get the filter search showing. The results are all topics, that include the keyword in the heading or the actual content and you also have the opportunity to set specific filters. When the user clicks on a topic, it shows the topic and additionally on the left side the structure of the document where it is located.

3.4.3 Import of the content and the facets into SchemaCDS

The content and its metadata from the CCMS was exported in the XML format and transformed into a zip.-file that could be imported into SchemaCDS. The facets can be delivered similar by importing a navigation.xml in the facet section of SchemaCDS. For more information about the transformation of data see: Data transformations from CMS to CDP enriched by semantics.

3.4.4 Output of the approach for deploying documents in SchemaCDS

For the approach of deploying documents the "content books" were imported that included all topics about one device and the "facet book". Fig. 4 demonstrates facet filters on the left sidebar. These facets are created by the "facet book" imported before. If the "facet book" included metadata that are not assigned to any "content book", they wouldn't show up in the sidebar. Another finding is, that there is no opportunity to search for metadata that are assigned to the topics contained in the books on this sidebar.

For filtering those specific topics there are two other options. One way is to type in a search word in the search field. Then it suggests all topics and documents that include that search word and also shows if the topic is a main chapter of a book or a lower chapter. Another way is to click on a document and open the filter criteria panel where you can also filter for topics within a document as displayed on the figure.

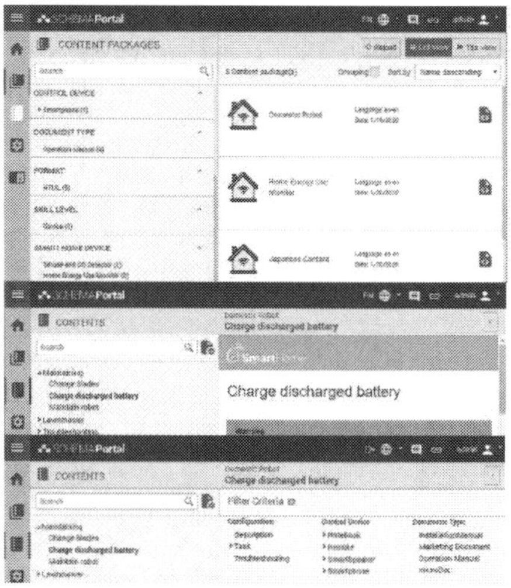

Fig. 4. Output of the approach for deploying documents in SchemaCDS

3.4.5 Output of the approache of deploying single topics in SchemaCDS

For the approach of deploying single topics the "content books" were imported that each included just one topic and the same "facet book" that we used for the approach for deploying documents.

Because every single topic book has assigned the metadata of the topic, all metadata are shown at the start at the left sidebar. It provides further opportunities to find your single topic right at the beginning of the users research without looking for them in whole documents. When the user clicks on a single topic, the filter criteria can also be expanded but since there is no book, there are no results when creating a filter.

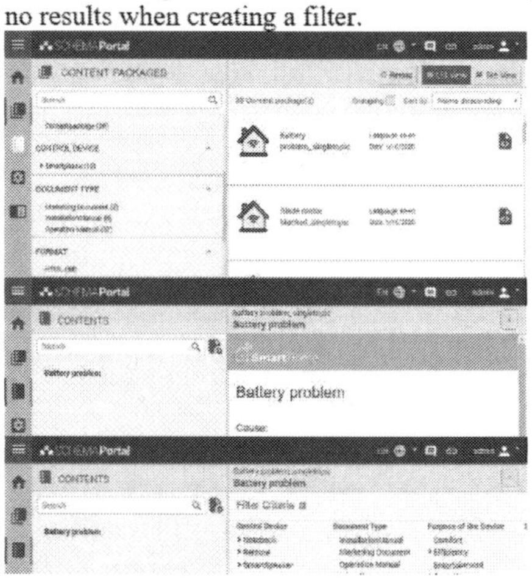

Fig. 5. Output of the approach for deploying single topics in SchemaCDS

3.5 Further approach to access single topics

Since the sidebar shows all facets that are assigned to the "content book" as metadata, it is very crowded when using the approach of providing topics. One way to reduce this information overflow, and support the user in his facet search, is to change the structure of the facets. The approach differs from the approach described in chapter 3.3 to restructure the PI-Concept to a small extent and to reformulate the terms in a user-friendly way and concentrates on structuring the facets into several small blocks. The structure is intended to be a list through which the user can click in order to get the desired information. In addition, the SchemaCDS offers the function that only facets that have been assigned to the account as metadata are displayed. This function helps the user to see what further information is available on his topic. An example is shown in Fig. 6. If the user is looking for installation instructions, he can see that there is also a troubleshooting available.

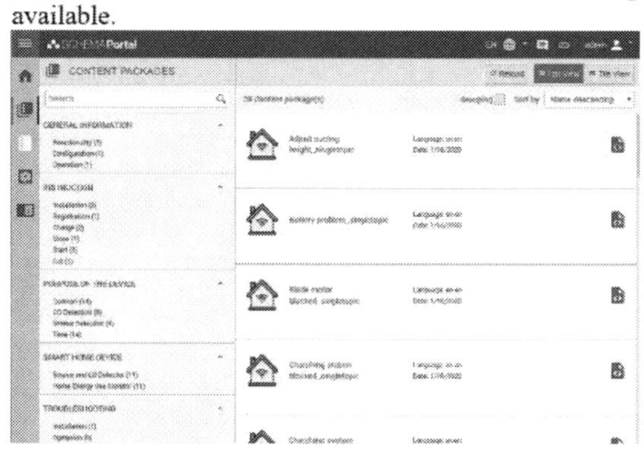

Fig. 6. Further approach for access of single topics in SchemaCDS

4 Discourse: microDocs

The comparison of documents and single topics that are deployed and accessed by a user in a Content Delivery Portal let us assume, that it depends on the use case which approach is the better one. It also showed, that both approaches are not ideal. There is another possibility to provide the user the content in the CDP. This possibility is relatively new and is called microDoc [5].

4.1 Definition microDoc

A microDoc [6] is a collection of a few topics that are contextual. For example, if a user wants to know how to install the app for the home energy monitor on his smartphone, he normally wants to know how to register and use the app as well. In a whole document, he could normally find this information in the next chapter. In single topics, he could find this information in topics with similar filter criteria. In a microDoc, he can find this contextual information at first glance.

4.2 Creation of microDocs

Because microDocs are relatively new, there is no common approach how to create them until now. Top level would be used, if you could create microDocs automatically based on rules on the metadata that combine some topics with similar metadata. Another efficient approach would be to track the users trace in a CDP to get to know which topics he needs, one after the other, and to create microDocs based on this tracking results.

4.3 Workaround creation of microDocs in this research

In the research it was not possible to use an automatic option for creating microDocs or to track the user. The first implementation phase was used for microDocs which means that the microDocs were created manually by hand. The microDocs were created by defined rules that can only be applied to the specific domain of the research: the content about smart home devices and specific defined use cases.

4.3.1 Topic types for microDocs

The content that was created and used within this research project consists of different topic types. These are: description, task, troubleshooting and glossary entry. The rules for the microDocs created from the content are affected by these topic types.

4.3.2 Specific rules for microDocs in this research field

1) A microDoc consists of at least 3 topics and at most 7 topics.
2) A microDoc can contain content about different smart home devices (for the use case general information).
3) Normally, a microDoc should only contain content about one specific smart home device.
4) A task (how to install the app) always comes with a description (what is the app) and if available the description of the app's functionality or a superordinated topic that helps to get to know where this information belongs.
   a) If there is a troubleshooting topic that helps to solve a problem to this specific task, it should be also contained in the microDoc.
   b) If there is a glossary entry topic for one of the words used in the task, it should be also contained in the microDoc.
5) If several different tasks must be performed to complete a task, they belong to one microDoc.
6) If the user cannot do anything with an instruction without further instructions, then further instructions belong in a microDoc until the result is satisfactory.
   a) e.g. task_install_the_app, task_setup_of_wifi, task_registration_at_the_app
7) A microDoc only consists of different troubleshooting topics in individual cases, if they should be coherent. Otherwise the user isn't interested in other problems.

5 Results

5.1 Single topics vs. document

We assumed, that people are used to document structures and use the table of content of the document to navigate. Therefore, the document offers a common access to the user. The single topics only offer the facet filter to navigate. Hence, the access to a single topics has to be in a clearly arranged structure. In a further step, the compatibility with different use cases would have to be tested in order to be able to make a statement about which approach is better suited for which applications. The foundation for this research was presented with this work.

5.2 microDocs

In our research, the ideal way of using the single topic books is with the described microDocs as an add-on. This would be an approach of combining the two aforementioned methods. MicroDocs do not provide as much information as whole documents do and do not provide too little information without context as single topic books do. The best way to implement microDocs would be by means of automated creation.

5.3 Compatibility of different tools

Using different tools can cause problems because of the missing standardization of exchange formats. Even with standardized exchange formats like iiRDS, using different tools can be complicated since the terminology of the metadata has to be exactly the same in both tools.

The authors would like to thank the International students' registry, the Faculty of Information Management and Media, the AStA Studierendenschaft HsKA, the Master's Program Communication and Media Management for financial support, Achim Steinacker from intelligent views GmbH, Tim Rausch from Schema GmbH and Ladivia Roehrl from Expert Communication Systems GmbH for great collaboration, insightful discussions and support and Professor Roy from University of Aizu for the organizational support.

References

1. Statcounter, Search Engine Market Share Worldwide. [Online]. Available: https://gs.statcounter.com/searchengine-market-share (2020)
2. S. Coss, Single Source Publishing – Modularer Content für EPUB & Co., 49, (2011)
3. P. Drewer, W.Ziegler, Technische Dokumentation-Übersetzungsgerechte Texterstellung und Content-Management, 367-371, (2014)
4. P. Drewer, W.Ziegler, Technische Dokumentation-Übersetzungsgerechte Texterstellung und Content-Management, 306-310, (2014)
5. W. Ziegler, Delivery zwischen Kontext und Content, technische kommunikation, vol. 6, 58-61, (2019)
6. W. Ziegler, Extending intelligent content delivery in technical communication by semantics: micro documents and content services, Proceedings of the ETLTC ACM Chapter International Conference. Aizuwakamatsu, Japan. (2020)

Data transformations from CMS to CDP enriched by semantics

Christina Salwitzek[1*] and *Christina* Steuer[1**]

[1]Karlsruhe University of Applied Sciences, Faculty of Information Management and Media, 76133 Karlsruhe, Germany

Abstract. Today's users no longer expect a classic manual, but short, clearly structured pieces of information that fit their application context, use case and role. Instead of conventional documentation, "intelligent information" is required that is modular, format-neutral and can be found via metadata and full-text search. The information is often created in a CMS and provided via CDPs. There are not always compatible interfaces between these systems, especially those of different software manufacturers. Therefore, the information created cannot be processed further. The purpose of this paper is to show that data transformations can provide accessibility for the information from a CMS for different CDPs. On this basis, data transformations were developed, enriched by semantics and implemented within the project. For the enrichment by semantics, metadata were used as well as a further approach based on metadata, called "microDocs". This approach describes the combination and aggregation of different topic-based information that are connected by defined use cases and a logical context. Some CDP manufacturers already support microDocs and it is expected that even more extensions will be implemented in the future. Accordingly, it is highly likely that microDocs will play an important role in the field of information delivery.

1 Introduction

To make information accessible, it must be published in a certain format in a specific system. To provide information that is fast, target group-based and context-based, the information can be published in a Content Delivery Portal (CDP). The data source for a CDP is in most cases a Content Management System (CMS).

For many companies, a CMS is a standard tool for creating documentation. The CMS is tasked with the systematic collection, creation, storage and refinement of structured information and media data in a single, finely granulated stock. [1]

To ensure an efficient delivery of the created information to the user, it is transferred to a CDP. The CDP is an online system for providing this information. The provision is done by modular or aggregated information that are accessed by different target groups using content-related search mechanisms. [2]

1.1 Content retrieval

To ensure that the information is selectively adapted to the user's situation and efficiently accessible, the concept of "Content Retrieval" is used within a CDP. Content Retrieval is the search for information in a specific portal, for example a CDP. Based on Content Retrieval there are two main approaches to search for information within a CDP [2]. These approaches include the direct and the structured search. The main difference of these approaches is the usage of metadata. [2].

1.2 Direct search

The direct search is based on a full-text database which already includes search terms and phrases [3]. It can be optimized, by using ontologies or terminology databases. An example for the direct search is the "Google Search".

1.3 Structured search

The structured search is based on metadata which is handed over by the CMS where the information is initially classified. For the structured search there are two different approaches which differ in their usage of metadata and use cases. The two different approaches are "navigation" and "filtering".

The navigation approach involves the use of navigation trees to follow along the "classical document structure including nested topics" [3]. The basis for the navigation is intrinsic and extrinsic metadata, variant properties and the document structure (see section 3.2.1 "Metadata Concept" for more details about these metadata types).

The filtering approach uses facets to search "corresponding to complex classification taxonomies or more simple metadata sets from CMS" [3]. The basis for

* Christina Salwitzek: sach1023@hs-karlsruhe.de
** Christina Steuer: stch1033@hs-karlsruhe.de

the filtering is intrinsic and extrinsic metadata as well as variant properties or functional metadata.

Within the project the navigation enabled the user to maneuver through modules in a document and localize his position within a document. The data which was used to implement this approach was the document structure, which was built previously in the CMS. The filtering was used to filter a document ("outer facets") and to filter modules within a document ("inner facets"). A more detailed explanation about the faceting possibilities can be found in section 2.3 "Data Transformation Process".

2 Data transformations

Content is often created in a CMS and provided via a CDP. However, there are not always compatible interfaces between these systems, especially between systems from different software manufacturers. These technical barriers prevent a platform-spanning delivery of information. In this case, data transformations enable the transfer of data from a CMS to variant CDPs that differ in the data format. Therefore, data transformations ensure accessibility of the content in several CDPs of different manufacturers.

2.1 Basics of data transformation

In order to understand the basics of data transformation the most important components need to be discussed in more detail (see Fig. 1). These components are:

A: Data input: XML document and media

B: Transformation process: XSLT Processor and XSL Stylesheet

C: Data output: content published in different formats for multiple use cases

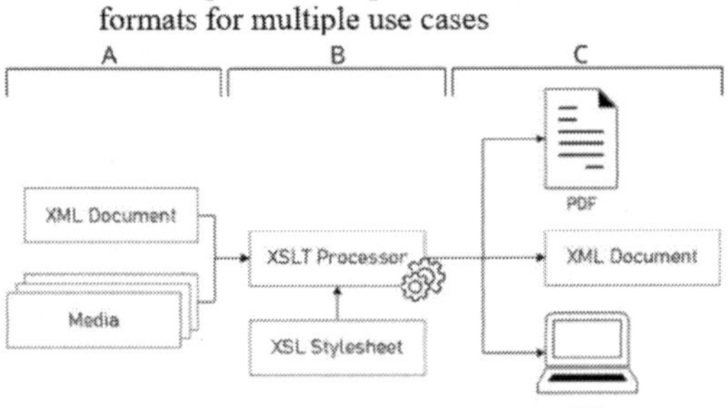

Fig. 1. Components of an XSL Transformation.

The basis of a data transformation is the input data itself. This data can include different content and formats, based on the use case and the source of the data. In order to process the data, an XSLT processor is required. The rules of processing are provided by an XSL stylesheet which is the core of the data transformation. Within the XSL stylesheet all transformation rules are defined for the appropriate output format. For each transformation, a batch file was used to automate this process. The result of the data transformation is the content from the input data in the required output format. This output format is used afterwards to publish the content. [4]

2.2 Data sources

The input for data transformations can be obtained from different data sources. Data sources that can be used for transformations are CMS, ontology editors and other databases (e.g. product information systems) [5]. The most common data source for a CDP is a CMS. Within a CMS the content is typically organized within modules in a certain XML structure, including metadata (see section 1 "Introduction"). Ontology editors as data sources are also getting more popular as ontologies enrich content by relations, which "improves the manual and automated search processes and allows a new and dynamic view on the information" [6]. Within an industrial context, not only CMS or ontology editors should be considered as data sources but also other databases within the company which provide useful information. Depending on the data sources, different output formats are provided. In general, most of the data sources provide the output format XML, which can be further processed via XSLT.

2.3 Data transformation process

The mentioned basics are part of the data transformation process in which certain content objects (also called topics) of a data stock, in this case a CMS, are transformed so that they can be correctly interpreted, indexed and found by the search system of an information portal, here the CDP. The data transformation process of this project can be divided into three essential stages: "preparation", "transformation" and "import".

2.3.1 *Preparation*

In the first stage, the preparation, the content must be created in the CMS editor in a standardized way and classified with metadata. The modularized content, which is to be published or exported, is compiled in a so-called "book". This book is exported in the descriptive mark-up language XML so it can be transformed with XSLT in the following stage. If the CMS content also contains graphics, a zip file will be created during the export, which includes the XML document and a separate folder with all graphic files (see Fig. 2). In order to be able to filter in the CDP according to different classification properties, an additional book, the metadata book, will be compiled which contains all possible metadata. This book is also exported as an XML document for further processing.

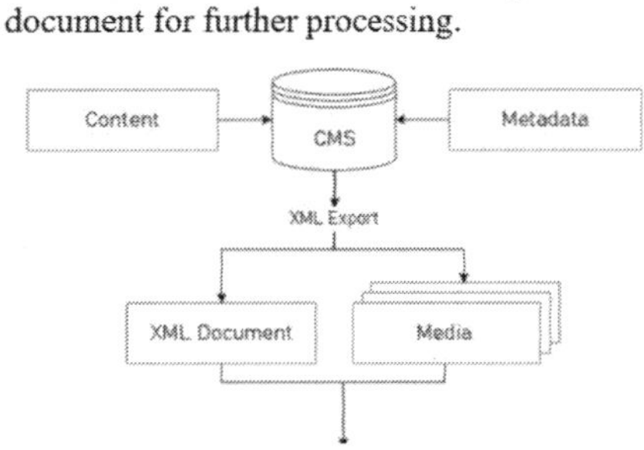

Fig. 2. Schematic illustration of the preparation stage.

2.3.2 Transformation

In the next stage, the actual data transformation, XSLT is used to convert the CMS content into the target format that can be interpreted by the CDP (see Fig. 3). By applying the XSLT stylesheet to the XML document, XSLT uses XPath to define parts of the XML document that should match one or more predefined templates. When a match is found, XSLT transforms the matching part of the XML document into the desired format [4]. As an outcome of the transformation, result documents are created from the source file. The individual transformations developed for the project generate result documents in HTML format for the CDP "CDS" (Schema Company) and "iviews content" (intelligent views Company), whereas the data transformation for the CDP "TopicPilot" (DOCUFY Company) generates documents in the system-specific format "DYXML", which is based on XML. As can be observed, the transformations are similar in their basic structure, but they differ due to system-specific adaptations, which are the result of manufacturer-specific implementations.

The XML document, which was exported from the metadata book in the preparation stage, is transformed into a so-called "facet file" using XSLT. Due to specific structural requirements that need to be fulfilled by the facet file, an additional data transformation was developed. The generated facet file is an XML document that contains all possible metadata and enables filtering in the CDP according to different classification properties, provided that the content has been classified appropriately in the preparation stage. The CDS portal allows a so-called inner faceting (searching for a module within a document) and outer faceting (searching for a document). In this case the facet file is responsible for the outer faceting. The inner faceting refers to filtering within the content packages. According to different classification properties, the system filters by topics that contain the selected property. For the inner faceting to work in the CDP, the corresponding metadata must be written into each topic during the transformation, therefore no separate (facet) file is needed.

The transformed data must be packed as a zip file so it can be imported into the CDP. This zip file must meet the system-specific requirements of the respective CDP manufacturer (e.g. a certain folder structure and designation), otherwise the upload of the zip file will fail. For an automated and therefore faster and error-free generation of the zip file, batch scripts were developed for the data transformations. The commands of the batch scripts not only zip the transformed files in the structure required by the CDP, they also trigger the data transformations. In the CDS portal and the TopicPilot portal, which were used for this project, these zip files are called "content packages". The previously mentioned facet file is not part of the content package, since it is generally valid for all content packages. Accordingly, although this file is transformed by the batch script transformation command, it is not zipped with the other files. This process can be controlled by specifying the batch script commands.

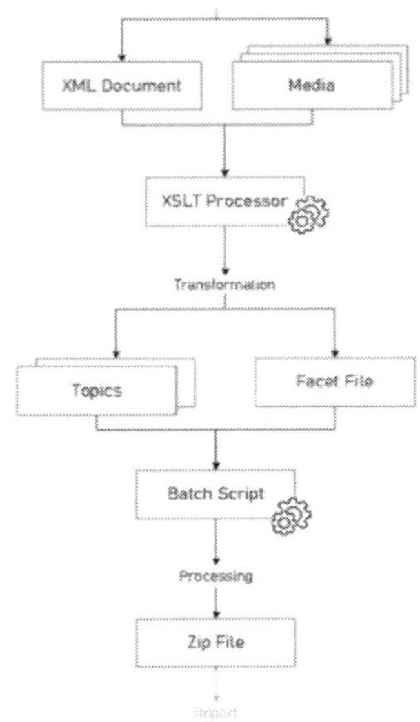

Fig. 3. Schematic illustration of the transformation stage.

2.3.3 Import

The last stage of the data transformation process describes the import of the data into the CDP. The previously mentioned content packages can be uploaded via the CDP import interface, whereas the facet file is imported separately via the facet interface. Once the upload is successful, the content packages and the possible filter options are displayed either in the content collection page or in the overview page (depending on the CDP). The inner and outer facets can now be applied to filter by topics or by content packages. The filter functions also offer the possibility to filter according to one or more properties to further narrow down the result. In addition, a navigation is provided, which is automatically generated by the structure of the content packages.

In summary, an interface was developed during the project between one CMS and the CDPs from several manufacturers. Therefore, the CMS content from Expert Communication Systems was transformed and imported successfully into the CDPs of Schema, intelligent views and DOCUFY.

3 Enrich data transformations

After describing how the first objective of the project was attained, the following sections explain the achievement of the second objective: transferring "intelligent content" from a CMS into CDPs.

3.1 Intelligent content

In general, "intelligent content is designed to be modular, structured, reusable, format free and semantically rich and, as a consequence, discoverable, reconfigurable, and adaptable" [7]. However, it is still difficult to delimit the concept of "intelligent content", as an unambiguous definition is not easy to present. In order to get a better understanding of the term itself and the multiple concepts of intelligent content in the context of technical communication, it is advisable to take a closer look at the "Intelligence Cascade" [2, 8].

The Intelligence Cascade consists of three levels. The first level is "Native Intelligence" and refers to the semantic structuring and classification of modular and format-neutral content, e.g. to automate processes in the CMS [6]. For a logical and standardized classification of content with metadata, classification methods like the "PI-classification scheme" can be used to "systematically express the validity [...] with regard to product components and information classes" [8]. The classification of content objects makes them machine-readable and supports navigation and filter functions, for example in CDPs. "Augmented Intelligence", the second level of the Intelligence Cascade, describes additional relations between different content objects, for example by ontologies as already mentioned in section 2.2 "Data Sources". The third level is "Artificial Intelligence" and refers to the automated extraction of metadata and knowledge by statistical methods [8]. This level was not considered within the project because of the limited time frame.

Regarding the project, content was created modular, format-neutral and structured within the CMS editor. Each content object, as well as the so-called books were classified with structured and semantic metadata. The term "structured" means here that typified metadata have been assigned, which follow a certain classification system, in this case the PI-classification. "Semantic" metadata refers to metadata whose meaning is formally defined. This allows the definition of formal axioms and allows conclusions to be drawn. Accordingly, semantic metadata can be used to make implicit knowledge explicit [9]. However, to ensure consistency and efficiency in creating, customizing and reusing the metadata as well as the content, a standardized metadata concept must first be established, which is described in more detail in the following section.

3.2 Enrich data transformations through a CMS

3.2.1 Metadata concept

As mentioned above, the content from a CMS and correspondingly also the data transformation can be enriched by using metadata. Within the project, the PI-classification scheme was used as a model to assign the content with semantic metadata. Using the PI-classification, a further distinction can be made between "intrinsic" and "extrinsic" metadata [1]. Based on the PI-classification, the metadata types were also extended with functional metadata (e.g. for error messages or code associated with topics) and variant properties (e.g. for technical configuration parameters or installation locations) [1].

Based on these metadata types a taxonomic metadata concept was developed and assigned for all modular information. The metadata concept was also used as a reference for the subsequent data transformation, in which both the facet file with all possible metadata, and the individual content objects or topics with the corresponding metadata were generated (see section 2.3 "Data Transformation Process").

3.2.2 MicroDocs

The previous paragraphs illustrate that metadata is the core of "intelligent content". Consequently, it is also possible to enrich content with further approaches based on metadata. One approach highlighted in the project was the approach of "microDocs" [10, 11].

"A microDoc is [...] the (sub)set of topics or other information units that are connected by defined use cases and a logical context and are available as a dynamic connection via a search or delivery system" [10]. Therefore, using the approach of microDocs in information portals like a CDP, further information that could be also relevant for the user, is displayed.

The following figure shows that a single topic usually cannot provide the user with enough information because it is a self-contained content module. On the other hand, the entire manual contains too much information and cognitively overwhelms the user. The microDoc is located in-between and shows not only one topic, but also the additional relevant topics for the specific use case [10, 11]. For instance: an end customer is looking for operating information and additional functions as well as possible operating errors or dangers are shown. So, a microDoc automatically provides him with information that he will eventually need in his situation.

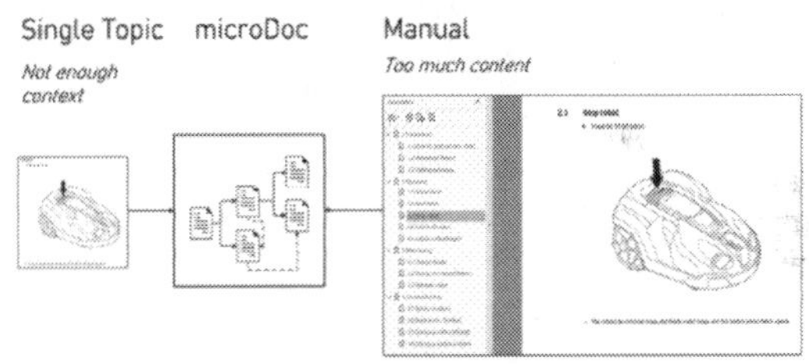

Fig. 4. The approach of microDocs compared to the individual topic and the entire manual. [figure based on 10]

Although the approach of microDocs is universal, there may be differences during implementation and the degree of dynamically generating a microDoc [10].

For example, microDocs can be generated for predefined use cases by a specific and static aggregation of topics by taking content from a CMS and zipping it into application-specific content packages for the CDP.

It is also possible to dynamically aggregate modular information units in CDPs based on semantic metadata, which is assigned in the CMS. The selection of the displayed content objects or links follows logical patterns for specific use cases, for example based on the PI-classification and different user roles.

Contextualization and linking through ontologies for the respective use case make it also possible to dynamically generate microDocs. Accordingly, the previously created ontology must be exported from the ontology editor so that the relations between the topics can be used for the data transformation. While the first two implementation options refer to the level of Native Intelligence, this implementation type includes the level of Augmented Intelligence (see section 3.1 "Intelligent Content").

Even though the term "microDocs" refers to a relatively new approach, some CDP manufacturers already have functions that support the approach of logically linking individual topics. In this respect, the focus during the project was on the CDS portal of Schema and it was discovered that different support functions for microDocs are already implemented at this moment.

One feature that supports the approach of microDocs is the "Related Topics" area. In this case, semantic links that intelligently extend the displayed topic are automatically generated by the metadata assignment in the individual topics and by predefined usage scenarios. The user is therefore shown topics that could be interesting for him as well.

4 Summary and outlook

This paper gave an insight regarding the need for data transformations to transfer content from a CMS to different CDPs, and the possibility to extend the content by semantics by using metadata and further approaches based on metadata.

After the basics of data transformations were mentioned, the transformation process of this project was described step by step. By successfully transforming the data from a CMS and importing it into three CDPs of different manufacturers, it was found that although the structure of the transformations is similar, system-specific rules must be met and adjustments need to be made, so that the content is transformed into the appropriate format of the respective CDP.

Content can become "intelligent" by enriching it with semantic metadata and further approaches based on metadata, for example "microDocs" that can support the user in the search for information by providing several topics that have the same logical context and fit to the user's use case. This logical connection can be created dynamically by assigning semantic metadata to the respective topics, for example by an ontology. Within the project, a specific system, the CDS portal, was focused on in detail and it was discovered that presently there are already integrated support functions for microDocs generated by semantic metadata.

In the future, it is expected that "intelligent information" will become even more important for an efficient and use case specific "Content Retrieval". As mentioned in this paper, there are already different approaches that are currently available, e.g. microDocs. Some CDPs already have first implementations for microDocs and it is expected that even more extensions will be implemented in the future. Moreover, the dynamic creation of microDocs could be supported by ontologies. A further step would be to get to the third level of the "Intelligence Cascade": Artificial Intelligence. Machine Learning and Deep Learning could make it possible that metadata is automatically assigned. For future projects also a closer look at ontologies could be interesting for new insights in the enrichment of data.

The authors would like to thank the International Office, the Faculty of Information Management and Media as well as the master's degree Program Communication and Media Management of Karlsruhe University of Applied Sciences for their support. Thank you to Dominik Kremer (DOCUFY Company), Tim Rausch (Schema Company) and to Lena Padeken (Karlsruhe University of Applied Sciences) for the great collaboration, insightful discussions and for their support. We would also like to thank Prof. Debopriyo Roy (University of Aizu) for the organizational support and Evan Stoddard for proofreading of this publication.

References

1. P. Drewer, W. Ziegler, *Technische Dokumentation: eine Einführung in die übersetzungsgerechte Texterstellung und in das Content-Management,* 2nd Edition, Vogel (2014)
2. W. Ziegler, *The Evolution of Content Management towards Intelligent Delivery Systems for Technical Communication*, Frontier, Official Journal of Japan Technical Communicators Association JTCA, 68-75 (2017)
3. W. Ziegler, *Semantic Information Development for Intelligent Content Delivery*, Frontier, Official Journal of Japan Technical Communicators Association JTCA, 18-29 (2019)
4. W3Schools, *XSL(T) Languages* (Retrieved February 17, 2020 from https://www.w3schools.com/xml/xsl_languages.asp 2020)
5. W. Ziegler, *Drivers of Digital Information Services: Intelligent Information Architectures in Technical Communication*, Proceedings of the ETLTC ACM Chapter International Conference, 48-52 (2019)
6. H. Fischer, L. Krägel, *Modeling of Complex Metadata in Technical Communication by Ontologies*, Proceedings of the ETLTC ACM Chapter International Conference, 11-16 (2019)
7. A. Rockley, C. Cooper, S. Abel, *Intelligent Content: A Primer*, XML Press (2015)
8. W. Ziegler, *Metadaten für intelligenten Content*, Intelligente Information: Schriften zur Technischen Kommunikation, **22**, 51-66 (2017)
9. W. Babik, H. Ohly, K. Weber, *Theorie, Semantik und Organisation von Wissen*, Fortschritte in der Wissensorganisation, **13**, 252-253 (2017)
10. W. Ziegler, *Delivery zwischen Kontext und Content*, technische kommunikation, **6**, 58-61 (2019)
11. W. Ziegler, *Extending intelligent content delivery in technical communication by semantics: micro documents and content services*, Proceedings of the ETLTC ACM Chapter International Conference (2020)

SAP Learning Journeys – a double bridge

Sven Leukert*

SAP SE, User Assistance CSI, 69190 Walldorf, Germany

Abstract. SAP Learning Journeys are a key element for providing a guiding path and framework for SAP users and implementation professionals to learn and stay current in their SAP product expertise. They also form a double bridge between the worlds of learning and technical documentation. On one hand, the Learning Journeys themselves are stored and maintained in the DITA content management system used for technical documentation, and then rendered both in the SAP Learning Hub and SAP Help Portal. On the other, the Learning Journeys allow the inclusion and referencing of technical documentation content into the learning offering modelled with the journeys. In this paper we will provide an account of how SAP Learning Journeys are managed and rendered, and what their evolving role is in the world of user enablement.

1 A double bridge

A Learning Journey is a defined path through a set of learning assets associated to a specific product, and often tailored to a specific role, structured into learning scenarios ranging from getting a first overview to becoming proficient, to extending one's skills.

Learning Journeys are visualized as interactive graphics, allowing to explore the details of the individual learning assets (each represented by a tile in the journey), even to navigate directly to the assets and begin learning (provided one already has the required access).

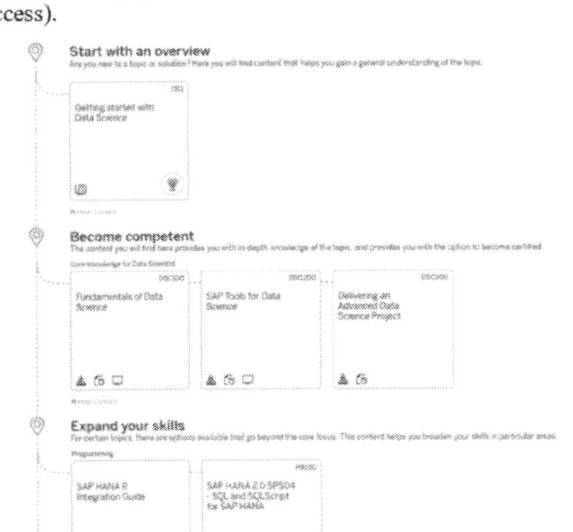

Fig. 1. Example of an SAP Learning Journey structure.

Filtering the Learning Journeys according to product, searching across all Learning Journeys for specific learning content, and within a single journey to filter by asset type are just some of the features provided with SAP Learning Journeys.

See Fig. 1 for an example of a Learning Journey structure or explore SAP Learning Journeys online on the SAP Help Portal [1].

Storing and managing the SAP Learning Journeys in a DITA content management system allows to take advantage of versioning and reuse concepts normally applied to technical documentation content, as well as automated production into different output formats, with rendering specifically adjusted to the respective channel. The Learning Journeys are rendered dynamically into SVG graphics, providing interactive features such as progressive disclosure or filtering.

On the other hand, certain technical content, for example "What's New" information for software products, has so far been included into Learning Journeys as an additional learning asset, often produced with some duplication based on the corresponding technical documentation. Including the What's New deliverables directly into the Learning Journeys eliminates the need for duplicate efforts and ties the two worlds closer together for the learner.

In this sense we have two connections between the worlds of technical documentation and learning – one on the data management side, and one on the content side. This is what we call the "double bridge" between the two worlds.

This article is not so much about ongoing or concluded research as it is an account of how this topic has evolved over the years at SAP. The author is therefore also not the only person responsible for the concepts and results, but there many other people involved in both the technical documentation and learning departments – too many to mention.

2 Learning Journeys in the DITA landscape

The source content for SAP Learning Journeys, including basic header information as well as required metadata, as well as the learning asset details are all maintained in the DITA content management system used for SAP technical product documentation. Each Learning Journey and each tile within the journey is represented by a single DITA topic, each supplied with

* Corresponding author: sven.leukert@sap.com

metadata, and grouped together into DITA maps for production and publishing purposes.

Hosting the Learning Journeys in the DITA content landscape provides a lot of benefits resulting from strong content management capabilities – from complex versioning to automated translation processes, and reuse on all levels of the content. There is also the flexibility to create different flavours of Learning Journeys for different target audiences, for internal learning purposes, and as guidance maps at SAP events.

2.1 Editing

As Learning Journeys and tiles are represented by DITA topics, editing them is essentially the same as for technical documentation topics – typically done in an XML editor, with support for DITA semantics. However, the visual structure of the final journey (as rendered in the output) is what authors have in mind when editing a journey, and very often they are not trained technical authors, so allowing a WYSIWYG approach is desirable.

The structural data of a Learning Journey is kept in a table, and customized style sheets are used within the XML editor to represent this table in a visual structure resembling the final output structure as much as possible. Additional functions built into the stylesheet support the authors with the assignment of metadata or setting proper cross references to standardized text elements reused across all Learning Journeys.

2.2 Production and publishing

As with the editing, Learning Journeys are produced and published just like the technical documentation content. Fully automated build cycles pick up and produce changed content multiple times per day, and after production the output is automatically pushed to the content delivery platform (CDP) underlying the SAP Help Portal, for final validation and publication into multiple consumption channels, including SAP Learning Hub and SAP Help Portal.

The content is produced into a mix of html, JSON and image files, which are later rendered dynamically into the actual Learning Journeys.

2.3 Rendering

To render the Learning Journeys from the produced html and JSON files into an interactive visual appearance, a mix of custom-developed and open source JavaScript libraries is used. The main journey graphic is rendered dynamically into a collection of SVG objects, arranged on the page and equipped with interactive elements, using the open source JavaScript library D3 [2].

2.4 Reporting

The structure of the topics used to represent the journeys and tiles, mostly in table format, lends itself nicely to content reporting – used for internal validation processes, reuse analysis, and consistency checking. This is done by producing the content into html files and then turning the aggregated data tables into dynamic tables, which allow filtering, sorting, searching, and export into spreadsheet format. All this is done using the open source DataTables [3] plugin for jQuery.

And as the Learning Journeys are published via the content delivery platform also used for technical documentation, its consumption reporting capabilities also automatically apply to the Learning Journey content. Predefined reports with consumption analysis information are produced automatically on a regular basis.

3 Reuse of content in Learning Journeys

On the non-technical side, the Learning Journeys also help to bridge the gap between the often-isolated content areas of learning and technical documentation. Separated content creation, production and publishing processes have led to some duplication of work, and unnecessary copy and paste activities.

Certain technical documentation deliverables can now be directly included into Learning Journeys as self-study learning assets. For example, What's New information for SAP's software products, often used by administrators and implementation consultants for planning the next upcoming projects, is now integrated into the "stay current" learning scenario of Learning Journeys as a learning asset. Likewise, blogs or videos related to specific product features and published in other channels can now be included into the product's learning journeys.

References

1. SAP Help Portal, public website, https://help.sap.com
2. Data-Driven Documents or D3.js. 4.4.0. 2016. Mike Bostock, https://d3js.org
3. DataTables. 1.10.13. 2016. SpryMedia Ltd, https://datatables.net

Levels of intelligent information access using ontology transformations

Lena Wenner[1*], and *Nergis* Kuru[1**]

[1] Karlsruhe University of Applied Sciences, Faculty of Information Management and Media, 76133 Karlsruhe, Germany

Abstract. Current techniques of intelligent information access have surpassed the mere provision of static information. They attempt to overcome the limitations of traditional content delivery processes by exploiting information retrieval techniques. While the existing literature has extensively explored the adoption of these techniques, comparatively little notice has so far been taken of their application as ontology transformations. This paper aims to explore levels of intelligent information access from a practical perspective. Applying the theoretical framework of information retrieval techniques, we identify and define levels of information access and propose respective ontology transformations. For this purpose, we decided to use an ontology-editing tool for modeling, transforming and displaying information about the domain of Smart Homes.

1 Introduction

Classic technical documentation still considers end-user products to be manufactured for a specific purpose and used in predefined and predictable situations. This understanding also applies to the rather static and extensive information products. However, as Leukert [1] points out, the expectations of users for the right amount of personalized, situation-dependent and contextual information are increasing. The approaches of the Internet of Things (IoT) and Industry 4.0 are changing the context in which (technical) information is embedded, accessed and used. The context can no longer be predefined, but rather evolves while using the products [2, 3].

Considering the paradigm shift from static information in classic manuals to on-demand delivery of information, the provision of *intelligent information* is becoming a fundamental requirement. In the context of this paper, the term *intelligent information* is understood as information that can be requested, processed and delivered both manually and automatically according to specific requests and use cases [4]. Information retrieval techniques evolved to give principled approaches to accessing *intelligent information*. These techniques aim at providing users with content that is both relevant and intelligible for them and their needs [5]. They can be brought into the field of ontologies to tackle the aforementioned challenges.

The existing literature has extensively explored the adoption and implementation of information retrieval techniques that have become the preferred form of information access [5]. However, our review of previous studies also suggests that the application of these techniques in the context of ontologies and ontology transformations is a topic that has not been sufficiently covered in the field of technical communication. Thus, the primary goal of this paper is to explore and compare different retrieval techniques from a practical perspective of both technical writers and ontology developers. To position our findings, we tailor these techniques to use cases and implement them as ontology transformations. By applying the latter to an ontology model, we propose opportunities to enhance the delivery of *intelligent information* and its access.

The structure of this paper is as follows: Section 2 is devoted to the basics of ontologies and ontology transformations. It also presents our research approach. Section 3 provides definitions of different levels of intelligent information access, combined with information retrieval techniques. Here, the focus lies on how these retrieval techniques were designed and implemented as ontology transformations. In section 4 we discuss the limitations of this study. Finally, section 5 reviews the main findings and provides a conclusion.

2 Background

Various authors have been discussing the many discourses and explanations for the term *ontology*. Guarino and Giaretta [6] even devote an entire paper to its terminological clarification and provide a list of several possible interpretations. These divergences in discourse suggest that the precise meaning of the term depends on the understanding of the disciplines in which ontologies are used. For this study, ontologies are defined as conceptualizations of knowledge and explicit

Corresponding authors:
Lena Wenner: lena.wenner@gmx.de,
**Nergis* Kuru: nergis.k@live.de

specifications of terms in a domain of interest (also domain of discourse) [7].

Ontologies are to model semantic networks and complex relations to enable a mutual understanding of the meaning of specific vocabulary terms and to facilitate information integration [8] across information sources. As such, they differ from existing approaches and methods like mind maps, thesauri, and hierarchical taxonomies.

Gruber [7] provides a detailed account of ontologies' nature. He explains that ontologies can be formally described by a set of objects (e.g. classes, instances, and relations) which are reflected in representational vocabularies, and which may differ depending on the ontology-editing tools used to represent the concepts of a domain and the relations among them. Given this explanation, ontologies are unambiguously formalized in logic-based representational vocabularies. Thus, their syntax and semantics are machine-interpretable that enables querying, logic-based reasoning [7], and "sense-making" in pursuit of meaningful knowledge. These mechanisms can be used to enhance more intelligent information search, delivery and access processes.

The representational vocabularies, their syntax and semantics form the backbone of ontology transformations. The meaning of the latter can be very broad. A more general definition by the Cambridge Dictionary considers transformations as a change in the appearance or character of something to improve itself in any way [9]. This is also the case in ontology transformations. As defined, they perform modifications on the formal semantics and ontology patterns, transforming (parts of) an ontology from one modeling choice to another. They do so by taking transformation instructions (specified as a set of rules or procedures) and an ontology as an input. An advantage worth noting is that the same conceptualization can be modeled and transformed in various ways [10].

The main purpose of ontology transformations is to convert information contained in ontologies into useful knowledge and valuable new insights. To conduct this, we decided to use the web-based tool Ontolis for modeling, displaying and transforming information about Smart Homes, which is the domain of discourse in this scenario. Consequently, the terminology we use to describe the practical implementation is ontolis-specific (terms are emphasized). While any ontology-editing tool could have been used, we chose Ontolis because it accommodates state-of-the-art semantic modeling and knowledge representation. Also, it supports sophisticated ontology transformations at different stages. For a profound explanation of the modeling methodology and the development practices in Ontolis, the reader is referred to a case study by Fischer and Krägel [11], which we deemed outside the scope of this paper.

2.1 Research approach

Ontology transformations strongly rely on the modeling of ontologies. Thus, the first steps of this research were to define the domain of discourse and develop specific use cases that guided many of the modeling decisions. These steps also had a significant impact on the application of the ontology transformations.

The ontology we developed for Smart Homes is intended to support end-users in retrieving high-level information on smart devices, e.g. a smart thermostat, smart lighting or smart speaker. For this projected task, we defined use cases according to the framework offered by Cockburn [12]. They go beyond single-session lookup tasks and consider more complex queries (such as in "Which smart devices are compatible with my existing ones controlled by the Apple Home Kit System?"). While defining a clear scope of information search and access scenarios, the use cases also provided the necessary scaffolding to develop the ontology.

Figure 1 presents an extracted part of the ontology in Ontolis. It consists of various components (represented as nodes) that constitute the semantic model and the information corpus for Smart Homes.

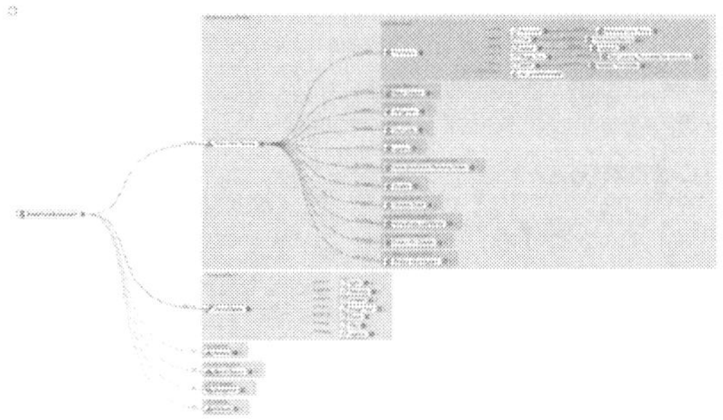

Fig. 1 Extracted part of the ontology model for Smart Homes developed in Ontolis.

The ontology model is not comprehensive in covering all possible topics and devices related to the domain of Smart Homes. However, it sufficiently describes and represents the classes, instances, attributes, and relations, which served as a suitable base for the ontology transformations.

3 Levels of intelligent information access

Intelligent information access attempts to overcome the limitations of current information delivery processes by exploiting information retrieval techniques. The latter normally use (direct or indirect) inputs and facilitate search and decision processes [13] to match information items from among large collections to the request [5]. This activity involves evaluating and weighting the information "so that each user can quickly find information that is both relevant and comprehensive for their needs." [5]

In the following, we define and summarize four levels of intelligent information access in the context of ontologies. We only focus on the fundamental notions needed for later references in the sections where ontology transformations are described.

3.1 Level 1: filtering

In general terms, filtering is understood as the removal of information rather than finding relevant content in a set of data. In this case, users are only provided with information that is not removed [14].

Although various filtering techniques share the goal of delivering only relevant information to users, we focus on rule-based filtering systems. The filtering component of those systems consists of a set of rules that are applied for information to be filtered. They instruct the filtering component to either filter out the information or to treat it as relevant as soon as the conditions of a rule are met [14]. The same applied to ontologies, their filtering components delete non-relevant information without changing the original structure of the ontology (see Figure 2).

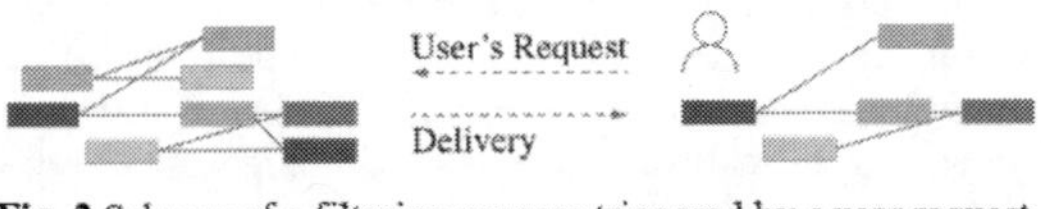

Fig. 2 Scheme of a filtering process triggered by a user request.

3.1.1 Implementation using Validity Rules

In Ontolis, we defined a set of *Validity Rules* that were able to include all elements of the ontology, namely classes, relationships, attributes and instances. Within these rules, all elements could be combined with logical operators such as AND, OR, XOR, and NOT, allowing more complex dependencies to be defined between them.

3.2 Level 2: semantic transformation

According to Roser [15], a semantic transformation specifies a transformation between two ontologies, a source ontology (SO) and a target ontology (TO).

Fig. 3 Scheme of a semantic transformation triggered by a user request.

Through semantic transformation, the elements of a SO can be transformed into another structure (see Figure 3) taking advantage of logical ontology patterns. These ontology patterns consist of links that indicate which elements of the SO need to be transformed into which elements of the TO. If they are equivalent to the elements in the SO, those elements are transformed into the same ones in the TO. If they differ from the elements in the SO, this results in a TO composed of different elements [15]. These links can be reflected in meta ontology, which defines a way of storage, tracing the links between input elements in SO and target elements in TO [16].

3.2.1 Implementation using QIRA

The mechanism described in section 3.2 was implemented using *QIRA*, an ontolis-specific query and transformation language. Building on this, we defined a set of declarative transformation rules to cause some modifications in a target ontology depending on queries. Since the current state of transformations is stored within these rules, *QIRA* can be understood as a meta ontology. The semantic transformation rules were initialized by user inputs. In our use case, users could select which specific smart device they wanted to receive information from. The resulting (TO) provided them with information that matched the query and the use case. Since the TO was completely transformed, it differed from its "origin" both regarding the number of elements and the structure.

To perform semantic transformations and to enable efficient query answering, *QIRA* uses an in-house developed engine that imitates a reasoner and exploits the functions of SQL queries and XSLT transformations. In general terms, a reasoner (also semantic reasoner or rules engine) is a software that infers logical consequences from explicitly asserted facts in ontologies [17].

Reasoners are key components for working with ontologies and ontology transformations, especially at higher levels of intelligent information access. This is due to the need for correctness and consistency of ontologies, which are essential to obtain correct query results and provide intelligent information. The reasoners verify if there are any inconsistencies and logical contradictions within the ontology [17]. Also, some of the knowledge modeled might not be explicit. In such cases, reasoners can draw conclusions based on inferences to deduce implicit knowledge and derive new facts [18].

In contrast to the previously described levels of intelligent information access (filtering and semantic transformation), the processes on the following levels can be additionally triggered through external events or certain conditions allowing higher automation of information delivery and access processes. Thus, the following levels and their respective retrieval techniques have been revolutionizing the way information is accessed.

3.3 Level 3: intelligent publication process

In the context of this paper, an intelligent publication process is defined as the dynamic aggregation and delivery of information in a non-ontological representation (see Figure 4). This means, information is converted into system-independent formats, such as HTML or PDF. As a result, information, or any content, can be provided on diverse domains and media platforms for different types of users. Intelligent publication processes generally build on semantic transformations (see section 3.2). The difference among them is that their results are not just a modified ontology model, but a different format. The ontology is validated and interpreted by a reasoner. Provided that very specific use cases are defined and represented in the ontology model, the reasoner identifies relevant information.

Fig. 4 Scheme of an intelligent publication process triggered by events.

On level of intelligent publication process, the delivery of content is usually context-, event- or process-driven [3]. According to Ziegler [3] such processes can be defined as push procedures, in which corresponding systems automatically gather information on operating conditions or product states, which can eventually trigger the information aggregation and delivery processes.

3.3.1 Implementation using the PublicForm

Based on our semantic transformation rules defined with *QIRA*, the elements of the ontology were converted to HTML elements upon user requests. Here, *QIRA* offered some genuine advantages. Particularly, the generic ability to retrieve relevant ontology elements and to redirect the transformation results to the so-called *PublicForm*. The latter was developed by Ontolis, to support the on-demand delivery of obtained information over the Internet.

We developed an interface that encapsulated the *PublicForm* and displayed information within a web browser by means of style sheets. Users were provided with read-only access to the information contained in the ontology. In this respect, the web-based interface did not provide explicit functionality for any direct modification of the underlying ontology model. Moreover, users could not see the actual semantic model.

Users were initially presented with four different categories that sought to simulate pre-filters. Selecting a certain category would lead them to the specification of the use case which was then presented as a summary, including the *PublicForm*. There, users could submit queries that triggered the corresponding ontology transformation. This process recomposed the information and presented the results as a coherent response.

Another means of performing this conversion is to use, for example, Quick Response (QR) codes, Radio-frequency identification (RFID) chips or user locations that can further automate the delivery and access processes driven by ontology transformations. Such automatic conversion processes hold great promise and can be seen as a key for intelligent and advanced methods of accessing information [19]. However, the premise for such approaches is that the relevant information or content should be semantically categorized and precisely described [2], and becomes therefore automatically retrievable, reusable, and reconfigurable [20]. This would also support the idea of *micro documents* aiming to provide information only to the extent required by users. Ziegler [3, 21] defines *micro documents* as logic-driven compositions of semantically linked information with limited context, bridging the gap between single topic delivery and monolithic documents. That means that search processes or requests can trigger content aggregation in the form of *micro documents*. The latter can benefit from additional enrichment of more complex semantic models, such as ontologies.

3.4 Level 4: intelligent content delivery

Within the process of intelligent content delivery, information from multiple heterogeneous information sources is aggregated through ontologies (see Figure 5). This can be done by linking the resources to ontologies through relations expressed via mappings. This mapping process is referred to as Database-to-Ontology Mapping. A general definition of this concept could be given as follows: an establishment of correspondences between the source components and the ontology components [22]. For further theoretical discussions on this topic, the reader is referred to Ghawi and Cullot [22] who propose several approaches to enable ontology-based information integration.

The level of intelligent content delivery uses the semantic patterns of ontologies to facilitate information integration across various information sources. During the process, information is extracted, aggregated and presented as a cohesive entity. This is in contrast to the previous levels described above, where information comes from a single source. The advantage of such information integration processes is that already existing information can be accessed and imported from different systems and, if needed, can be seamlessly combined with other information that might not be directly available to users.

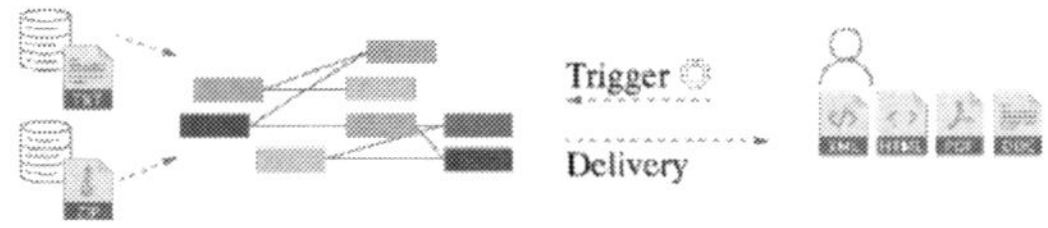

Fig. 5 Scheme of an intelligent content delivery process triggered by events.

3.4.1 Possible future implementation scenarios

In future projects, we would like to relate information from various information sources, such as Content Management Systems (CMS), and transform them into a single target form by using ontologies as semantic middleware [3]. Especially in the realm of technical communication, much attention has been paid to CMS, which store, retrieve and use granular (technical) information on end-user products, while enabling single-sourcing mechanisms [23]. In such systems information can be used and flexibly, or even automatically, retrieved during composing activities [24]. This means information is repurposed and reassembled to create a variety of information products addressing different needs.

To bridge the heterogeneity between different information sources (e.g. CMS), the sources must be mapped to ontologies which will express their semantics. In other words, both a source and an ontology need to be semantically related on a conceptual level [22]. This would require first the identification of the sources, which may contain different types of information. Secondly, the information stored in those sources would be unequivocally defined using metadata. From here, the mapping process would start which includes following sequential process steps: a transformation of the source schema into the ontology structure followed by a migration of the source components into ontology components. The latter, also referred to as ontology population, can be realized as a query-driven process that transforms the information resulting from a given query [22]. The outlined mapping process is fairly dynamic and starts running as soon as updates are made within the source(s).

The query results can be redirected to web services, such as Content Delivery Portals (CDP). Such portals are increasingly used to enable the interoperability between several and distributed sources. They aim to answer user queries and deliver the right amount of corresponding information [25].

Logical semantic patterns of ontologies can bridge the gap between data integration and migration. This can ultimately foster the efficient reuse of often already existing information from multiple (distributed) information sources. Therefore, building on intelligent content delivery processes and making use of ontology transformations can support the idea of accessing intelligent, semantically enriched information.

4 Study limitations

The present paper has certain limitations. First and foremost, both the ontology model (for Smart Homes) and ontology transformations were defined and carried out in Ontolis. Thus, they are limited to the functional capabilities and scope of this tool. However, the validity of the findings described and presented could be extended, for example, by examining the levels of information access in different ontology-editing tools to find any similarities or differences in the conclusions.

Another limitation has to do with the ontology itself. According to Staab and Studer [26], ontologies should express a consensus, that is a shared view between multiple parties rather than a single view. Even though attempts were made to include different perspectives on the domain of Smart Homes, the possibility of relevant omissions and researcher biases remains. Therefore, our recommendation for future research on the same topic would be to develop an ontology model based on use cases and evaluate the ontology by discussing it with experts from the field. This could enable the analysis of even more realistic information access scenarios and ensure real-world application.

5 Conclusion

Ontology transformations can process large semantic models effectively and provide personalized and use-case specific information. As for the definition of intelligent information in section 1, ontology transformations can improve making information truly intelligent. However, the outcome of transformations does not offer the same value among all user groups. On the one hand, end-users only benefit if the results are presented in a media-specific format. Information tagged with standard HTML tags, provides the ability for end-users to simply view and "consume" the aggregated information [27]. In this project, we managed this by starting at the level of intelligent publication process.

Ontology developers and domain experts on the other hand use ontologies to store, effectively organize, share and annotate large sets of information [27] in their fields enabling collaboration in modeling and within companies. They can use ontology transformations to narrow down the domain of interest to a specific information need or to extend the set of information contained within the ontology.

We have described approaches by which the delivery of *intelligent information* and its access can be enhanced by using ontology transformations. We have shown how information retrieval techniques can be applied as ontology transformations. Depending on the level of implementation, ontology transformations offer in-time and on-demand access to personalized, contextualized information. From this perspective, both ontologies and ontology transformations can be portrayed as very promising approaches of intelligent information access. However, it needs to be considered that the development of use cases, ontologies and ontology transformations is a "process of iterative design [that] will likely continue through the entire lifecycle of the ontology." [28]

We would like to thank the International Office, the Faculty of Information Management and Media, the AStA Students Union, the master's program Communication and Media Management from Karlsruhe University of Applied Sciences for the financial support. We also thank Thomas Weinmann and Christian Koller from Ontolis for great collaboration, insightful discussions, and their support as well as Professor D. Roy from the University of Aizu (UoA) for the organization of the conference at UoA.

References

1. S. Leukert: Wandel des Kontextbegriffs. In J. Henning, M. Tjarks-Sobhani (Eds.): Intelligente Informationen. Schriften zur Technischen Kommunikation. 22nd ed. Stuttgart: tekom e.V., pp. 103–110. (2017)
2. W. Ziegler: Semantic Information Development for Intelligent Content Delivery. In *Official Journal of Japan Technical Communication Association JTCA*, pp. 18–29. (2019)
3. W. Ziegler: Drivers of Digital Information Services: Intelligent Information Architectures in Technical Communication. In D. Roy (Ed.): ACM Chapter Proceedings on Educational Technology, Language and Technical Communication. Aizu, Japan: The University of Aizu, pp. 48–53. (2019)
4. T. Nguyen, W. Ziegler: Interactive Content Delivery: Technologies, Use Cases and Industrial Applications for IoT Scenarios. In tekom e.V. (Ed.): Intelligente Informationen. Stuttgart. tcworld conference, pp. 142–144. (2017)
5. C. D. Manning, P. Raghavan, H. Schütze: Introduction to Information Retrieval. Cambridge: Cambridge UP. (2009)

6. N. Guarino, P. Giaretta: Ontologies and knowledge bases: Towards a terminological clarification. In N. Mars (Ed.): Building and sharing very large-scale knowledge bases. Towards very large knowledge bases. Amsterdam: Ios Pr. (1995)
7. T. R. Gruber: A translation approach to portable ontology specifications. In *Knowledge Acquisition* 5 (2), pp. 199–220. (1993)
8. S. Spaccapietra: Journal on Data Semantics XI. Berlin: Springer. (2008)
9. Cambridge Dictionary: Transformation | meaning in the Cambridge English Dictionary. Cambridge University Press. Available online at https://dictionary.cambridge.org/dictionary/english/transformation, checked on 3/5/2020. (2020)
10. O. Šváb-Zamazal, V. Svátek, F. Scharffe, J. David: Detection and Transformation of Ontology Patterns. In A. Fred, J. L. G. Dietz, K. Liu, J. Filipe (Eds.): Communications in computer and information science, Bd. 128, Knowledge Discovery, Knowledge Engineering and Knowledge Management: First International Joint Conference, IC3K. Funchal, Madeira, Portugal, pp. 210–223. (2009)
11. H. Fischer, L. Krägel: Modeling of Complex Metadata in Technical Communication by Ontologies. In D. Roy (Ed.): ACM Chapter Proceedings on Educational Technology, Language and Technical Communiacation. Aizu, Japan: The University of Aizu, pp. 11-16. (2019)
12. A. Cockburn: Writing effective use cases. Boston: Addison-Wesley. (2006)
13. G. Armano, M. Gemmis; Semeraro, Giovanni; Vargiu, Eloisa: Intelligent Information Access. Berlin, Heidelberg: Springer-Verlag Berlin Heidelberg. (2010)
14. N. J. Belkin, W. B. Croft: Information filtering and information retrieval: two sides of the same coin? In *Communications of the ACM* 35 (12), pp. 29–38. (1992)
15. S. Roser, B. Bauer: Ontology-Based Model Transformation. In J. Bruel (Ed.): Satellite events at the MoDELS 2005 conference. MoDELS 2005 international workshops, Berlin: Springer, pp. 355–356. (2006)
16. B. Wouters, M. Gervais: Ontology Transformations. In C. Chi (Ed.): 2012 IEEE 16th International Enterprise Distributed Object Computing Conference (EDOC). pp. 71–80. (2012)
17. S. Abburu: A Survey on Ontology Reasoners and Comparison. In *International Journal of Computer Applications* (17). (2012)
18. D. Moshman: From inference to reasoning: The construction of rationality. In *Thinking & Reasoning* 10 (2), pp. 221–239. (2007)
19. J. Oevermann, W. Ziegler: Automated Classification of Content Components in Technical Communication. In *Computational Intelligence* (33). (2017)
20. A. Rockley, C. Cooper, K. Halvorson: Managing enterprise content. A unified content strategy. 2nd ed. Berkeley, CA: New Riders. (2012)
21. W. Ziegler: Extending intelligent content delivery in technical communication by semantics: micro documents and content services. In D. Roy (Ed.): Proceedings of the ETLTC ACM Chapter International Conference. Aizuwakamatsu, Japan. (2020)
22. R. Ghawi, N. Cullot (Eds.): Database-to-Ontology Mapping Generation for Semantic Interoperability. Vienna. Third International Workshop on Database Interoperability. (2007)
23. S. Closs: Single-Source-Publishing. Topicorientierte Strukturierung und DITA. Frankfurt am Main: entwickler.press. (2007)
24. C. Oberle, W. Ziegler: Content Intelligence for Content Management Systems. tcworld. Available online at http://www.tcworld.info/rss/article/content-intelligence-for-content-management-systems/, updated on 10/2012, checked on 3/4/2020. (2012)
25. W. Ziegler: The Evolution of Content Management towards Intelligent Delivery Systems for Technical Communication. In *Frontier, Official Journal of Japan Technical Communicators Association JTCA*, pp. 68–75. (2017)
26. S. Staab, R. Studer: Handbook on Ontologies. Dordrecht: Springer. (2009)
27. T. E. Potok, M. T. Elmore, J. W. Reed. N. F Samatova: An ontology-based HTML to XML conversion using intelligent agents. In R. H. Sprague (Ed.): Proceedings of the 35th Annual Hawaii International Conference on System Sciences. Los Alamitos, Calif: IEEE Computer Society Press, pp. 1220–1229. (2002)
28. N. F. Noy, D. L. McGuinness: Ontology Development 101: A Guide to Creating Your First Ontology. Stanford, CA: Stanford University. (2001)

Extending intelligent content delivery in technical communication by semantics: microdocuments and content services

Wolfgang Ziegler[1*]

[1] Karlsruhe University of Applied Sciences, Faculty of Information Management and Media, 76133 Karlsruhe, Germany

Abstract. We address and develop a new concept for the dynamic delivery of topic-based content created within the domain of technical communication. Corresponding content management environments introduced within the last decades, focused so far on semantically structured and mostly XML-based information models and, more recently, on semantic metadata using taxonomies leading together to concepts of so-called intelligent content. Latest developments attempt to extend these concepts with additional explicit semantic approaches modelled and implemented, for example, by using ontologies and related technologies. In this article, we propose how content users might benefit from these semantic concepts by the delivery of sets of logically connected topics, which can be described as microdocuments ("microDocs"). This generic approach of topic assemblies might also play a role in the provisioning of content by web-services being integrated into different types of content processing and content delivery applications.

1 Introduction

The delivery of so-called intelligent information in technical communication (TC) scenarios is driven by topic-based content enriched by semantics from XML-structuring and corresponding metadata [1, 2]. Content considered in TC is created typically within component content management systems (CCMS). Dynamic user access can then be provided by content delivery portals (CDP) and corresponding interfaces [3]. While these applications allow for metadata-based facetted search, document navigation and full text search, the underlying concepts and technology can vary considerably.

One of the recently discussed enhanced concepts are ontology models. They are well-known in computer science and gained increasing interest in TC to improve model-based content creation processes or effectivity of search and delivery processes. We attempt to expand these considerations by combining topic-based content provisioning, semantics and ontology modelling in a new way. We explore semantic aspects of so-called microdocuments (microDocs) as a use-case driven content provisioning, bridging the gap between single-topic delivery and large-document search. Hereby, the need for context and content amount should be satisfied in a better way.

2 Technological background

In this section, we clarify the technological and methodological background of semantics used so far in the domain of technical communication. In a most general sense, semantic technologies try to define and implement explicitly machine-readable and also human-interpretable representations of data. Following this, we will focus on topic-based content management applications and the corresponding processes. Thus, we will describe and consider content at the level of native intelligence introduced in [4, 5]. In the second subsection, we will summarize a special classification scheme used in TC representing the basis for implementations of higher intelligence levels within the intelligence cascade of content.

2.1 Semantics of natively intelligent content

Semantics has been introduced in TC early on within content creation processes by structured information models and mostly as DTD/XSD-based XML structures. Subsequently, semantic information became important on a larger scale with the spreading of CCMS. Technical writers apply semantic structuring and tagging to topic-based, reusable content. In turn, structured content should follow and can be controlled by linguistic rules. Moreover, semantically tagged content allows for many data processing scenarios like specific publishing for multiple media, formats, document types, target groups, markets, etc.

The next step in the use of semantics in TC was done by concepts of semantic metadata. The term semantics should be even more clarified in this context: Metadata has been introduced to describe content contained in topics, for retrieval of topics and for process automation. But types, logics and implementations of metadata in

* Email: wolfgang.ziegler@hs-karlsruhe.de

CCMS are varying strongly. Beside non-semantic plain-text metadata, metadata are somtimes implemented and processed as XML-attributes included in content object code like *<topic audience="admin" >...<topic>*. Or, even more generic, as XML-encoded label-value pairs separated from the content. By the latter, one can even describe hierarchical metadata modelled as taxonomies, like in the following example of Fig. 1, where labels (here called "class") and values stem from the PI-classification scheme described later.

```
<metadata class="Component" value="PI-Fan" >
    <metadata class="Component" value="MountingBracket">
        <metadata class="Component" value="Base">
            <metadata class="Component" value="BasePlate"/>
            <metadata class="Component" value="TelescopicRod"/>
        </metadata>
    </metadata>
</metadata>
```

Fig. 1. Example of XML metadata definition file for hierarchical metadata. Metadata values are assigned within CCMS authoring process to topics.

In this regard, metadata are in fact implicitly semantic and machine-processable. But the conceptual interpretation, i.e. meaning and human understanding might be still limited to the domain of the application, for example to system users within a company. The domain range will, of course, extend when using standards like DITA, ATA ISpec 2200 or S1000D. In the latter, not only metadata labels but also metadata values are standardized for military and aviation industries [6]. So far, in summary, CCMS implementations manage and process modularized content within topics and enriched by implicitly semantic metadata. Depending on the CCMS implementation, metadata are stored within topics or, more often, kept separately in databases as data, resp. relations. Separate XML metadata-objects as in Fig. 1 are used, for example, also for data export, exchange or reporting.

2.2 Metadata by PI-classification

One way to add systematically native intelligence to CCMS managed content is the well-established method of PI-classification [2]. Modularized, topic-based content can be assigned to four basic classes of metadata. These classes are organized with respect to products (P) and to information (I):

• intrinsic product classes, stating the physical or virtual product components the content is directly connected to. They can form complex and multi-level taxonomies.

• intrinsic information classes, defining precisely the information contained in the topic. Taxonomies are given by information types (e.g. procedural, descriptive, conceptual, safety). Subclasses thereof can describe more specific information (maintenance, repair, regulations, functions, etc.)

• extrinsic product classes describe the validity of topics with regard to individual products and reflect the portfolio of offered or delivered products.

• extrinsic information classes can be used for the assignment to output media, document types, markets or target groups.

The intrinsic metadata classes define the modular topic concept for authors, while the extrinsic metadata are used for process automation and variant management.

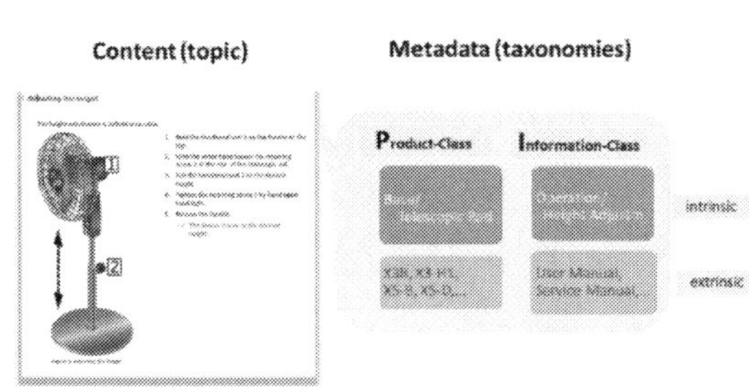

Fig. 2. Basic PI-Classification example for a topic (left side) of the PI-Fan reference content. The assigned classification values are usually stored in CCMS databases as hierarchical metadata separately from the topic.

This method of a multidimensional information space of metadata has been extended by two additional metadata dimensions: functional metadata and variant properties By functional metadata, delivery functionalities can support IoT-requirements (e.g. error code handling of content), work time calculations or run-time-based functions (e.g. maintenance intervals) [7]. Variant properties, on the other hand, should cover all additional configuration parameters needed for product-specific information delivery [8]. Hence, in the most general description, information architects end up with formally six-dimensional information space depicted in Fig. 3. The classes and values originate here from the reference content of the PI-class method consisting of a virtual product called the PI-Fan [9]. In industrial applications, the abstract dimensions of functional metadata and variant properties split into a manifold of parameters according to delivery use cases and to the specific product domain.

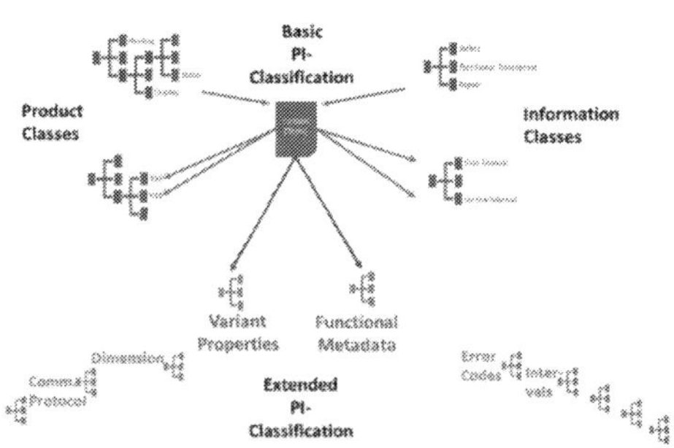

Fig. 3. Metadata information space for topic-based content (center) given by the extended PI-Classification (lower section) and some examples of classes. Basic classification is depicted in the upper section. In/outgoing arrows depict condeptual single-/multi-valued assignments of classes.

It should be noted that in Fig. 1, for simplicity, only the intrinsic base dimension of product components has been included in the code. It also is derived from the PI-Fan reference implementation. In practical applications, all classes (labels) have to be engineered specifically as custom CCMS implementations. Applying this method, semantic PI-classified metadata leads systematically to natively intelligent content and allows for higher CCMS process support and automization. However, the concept range might be limited because the implementations are system- and domain-dependent and therefore, still implicit.

3 Explicit semantics in TC

On the next methodological level of the intelligence cascade, the level of augmented intelligence, ontologies introduce more formalized and therefore explicit semantics. Ontological approaches are not new in the history of philosophy, linguistics, knowledge management [10] and, of course, semantic web technologies. But they gained recent interest in TC because increasing data, content and process complexity urges information architects to seek for more suitable technologies.

In this section, we will first focus on elementary and formal aspects to understand explicitness of semantics given by ontologies. We then give a short overview over applicability of corresponding implementations in the domain of TC.

3.1 Formal representation of semantics

Ontologies consist of definitions of object classes and instances thereof, their properties and relations between each other. There are lightweight and less complex ontology representations, often using the syntax of the resource description framework (RDF) and RDF-schema (RDFS) [11]. Heavy-weight ontologies can include additional rules and restrictions being represented, for example, within the ontology web language OWL [12]. The manifold of objects included in an ontology depends on the considered use case. Metadata classes and topic-based content classes are therefore just a small subset of possible ontological models. Ontologies can be visualized typically as semantic networks.

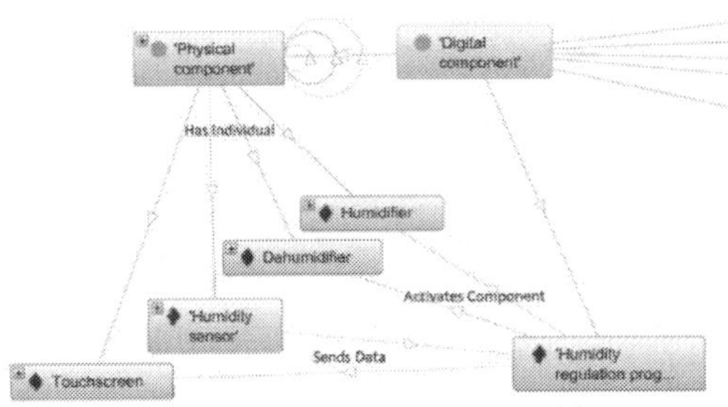

Fig. 4. Ontology detail of classes (circles) and instances (diamonds) defined in the Protégé modelling software [13]. Labelled lines depict different types of explicit relationships.

In Fig. 4, we depict a cut out of product details as a possible extension of the PI-Fan reference model. Classes and their instances of digital and physical components show relationships among each other. As a simple example, the model includes a digital software component (humidity regulation program) activating a humidifier hardware component.

Semantics of relations and classes, resp. instances is expressed explicitly by the above-mentioned ontology representations like OWL/RDF(S). In Fig. XY some corresponding code excerpts of the model are illustrated. One finds the definition of a relation "Activates_component" between digital or physical components (domain) activating physical components (range). The individual relation is then given between specific instances as introduced above.

Similarly, one can also define relationships between metadata as outlined implicitly in the previous section. Using ontology languages, one can express and subsequently even visualize explicitly, for example, common taxonomic (is subclass of) or partitive (is part of) relationships or any other system of logically ordered metadata values.

```
<owl:ObjectProperty rdf:about="http://.../DemoOnto#Activates_component">
        <rdfs:subPropertyOf rdf:resource="http://http://.../#Intra-class_relations"/>
        <rdfs:domain rdf:resource="http://.../DemoOnto#Digital_component"/>
        <rdfs:domain rdf:resource="http://.../DemoOnto#Physical_component"/>
        <rdfs:range rdf:resource="http://.../DemoOnto#Physical_component"/>
        <rdfs:label xml:lang="en">Activates component</rdfs:label>
</owl:ObjectProperty>

<owl:NamedIndividual rdf:about="http://.../DemoOnto#Regulate_humidity">
    <rdf:type rdf:resource="http://.../DemoOnto#Digital_component"/>
    <Activates_component rdf:resource="http://.../DemoOnto#Dehumidifier"/>
    <Activates_component rdf:resource="http://.../DemoOnto#Humidifier"/>
    <Sends_data_to_component rdf:resource="http://.../DemoOnto#Touchscreen"/>
    <rdfs:label xml:lang="en">Humidity regulation program</rdfs:label>
</owl:NamedIndividual>
```

Fig. 5. Code excerpt of the example ontology of Fig. 4: Definition of the relation described in the text and the individual relation between component instances in OWL/RDF representation. Class definitions of components have been omitted for simplicity.

But still, the domain range and the widely understanding and interpretation of relationships is an open question. It is usually answered by standardization and, necessarily, a broad acceptance of standards. As an example, the intelligent information request and delivery standard (iiRDS) has been developed basically for the exchange of modularized technical information [14]. Therefore, one intends to standardize content exchange focusing first on the exchange between CCMS and CDP. The core metadata model for topic classification is based on the PI-classification method introduced earlier. iiRDS defines a packaging mechanism on-top and uses RDFS for the representation of taxonomic metadata. More complex cross-relations would have to be modelled as extensions, thereby, potentially reducing the domain range again.

3.2 Ontology applications in TC

Recently, information and TC system architects started to take advantage of the semantical richness of ontologies. One can find several application types and corresponding process steps where ontologies can be applied by:

• Type I support model-based content engineering aligned with product-modelling. Modular content creation, variant and configuration management is modelled with the aid of partitive, functional or other relations given by product engineering and corresponding component classes. Semantic modelling software visualizing complex product dependencies might also interact by interfaces with CCMS to reduce or control metadata complexity in the authoring environment [15].

• Type II improve search and retrieval of information using CDP or other search environments. Here, semantic relations are modelled to optimize relevance and precision of search results. Relations are modelled along the use cases and business cases of content delivery. Also, content from other sources then CCMS can be included.

• Type III connect multiple data sources: Semantic software and contained models can act as a middleware between data sources and content consuming applications. Semantic networks are used to map data, various content types and documents along with their specific metadata environments. This is going beyond the scope of TC and therefore, CDP are just one of the possible delivery channels.

In this paper, we focus on the technical side of information systems. But, of course, TC-relevant ontologies are also well-known within linguistic sciences and terminology management, which is strongly related to the metadata development described so far.

For the first two application types of TC mentioned above, a schematic picture can be found in Fig. 6. Content transfer is achieved by packaging of content and metadata, which is done in proprietary formats or, for example, according to DITA-conform topic assemblies (maps). Another standardized approach would be the use of the above-mentioned iiRDS packaging format including RDFS syntax for taxonomic metadata.

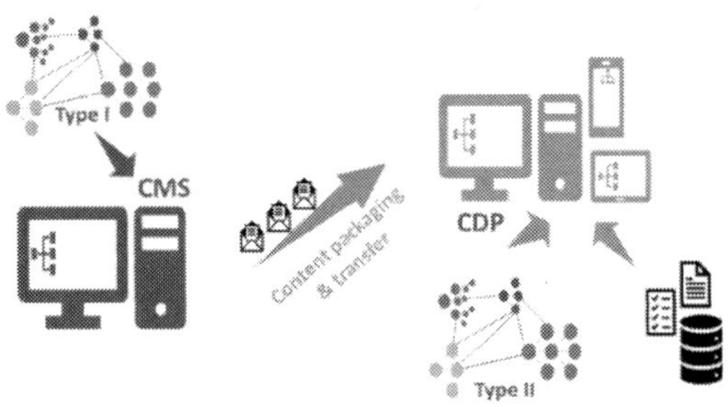

Fig. 6. Ontologies used in TC depicted as networks can support content creation (application type I on CCMS side) and search and delivery processes (application type II on CDP side).

4 Extending content delivery

In this section, we will combine the above investigated concepts of semantics with CDP functionalities. Starting point is the search and delivery of topic-based content from CCMS applications.

4.1 Dynamic deliverables as micro-documents

Delivery applications are understood in many cases as search interfaces adapted to the TC domain. This means, users can search manually for content using facets, direct text search or by navigation within document structures. Facets are usually derived from taxonomic metadata stemming from CCMS or, as described above, from classes and instances of a semantic model (application type II). The search results, i.e. the deliverables consumed by users consist either in single topics or in documents. The latter can be monolithic or assemblies of topics following traditional table-of-content (toc) structures. We now claim that even if topics are developed self-contained and therefore follow intrinsic classification, there is, in many cases, a lack of context or required correlated content. On the other hand, in traditional documents, there is potentially an abundance of content because documents are developed typically as a normatively or product-driven most complete set of information. But users in a specific use case and in a specific role need a relevant, precise and reduced, but sufficient amount of information. This has been the initial idea of content delivery in TC.

Preciseness of primary search results in CDP should be ensured by metadata quality from taxonomic classification. Then, in addition, the relevance of contextual content and the sufficiency of delivered topics should be expressible by rules. These rules can, in general, also depend on use cases and user roles. So, the user can finally define corresponding dynamic deliverables received upon request by users as micro-documents (microDocs): A microDoc is a (sub-)set of topics required by predefined use cases and connected by a logical concept as a dynamic publication in search media. [16]

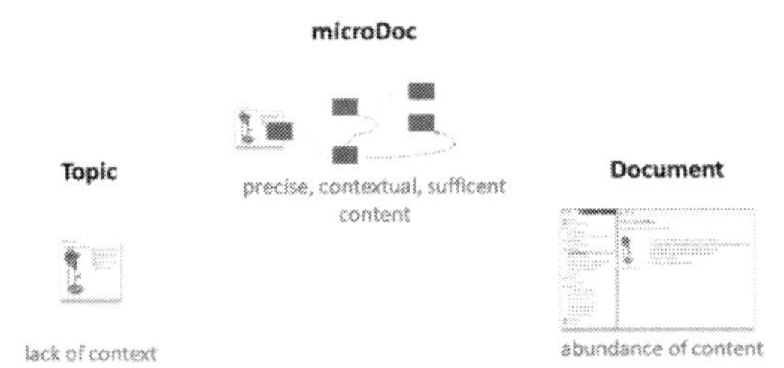

Fig. 7. microDocs as a rules-based content search and delivery optimization method with respect to required context and content amount.

It is now a question of involved technologies, i.e. the prevailing intelligence cascade level, how the respective logical concept can be implemented as rules for correlating content. Consequently, there will be several implementation levels of microDocs with increasing complexity:

a) Static documents predefined as topic assemblies on CCMS-level for selected and potentially most relevant use cases.

b) Dynamic topic arrangement within CDP and within the retrieval process. The arrangement is based on rules, applied to taxonomic metadata of topics.

c) Arrangement of content following rules predefined by semantic relations, properties of ontology classes and their instances.

Note, that the arrangement of topics and content objects in more general search systems might be realized in very different ways in the front-end applications. Examples might be aggregations in document-style or as topic clouds, reduced semantic networks, generated links, filtering of documents etc. And of course, there can be transitions and mixtures between the above introduced levels.

It is now still an open question, from where the afore-mentioned rules can be logically derived. As a starting point, TC information architects and writers can define

the most important rules, for example, according to already known user feedback, problem analysis, didactics or implied task logics and required prior knowledge. Once delivery is initiated, one can consider two additional levels:
d) Improvement of rules by web-analytics. Hereby, search behavior as well as quality of search results and other indirect or even direct feedback can be analyzed. Analytics is done at this level by humans and implications will change rules and even semantics.
e) Improvement of rules by artificial intelligence. Machine-learning algorithms can analyze search interactions and can derive, express and improve rules automatically. This would match scenarios of so-called predictive content.

These two levels d), e) could also be understood as quality assurance measures of a)-c) and not as independent levels themselves. Moreover, if further advanced deep-learning technologies like neural networks were introduced to the process, this next level would then not even impose the existences of rules set or explicitly understood by humans.

4.2 Content services

The information architecture derived so far, has especially on delivery side further consequences on the architecture of involved systems. In the architectural picture drawn for CDP, the user front-end is part of the delivery-application. But recent developments also tend to an architecture where CDP can act as a content service application (CSA), also known as headless CDP, resp. headless CMS.

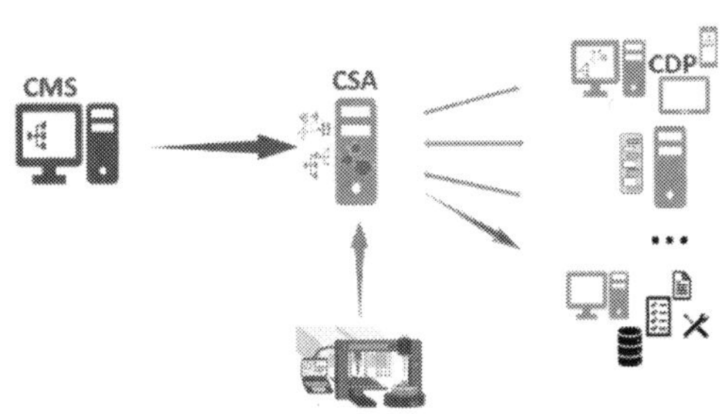

Fig. 8. Content service application CSA in the center providing content-based web-services upon request to a variety of content consuming applications like front-end CDP or chatbot applications. MicroDocs can be generated by processing rules applied to semantic relations within CSA. In the lower part, a push scenario is sketched.

The advantage of such a web-service architecture shown in Fig. 8. is, that a larger variety of content consuming applications can request, process and deliver content according to their specific use case and independently from the internal logic of the intermediate CSA server. Traditional search interfaces and facetted CDP search are only some of the possible content consumers. Others might be chatbots, social media platforms, service management applications, sales applications, help-desk support applications and many more. In this sense, CSA resemble partially to the application type III of ontology applications as an information hub. The difference would be the more limited side of content sources focusing CCMS-based content or, at least, information objects classified according to a common metadata concept.

In Fig. 8 the visualization of the corresponding architectural concept can be found. Combining the theoretical considerations of microDocs and the recent approaches of service-oriented architectures, one can understand microDocs as dynamic microservices supporting predefined front-end applications and use cases by dynamically optimized content assemblies. They could be transferred to front-end CDP upon request as standardized iiRDS packages, whereas other applications might request different packaging formats or just simple web-formats. The logic, i.e. the rules defined in the CSA, can act on taxonomies or ontologies, depending again on the intelligence level of involved technologies. But in such a case, rules don't have to be implemented in the front-end CDP. So far, we considered pull, technologies delivering information upon request. But of course, event-driven push technologies can also be supported as shown also in Fig. 8. There, a software-detected event within a machine can trigger the automized delivery of topics or microDocs to a service application without an active request.

5 Summary

In this article, we gave a basic introduction into the recent situation of semantics and how it is introduced via intelligent content in the domain of technical communication. We focused first on the information architecture of topic-based content used in CCMS and outlined the transition from natively intelligent content of metadata taxonomies to more explicit semantics of ontologies and so-called extended intelligence. Thereby, we used the PI-classification and its formulation as OWL/RDF representation to clarify explicitness of ontological approaches. Standards like iiRDS based on RDF and PI-classification with a normatively given vocabulary can then increase the domain range and acceptance of such technologies. iiRDS packaging, is thereby intended for data transfer between CCMS and delivery systems.

Furthermore, we introduced a new concept of microdocuments to optimize content relevance of requested information via CDP. This is done by bridging the gap between topic-based and document-based delivery by building a new type of rules-based and use-case-dependent dynamic topic assemblies. The logical concept of these microDocs, i.e. the relevant context and the amount of required content, should be derived at different levels from semantic rules and models. These models then can be either taxonomies or ontologies.

Finally, we gave an outlook on implications for recent system architectures of CDP. We focused on content service applications as a middleware between CCMS and a variety of front-end applications. Semantic rules are processed within CSA to generate and deliver microDocs in push and pull scenarios. Therefore, microDocs can be understood as microservices providing more contextual rich content than just single topics in CDP scenarios.

The author acknowledges support with ontology modelling of a modified and extended PI-Fan product model by A. Ahmadpour.

References

1. A. Rockley, *Managing Enterprise Content. A Unified Content Strategy*. New Riders. (2012)
2. W. Ziegler, *Basic Concepts Which Support the Management and Delivery of Intelligent Content*, Frontier, Official Journal of Japan Technical Communicators Association JTCA, p. 84-91, (2017)
3. W. Ziegler, H. Beier, *Content delivery portals: The future of modular content*, tcworld e-magazine 02/2015
4. W. Ziegler, *The Evolution of Content Management towards Intelligent Delivery Systems for Technical Communication*, Frontier, Official Journal of Japan Technical Communicators Association JTCA, p. 68-75, (2017)
5. W. Ziegler, *Drivers of Digital Information Services: Intelligent Information Architectures in Technical Communication,* ACM Chapter Proceedings on Educational Technology, Language and Technical Communication ETLTC, ISSN: 2434 – 9526, p. 48-52, **1** (2019)
6. ASD, *S1000D International Specification for Technical Publications,* http://public.s1000d.org/Pages/Home.aspx
7. W. Ziegler, *Intelligente Informationen*, Schriften zur Technischen Kommunikation, Vol. 22, p. 51-66, Ed. Hennig J., Tjarks-Sobhani M., tcworld GmbH, (2017)
8. W. Ziegler, U. Parson, J. Sapara, *iiRDS for technical writers – Introduction to the Metadata*, Tutorial Presentation & Proceedings tcworld conference, p. 225-228 (2017)
9. W. Ziegler, *Content management systems tested: Introducing the PI-Fan*, tcworld e-magazine 10/2016
10. N. Guarino, *Formal Ontology, Conceptual Analysis and Knowledge Representation*. Int. J. Human-Computer Studies 43, (1995)
11. W3C, *RDF Schema 1.1,* https://www.w3.org/TR/rdf-schema/ (2014)
12. W3C, *Web Ontology Language (OWL)*, https://www.w3.org/OWL/ (2012)
13. *Protege Desktop User Documentation*, https://protegewiki.stanford.edu/wiki/Protege4UserDocs, (2019)
14. iiRDS – The International Standard for intelligent information Request and Delivery https://iirds.org/material-downloads/iirds-version-1-0-1/
15. C. Deschner, W. Ziegler, *Informationsmanagement und Ontologien – entwicklungsnahe Produktdokumentation in der Medizintechnik*, Presentation & Proceedings tcworld conference, p. 98-99 (2018)
16. W. Ziegler, *Alles hängt mit allem zusammen: Content vom Anfang bis zum Ende gedacht*, Presentation & Proceedings tcworld conference, (2019)

https://doi.org/10.1051/shsconf/20207704001

"Pool of Toys": Multimodal Visual Music Rendering of Sequenced and Real-time Control Events

Satsuki Kawahara[1] *& Michael Cohen*[1]

[1] Spatial Media Group, Computer Arts Lab., University of Aizu; Aizu-Wakamatsu, Fukushima 965-8580; Japan

Abstract. The goal of this study is to display music visually to aid recognizing each component, enjoying music not just aurally but visually as well. Elements of western music comprise multiple aspects (e.g., rhythm, melody, harmony, and orchestration). To express them, we introduce a "live song" called "Pool of Toys." A pool filled with toys is used as a motif in a game engine (Unity). A multitimbral song including musical elements was created using DAWs (GarageBand and then Ableton Live). Each part is imported as a MIDI track into Unity, controlling the attributes of visual elements (floating toys) at runtime. A surface grid controller (Launchpad Pro) is used at runtime along with the precomposed music so that performers can synchronously play the MIDI terminal with output displayed in realtime.

1 Introduction

Music is basically auditory information. Vibrations in air reach our ear and move the eardrum. By the complex structure of ear, this vibration is converted into neural signals and processed in the brain. The percentage of each human sense occupied in our brain information is approximately as follows: Taste 1.0%, Tactile 1.5%, Smell 3.5%, Hearing 11.0%, and Visual 83.0%. Visual modality occupies the largest portion (83.0%), while auditory modality is slightly above 1/10 of it. Sometimes we feel people who have never learned musical instrumentals experience difficulty in recognizing detailed parts in songs. Visualizing music can support recognizing song details. At some concerts, performers often project video that provides visual effects matching the rhythm and the story of songs. Precise visual effects are possible thanks to the technological advancement. Recently, there is research on visual effects in hearing [3] and improved performance in music using visuals and sounds together [4]. In this research, we aim to develop a system that allows people to enjoy multisensory experience (visual and auditory) when listening to music. We implement the system using the game engine Unity and various accompanying tools. Our system supports audition with visuals, and it can help listeners recognize music details.

2. Methodology

2.1 Multitimbral Synthesis

Multitimbrality describes the multiplicity of parts that can be played by an instrument or synthesizer [5]. Generally, these parts are assigned different MIDI channels to be controlled independently. (This is not the same as polyphony, or the number of notes that can be generated at the same time). When musical instruments (synthesizer, sampler, etc.) can generate more than one timbre, they are called multitimbral.

2.2 Polyphony

Polyphony in music is simultaneously combination of multiple tones or melody lines [6]. Therefore, simplex interval composed of harmony of multiple simultaneous tones, such as a chord, is polyphony. Counterpoint is pattern of polyphonic voices, such as parallel melody lines.

2.3 DAW (Digital Audio Workstation)

A DAW (Digital Audio Workstation) is music creation software. It integrates various functions (MIDI sequencer, musical composition, multitrack recording, audio editing, mixing, mastering, etc.) and completes musical composition to output audio files. In this study, a song was composed using Ableton Live.

2.4 MIDI

MIDI is a protocol for recording and playing music on digital devices [7]. It encodes and distributes information related to the production of music, using assumptions about audio synthesis timbre or "patch," but doesn't directly indicate sounds. The command set includes note on (with key velocity), note off, pitch event, and other ways of controlling synthesis.

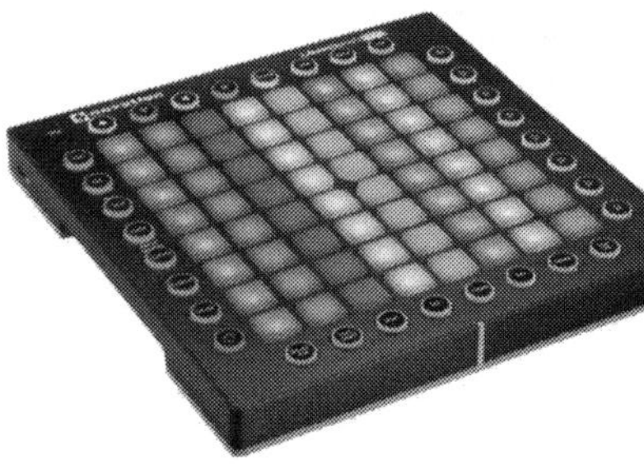

Figure 1: Novation Launchpad Pro

Novation Launchpad Pro [8] is a MIDI surface controller triggering multitrack instruments and tone for arbitrary music software, using an 8×8 gridded RGB touchpad (Figure 1). For example, it can control drums and keyboard played at the same time. There are a variety of layouts (Note, Drum, Fader, and Programmer). In this study, Ableton Live is chosen to use Launchpad Pro. Launchpad Pro switches layouts automatically, remapping MIDI commands sent by the respective buttons.

2.5 Unity

Unity [9] is a cross-platform game engine. It is a development environment used for making games that integrates 2D/3D description, playing sounds, management of user interface, and data management/creation.

2.5.1 Sequenced Control: MIDI Tool Kit

Figure 2: MIDI Player Toolkit

MIDI Tool Kit [10] is a Unity component (available from the Asset store) for playing sounds from a MIDI file (.mid) without requiring C# or JavaScript programming. It defines music using custom inspectors and synchronizes MIDI events and application responses. As shown in Figure 2, it is installed as a Unity plug-in module including a menu, the name of which header is the initials of "MIDI Player Tool Kit".

2.5.2 Realtime Control: MIDI Jack

MIDI Jack [11] is used as MIDI input API for Unity. Using MidiMaster Class, it performs basic functions such as parsing note on/off opcodes, obtaining note velocity,

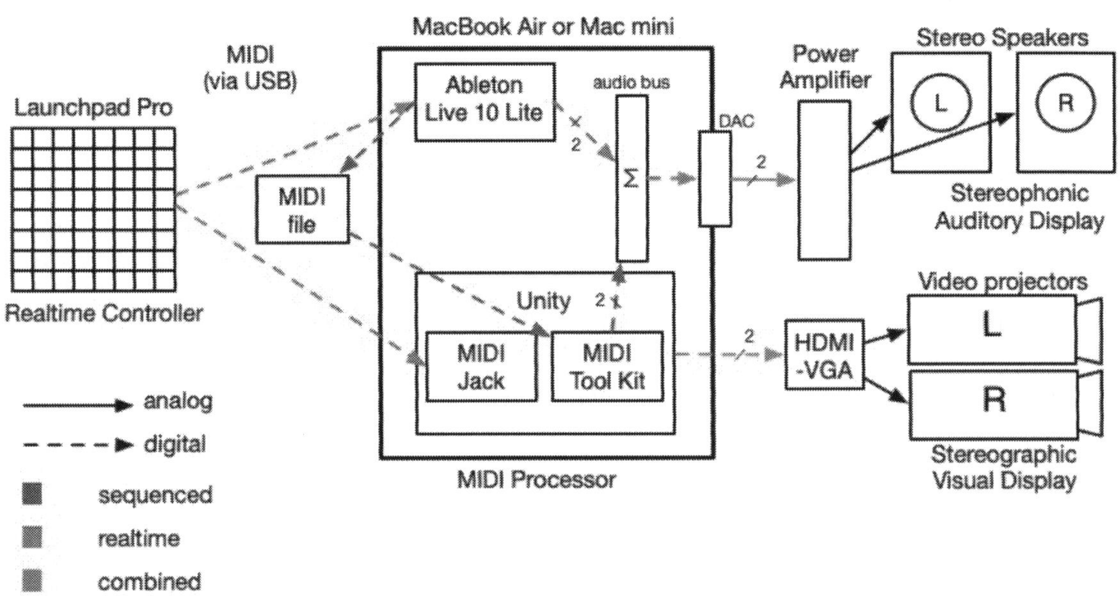

Figure 3: System architecture and data flow

interpreting performed key presses/releases, and obtaining controller values. Such given functions are displayed in a MIDI monitor window list of active devices and MIDI messages received.

3 Implementation

3.1 Overview

3D rendering was developed using macOS (on MacBook Air and Mac Mini) using Unity version 2019.3.04a with the programming language C#. Each imported MIDI track controls (modulates) the attributes of scene objects. Performers can play MIDI terminals, and the output is reflected in real-time. System diagram and flow are shown in Figure 3.

3.2 Design

Figure 4: Swimming pool (basic empty space)

The motif of the titular pool is a swimming pool, as illustrated in Figure 4, and we used game objects arranged in Unity. Toys and water objects were imported from Unity Asset Store. The expression of buoyancy was created using Unity-Water Buoyancy Simulation for Unity Engine [12], simulating toys floating in the water.

3.3 Sequenced MIDI Event

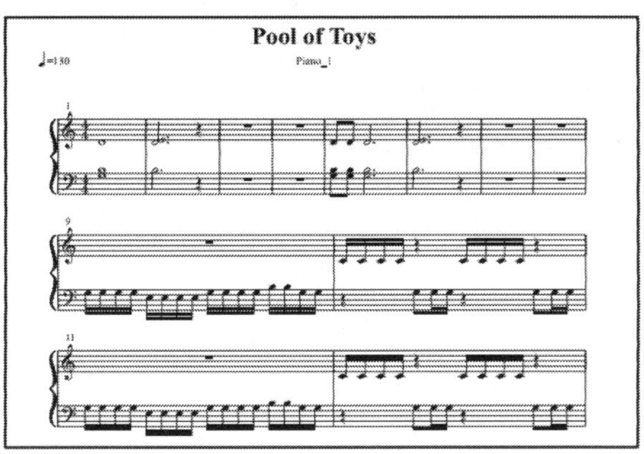

Figure 5: Piano part 1 for "Pool of Toys"; 「おもちゃのプール」

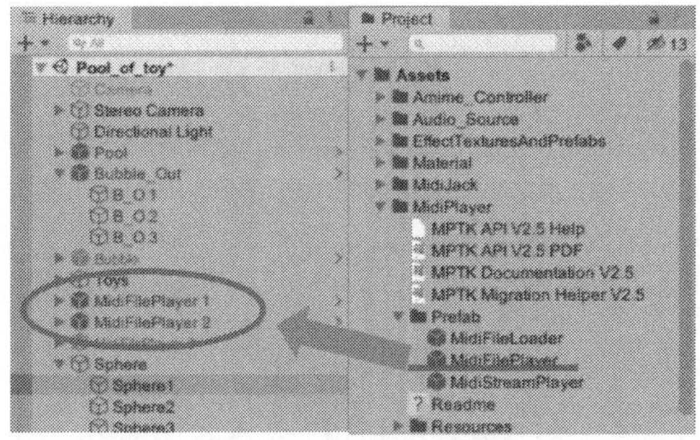

Figure 6: MIDI File Player added to Unity scene

We originally used Garage Band (DAW in Mac), but it had trouble exporting MIDI files (loop → MIDI). The song "Pool of Toys"; 「おもちゃのプール」 (Figure 5) was composed using Ableton Live, imported into Unity as a MIDI file (.mid). Ableton Live enables direct export of separated parts as .mid tracks. The earlier version was composed using Apple GarageBand on macOS, but it did not allow us to directly export MIDI tracks. The composition contains two tracks (both piano parts).

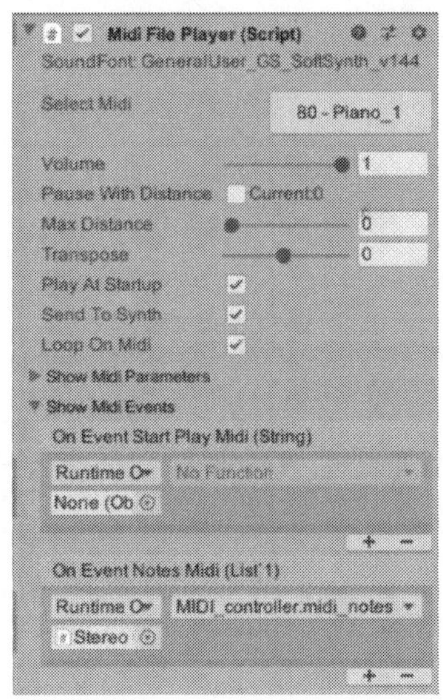

Figure 7: Select MIDI and add Event Note MIDI

Sequenced MIDI Event handler was created using MIDI Tool Kit on Unity. .mid was added to Unity via MPTK Midi File Setup (Figure 3). MidiFilePlayer (object can play .mid) from Prefab was added to Hierarchy (Figure 6), and a function (MIDI_controller.cs) that modulates objects (such as spherical bubble) when getting note from .mid was devised. The function was attached to the Main Camera,

https://doi.org/10.1051/shsconf/20207704001

and event was added and event (MIDI_controller.midi_notes) was selected (Figure 7). During this procedure, MidiFilePlayer references both piano sounds because it is possible to input only one file. Spherical bubbles were designed as Game objects. Each bubble is generated dynamically upon the recognition of respective `note on` event and disappears ("times-out") after "deathspan," determined as a fraction of its sustained lifetime.

3.4 Realtime MIDI Event

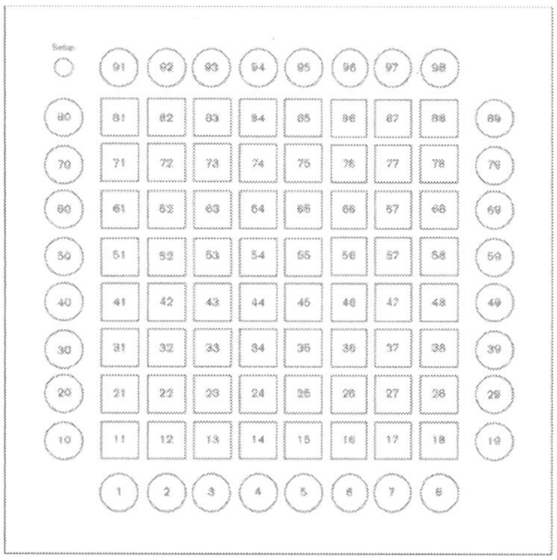

Figure 8: Launchpad Pro grid controller lay-out MIDI values

Real-time MIDI events arise from controller signal, outputting audio from Ableton Live (not from Unity). The sound is polyphonic. Programmer Layout [13] of controller was used on Unity. Numbers used and an example of how they can be allocated are shown in Figure 8. Function changes moving objects (toys) and used function in Midi Jack identifies the control based on the signal from the controller. At this stage, tones are generated as one-shot or looping sounds. Notes played by performers are displayed visually as well as aurally. Sounds include drums, synthesizer, bass and guitar, synthesized by Ableton Live. Using functions such as Animator in Unity, what is visually expressed is the movement of objects or the changing colors of them.

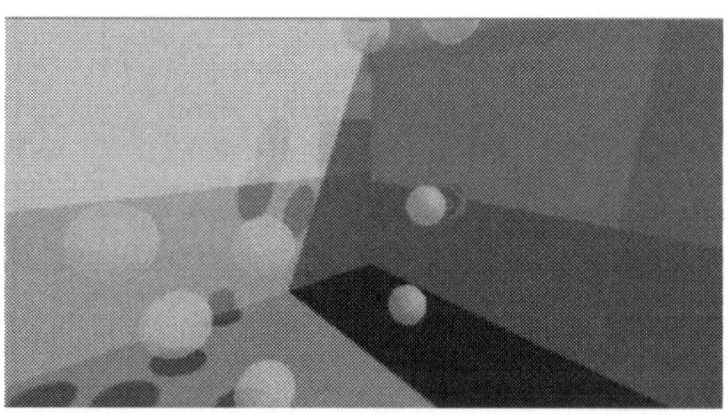

Figure 9: Sequenced MIDI events: outputting bubbles

4 Results

With our system and Pool of Toys, one can listen to and see the visual effect of both events (composed offline and online MIDI events). Performers push a controller button, and the colors and movement of rigged toys change. The prototype supports both sequenced and real-time events, generated by controller, as shown in Figures 9 and 10.

5 Future Work

Figure 10: Realtime MIDI events : modulating scene color of toys (changing from yellow to red)

Remaining issues include the quality of the moving objects, such as water surface animation (shadows, caustics, etc.). We would also like to experiment with spatial sound and perspective (standpoint) adjustment so that users can virtually walk or swim around the underwater scene, enjoying various visual and auditory stimuli. In a song, there is a chord (harmony) progression. With each changing chord, listeners can feel the changing mood with the changing sound. So, performers can play displayed chord whose position is set by the controller more easily on Game Display of Unity. For doing this, we hope to make a system to read the chord progression from MIDI and modulate the scene accordingly.

5 Acknowledgements

We thank Camilo Arévalo and members of the Spatial Media Group for helping us.

References

1. 音が聞こえるとは
   https://www.toa.co.jp/otokukan/otomame/theme1/1-1.htm
2. 情報の伝わりやすさと視覚の関係
   『産業教育機器システム便覧』P4「図 1.2 五感による近くの割合」教育機器編集委員会編 日科技連出版社 1972
3. P. Friedrich and K. Reinhard, 2012. *When the Eye Listens: A Meta-analysis of How Audio-visual Presentation Enhances the Appreciation of Music Performance.* Music Perception: An Interdisciplinary Journal, Vol. 30, No. 1, Sept. 2012; (pp. 71–83). DOI: 10.1525/mp.2012.30.1.71
4. E. G. Sharon, A. G. Lee, and B. Randolph, 2005. *Hearing What the Eyes See: Auditory Encoding of Visual Temporal Sequence.* Psychological Science 16(3): 228–235, March 1, 2005, DOI: 10.1111/j.0956-7976.2005.00808.x
5. Multitimbral Synthesis
   https://www.sweetwater.com/insync/multitimbral/
6. Polyphony
   https://www.britannica.com/art/polyphony-music
7. MIDI
   https://whatis.techtarget.com/definition/MIDI-Musical-Instrument-Digital-Interface
8. Launchpad Pro
   https://novationmusic.com/launch/launchpad-pro
9. Unity
   https://unity.com/
10. MIDI Tool Kit
    https://paxstellar.fr/
11. MIDI Jack, Keijiro Takahashi, 2013-2015.
    https://github.com/keijiro/MidiJack
12. Floating Object in Water, Denis Rizov, 2015.
    https://github.com/dbrizov/Unity-WaterBuoyancy
13. Launchpad pro programmer's Reference Guide
    https://d2xhy469pqj8rc.cloudfront.net/sites/default/files/novation/downloads/10598/launchpad-pro-programmers-reference-guide_0.pdf

Optimizing Deep-Neural-Network-Driven Autonomous Race Car Using Image Scaling

Yaqub Mahmoud[1,*], *Yuichi* Okuyama[1,**], *Tomohide* Fukuchi[1,***], *Tanaka* Kosuke[1,****], and *Iori* Ando[1,†]

[1]School of Computer Science and Engineering, The University of Aizu, Aizuwakamatsu, Japan

Abstract. In this work we propose scaling down the image resolution of an autonomous vehicle and measuring the performance difference using pre-determined metrics. We formulated a testing strategy and provided suitable testing metrics for RC driven autonomous vehicles. Our goal is to measure and prove that scaling down an image will result in faster response time and higher speeds. Our model shows an increase in response rate of the neural models, improving safety and results in the car having higher speeds.

1 Introduction

Autonomous driving algorithms give vehicles the capability of sensing their environment and moving safely with little or no human input. Autonomous Driving (AD) scenarios are considered very complex environments as they are highly dynamic containing multiple object classes that move at different speeds in diverse directions [1]. Since the DARPA Grand Challenge competition [2], autonomous driving has been actively researched [3]. Significant progress in Machine Learning (ML) techniques like Deep Neural Networks (DNNs) over the last decade has enabled the development of safety-critical ML systems like autonomous cars. Several major car manufacturers including Tesla, GM, Ford, BMW, and Waymo/Google are building and actively testing these cars [1].

Modern autonomous vehicles combine a variety of sensors and cameras to perceive their surroundings and utilize advanced control systems to interpret the sensory information to identify appropriate navigation paths. These various sensors each have their own advantages and disadvantages. For instance, ultrasonic sensors provide good performance of depth measurement for close obstacles but they lack semantic information and perform poorly for far objects. Camera sensors, on the other hand, provide rich color information from which scene semantics can be extracted. However, they lack information on depth and rely on scene illumination [2]. One goal of autonomous driving is to make a vehicle sense its environment and navigate without human input [4], and to maintain control similarly to humans so that the vehicle's motion is interpretable and comfortable [3].

Now, the major challenge becomes how to get the neural networks into series production cars, in a safety-conform way [5]. There have been a lot of strides recently in the development of open source software for small portable autonomous vehicles. These portable vehicles are aimed at enthusiasts who are curious about machine learning and also at researchers who want to develop better and more enhanced autonomous driving algorithms. They are cheaper than actual autonomous cars and offer an environment to speedily develop and test the driving algorithms.

However, before a neural network finds its way into series production cars, it has to first undergo strict assessment concerning functional safety [5]. Although open-source and widely available, limited testing has been done on the true capabilities of these small portable vehicles and more work is needed to see if the results they provide us with can be consistent and reliable. This research downscales the images from a portable autonomous racing car and tests both the modified and pre-modified system with the aim of achieving an increase in speed and response rate of the autonomous vehicle. The goal is to increase the speed and response rate of the autonomous vehicle while assessing its reliability for research.

There have been several research using RC cars, however, no one has asked the question of how varying degrees of image sizes affects the overall behaviour of a deep-neural-network-driven autonomous car. To our best knowledge, we are the first to look into and question whether or not RC vehicles are suitable for research activities. We also believe that we are the first to look at the influence of image resolution on vehicle speed. The contributions of our work are as follows:

- We demonstrate that downscaling the image size of an autonomous vehicle results in higher speeds.
- We also show downscaling images results in faster response rate and thus increases safety.
- We analyze the different neural network models available in the system.

*e-mail: m5222108@u-aizu.ac.jp
**e-mail: okuyama@u-aizu.ac.jp
***e-mail: m5222102@u-aizu.ac.jp
****e-mail: s1260138@u-aizu.ac.jp
†e-mail: s1260211@u-aizu.ac.jp

- We provide a testing framework for research using RC based autonomous vehicles.
- We perform testing on the capabilities of RC driven autonomous vehicles.
- We provide experimental evidence proving our hypothesis.

The rest of this paper is organized as follows: Chapter 2 provides more background information on deep learning and RC autonomous cars. In Chapter 3, we provide detailed information on the neural network models available for use in the system. Chapter 4 describes the system model in use. Chapter 5 describes our simulation and experiment setup. In Chapter 6, we present our results. Finally, Chapter 7 concludes the paper.

2 Background

2.1 Deep Learning for Autonomous Driving

Classical methods provide of general self-driving poor performance compared to deep learning methods in addition to high complexity due to complicated pipelines used. Deep learning algorithms are becoming successful beyond object detection [4, 2]. Deep learning can be applied to a self-driving car to recognize objects in front of the vehicle or to judge for itself when any situation arises. But to make these judgements, we need a lot of data as training data [5, 6]. In this paper, we collect learning data with an end-to-end method [1] and an autonomous driving technique announced by Nvidia using car games [7].

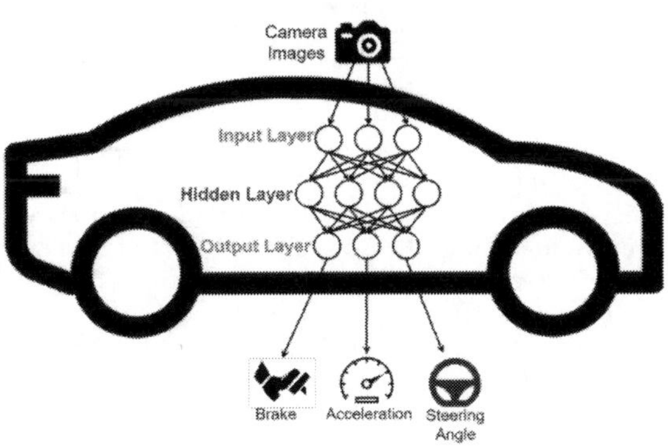

Figure 1: Deep-Neural-Network-Driven Autonomous Car

The key component of an autonomous vehicle is the perception module controlled by the underlying Deep Neural Network (DNN). Fig. 1 shows an autonomous car with a deep-neural-network. The DNN takes input from different sensors like camera, light detection and ranging sensor (LiDAR), and IR (infrared) sensor that measure the environment and outputs the steering angle, braking, etc. necessary to maneuver the car safely under current conditions. The first few layers of an autonomous car DNN extract low-level features such as edges and directions, while the deeper layers identify objects like stop signs and other cars, and the final layer outputs the steering decision (e.g., turning left or right). Each layer of a DNN consists of a sequence of individual computing units called neurons. The neurons in different layers are connected with each other through edges and each edge has a corresponding weight [1].

2.2 Donkey Car

Donkey car is an open source Do-It-Yourself (DIY) self-driving platform for small vehicles. Donkey is a high-level self-driving library written in Python, developed with a focus on enabling fast experimentation and easy contribution [8]. It uses Raspberry Pi 4, or similar boards, together with a camera to control an RC car to drive through tracks autonomously. It is one of the most popular RC cars used by both enthusiasts and researchers who are striving to further develop the field.

3 Neural Network Architecture

In this section, we detail the different neural network architectures available in donkey car. Neural networks have proven to be a very good way of training images that have been collected [9]. It is crucial to perform testing on neural networks to make sure they are consistent in their results. Keras is a high-level neural network API written in Python. It is good for fast implementation and capable of running on TensorFlow. Donkey car uses keras to reproduce the steering and throttle based-on the image the camera sees [8]. Table 1 provides a summary of the different neural network models used in donkey car.

4 System Model

In this section we have provided a detailed list of the various components used in the system and also highlighted their importance.

4.1 Autonomous Driving System

Creating a system specification is one of the major challenges in testing a complex neural-based system like autonomous vehicle [1]. Fig. 2. shows an overview of our autonomous self-driving system that we used in this paper. Autonomous driving is achieved by recording images and your inputs while you're driving it. The data is then retrieved and fed into a neural network to train the data and output a file. Finally, the output is then placed into the car and it will use this for inference in order to achieve self-driving.

In summary, our car drives in the following steps:

- Use a controller to move the car and simultaneously collect data using the camera.
- Train the data collected on a google colaboratory server.
- Transfer the deep learning output from the server to the car.
- Input commands for self-driving.

Table 1: Description of Neural Networks of the System

Neural Network	Network Structure	Output
Keras Linear	5 conv. layers 2 dense layers	2 dense layers with 1 scalar output each for steering & throttle
Keras Categorical	5 conv. layers 2 dense layers	2 dense layers 16 & 20 w categorical output
Keras IMU	5 conv. layers 2 dense layers 3 dense layers for vector data	2 dense layers with 1 scalar output each for steering & throttle
Keras Latent	5 conv. layers to a 10x1x1 vector 6 Conv2dTranspose layers (b4 outputting images)	2 dense layers with 1 scalar output each for steering & throttle Outputs Images
Keras RNN	4 time distr. conv. layers 2 LSTM layers 3 dense layers Driving controls	1 dense layer with 2 scalar outputs for steering & throttle
Keras 3D	4 3D conv. layers (each with max pooling) 2 dense layers Driving controls	1 dense layer with 2 scalar outputs for steering & throttle
Keras Behavior	5 conv. layers 2 dense layers Driving controls	Categorical steering Throttle is similar to keras linear
Keras Localizer	5 conv. layers 2 dense layers	2 dense layers with 1 scalar each output for steering & throttle 1 categorical output for location

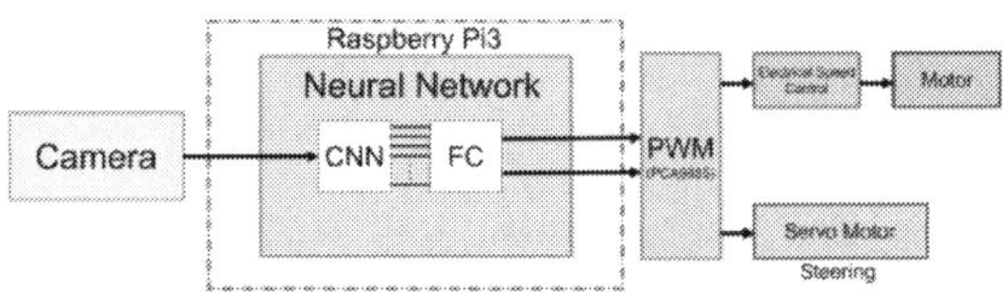

Figure 2: Overview of Autonomous Driving System

4.2 Data Acquisition

Cameras are a very common way of getting input data for autonomous vehicles. They have proven to excel in providing rich colors and a very comprehensive and detailed "world view". A. Ghofrani et. al. [10] used an end-to-end RGB-based Indoor Camera Positioning System using deep convolutional neural networks. R. Blin et. al. [11] has demonstrated road scene analysis by using polarization-encoded images. We gathered over 10,000 images and each image has its own JSON file associated with it as shown in Fig. 3(a). Inside each JSON file, the steering angle, throttle speed and time is recorded for each image frame. Fig. 3(b). shows the distribution of the image data with number of images on the y-axis and steering angle on the x-axis. A +ve x-axis value indicates that the car was moving to the right while a -ve value indicates that the car was moving to the left side.

4.3 Raspberry Pi Controller

Several projects including [12, 7] have used raspberry pi in their implementations. And while raspberry pi can be used for various computations, it falls short when trying to run deep learning models on it [7]. For this reason, we only use the raspberry pi for the least computationally intensive tasks such as inference and we reserved running deep learning models on google colaboratory. We also keep in mind the limited processing power of raspberry pi when making changes to the system. To achieve inference, we first installed raspian as a fundamental linux-based OS. We then installed python because it is the de-facto programming language for AI development. We then installed Tensor-flow as a library for deep learning. Finally, we installed the donkey car software to provide the controls necessary for donkey car hardware.

4.4 Google Colaboratory

Rendering a collection of images sufficiently large for machine learning algorithm training and evaluation is prohibitively slow with only one machine. Using cloud resources, in our case the Google Cloud Platform, we created many images in parallel to create a significant data set in a practical amount of time. Donkey car has both inference and training capabilities. But due to limited computation, we only use it for inference. For training, we use Google Colaboratory because it provides free powerful computational resources. Images were modified using image manipulation techniques borrowed from [13, 14]. We then modified the system to be able to operate on all varying degree of input image resolutions.

5 Simulation and Experiment

5.1 Simulation Setup

We set up a simulation experiment of donkey car on the Linux Ubuntu operating system as shown in Fig. 4. We obtained over 10,000 frames with the accompanying data entries as shown in Fig. 3(a). After that, the images were then down-scaled from the default resolution of 160x120 to the resolutions 120x90, 80x60 and 40x30 pixels. A

 https://doi.org/10.1051/shsconf/20207704002

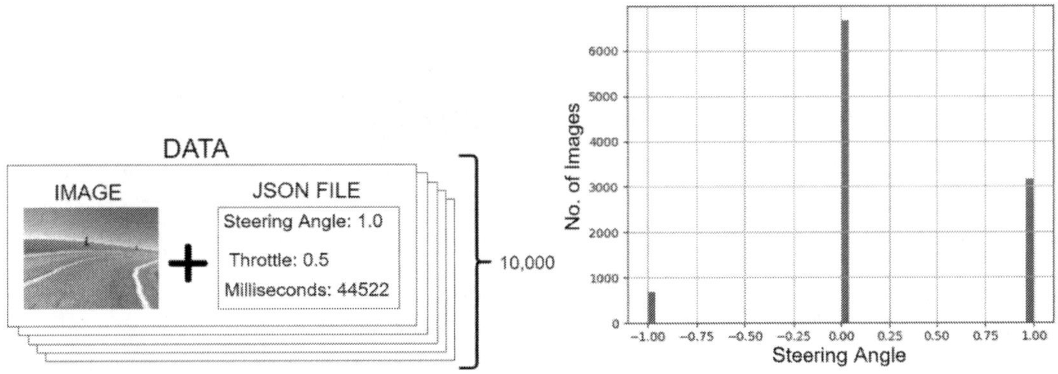

(a) Data Composition

(b) Data Distribution

Figure 3: Image Data Visualization

Figure 4: Donkey Car Simulation in Linux Environment

thing to note is that all new resolutions have the same aspect ratio of 4:3 as the default resolution. This was done so as to maintain a level of consistency in our tests and results.

After rescaling the image data as shown in Fig. 5(a), we uploaded them separately to google colaboratory for training. The training results in a H5 file. The H5 file is then uploaded to the simulation vehicle to be used for inference that will result in self-driving. Testing was done only for the Keras Linear and Keras Categorical neural network models.

5.2 Experiment Setup

We also set up an experiment by creating a simple real-world to obtain 10,000 frames and then test the autonomous car driving around the course multiple times. We explored the influence of reducing the resolution of an image on the speed of the self-driving vehicle. An assessment of network resilience in terms of accuracy has been done by Blasinski et al.[9]. But our system seeks to see an increase in speed given lower resolution images. Our proposed method downscales the image size from 160x120 to 120x90 pixels as shown in Fig. 5(b). Both of which have an aspect ratio of 4:3. Having tried various image resolutions, we found 120x90 to be the perfect mix between increasing the driving response and retaining as much relevant information as possible for self-driving.

We then performed evaluation on both the default system and also the modified system. To evaluate the system, we first got training data from the autonomous vehicle using the Keras IMU model. Since Keras IMU has all the inputs required by other models, and since colaboratory automatically parses the data needed for each model, the other models can use the same training data. In other words, there is no need of obtaining training data from each and every model. To evaluate the system we chose to measure the frames-per-second (FPS) and lap time of the vehicle. Testing for the above criteria was done for the Keras Linear and Keras Categrical neural network models. Donkey car currently only supports the old IMU MPU6050. We found a way to implement a newer version of IMU MPU9250 which provides more accurate relay signals and we made donkey car support it.

6 Results

We tested each neural network 5 times for each evaluation criteria and showed the average in the results section. We then separated the results of testing into 2 main categories: when the system is default and when the system is changed.

6.1 Simulation Result

Fig. 6 shows results from testing of inference of the autonomous car in the simulation. We obtained four different

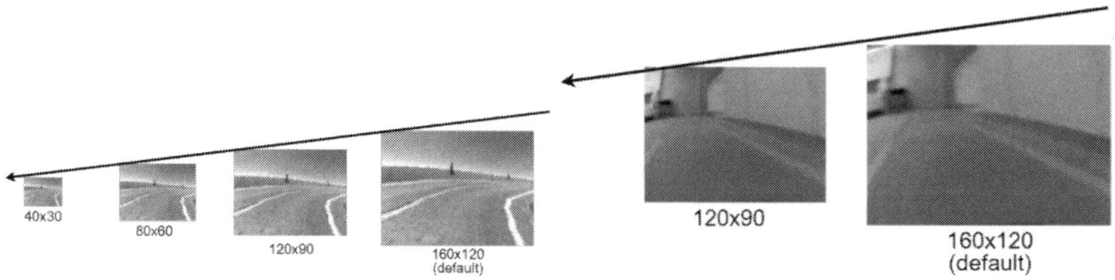

(a) Downscaling Simulation Images (b) Downscaling Experiment Images

Figure 5: Downscaling Images to Different Resoultions

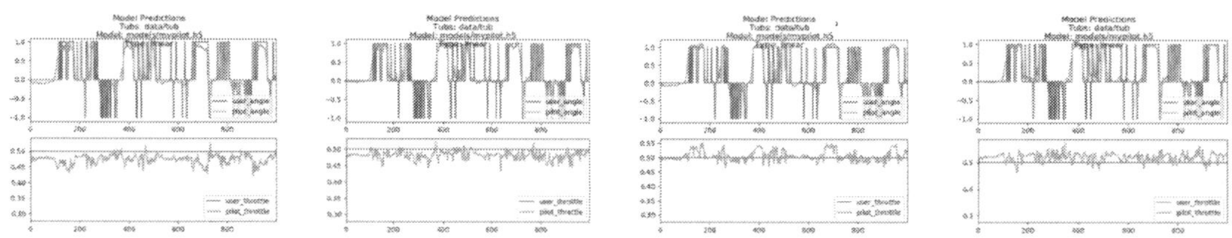

(a) 160 x 120 (default) (b) 120 x 90 (c) 80 x 60 (d) 40 x 30

Figure 6: Simulation results showing a gradual increase of speed as the scale of the image decreases

graphs, one for each image size. The bottom half shows the speed at which the car self-drove itself. The results show an increase in speed the lower the resolution gets. Thus, with regards to our goal of increasing the speed of self-driving, we have been successful in the simulation.

6.2 Frames-Per-Second (FPS)

We developed a frame rate recording application into the system to record the fps during the inference stage when the car is driving itself. This give us more insight into the performance of the autonomous algorithms in play. The code below was implemented in the vehicle.py file of donkey car.

```
start_time = time();
counter = 0;
while(1){
    counter++;
    if(conter == 10){
        fps = 10 / (time() - start_time);
        counter = 0;
        start_time = time();
    }
}
```

Fig. 7 shows an improvement in frames-per-second after changing the image size. This shows that a lower image size increases the response rate of the vehicle.Compared to [2] our system is at least 80% faster in frames-per-second and thus more responsive.

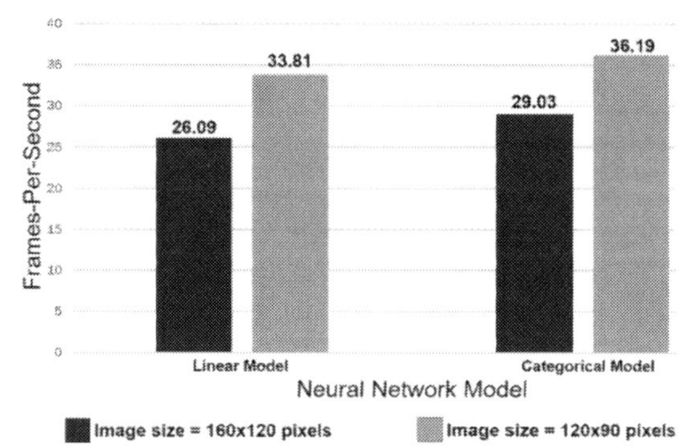

Figure 7: Average Freames-Per-Second

6.3 Lap Time

We set up a track and Donkey car was allowed to run 5 laps around the track for each neural network model for both the 160x120 and 120x90 image resolutions. The total time taken to complete the 5 laps was then recorded. Fig. 8 shows a decrease in total time taken to go round the track once the image has been downscaled from 160x120 to 120x90 pixels. This means that we achieved an increase in speed after downscaling the image size.

https://doi.org/10.1051/shsconf/20207704002

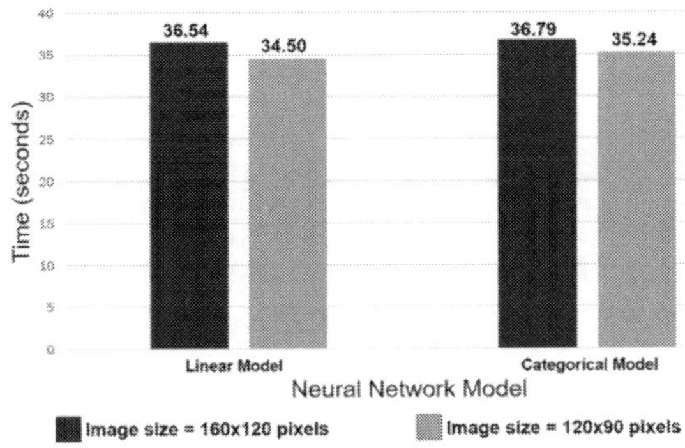

Figure 8: Total Lap Time

7 Conclusion

In this work, we succeeded in making an RC car run faster and have a higher response rate by downscaling the image size. We have shown that we were able to obtain and measure an increase in speed and response time for both the simulation and on the real-world race track. By increasing response time, we have made the system faster. From our results we deduce that the categorical model is the best in terms of consistency and reliability for research. However, better standards and processes are required in order to allow the creation of algorithms with better predictability and safety in mind. And although open-source autonomous vehicles have come a long way, more work is needed if they are to be used for serious research work requiring very high degrees of accuracy. We hope that this study encourages further investigation into making RC vehicles more adaptable for use in research activities.

8 Ackowledgements

To the Fabo Company, Japan for assisting with their expertise. The first author had received financial support from the Otsuka-Toshimi Scholarship Foundation.

References

[1] Yuchi Tian et al. "Deeptest: Automated testing of deep-neural-network-driven autonomous cars". In: *Proceedings of the 40th international conference on software engineering*. 2018, pp. 303–314.

[2] Hazem Rashed et al. "Fusemodnet: Real-time camera and lidar based moving object detection for robust low-light autonomous driving". In: *Proceedings of the IEEE International Conference on Computer Vision Workshops*. 2019, pp. 0–0.

[3] Justin Zheng, Kazuhide Okamoto, and Panagiotis Tsiotras. "Vision-Based Autonomous Vehicle Control using the Two-Point Visual Driver Control Model". In: *arXiv preprint arXiv:1910.04862* (2019).

[4] Xinlei Pan et al. "Virtual to real reinforcement learning for autonomous driving". In: *arXiv preprint arXiv:1704.03952* (2017).

[5] Qing Rao and Jelena Frtunikj. "Deep learning for self-driving cars: chances and challenges". In: *Proceedings of the 1st International Workshop on Software Engineering for AI in Autonomous Systems*. 2018, pp. 35–38.

[6] Qi Zhang and Tao Du. "Self-driving scale car trained by Deep reinforcement Learning". In: *arXiv preprint arXiv:1909.03467* (2019).

[7] Juntae Kim et al. "Deep learning algorithm using virtual environment data for self-driving car". In: *2019 International Conference on Artificial Intelligence in Information and Communication (ICAIIC)*. IEEE. 2019, pp. 444–448.

[8] *Donkey Car Documentation*. URL: docs.donkeycar.com.

[9] Henryk Blasinski et al. "Optimizing image acquisition systems for autonomous driving". In: *Electronic Imaging* 2018.5 (2018), pp. 161–1.

[10] Ali Ghofrani, Rahil Mahdian Toroghi, and Seyed Mojtaba Tabatabaie. "ICPS-net: an end-to-end RGB-based indoor camera positioning system using deep convolutional neural networks". In: *Twelfth International Conference on Machine Vision (ICMV 2019)*. Vol. 11433. International Society for Optics and Photonics. 2020, p. 1143323.

[11] Rachel Blin et al. "Road scenes analysis in adverse weather conditions by polarization-encoded images and adapted deep learning". In: *2019 IEEE Intelligent Transportation Systems Conference (ITSC)*. IEEE. 2019, pp. 27–32.

[12] Raj Shirolkar et al. "Self-Driving Autonomous Car using Raspberry Pi". In: *International Journal of Engineering Research Technology (IJERT) Volume 08, Issue 05* (2019).

[13] Anju Sudhakaran and Manju Manuel. "High-Quality Image Scaling Using V-Model". In: *2018 International Conference on Circuits and Systems in Digital Enterprise Technology (ICCSDET)*. IEEE. 2018, pp. 1–4.

[14] Yunfeng Zhang et al. "Single-image super-resolution based on rational fractal interpolation". In: *IEEE Transactions on Image Processing* 27.8 (2018), pp. 3782–3797.

Architecture and Design of a Spiking Neuron Processor Core Towards the Design of a Large-scale Event-Driven 3D-NoC-based Neuromorphic Processor

Mark Ogbodo[1,*], *Khanh* Dang, *Fukuchi* Tomohide, and *Abderazek* Abdallah

[1]Adaptive Systems Laboratory, Graduate School of Computer Science and Engineering, The University of Aizu, Japan.

Abstract. Neuromorphic computing tries to model in hardware the biological brain which is adept at operating in a rapid, real-time, parallel, low power, adaptive and fault-tolerant manner within a volume of 2 liters. Leveraging the event driven nature of Spiking Neural Network (SNN), neuromorphic systems have been able to demonstrate low power consumption by power gating sections of the network not driven by an event at any point in time. However, further exploration in this field towards the building of edge application friendly agents and efficient scalable neuromorphic systems with large number of synapses necessitates the building of small-sized low power spiking neuron processor core with efficient neuro-coding scheme and fault tolerance. This paper presents a spiking neuron processor core suitable for an event-driven Three-Dimensional Network on Chip (3D-NoC) SNN based neuromorphic systems. The spiking neuron Processor core houses an array of leaky integrate and fire (LIF) neurons, and utilizes a crossbar memory in modelling the synapses, all within a chip area of $0.12mm^2$ and was able to achieves an accuracy of 95.15% on MNIST dataset inference.

1 Introduction

Neuromorphic computing which is aimed at modeling the biological brain on hardware has gone through decades of research [1], and the ability of the biological brain to carryout rapid parallel computations in real time, in a fault tolerant and power efficient manner is the inspiration behind it [2]. The third generation of Artificial Neural Network (ANN) Spiking Neural Network (SNN) has proven to be more effective than its predecessors in this aim, mimicking more closely, the behavior of a biological neuron. The computation of Spiking neurons, like biological neurons are event triggered and communicate via spikes which could be sparse, and this makes them process information only when spikes are received. Neuromorphic architectures take advantage of the sparsity of spikes in SNN to reduce power consumption by power gating parts of the network that are not receiving spikes at any point in time. However, an efficient neuromorphic hardware targeted towards edge application and scalable neuromorphic architecture with large number of synapses requires building small sized neural Processors with low power consumption, efficient neuro-coding scheme, and fault tolerance.

To enable scalability while maintaining minimal power consumption and footprint, we presented in our previous work [3] a Three Dimensional Network-on-Chip (3D-NoC) SNN based architecture, a different approach from the conventional 2D-NoC which is limited in scalability, and consumes more power with increased latency and foot print, when scaling is attempted. The 3D-NoC based SNN architecture utilizes the merits of Network-on-Chips and 3D-Integrated Circuits [4] to enhance the parallelism and scalability of a neuromorphic processor in the third dimension, minimizing power consumption and communication latency as a result of the brief length and low power consumption of the Through Silicon Vias (TSVs) [5] employed in inter-layer communication [6][7]. The 3D-NoC SNN based architecture has the spiking neuron processor cores as the processing elements. These processing elements are connected in a 2D mesh topology to form tiles, and then stacked to form the 3D structure. Communication among the processing elements are made possible with 3D routers [8] (one for each spiking neuron processor core).

In this work, we present the architecture and design of a spiking neuron processor core described in Fig 1 suitable for the 3D-NoC based SNN architecture. The spiking neuron processor core is designed using the leaky integrate and fire (LIF) spiking neuron model which accumulates incoming spikes as membrane potential and stores in the buffer while experiencing leak, then fires an output spike when the membrane potential crosses a threshold. We have chosen the LIF spiking neuron model because of its simplicity, while maintaining some degree of biological plausibility, making it easier to implement. In designing the spiking neuron processor core, we utilized an SRAM for the N×N crossbar based synapse (N is the number of neurons) which has the synapse at the intersection of horizontal and vertical wires that represent the axons and dendrites of the neurons. An SRAM is also used for the neuron and synapse memory. A control unit implemented as a finite state machine is used to control the operations of the spiking neuron processor.

*Corresponding author e-mail: d8211104@u-aizu.ac.jp

 https://doi.org/10.1051/shsconf/20207704003

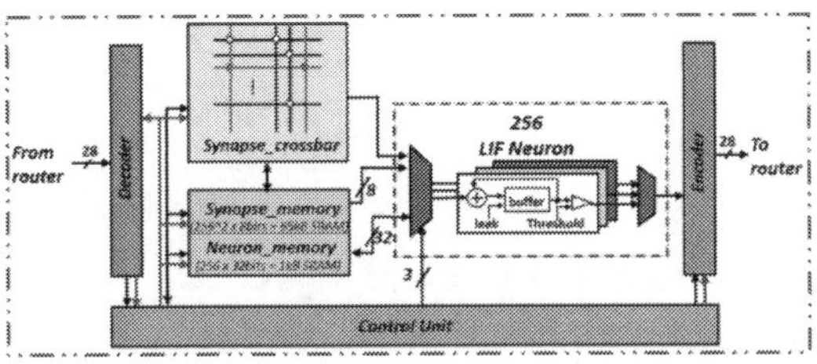

Figure 1. Spiking Neuron Processor Core Architecture.

2 Methodology

The spiking neuron processor core design is described using Verilog-HDL. Cadence tools were used for the synthesis and simulation. The hardware complexity is evaluated for power and area. For performance evaluation, the neuro-core is used to classify MNIST dataset [9] of 60,000 training, and 10,000 inference images on an SNN with an architecture of 748×48×10 trained off-chip with backpropagation as an ANN, then converted to SNN [10]. The MNIST images are converted to spikes using Poisson distribution before being sent to the network for classification. Finally, the result is compared with some existing work and presented in Figure 2.

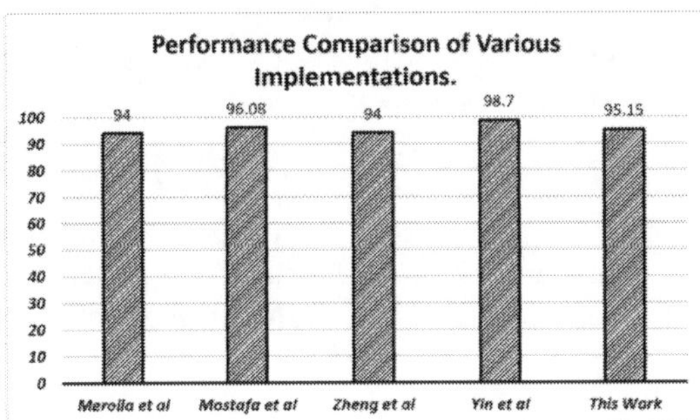

Figure 2. Area and Accuracy comparison

3 Result

The spiking neuron processor consumes an estimated power (leakage and dynamic) of $493.5018mW$, covers a chip area of $0.12mm^2$ and achieves an accuracy of 95.15% on MNIST dataset inference. The result was compared with some existing works reviewed in [11]. The comparison shows that the spiking neuron processor core has a good trade-off between area and accuracy

4 Conclusion and Future Work

This work presents the architecture and design of a spiking neuron processor core for 3D-NoC SNN, and evaluated its hardware complexity and performance. Future works towards realizing the 3D-NoC SNN architecture will require integrating the spiking neuron processor core into it, and exploring applications that will leverage the architecture.

References

[1] D. Monroe, *Neuromorphic computing gets ready for the (really) big time* (Association for Computing Machinery (ACM), 2014), Vol. 57, pp. 13–15

[2] T. Wunderlich, A.F. Kungl, E. Müller, A. Hartel, Y. Stradmann, S.A. Aamir, A. Grübl, A. Heimbrecht, K. Schreiber, D. Stöckel et al., *Demonstrating Advantages of Neuromorphic Computation: A Pilot Study* (2019), Vol. 13, p. 260, ISSN 1662-453X

[3] T.H. Vu, O.M. Ikechukwu, A. Ben Abdallah, *Fault-Tolerant Spike Routing Algorithm and Architecture for Three Dimensional NoC-Based Neuromorphic Systems* (2019), Vol. 7, pp. 90436–90452, ISSN 2169-3536

[4] K.N. Dang, A. Ben Ahmed, X. Tran, Y. Okuyama, A. Ben Abdallah, *A Comprehensive Reliability Assessment of Fault-Resilient Network-on-Chip Using Analytical Model* (2017), Vol. 25, pp. 3099–3112

[5] K.N. Dang, A.B. Ahmed, Y. Okuyama, B.A. Abderazek, *Scalable design methodology and online algorithm for TSV-cluster defects recovery in highly reliable 3D-NoC systems* (2017), pp. 1–1

[6] K.N. Dang, M.C. Meyer, A.B. Ahmed, A.B. Abdallah, X. Tran, *A non-blocking non-degrading multiple defects link testing method for 3D-Networks-on-Chip* (2020), pp. 1–1

[7] K.N. Dang, A.B. Ahmed, A.B. Abdallah, X. Tran, *TSV-OCT: A Scalable Online Multiple-TSV Defects Localization for Real-Time 3-D-IC Systems* (2019), Vol. 28, pp. 672–685

[8] H.T. Vu, Y. Okuyama, A. Ben Abdallah, *Analytical performance assessment and high-throughput low-latency spike routing algorithm for spiking neural network systems* (2019), Vol. 75

[9] Y. LeCun, *Mnist database of handwritten digits*, http://yann.lecun.com/exdb/mnist/ (2020-03-28)

[10] P.U. Diehl, D. Neil, J. Binas, M. Cook, S. Liu, M. Pfeiffer, *Fast-classifying, high-accuracy spiking deep networks through weight and threshold balancing*, in *(IJCNN)* (2015), pp. 1–8

[11] M. Bouvier, A. Valentian, T. Mesquida, F. Rummens, M. Reyboz, E. Vianello, E. Beigne, *Spiking Neural Networks Hardware Implementations and Challenges: A Survey* (ACM, June 2019), Vol. 15, pp. 22:1–22:35, ISSN 1550-4832

A Study on QoE Improvement of Online Games with UDP Multipathization by SDN

Sou Takabayashi[1], *Yoshihiro Ito*[1]

[1]Nagoya Institute of Technology, Japan

Abstract. This paper studies QoE improvement of Online games by applying the UDP/TCP multi-pathization method by SDN. The method can distribute packets for one stream to multiple paths by controlling the network with software with-out any new transport layer protocol. The author evaluates QoE for two actual online games using the multi-pathization method by experiments with subjects. The experimental results show the following. The authors show that multi-pathization by SDN is effective for online games. However, to further improve QoE, it is necessary to investigate and examine the packet length threshold that is appropriate for online games when distributing packets to each path.

1 INTRODUCTION

In recent years, the market for online games has been expanding in the world. The market size has exceeded 1000 million dollars and it is expected to reach 1700 million dollars by 2022[2]. Especially attention has been focused on `e-Sports', which refers to competitions and sports played against computer games and video games. E-Sports com- petitions are held all over the world, and the competition population including the audience is said to be 350 million.

As online games develop, a more comfortable environment for users is desired. In order to consist of such environments, a network with low communication delay and packet loss is required. However, the number of online game services be- comes large, the amount of traffic generated by them also in- creases. This causes congestion over the network and makes high communication delay and many packet losses.

To solve the above problem, we consider network control by SDN. SDN is an abbreviation of Software Dened Net- working and is a generic term for technologies that can control network devices centrally with a single software and it can change network configurations and settings flexibly and dynamically. For example, UDP cannot use multiple paths simultaneously. However, by SDN, it is possible to realize UDP data transmission over multiple paths without any new protocol that supports multiple paths, such as MPUDP [3]. If the transmission over multiple paths can be performed by SDN, network congestion will be suppressed by distributing the load to multiple paths without changing any existing configurations on terminals. Furthermore, even if a part of a network is disconnected, the UDP data transmission can be compensated by the other paths. That is, the connectivity between end terminals can be kept.

As such a control, [1] proposes TCP/UDP multi-pathization method by SDN. In this method, OpenFlow switches are controlled by the OpenFlow controller, and packets are distributed to multiple paths. At that time, network congestion can be suppressed by checking congestion for each route and controlling switches. Reference [1] studies the application of the multi-pathization method to Web services. We think that the method is also effective for online games, and we investigate the effectiveness of it by evaluating the user's quality of experience (QoE) through subject experiments.

This paper is organized as follows. Chapter 2 describes the multi-pathization method by SDN. Chapter 3 and Chapter 4 show our experiments and the results, respectively. Chapter 5 concludes our paper.

The use of sections to divide the text of the paper is optional and left as a decision for the author. Where the author wishes to divide the paper into sections the formatting shown in Table 2 should be used.

2 Multi-Pathization Method by SDN

In the conventional communication method using UDP, only a single path can be used. Therefore, if the amount of traffic on this path increases, congestion occurs, and the service provided by UDP deteriorates. Therefore, there is a need for a network that can distribute packets to multiple paths and reduce congestion. In [1], the multi-pathization method by SDN is adopted as such network control.

As described in Chapter 1, SDN refers to dynamically con- trolling a network with software and its architecture. In the conventional network, when sending data from the server to the client, the transmission path is determined by each net- work device individually, and it is di-cult to change to the optimum path according to the congestion. Besides, changing the network requires a lot of work because it requires setting up a large numer of devices. However, SDN separates the path control and data transfer processing that has been performed by each network device one by one, and dynamically controls the device that performs data transfer processing by software. This enables flexible network control.

In the multi-pathization method used in the [1], when congestion occurs in the network, SDN control the network to send packets using a path without congestion. As a result, congestion on the network can be suppressed and the throughput of packet transfer can be improved. Further- more, by using this method, end-to-end connectivity can be improved by using other paths even if there is a failure in one path. Also, SDN can be used to communicate with conventional protocols such as TCP and UDP without using new protocols such as MPTCP and MPUDP.

[1] uses OpenFlow as a technology for implementing SDN. OpenFlow performs path control with the OpenFlow controller and performs data transfer processing with the Open-Flow switch. In this experiment, We use OpenFlow to implement SDN.

3 Experiment

3.1 Purpose

We apply multi-pathization method by SDN to online games and assess QoE. For comparison, We assess QoE of online games even in an environment using a conventional UDP communication method. The purpose is to investigate the effectiveness of this multi-pathization method for online games.

3.2 Experimental environment

Our experimental network is shown in Fig. 1. This net- work consists of two game terminals (game terminal 1 and game terminal 2), a load client, a load server, an Open- Flow controller, four OpenFlow switches (OpenFlow switch 1 through OpenFlow switch 4) and a network emulator. We use Trema as an OpenFlow controller. Trema [5] is one of the frameworks of OpenFlow controller. We adopt Open vSwitch as openow switches. The threshold value of the packet length used to assign packets to paths is set to 300 bytes as the same with [1]. Due to the circumstances of the experimental environment, subjects play the game on game terminal 1. Since game wins and losses may affect QoE, I always play as an opponent on game terminal 2 to maintain fairness.

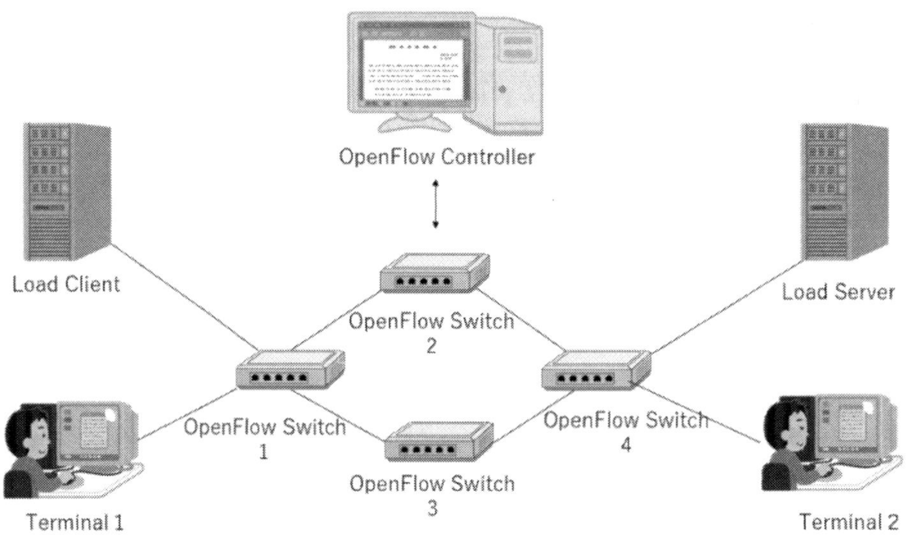

Fig. 1. Experimental configuration diagram

For comparison, we assess not only QoE with the multi- pathization method but also that without the method. Here we prepare two paths (Path1 and Path2) over the experimental network. Path1 and Path2 are constructed via OpenFlow switch2 and OpenFlow switch 3, respectively.

When we assess QoE without the multi-pathization method, the traffic between the game terminals passes through Path1. On the other hand, for the assessment of QoE with the multi-pathization method, we use both of Path1 and Path2. In either case, we generate load traffic, which makes a path congested over only Path1. In order to generate the load traffic, we use iPerf[7]. Moreover, we add delay by a net- work emulator which is between OpenFlow switches. When we assess QoE without the multi-pathization, we add de- lay between OpenFlow switch1 and OpenFlow switch2. For assessment QoE with the multi-pathization, we add delay between OpenFlow switch1 and OpenFlow switch2, and be- tween OpenFlow switch1 and OpenFlow switch 3.

We consider the satisfaction, which is one of the usability scales standardized in ISO 9241-11, as a QoE parameter. We use the SD method [6] to assess satisfaction. The SD method is a psychological method that evaluates an individual's impression of a problem using conflicting adjective pairs. Each adjective pair is evaluated on a 5-point scale, and 20 sets of questions are used for the evaluation. The satisfaction in this paper is the mean of the voted score for the 20 pairs of questions. We used items related to video, related to sound, related to operability, and related to the quality of experience such as `interesting' and `satisfied'. Fig. 2 shows the adjective pairs used in this experiment.

about video
natural 5 —— 4 —— 3 —— 2 —— 1 unnatural
coherent 5 —— 4 —— 3 —— 2 —— 1 collasped
smooth 5 —— 4 —— 3 —— 2 —— 1 rough
ease to see 5 —— 4 —— 3 —— 2 —— 1 difficult to see
beautiful 5 —— 4 —— 3 —— 2 —— 1 ugly
about sound
natural 5 —— 4 —— 3 —— 2 —— 1 unnatural
beautiful 5 —— 4 —— 3 —— 2 —— 1 ugly
smooth 5 —— 4 —— 3 —— 2 —— 1 rough
about operation
stable 5 —— 4 —— 3 —— 2 —— 1 unstable
light 5 —— 4 —— 3 —— 2 —— 1 heavy
good at responsiveness 5 —— 4 —— 3 —— 2 —— 1 bad at responsiveness
sensation of user
interesting 5 —— 4 —— 3 —— 2 —— 1 boring
pleasant 5 —— 4 —— 3 —— 2 —— 1 unpleasant
confortable 5 —— 4 —— 3 —— 2 —— 1 unconfortable
favorite 5 —— 4 —— 3 —— 2 —— 1 unfavorite
approachable 5 —— 4 —— 3 —— 2 —— 1 inaccessible
easy 5 —— 4 —— 3 —— 2 —— 1 difficult
laborless 5 —— 4 —— 3 —— 2 —— 1 tiring
attractive 5 —— 4 —— 3 —— 2 —— 1 unattractive
satisfied 5 —— 4 —— 3 —— 2 —— 1 dissatisfied

Fig. 2. Question items for experiments

In this study, we target two online games: Paintball Party 2[8] and SuperTuxKart[9]. Paintball Party 2 is a game that multiple players shoot guns and defeat each other. Players move on the 2D field using dash or jump and use items that are falling on the field. The winner is the player who defeated more opponents in time. Another game, SuperTuxKart is a car racing game. Players aim at the goal faster than other players by using not only the accelerator but also brake and drift. It is also possible to pick up items falling on the course and attack or accelerate using them. Paintball Party 2 can be played with up to 16 players, and SuperTuxKart can play with up to 8 players in a local environment, but in this experiment, two players play one-on-one in each online game. Fig. 3 shows the Paintball Party 2 game screen, and Fig. 4 shows the SuperTuxKart game screen.

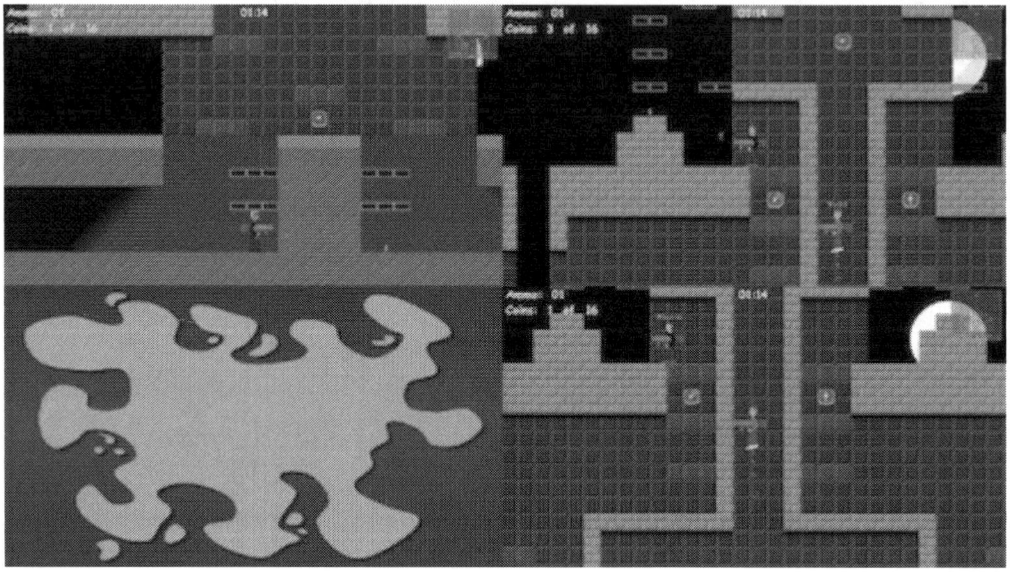

Fig. 3. Game screen of Paintball Party 2

Fig. 4. Game screen of SuperTuxKart

In this paper, we treat 12 environments. Fig. 6 shows environment for Paintball Party 2 and Fig. 5 shows environment for SupertuxKart. Environments 5 to 12 use the multi-pathization method and environments 1 to 4 without it. Among them, the experiment is divided into environments with no load or delay, environments with the only load, environments with the only delay, and environments with both load and delay. For example, about Paintball Party 2, the number of connections when applying load was set to 374, and the delay was set to 200ms. If the load and delay are too small, users can play the game without com- plaints and if it is too large, they cannot be able to play the game. In order to avoid this, the load and delay values were set by the author in a preliminary experiment and found to be just right.

environment	path	number of connections	delay of path1(ms)	delay of path2(ms)
Env1	normal	0	0	
Env2			200	
Env3		374	0	
Env4			200	
Env5	Multi-pathization	0	0	0
Env6				200
Env7			200	0
Env8				200
Env9		374	0	0
Env10				200
Env11			200	0
Env12				200

Fig. 5. Communication environment of Paintball Party 2

environment	path	number of connections	delay of path1(ms)	delay of path2(ms)
Env1	normal	0	0	
Env2			500	
Env3		374	0	
Env4			500	
Env5	Multi-pathization	0	0	0
Env6				500
Env7			500	0
Env8				500
Env9		374	0	0
Env10				500
Env11			500	0
Env12				500

Fig. 6. Communication environment of SuperTuxKart

4 Results

We investigate the results for PaintParty2. First, we consider the case with no load. To compare with QoE of Env1(SINGLE), which is no delay and no load, Env 5(MULTI) is close to Env1 but Env6(MULTI) is lower than Env1. This reason is that in Env6 send packets using Path2 but the delay of Path2 is 200ms, so the assignment of packets to Path2 causes the deterioration of QoE. On the other hand, QoE of Env2(SINGLE), which is no load and with delay, is lower than Env7(MULTI) but higher than Env8(MULTI). This is probably because most of the packets used in this game use path 2. From the result, the multi-pathization with heterogeneous paths may degrade QoE of PaintParty2 with no load environment.

Next, let us consider environments with load. QoE of Env3(SINGLE), which is with load and no delay, is slightly but lower than that of Env9(MULTI). But QoE of Env4(SINGLE), which with load and with delay, is less than both of Env10(MULTI) and Env11(MULTI).

This might be because the influence of the load could be reduced by using the multi-pathization method. Therefore, for PaintParty2, under congested environment with long delay, the multi-pathization method is effective.

Next, we consider the cases of SuperTuxKart. Under environments of Env2, Env 4, Env6, Env8, Env10 and Env12, QoE is degraded. That is, for SINGLE, when with no delay, QoE becomes high regardless of the load. On the other hand, for MULTI, QoE is high when no delay for Path2. Also, in SuperTuxCart, the multi-pathization method assigns almost packets to Path2. Therefore, if we modify the multi- pathization method to select a path according to RTT of paths, QoE of these games will be higher than that of this time's experiments. So, we need to investigate the packet lengths in these games and consider the optimal threshold for assigning them.

From the results of experiments on two games, we found that the multi-pathization method used in this experiment is effective for online games because it can avoid congestion and delay. However, for future works, we examine the thresholds for distributing packets not only for the two games used in this experiment but also for various games.

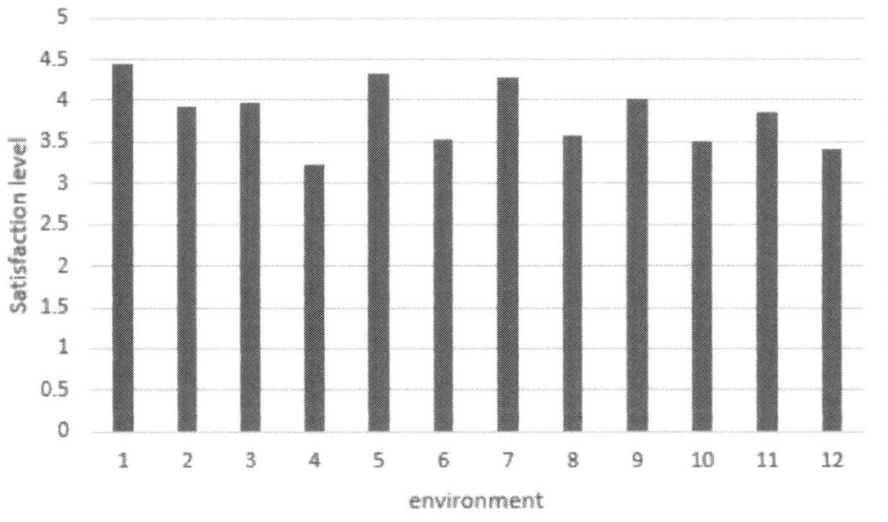

Fig. 7. Result of Paintball Party 2

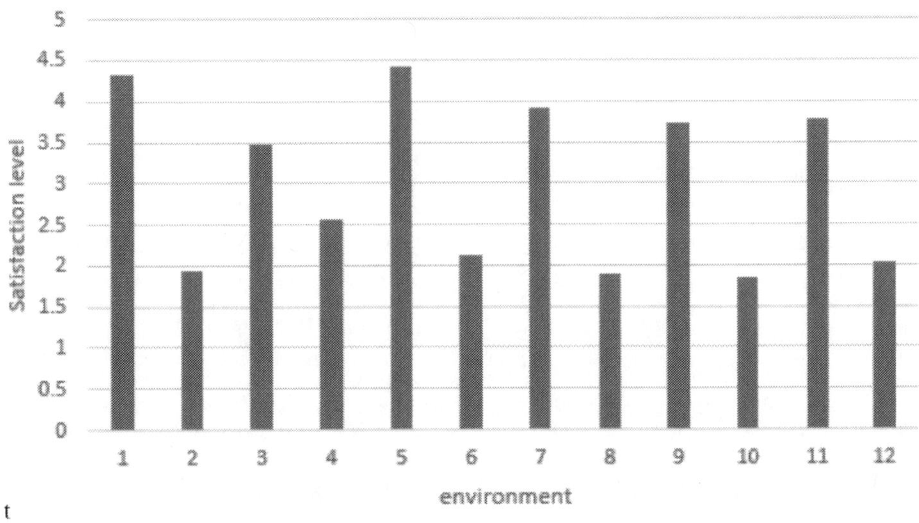

t **Fig. 8**
Result of SuperTuxKart

5 Conclusions

This paper studied the application of the multi-pathization method by SDN to online games by experiments with subjects. Experimental results show that this method is effective for online games.

However, it is not clear that the packet length threshold used to distribute used in this experiment is most effective for online games. Therefore, as future work, we will investigate the most effective threshold for online games.

6 Acknowledgments

The authors would like to thank Ms.Kaori Iwata and the member of our laboratory for their assistance in our research. In addition, we also thank the subjects who cooperated in our experiment.

References

[1] K. Iwata and Y. Ito. " Proposal and Development of TCP Multi-Pathization Method with SDN by IoT Devices " . Proceedings of ITNAC, pp.1-16, November 2017.
[2] https://www.statista.com/statistics/490522/global esports-market-revenue/
[3] S Liu, W Lei, W Zhang, H Li." MPUDP: Multipath Multimedia Transport Protocol over Overlay Network. " 5th International Conference on Machinery, Materials and Computing Technology (ICMMCT 2017), vol.126,pp731-734, April 2017
[4] A. Ford, C. Raiciu, M. Handley, and O. Bonaventure. TCP Extensions for Multipath Operation with Multiple Addresses. RFC 6824 (Experimental), January 2013.
[5] _Trema_. https://trema.github.io/trema/.
[6] _Semantic Di_erential_.Scalehttps://businessjargons.com/semantic-di_erential scale.html
[7] _ What is iPerf_. https://iperf.fr/
[8] _Paintball Party 2_. http://www.t3-i.com/pages/project.php?id=paintball_party_2

[9] _SuperTuxKart_.https://supertuxkart.net/Main_Page

Akabeko Ensemble: Cultural multimodal helical computer music installation

Yoshiki Tokumitsu[1] *& Michael Cohen,*[1]

[1] Spatial Media Group, Computer Arts Lab., University of Aizu; Aizu-Wakamatsu, Fukushima 965-8580; Japan

Abstract. In this study, we made "Aka-beko" choral ensemble. It comprises an octave of a chromatic musical scale, arranged in a helix and populated by animated oxen, instances of a regional mascot, who lift their heads and sing when triggered by events from a realtime MIDI keyboard controller. The application installation in the University of Aizu UBIC 3D Theater features stereographic display and spatialized sound.

1 Introduction

1.1 Visual music

Visual music displays music multimodally, synesthetically rendering musical information visually as well as acoustically. In this research, we developed a multimedia music performance application designed especially to flatter special features of a University of Aizu venue, the so-called UBIC 3D Theater. CAD software Blender was used to make an Aka-beko (red ox) model, which was imported into game engine Unity [3] for procedural instantiation, parametric livery (color), arrangement (3D position, including location and orientation), rigging (connection between physical controller and virtual object), animation (idling gesture of head-bobbing and occasional head-raising singing howls), and audio clip cueing.

1.2 Helical structure of scales

Musical scales can be modeled as helices, with circumplex (azimuthal) dimension corresponding to pitch class (Do, Do#, Re, etc.) and longitudinal dimension corresponding to absolute pitch, basically the fundamental frequency of a complex tone. Notes arranged in such fashion revolve around a notional listener in the tube of the helix as they climb a scale [1]. We preserve the customary left-to-right order of ascending scales (reflecting cultural preference for left-to-right literacy, perhaps based on awkwardness of writing right-to-left with a right hand). To highlight this structure, the oxen were arranged to have a somewhat redundant coding, rotated to face the center of the left-handed helix, and colored (their name notwithstanding) according to hue on a color wheel [4].

In such a convention, then, a red ox is at 'north' or '12 o'clock,' an orange one 30 degrees clockwise at a little past 'north-north-east' or '1 o'clock,' etc. For a chromatic octave (including accidentals as well as the diatonic scale), the number of notes including the doubled first note is 13.

1.3 Procedural modeling

We used programmatic specification of objects (in our case, Akabeko position, color, etc.), rather than manual arrangement. A single "prefab," with an exemplar generic template, is instantiated 13 times at runtime, all of them together performing a little dance-like ceremony as they are introduced, somewhat resembling the parade of sumo wrestlers before a tournament.

Using parametric specification of cylindrical coordinates to naturally express the location (azimuth around a ring of fixed radius), orientation (facing direction), and color of each ox, the angular bearing and rotational yaw are determined by

$$\text{bearing} = n * 360 / N,$$

$$\text{yaw} = 180 - \text{bearing},$$

where n is index of the Akabeko object and N is the total number of them in an octave, which is a dozen in our case (since the octave doubling of the tonic shouldn't be counted for the number of semitones in a single octave). Likewise, the altitude, which corresponds directly to pitch, is also proportional to note index:

$$\text{height} \propto n * 360 / N$$

2. Implementation

2.1 Blender

CAD software Blender was used to create an Akabeko model, imported into Unity as prefab (template). The Blender model comprises two parts, head and body, with the head suspended from the body through a neck hole. The model was augmented with a default "idling" head-bobbing animation and a head-raising singing gesture. The bobbing animation is a sinusoidal-like motion which starts in a neutral position, raises the head (¼), then lowers through that datum (2/4) all the way down (¾), finally raising it again (4/4) before repeating the cycle. The head-raising singing gesture, triggered by a "`note on`" MIDI event, resembles the corresponding phase of the head-bogging gesture, its "first quarter," but has greater amplitude, emphasizing the singing. The singing head is kept in raised position until the corresponding "note off" event is received, at which point the head drops back into its default bobbing, awaiting more singing cues.

Figure 1: 3D Akabeko Model

2.2 Unity

Unity is one of the most popular real time 3D development platforms. It can be used to develop various software including 2D, 3D, VR and AR environments and experiences. It is used to arrange, animate, and project stereographic rendering.

2.3 MidiJack

MidiJack [2] is middleware for connecting a MIDI controller to Unity rigging (connection between real controller and virtual object). It is used to trigger respective choral events, mapping between the tones across one octave (chromatic scale) to corresponding Akabeko ensemble members.

Ensemble voices (instrument, timbre, or "patch") are supplied by Shakuhachi notes, prerendered by Mathematica as audio files, imported into Unity as audio clips. They are triggered at runtime by MIDI events, auditorily rendered along with singing gesture.

2.4 Animation

The cultural Akabeko has a natural "head-bobbing" or "bobble-head" default nodding, used in our application as a default "idling gesture." This gesture was originally developed in Blender by creating several key poses (Figs. 1, 2, 3) and inserting them into keyframes (Fig. 4), finally adjusted to interpolate smoothly.

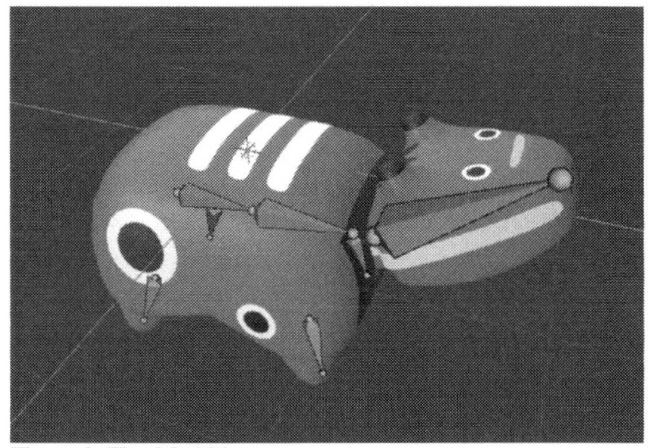

Figure 2: Head-bobbing, up

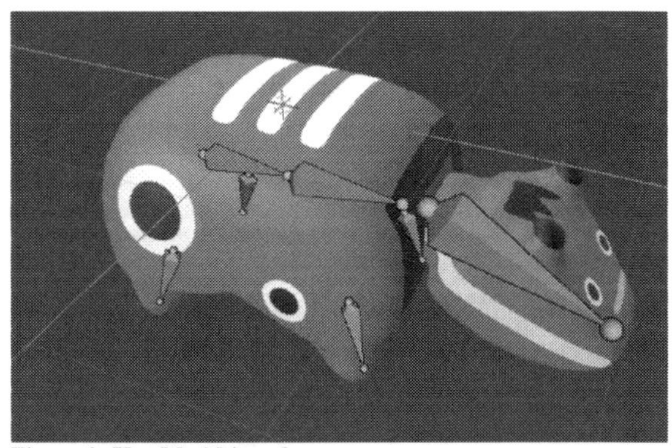

Figure 3: Head-bobbing, down

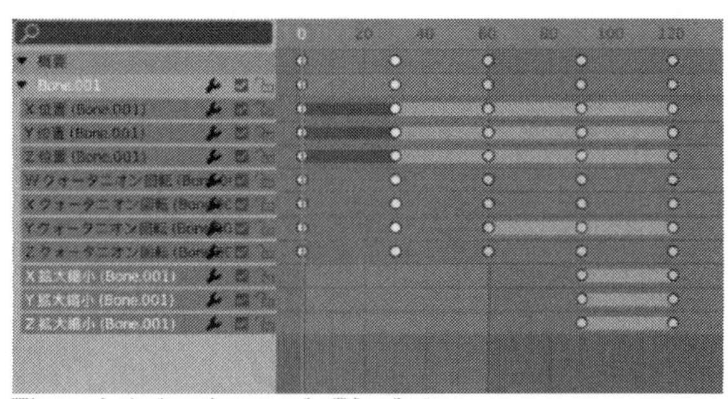

Figure 4: Animation graph (Blender)

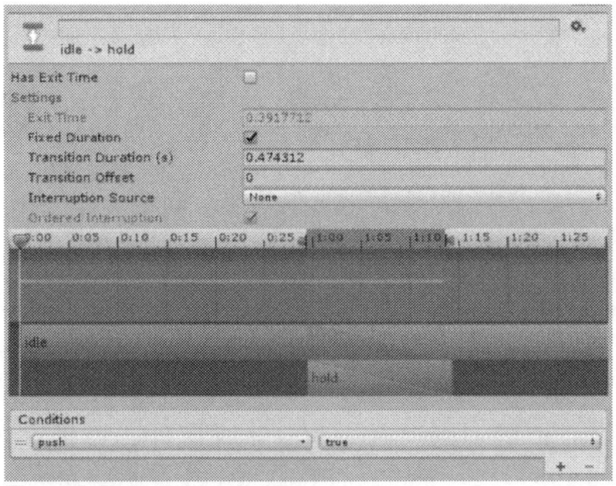

Figure 5: Unity animator

Unity automatically transitions between the two animations [5], adjusting the animation switching time with Fixed Duration (Fig. 5). The transition animation with the transition duration value 1 takes the same amount of time as the animation above. The animation is played below from the middle by changing the value of Transition Offset. A natural gesture when singing is to raise (not lower) head. We smoothly integrate default head-bobbing idling gesture with singing gesture when respective note is played.

2.5 Stereographic display

Having arranged separate but attached left and right cameras for stereographic display, we configured separate rendering windows, driving separate, passively polarized filtered projectors. The overlaid stereo pair is projected on a "silver screen" that preserves polarization. Circularly polarized lenses eyewear (corresponding to projector filters) worn by users separate left and right views for binocular viewing.

2.6 Displaced multimedia perspectives

Our scene is not "virtual reality," which features an intimate, egocentric, 1st-person perspective on a virtual world, but an abstract 3rd-person experience: the visual perspective, represented by the virtual stereo camera, is best placed outside the helix, typically behind 6 o'clock (or south), the better to see the entire Aka-beko ensemble. However, the virtual spatial microphone is best located in the tube of the helix, the better to appreciate the directionalized notes. By separating the virtual microphone and virtual camera, graphical rendering is from outside of helix, whereas acoustic rendering is from within the helix.

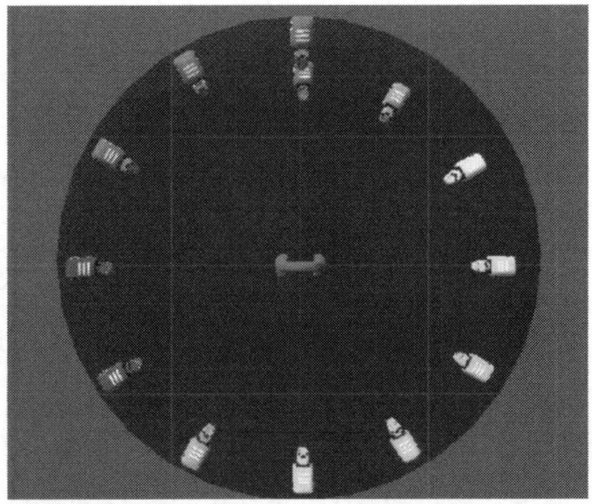

Figure 6: Modulate color and arrange as helix

2.7 Zig Sim

Zig Sim [6] is smartphone application for networked control. It uses embedded IMU sensor such as smartphone and wireless LAN module such as Wi-Fi, as shown in Fig 7. Quaternion function was used to rotate camera rotates around Akabeko helix while revolving, always facing center of scene.

2.8 Spatial Sound & Rendering

Audio clips were prepared "offline" using Mathematica's Shakuhachi instrument, one for each of the 13 notes represented from the chromatic scale. These were attached to the respective oxen, one note each. These audio sources are configured as "2D" sources, like non-diegetic scene elements, so when triggered they are not immediately directionalized or spatialized by the game engine, but instead simply sent to the workstation audio output as an unmodified mono signal. The speaker array mixer is simultaneously configured to route such display to the respective ceiling-mounted speaker or more generally panned between a pair of speakers.

https://doi.org/10.1051/shsconf/20207704005

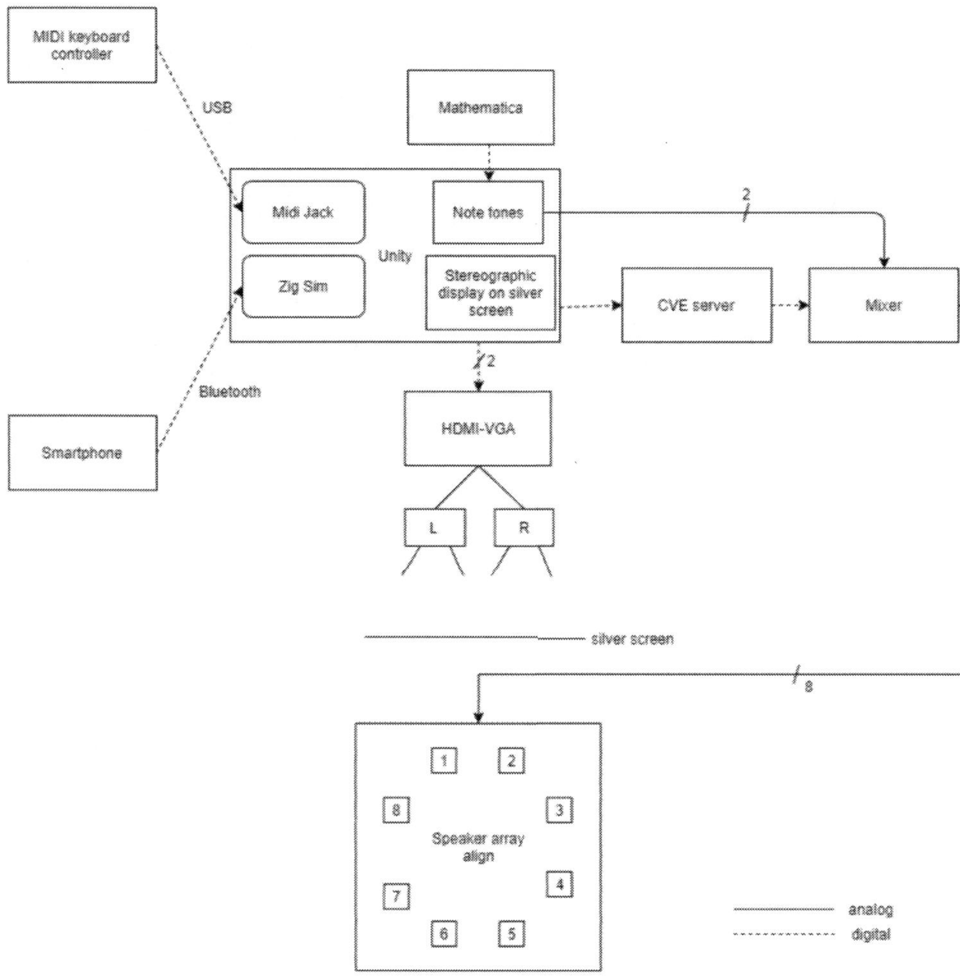

Figure 7: System schematic

2.9 Data flow for deployed application

Akabeko ensemble is hosted on a workstation (Mac Mini) running game engine. A MIDI keyboard controller is attached via USB, and a smartphone running Zig Sim connects via Wi-Fi. After a ceremonial "splash" (introductory cut scene), the virtual objects await triggers from the controllers: the oxen await musical cues to sing, and the camera awaits rotational imperatives to rotate and revolve around the ensemble helix in a phase-locked-loop "inspection gesture." Parallel game windows with runtime renderings from perspective of left and right halves of virtual stereo camera are connected to passively polarized stereo projectors, which imagery bounces off a silver screen that preserves such polarity, whence guests can see stereo imagery through complementary eyewear, a.k.a. "3D glasses."

3. Conclusion and Future Work

Our proof-of-concert has several restrictions. Because unextended analog audio output jack on workstation is stereo, only 1 or at most 2 output channels could be directly diffused by the speaker array. This means that the system is "monophonic": only 1 note can be rendered at once without confusing collision of a chord tones, at the location of the last-played note of an arpeggio. To work-around this limitation, we could deploy an audio interface, a digital "fan-out" that allows distribution of more than two audio channels. (Such interfaces had been based on Firewire or USB, and modern USB-C bandwidth can support many audio channels.) Our sound spatializer mixer has eight inputs, so that level of polyphony could be supported. We would have to cull or aggregate some of the keys to accommodate extended but still limited input receptivity, the diatonic scale (just the "white notes") being a natural selection. Only songs within a certain key (such as C or A minor) could be played properly, but polyphony would be full. Since the scale wraps around, notes in the same pitch class map to the same azimuthal direction, since our speaker array doesn't model altitude, height, or elevation.

4. Acknowledgements

We thank Ryouhei Hashimoto for his assistance.

References

[1] Jens Herder and Michael Cohen. "The Helical Keyboard: Perspectives for Spatial Auditory Displays and Visual Music". In: JNMR: J. of New Music Research 31.3 (2002). Ed. by Gunnar Johannsen and Giovanni De Poli, pp. 269–281. ISSN: 0929-8215.
DOI: 10.1076/jnmr.31.3.269.14180.

[2] MIDI Jack. https://github.com/keijiro/MidiJack

[3] Unity User Manual. https://docs.unity3d.com/Manual

[4] 【Unity】スクリプトで RGB と HSV を相互に変換する方法. http://nn-hokuson.hatenablog.com/entry/2017/04/12/194631

[5] 【Unity 開発】Animator Controller の遷移設定 (Duration 等)【ひよこエッセンス】 https://hiyotama.hatenablog.com/entry/2015/06/29/090000

[6] Zig Sim. https://zig-project.com

Narrowcasting visualization using particles for spatial sound conferencing

Koki Tsuda,[1] *Michael Cohen,*[1] *& Rintarō Satō*[1]

[1] Spatial Media Group, Computer Arts Lab., University of Aizu; Aizu-Wakamatsu, Fukushima 965-8580; Japan

Abstract. The goal of this study is to visualize duplex auditory communication filtered with narrowcasting. Narrowcasting is technology that enables media stream filtering for privacy. Audio narrowcasting has four operations (solo & mute and attend & deafen). In this research, communication from source to sink is determined according to these four operations, including "autofocus" determination of multipresent sinks, and visualized using flying particles. Soundscapes are compiled according to narrowcasting attributes. With such multimodal representation, users can more easily understand narrowcasting communication.

1 Introduction

1.1 Related Research

An audio narrowcasting interface was developed by the Spatial Media Group [1]. We can use a CVE (Collaborative Virtual Environment) to connect heterogeneous clients. We can connect our phone to Unity game engine, control player directions, and audition (listen to) spatial sound.

1.2 Narrowcasting

Narrowcasting is technology in communication applications such as chat-spaces or conferences that enables media stream filtering. It extends broadcast and multicast systems with articulated control. For audio communication, a source is a speaker, such as a mouth. A sink is listener, represented by ears. Narrowcasting has four attributes: solo & mute (for sources) and attend & deafen (for sinks).

1.3 Multipresence

Multipresence means having (virtual) presence in multiple places at once. In our application, a user designates multiple avatar icons as "self" to realize multipresence.

1.4 Autofocus

Multipresence introduces some ambiguity, as sources can be in the presence of multiple self-designated sinks. Each source must determine which single sink can hear its sound. Such determination is called "autofocus." For our simplified model, sources are considered omnidirectional, and orientation is not considered for estimation of loudness. Since intensity falls off with distance, active sources are each autofocused to their closest sink.

1.5 Narrowcasting predicate calculus formalization

The general expression of narrowcasting activation is

```
active(x) = ¬exclude(x) ∧
     ((∃y (include(y) ∧ (self(x)⇔self(y))))
     ⇒ include(x)),
```

where '¬' means "not," '∃' means "there exists," '∧' means "and," and '⇔' means equivalence.

A channel is active unless it has been explicitly disabled or a relevant peer has been focused upon to the exclusion of the respective object under consideration. So, for mute and select (solo), the source relation is

```
active(source x) = ¬mute(x) ∧
      ((∃y (select(y) ∧ (self(x)⇔self(y))))
      ⇒ select(x)).
```

For deafen and attend, the sink relation is

```
active(sink x) = ¬deafen(x) ∧
      ((∃y (attend(y) ∧ (self(x)⇔self(y))))
      ⇒ attend(x)).
```

1.6 Unity

Unity is a game engine for multiple platforms that can manage development tools, 2D/3D graphics, sound reproduction, and user interface management. It can be programmed in the C# and JavaScript programming

https://doi.org/10.1051/shsconf/20207704006

languages. Unity was used to develop a particle animation to visualize the narrowcasting interface.

1.7 Sources and Sinks

For auditory modeling, a source is virtual speaker, and its metaphorical organ is a mouth. A sink is a virtual listener, and its corresponding metaphorical organ is an ear. Narrowcasting operations include four commands— mute & deafen (excluding operations) and solo & attend (focusing operations). We use a 2D iconography to express these four orthogonal (independent) states (Fig. 1).

exclud

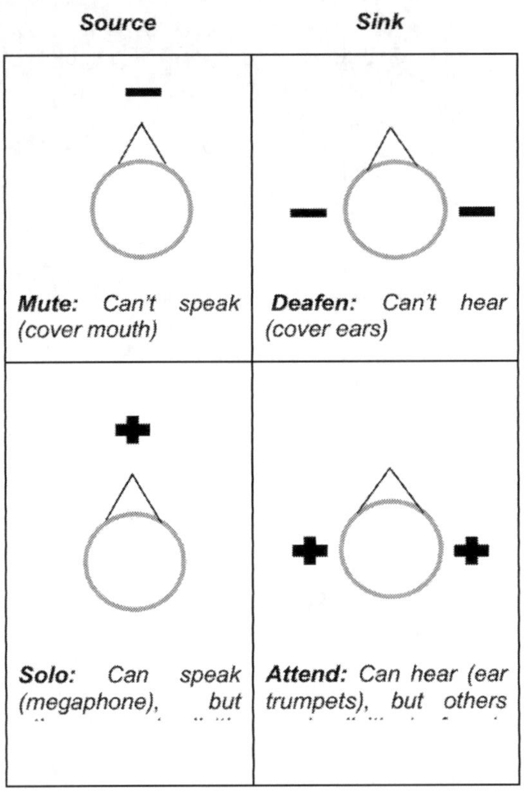

Fig. 1: Auditory narrowcasting attributes iconic representations

1.8 Particle

Particles were animated with Unity's particle system. Settings from the particle system components of Unity can be used to create various effects. For example, one can create effects such as rain, snow, and fire. We adjusted various parameters (duration, looping, start lifetime, speed, size, color, simulation space, emission, shape, triggers, renderer) to implement narrowcasting visualization particle animation.

2. Implementation

2.1 Make particle animation

We used Unity to extend narrowcasting interface, developing in the C# programming language. We extended a script written in C# (Channel Manager KJM) to implement particle animation in the narrowcasting interface. We configured this particle animation using Unity's particle system. As seen in Figs. 2 and 3, we used various parameters (duration, start lifetime, speed, size, color, simulation space, emission, shape, triggers, renderer) to animate particle flow from sources to sinks. Particles are continuously generated. We set particles as follows.

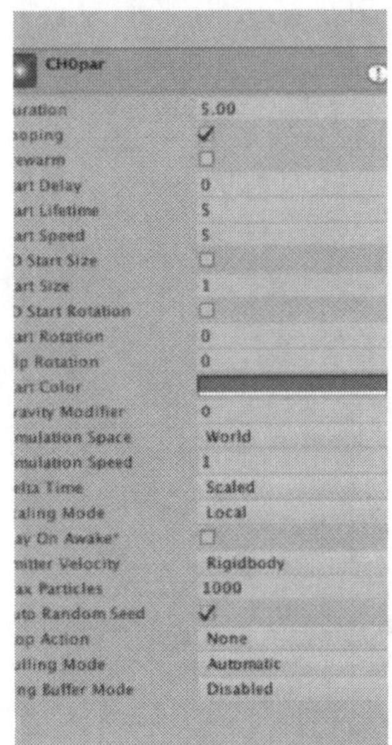

Fig. 2: Unity particle parameters

For Start Color attribute, color is that of source. For Simulation Space attribute, we used "`World`". By doing so, particles fly automatically from each source to their respectively determined ("autofocused") sink.

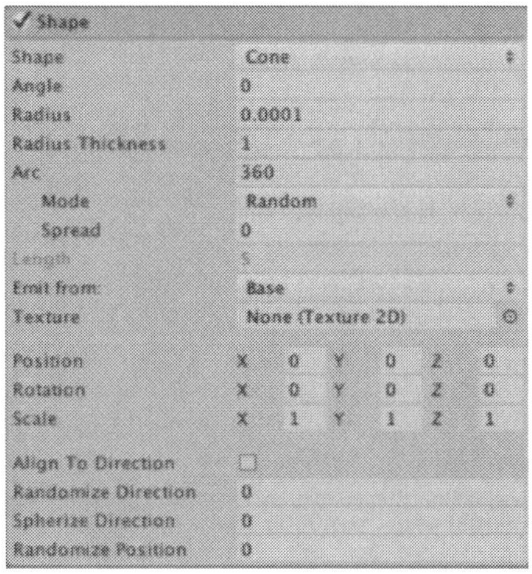

Fig. 3: Unity particles Shape module

Shape attribute: Shape is Conical. Angle is 0°. Radius is 0.0001, very tightly beamed, because it is necessary to make the particle fly in nearly straight direction.

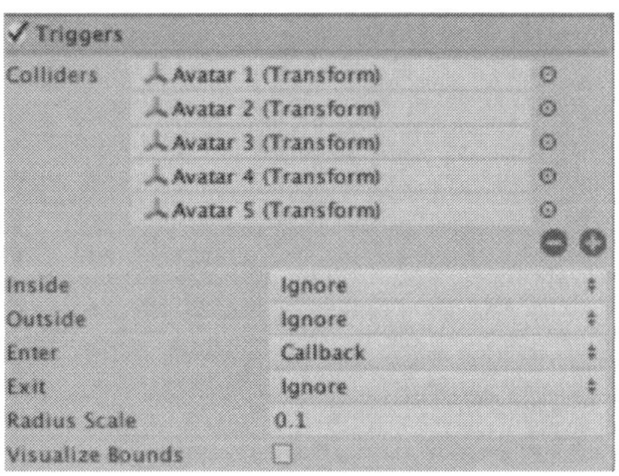

Fig. 4: Unity Triggers module

The `Colliders` attribute sets the collider of an object to trigger when a particle touches it. The `Enter` attribute is configured to invoke the `OnParticleTrigger` method with callback when a particle enters the collider. When each particle reaches its respective sink, the size of the colliding particle is set to 0.

2.2 Launch particles

Particle color (livery) is set to match that of its source. We use the function `Makeparticle` to launch particles towards the determined (autofocused) sink (as shown in Fig. 5).

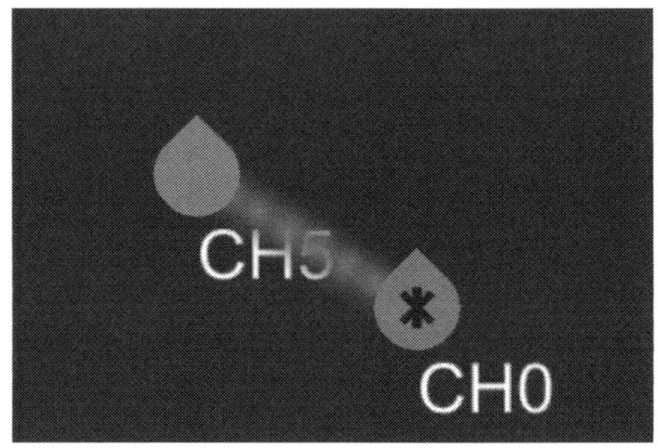

Fig. 5: Particle animation– Source is CH5; sink (asterisked) is CH0.

2.3 Control stop of particles

We use the `StopParticle` function to arrest the particles, thereby preventing them from continuing to move after they have reached their "destination."

2.4 Control particle collision

We use triggers to make particles disappear when they reach their respective sink. But it doesn't work because trigger reacts with other sinks along the flight path. Therefore, we developed a script written in C# (`Collision`) to solve the problem. By using the function of `OnParticleTrigger`, trigger responds only to the specified sink.

2.5 Compose music

 https://doi.org/10.1051/shsconf/20207704006

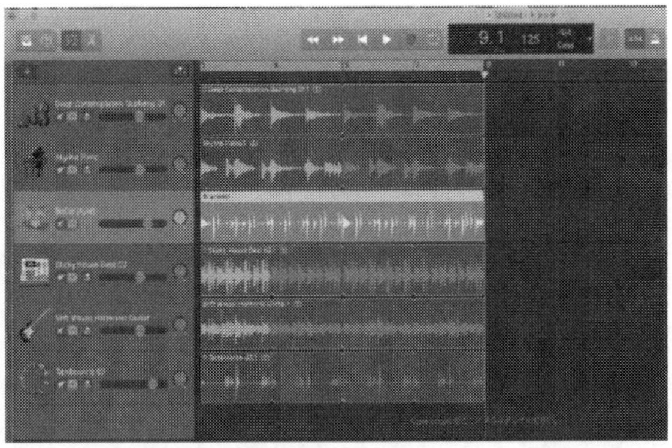

Figure 6: Demonstration music

We composed polyphonic music using GarageBand specifically for demonstrating this system, as shown in Fig. 6. The composition is intended to foster a calm mood.

3. Conclusion

We were able to visualize the state of narrowcasting communication, as shown in Fig. 7.

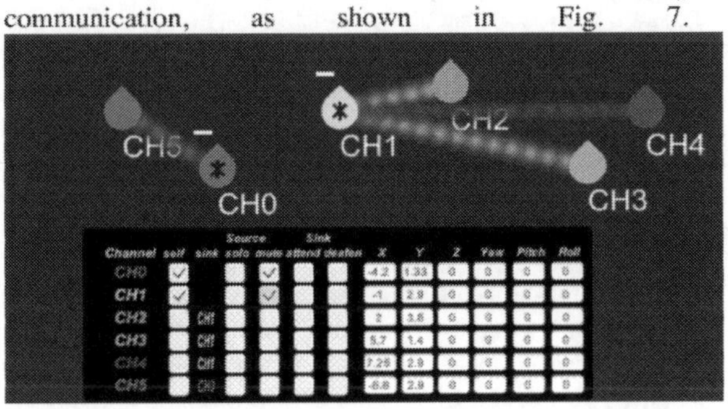

Fig. 7: Narrowcasting visualization– CH5 is auditioned by CH0, and CH2, CH3, and CH4 are auditioned by CH1.

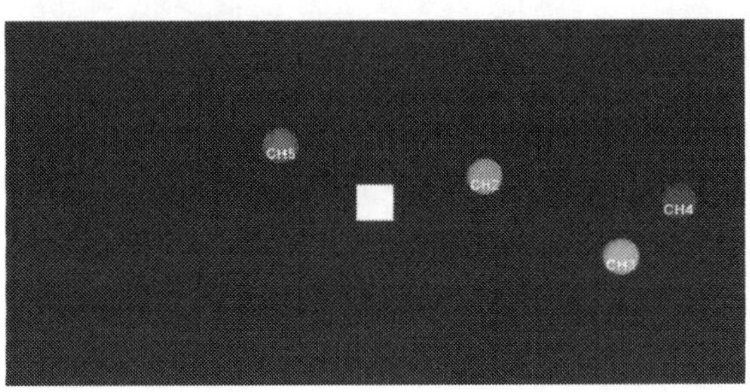

Fig. 8: Egocentric soundscape collapse

We could also deploy this program as native iOS & iPadOS application.

4. Future Work

In future work, we would like to apply technique applicable to immersive interface, such as that presented by HMD for VR or AR. We also plan to compose music specifically for demonstrating this system. Finally, the system is currently stand-alone, without networked media streams (only signaling), so it is appropriate only for offline music audition, not realtime conferencing. We hope to integrate realtime audio networking to test practical groupware applications.

5. Acknowledgements

We thank members of the Spatial Media Group. Yoshi Hoshino did the iOS & iPadOS port.

References

[1] Michael Cohen and Hiromasa Kojima. "Multipresence and Autofocus for Interpreted Narrowcasting". In: AES: Audio Engineering Society Int. Conf. on Spatial Reproduction — Aesthetics and Science. Tokyo, Aug. 2018. ***http://www.aes.org/e-lib/browse.cfm?elib=19653***

[2] Unity https://unity.com

[3] ParticleSystem (Shuriken) https://docs.unity3d.com/jp/460/Manual/class-ParticleSystem.html

[4] Unity5.4 の Particle System の Trigger と Collision モジュールの使方：http://hajimete-program.com/blog/2016/09/23/unity5-4 の particlesystem の trigger と collision モジュールの使い方/

[5] Unity's Particle Trigger Technique: https://docs.unity3d.com/ja/current/ScriptReference/MonoBehaviour.OnParticleTrigger.html

Assessment of TCP Multi-Pathization Method on IoT Devices by SDN based on WebQoE

Yuki Yoshida[1,*] and *Yoshihiro* Ito[1,**]

[1]Nagoya Institute of Technology, Graduate School of Engineering, Computer Science and Engineering, Gokiso, Nagoya city, Aichi prefecture, Japan

Abstract. This paper assesses QoE for a Web service (WebQoE) for the TCP multi-pathization method by SDN by experiments with subjects. The multi-pathization method is one of the QoS controls for IoT networks; it can multi-pathize a TCP connection without any changes of terminals or protocols. The previous work of the authors has evaluated QoS of Web services but has not assessed QoE. This paper assesses QoE of an online map service for the multi-pathization method by experiments with subjects. In the experiment, the authors treat various environments which differs in the amount of load traffic. The obtained results show that WebQoE for the multi-pathization method is always higher than that without the method. Consequently, the paper confirms that the multi-pathization is effective from point of users' view.

1 Introduction

With the development of the Internet and sensing technology, IoT (Internet of Things) devices, which connect various things such as home appliances and vehicles to the Internet, are increasing. As the number of services concerning IoT grows, the traffic generated by IoT devices will also rise rapidly. This causes congestion over a network and then degrades its quality of service (QoS).

In order to avoid congestion, traffic control over the network is inevitable. Especially, considering networks for IoT, such control needs to meet the following two requirements. Firstly, since a network for IoT is easy to change in configuration, it is necessary for the control to have the flexibility to change the network setting dynamically. Secondly, because IoT devices are unreliable, it is necessary that the control must be fault tolerant so that communication will not be interrupted if a part of the network is broken. However, since services using IoT are not assumed at the time when the standard protocols of the Internet were standardized, it is difficult to realize such network control only with existing protocols. For example, although it is conceivable to improve fault tolerance by using multiple network interfaces such as Wi-Fi and 4G, TCP cannot use multiple paths simultaneously.

Instead of TCP, it is possible to use multiple paths with MPTCP (MultiPath TCP [1]), which is the next-generation transport layer protocol. However, in order to replace TCP with MPTCP, it is necessary to modify all terminals and servers, this takes much time and cost.

In order to solve the above-mentioned problems, [2] proposes TCP multi-pathization method with SDN (Software Defined Networking [3]). Since this method is performed by SDN, a control which satisfies the above two requirements can be realized without using any new protocols such as MPTCP.

On the other hand, it is expected that Web services will be used on IoT devices due to the improvement of performance of IoT devices. As a result, it is required to study an application of the method of [2] to Web services. Reference [4] evaluates the QoS when using Web service with TCP multi-pathization method with SDN, and confirms the effectiveness to the Web service of the multi-pathization method. However, [4] does not treat QoE. In Web services, QoE is the most important because users finally decide the QoS of a Web service. It is indispensable to assess QoE of the TCP multi-pathization method for Web services.

In this paper, we assess QoE for a Web service(WebQoE) with TCP multi-pathization method by SDN by experiments with subjects and confirm its effectiveness from the viewpoint of QoE. The paper is organized as follows. Section II shows the TCP multi-pathization method we use in this study. Section III describes the details of the experiment. Section IV concludes this paper.

2 TCP Multi-Pathization method

The TCP multi-pathization proposed in [2] has the following four advantages.

- By using SDN, the method can be realized without modifying the end terminals.
- Under congestion, throughput can be improved by using multiple paths.
- It is possible to suppress the congestion on the network by branching the traffic into multiple paths.

*e-mail: yuki@en.nitech.ac.jp
**e-mail: yoshi@en.nitech.ac.jp

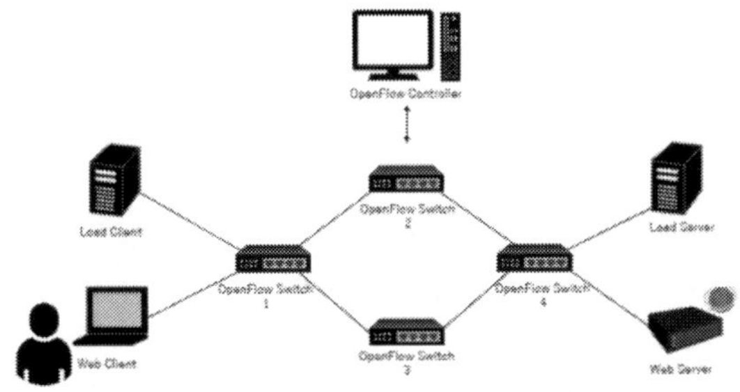

Figure 1. Experiment environment

- When one path breaks, end-to-end fault tolerance can be improved by using another path.

The multi-pathization method adopt OpenFlow as SDN. In this method, a TCP connection is multi-pathed by distributing packets to the paths on the OpenFlow switch where the path branches according to the congestion degree of the path and the packet length. The OpenFlow switch on each path sends statistics of its own network interface to the OpenFlow controller at a regular interval. The OpenFlow controller calculates the amount of traffic per unit time for each path. Based on this, the OpenFlow controller controls the OpenFlow switch to transfer packets whose packet length is more than or equal to the threshold value to a path with high traffic volume, and other packets to a path with low traffic volume.

3 Experiment

3.1 Purpose

In this experiment, we assess WebQoE of the TCP multi-pathization method by SDN. Note that we also compare it with normal TCP(single path).

3.2 Experiment environment

Our experiment environment is shown in Fig.1. This environment is composed of an OpenFlow controller, four OpenFlow switches(we refer to them as OpenFlow Switch 1 through OpenFlow Switch 4), a Web client, a Web server, a load client, a load server, and a network emulator. As an OpenFlow controller framework, we adopt Trema(0.4.6)[5]. The OpenFlow switches are realized with Open vSwitch(2.8.90)[6], which is virtual OpenFlow switch software.

3.3 Evaluation scale

We treat the usability defined in ISO 9241-11 [7] as WebQoE parameters and select one scale of them: the satisfaction. In order to assess the satisfaction for a Web service, we utilize the five-grade rating scale method[8] whose terms for evaluation are ‘very satisfied’, ‘satisfied’, ‘neither satisfied nor dissatisfied’, ‘dissatisfied’, and ‘very dissatisfied’. The terms for evaluation are assigned a number from 5 to 1, respectively. Thus we treat the mean of the voted score as a QoE parameter.

Table 1. experimental environments

No.	method	Number of TCP connections of load traffic
Env1	normal TCP	50
Env2	normal TCP	100
Env3	normal TCP	150
Env4	multi-pathization	50
Env5	multi-pathization	100
Env6	multi-pathization	150

3.4 Experiment contents

3.4.1 QoE evaluation experiment

In our experiment, we prepare two paths between the Web client and the Web server(Path1, Path2). Path 1 is the upper path via OpenFlow Switch 2 in Fig.1; Path 2 is the lower path via OpenFlow Switch 3. Note that only path 1 is used for communication by normal TCP(single path). In order to generate congestion over one of the paths, load traffic is generated over Path 1 for normal TCP and over Path 2 for multi-pathization method. To change the amount of traffic over the path, we change the number of TCP connections of the load traffic. As shown in Table 1, this experiment uses six experimental environments: Env1, Env2, Env3, Env4, Env5, and Env6. This paper utilizes a map service, which are Web services widely used around the world, as a target. We construct a map service as a Web server, based on the information published in OpenStreetMap[9], which is a project aimed at creating geographic information data. The subjects access the Web service on the Web client and use the map service for 90 seconds while the experimenter changes the delay and load traffic. The number of subjects is 10.

In each experimental environment, delay is added between OpenFlow Switch 1 and OpenFlow Switch 2 by the network emulator. In this experiment, six round trip delay values of 0 ms, 25 ms, 50 ms, 100 ms, 150 ms, and 200 ms are utilized. Also, the threshold of packet length used to determine the packet branching in this method is set to 300 bytes in [2] which is the proposal source of this method. However, we believe that this threshold needs to be reexamined when applying this method to Web services. Therefore, the following preliminary experiment will be conducted.

3.4.2 Threshold examination experiment

In order to investigate the threshold used for packet branching in this method, we perform QoS evaluation experiments with multiple thresholds. The experimental environment is the same as the QoS and QoE evaluation experiment. TCP throughput is used as an evaluation scale. The TCP throughput here is defined as the amount of

TCP data transfer(Kbyte/sec) per unit time between sending and receiving. ApacheBench is used to measure TCP throughput. ApacheBench is a web server benchmark tool bundled with Apache HTTP Server[10].

In order to determine the threshold options, we investigate the packet length distribution when communicating from the Web client to the map service in the Web server. Figure 2 shows the measured packet length distribution. By examining the details of each packet, we found the following. Packets for establishing/disconnecting TCP connections such as SYN packets and FIN packets are distributed in a group of 40 to 79 bytes. HTTP communication packets are distributed in a group of 160 to 319 bytes. ACK packets are distributed in a group of 1514 bytes.

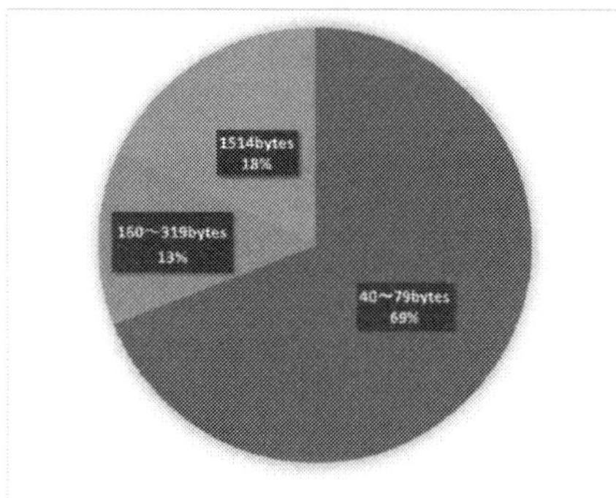

Figure 2. The packet length distribution

Packets for establishing/disconnecting TCP connections such as SYN packets and FIN packets are important because of the large number of TCP connections in Web service communication. Also, in this method, packets smaller than the threshold value are branched to an uncongested path. Therefore, there are two threshold options: 80 bytes that emphasize only TCP connection establishment/disconnection, and 300 bytes that also emphasize HTTP communication. Using the multi-pathization method that set these two threshold the single-path communication method, we measured TCP throughput when communication is performed between the Web client and the Web server for one minute with load and delay. The number of TCP connections for load traffic is five, and five types of delays of 0, 10, 25, 50, and 100 ms are used. The result is shown in Figure 3.

Looking at the figure 3, it can be seen that the throughput is highest when the threshold is 300 bytes. In addition, when the threshold is 80 bytes, the overall throughput is slightly lower than when the threshold is 300 bytes. Based on the above results, in this study, the packet length threshold used to determine packet branching in the multi-pathization method is set to 300 bytes.

3.5 Results and Discussion

Figure 4 depicts the satisfaction: In Fig. 4 the abscissa axis is the delay for Path 1 and the ordinate axis is the satisfaction value. For comparison, we also show QoS results of [4] in Fig. 5. The communication environment and network topology of [4] are all the same as those of this paper. Reference [4] measures the TCP throughput as a QoS parameter. Figure 5 depicts the measured TCP throughput; the abscissa axis is the delay for Path 1 and the ordinate axis is the TCP throughput; it also shows the regression lines in which the delay is an independent variable and the TCP throughput is a dependent variable.

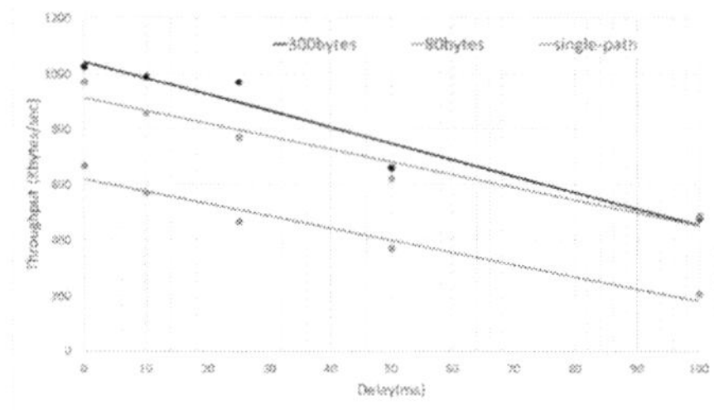

Figure 3. TCP throughput by threshold

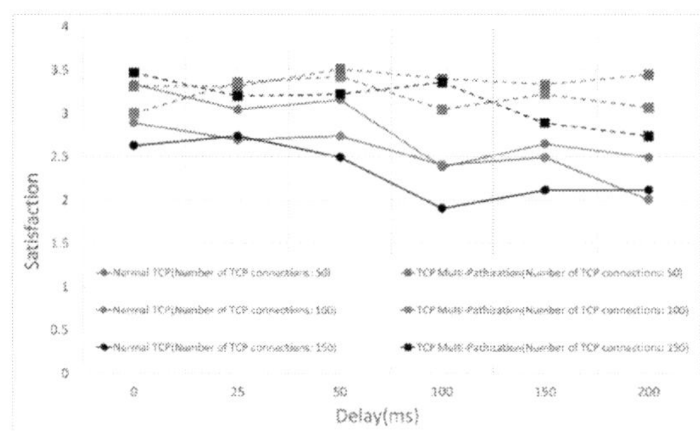

Figure 4. Satisfaction

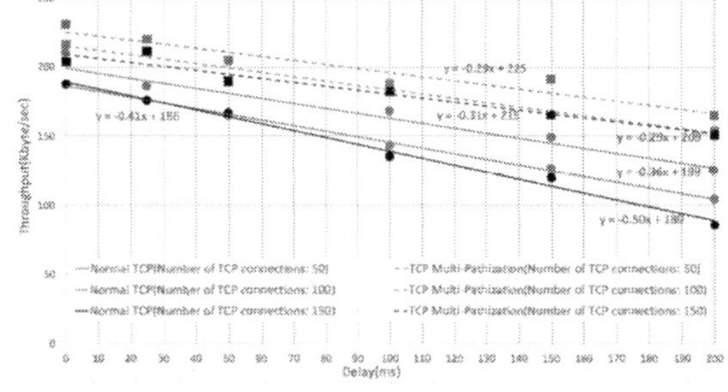

Figure 5. TCP Throughput [4]

From Fig.4, we see that the satisfaction of this method is always higher than that of normal TCP regardless of the delay when the number of load TCP connections is same like the TCP throughput. Also, in normal TCP, regardless of the number of load TCP connections, the satisfaction decreases so much as the delay increases. However, in this method, when the number of load TCP connections is 50 or 100, the satisfaction does not decrease so much as the delay increases. Contrary to this, when the number of load TCP connections is 150, the satisfaction decreases as normal TCP. Therefore, when the load on the path is large, although the satisfaction is higher than that of normal TCP, we can see that the influence of delay appears in the degree of satisfaction. Here, Fig. 5 shows that the QoS(TCP throughput) decreases as the delay increases even when using this method, regardless of the number of load TCP connections. However, from Fig. 4, except when the number of load TCP connections is 150, the increase of the delay does not degrade the satisfaction by this method so much.

From the other point of view, in normal TCP, the satisfaction decreases as the number of load TCP connections increases. However, in this method, the satisfaction can keep high even if the number of load TCP connections increases. Also, we see that, when TCP connections of load is 50 or 150 and the delay is from 50 ms to 100 ms, the satisfaction is greatly reduced in normal TCP. However, in this method, regardless of the number of load TCP connections, the increase of the delay does not degrade the satisfaction. Therefore, even if the delay increases while using Web services, QoS degrades but QoE does not deteriorate significantly. That is this method can maintain a high user experience for Web service from point of users' view.

From the above, we confirm that this method can provide higher satisfaction than normal TCP, and it is easy to maintain QoE against deterioration of communication environment such as increase of load TCP connections and delay. Therefore, we confirmed the effectiveness of this method for using Web services from the viewpoint of QoE.

4 Conclusion

In this study, we evaluated the effectiveness of the TCP multi-pathization method by SDN from the viewpoint of QoE. As the result of the experiments with subjects, the satisfaction of the multi-pathization method is always higher than that of the normal TCP, and the effectiveness in using Web services is confirmed.

As our future works, we consider evaluating in other web services such as shopping services. Also, the threshold of packet length used for packet branching in the multi-pathization method is set to 300 bytes in this study. In the future, we will investigate appropriate thresholds for each Web service, and enable them to be changed dynamically for each Web service.

Acknowledgment

The authors would like to thank the people of the National Institute of Information and Communications Technology and related people. In addition, they thank the member of their laboratory for assistance in research.

References

[1] A. Ford, C. Raiciu, M. Handley, O. Bonaventure, "*TCP Extensions for Multipath Operation with Multiple Addresses*", RFC 6824 (Experimental) (2013)
[2] K. Iwata, Y. Ito, Proc. ITNAC (2017)
[3] "*SDN*", https://www.opennetworking.org/sdn-resources/sdn-definition
[4] Y. Yoshida, Y. Ito, Communication Society / Technical Committee on Internet Architecture (2019)
[5] "*Trema*", https://trema.github.io/trema/
[6] "*Open vSwitch*", http://openvswitch.org/
[7] "*Ergonomic requirements for office work with visual display terminals(VDTs) - Part11: Guidance on usability*", ISO 9241-11 (1998)
[8] J.P. Guilford, "*Psychometric methods*", McGraw-Hill (1954)
[9] "*Open Street Map*", https://www.openstreetmap.org/
[10] "*Apache HTTP Server*", https://httpd.apache.org/

Wearable device for automatic detection and monitoring of freezing in Parkinson's disease

Michelle Millán[1]*, *Hiram* Cantú[2]

[1]Departamento de Ingeniería Biomédica, Vicerrectoría de Ciencias de la Salud, Universidad de Monterrey, 66238 San Pedro Garza García, Nuevo León, México
[2]Departamento de Ingeniería Biomédica, Vicerrectoría de Ciencias de la Salud, Universidad de Monterrey, 66238 San Pedro Garza García, Nuevo León, México

Abstract. Freezing of gait (FOG) in Parkinson's disease (PD) is described as a short-term episode of absence or considerable decrease of movement despite the intention of moving forward. FOG is related to risk of falls and low quality of life for individuals with PD. FOG has been studied and analyzed through different techniques, including inertial movement units (IMUs) and motion capture systems (MOCAP), both along with robust algorithms. Still, there is not a standardized methodology to identify nor quantify freezing episodes (FEs). In a previous work from our group, a new methodology was developed to differentiate FEs from normal movement using position data obtained from a motion capture system. The purpose of this study is to determine if this methodology is equally effective identifying FEs when using IMUs. Twenty subjects with PD will perform two different gait-related tasks. Trials will be tracked by IMUs and filmed by a video camera; data from IMUs will be compared to the time occurrence of FEs obtained from the videos. We expect this methodology will successfully detect FEs with IMUs' data. Results would allow the development of a wearable device able to detect and monitor FOG. It is expected that the use of this type of devices would allow clinicians to better understand FOG and improve patients' care.

1 Introduction

Parkinson's disease (PD) is defined as a neurological condition that evolves progressively and it is characterized by the appearance of hypokinesia, akinesia, tremor, rigidity and postural instability. These movement disturbances are associated with gait altered patterns, such as short and slow steps. In most of the cases, PD tend to affect elderly, which results in performance complications during specialized motor tasks like walking, writing and talking [1].

In addition to these symptoms, some individuals with PD experience episodic movement arrests that usually occurs in advanced stages of the disease, better known as freezing. Freezing is more commonly studied in gait (freezing of gait, FOG) [2-9] and it is described

* Corresponding author: michelle.millan@udem.edu

as a short-term episode of absence or considerable decrease of movement despite the intention of moving forward [8]. However, 80% of the PD patients will never go through FOG at any stage of the disease [10].

This phenomenon is related to risk of falls and low quality of life for individuals with PD. While the disease progresses, FOG becomes more frequent and disabling usually leading to falls [10-13]. One of the most feared consequences from falls are hip fractures which typically lead to nursing home admission. Hip fractures are related to a high mortality and high morbidity in PD [14]. According to Hosseinzadeh and colleagues' study [15], PD almost tripled the risk of hip fracture, implying a direct association between PD and fracture risk.

Currently, there is only one tool validated to identify FOG, a self-assessment questionnaire in which PD patients self-report how often they experience freezing [16, 17]. This tool is highly sensitive in identifying those individuals with PD who experience freezing (freezers) from those who do not (non-freezers). However, the Freezing of Gait Questionnaire (FOGQ) is subjective and does not help to quantify the specific time when this phenomenon occurs.

Based on the FOG definition previously described, it is suggested that the influence of freezing can vary from temporary gait pattern disruptions to a complete gait cycle arrest [18]. Therefore, several objective approaches that fit the definition have been used to identify and study freezing from different perspectives (i.e. kinematics, kinetics) to minimize its effects [3], [11], [19-21]. From all these approaches, complete movement arrests and initial amplitude decreases are the most common criteria used to identify freezing in PD [22-26], two different methodologies that raise the need of a standardized method to ensure the same phenomenon is being studied and allow comparisons across studies.

The use of inertial movement units (IMUs), such as accelerometers, has been a popular method to identify and quantify FOG in real time along with robust algorithms. Tripoliti and colleagues [27] identified FOG by analyzing data obtained from accelerometers during gait tasks using a Random Forests classification algorithm with 81.94% sensitivity. Moreover, Cole and colleagues [28] created a Dynamic Neural Network for freezing detection using accelerometers during unscripted activity reaching 83% of sensitivity. Rezvanian and Lockhart [29] used the continuous wavelet transform (CWT) to decompose acceleration data obtained from IMUs by taking into account the frequency and time domains, reaching a sensitivity of 84.9%.

Although many efforts have been made in order to study FEs, there is no standardized methodology to identify nor quantify them, which prevent comparison among different studies. Despite the fact that many studies coincide between technologies, IMU methods are often unclear. If IMUs are expected to be used as a substitute for motion capture systems (MOCAP), IMUs methods are required to be reliable and reproducible [30].

Based on our recent results using position data obtained from MOCAP [31], it was shown that a freezing method based on complete movement arrests rather than amplitude decrease better discriminates freezing from normal movement during a gait related task. Moreover, higher sensitivity (88.3%) was obtained by using this new method that considers: (i) complete movement arrests as freezing criteria, (ii) 0.5 seconds as the minimum duration of a freezing episode, (iii) a minimum time of 2 seconds to overcome a freezing episode, and (iv) a robust algorithm that considers both, time and frequency characteristics of the signal (CWT).

The purpose of this study is to determine whether this method is equally effective detecting FEs when using IMUs (i.e. acceleration data). Moreover, we aim to define the most optimal anatomical landmark to place IMUs that would better differentiate freezing from normal movement. We define sensitivity as the probability for our method to identify FEs when FEs occur, and specificity as the probability for our method to identify normal movement when FEs do not occur. To address these objectives, individuals with PD will perform an experimental protocol, which includes specific tasks, in order to obtain data from IMUs. Twenty participants with PD will be recruited: 10 freezers and 10 non-freezers, classified according to their FOGQ results. We assumed that the proposed tasks will trigger FEs in individuals with PD.

We expect that (i) the methodology used in data obtained from motion capture system will be equally effective to identify and quantify FEs in data obtained from IMUs, also with the obtained results it will be possible to (ii) develop a methodology to predict FOG using IMUs, (iii) develop a wearable device able to detect and monitor FOG by the implementation of the proposed methodology, and (iv) objectively evaluate FOG quantification.

Movement analysis of PD individuals with FOG focuses, among other purposes, on identifying and quantifying FOG through different methodologies. Development and implementation of new methodologies for FOG detection enhances the design and creation of wearable devices capable of detect and monitor FOG. As a result of this research, a new methodology could be implemented in a wearable device for detection and monitoring of FOG in PD patients. The study and analysis of FOG is essential for the development of technologies, which can provide novel insight to the experts, such as neurologists, geriatricians, rehabilitation specialists, physiotherapists and nurses, who work closely with FOG.

2 Methodology

2.1 Subjects

Twenty participants with PD (10 reporting FOG, and 10 without FOG) will be recruited for this study. Participants will be classified as freezers if a score ≥1 is met on item 3 of the Freezing of Gait Questionnaire (FOGQ): "do you feel that your feet get glued to the floor while walking, making a turn or when trying to initiate walking?" [16]. Freezers and non-freezers will be matched for disease severity. The inclusion criteria will be: (i) idiopathic PD, (ii) age between 50 and 80 years, (iii) Hoehn and Yahr stage I, II, III, or IV, where bilateral impairment movements can be identified, but individuals are still able to walk or stand unassisted [31], and (iv) use of levodopa medication. The exclusion criteria will be: (i) mild cognitive impairment defined by a score ≤25/30 on The Montreal Cognitive Assessment (MoCA), (ii) neurological, orthopedic, or muscular disorders other than PD, (iii) currently having implanted deep brain stimulation (DBS) electrodes or (iv) history of diabetes.

A control group of 10 healthy age- and sex-matched participants will also be recruited. Control subjects (i) presenting history or evidence of neurological, orthopedic, or muscular disability, (ii) self-reporting postural impairments or unexplained falls in the last year, (iii) taking medication that might affect balance (i.e. ototoxic drugs such as antidepressants, anti-seizure, diuretics), (iv) complaining of paresthesia characterized by the sensation of tingling skin and/or a limb falling asleep, or (v) with a history of diabetes will be excluded from this study. All participants will provide written informed consent prior to their participation in the study.

2.2 Clinical evaluation

First, participants with PD will be clinically assessed with (i) a medical history questionnaire, (ii) the MoCA test, (iii) the Unified Parkinson Disease Rating Scale Part 3 (UPDRS-III), (iv) the Hoehn and Yahr (H&Y) scale, and (v) the FOGQ.

2.3 Experimental protocol

The experimental protocol includes two different tasks. First task consists of performing a stepping-in-place (SIP) task, a gait-like activity that consists on participants raising the legs alternately and continuously at a comfortable height (see Fig. 1). The SIP has been successfully used to identify freezing episodes in individuals with PD [32]. Participants will be asked to perform the task at a comfortable and self-selected pace that will be obtained from practice trials.

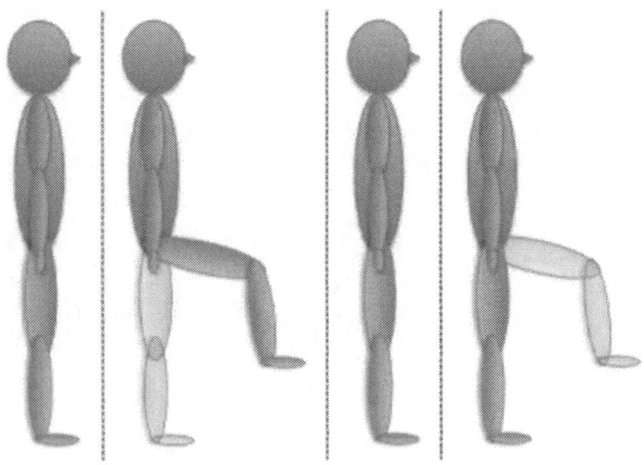

Fig. 1. Schematic representation of the stepping-in-place task.

The experimental protocol includes two trials of the SIP task, the first of 30 seconds and the second of 120 seconds duration. Before starting the task, participants will be provided with a 10-beat auditory feedback from a metronome set at the self-selected pace and they will be asked to memorize and perform the task following this rhythm.

Second task consists of performing different activities of daily life. As shown in Fig. 2, participants will (a) stand up from a chair, (b) walk straight for 6 m in a designated path of 50 cm wide, (c) turn 180°, (d) return to the chair while walking the 6 m and, (e) sit for 1 minute in the chair. According to Schaafsma and coleagues [33] this type of activities can trigger FOG.

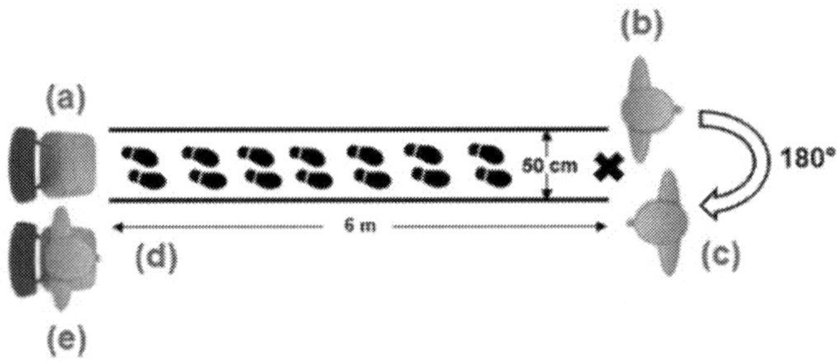

Fig. 2. Schematic representation of the daily life activities task.

Video data will be obtained by filming each session of the experimental protocol with a video camera placed in the frontal and sagittal plane. Kinematic data will be recorded during the whole trials and 5 seconds before initiating the SIP task in order to have a quiet stance baseline.

2.4 Data acquisition

Spatiotemporal measures of gait (accelerations) will be obtained from Trigno Avanti Sensors (Trigno™ Wireless Biofeedback System, Delsys Inc., Natick, MA). Participants will wear 8 wireless IMUs (triaxial accelerometers, gyroscopes and magnetometers) on the back and the lower limbs (thoracic and lumbar region, bilateral upper thigh, bilateral lower shank, and bilateral feet) as shown in Fig. 3.

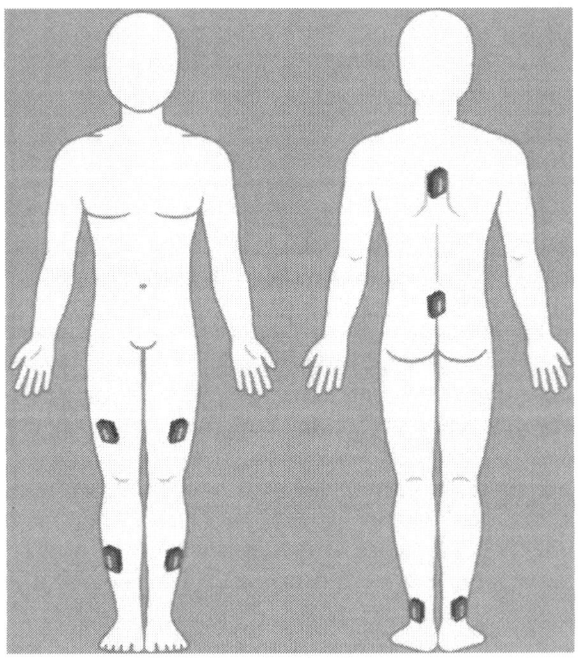

Fig. 3. Sensors placement.

2.5 Data analysis

A freezing episode will be defined as a period lasting at least 0.5 seconds of movement arrest, in which one or both limbs display no movement. Moreover, a minimum time of 2 seconds between two freezing episodes will be required to consider it as 'normal movement'.

A pair of trained observers will inspect visually and independently inspected the videos for each participant in all trials to freezing occurrence. They will identify the number of FEs, duration time and the time when they occur. If no agreement is met between observers, videos will be reviewed by each of them.

Automated detection of FEs will be performed in 3D acceleration data obtained from each of the IMUs with the method previously described by computing the algorithm in Matlab (MathWorks, Massachusetts, USA). Number, duration time, and time of occurrence of the FEs will be obtained. Differences between the acceleration data and the video data (reference) then will be calculated for each outcome measurement.

2.6 Statistical analysis

For all the statistical analysis, significance levels of .05 will be used. Inter-rater reliability of the values reported by each observer prior to reaching consensus will be assessed using Cohen's kappa for the rating of the number, duration and time of occurrence of the freezing episodes. The differences of number and total duration of freezing episodes between the videos and acceleration data will be compared by means of a non-parametric repeated measures Friedman test for equal sample sizes. The accuracy to identify time of occurrence of a freezing episode between the videos and the acceleration data will be compared using a non-parametric repeated measures Cochran's Q test for unequal sample sizes. If significant differences are found in non-parametric tests, Wilcoxon post-hoc comparisons will be performed to determine pair-wise differences with Bonferroni corrections. The accuracy to identify freezing episodes on the acceleration data and on every different anatomical landmark will be described by the area under the receiver operating characteristic (ROC) curve in terms of sensitivity and specificity. Sensitivity refers to the probability that the algorithm applied to the acceleration data detects a freezing episode when freezing is present, while specificity indicates the probability that the algorithm detects normal movement when there is no freezing.

3 Conclusion

Currently, this research is underway. The proposed methodology will be applied in data obtained from IMUs in order to identify and quantify FOG in individuals with PD. Further analyses from IMUs data, as well as data from video recordings, will be used to determine if the proposed methodology is effective identifying FOG. From the obtained information, we expect to determine the optimal anatomical placement of the IMUs that better discriminate FOG from normal movement. It is expected that the closer the IMU is to the ground (e.g. ankle and/or heel) the better would be in identifying FOG. Results would allow the design of a wearable device prototype, which integrates the proposed methodology. These devices would allow the monitoring of individuals with PD who suffer FOG in order to reduce risk of falls, and also provide novel knowledge to help clinicians to tackle with improved rehabilitation therapies and medicine doses.

References

1. M. E. Morris, F. Huxham, J. McGinley, K. Dodd, and R. Iansek, "The biomechanics and motor control of gait in Parkinson disease," *Clin. Biomech.*, vol. **16**, no. 6, pp. 459–470, (2001)
2. Q. J. Almeida and C. A. Lebold, "Freezing of gait in Parkinson's disease: A perceptual cause for a motor impairment?," *J. Neurol. Neurosurg. Psychiatry*, vol. **81**, no. 5, pp. 513–518, (2010)
3. K. A. Ehgoetz Martens, F. Pieruccini-Faria, and Q. J. Almeida, "Could Sensory Mechanisms Be a Core Factor That Underlies Freezing of Gait in Parkinson's Disease?," *PLoS One*, vol. **8**, no. 5, (2013)
4. U. M. Fietzek, J. Zwosta, F. E. Schroeteler, K. Ziegler, and A. O. Ceballos-Baumann, "Levodopa changes the severity of freezing in Parkinson's disease," *Park. Relat. Disord.*, vol. **19**, no. 10, pp. 894–896, (2013)
5. Y. Kwon *et al.*, "A practical method for the detection of freezing of gait in patients with Parkinson's disease," *Clin. Interv. Aging*, vol. **9**, pp. 1709–1719, (2014)
6. S. H. G. Mensink *et al.*, "Additional weight load increases freezing of gait episodes in Parkinson's disease; an experimental study," *J. Neurol.*, vol. **261**, no. 5, pp. 999–1008, (2014)
7. A. Nieuwboer and N. Giladi, "Characterizing freezing of gait in Parkinson's disease: Models of an episodic phenomenon," *Mov. Disord.*, vol. **28**, no. 11, pp. 1509–1519, (2013)
8. J. G. Nutt, B. R. Bloem, N. Giladi, M. Hallett, F. B. Horak, and A. Nieuwboer, "Freezing of gait: Moving forward on a mysterious clinical phenomenon," *Lancet Neurol.*, vol. **10**, no. 8, pp. 734–744, (2011)
9. J. Spildooren, S. Vercruysse, K. Desloovere, W. Vandenberghe, E. Kerckhofs, and A. Nieuwboer, "Freezing of gait in Parkinson's disease: The impact of dual-tasking and turning," *Mov. Disord.*, vol. **25**, no. 15, pp. 2563–2570, (2010)
10. B. R. Bloem, J. M. Hausdorff, J. E. Visser, and N. Giladi, "Falls and freezing of Gait in Parkinson's disease: A review of two interconnected, episodic phenomena," *Mov. Disord.*, vol. **19**, no. 8, pp. 871–884, (2004)
11. J. V. Jacobs, J. G. Nutt, P. Carlson-Kuhta, R. Allen, and F. B. Horak, "Dual tasking during postural stepping responses increases falls but not freezing in people with Parkinson's disease," *Park. Relat. Disord.*, vol. **20**, no. 7, pp. 779–781, (2014)
12. G. K. Kerr, C. J. Worringham, M. H. Cole, P. F. Lacherez, J. M. Wood, and P. A. Silburn, "Predictors of future falls in Parkinson disease," *Neurology*, vol. **75**, no. 2, pp. 116–124, (2010)
13. S. Vercruysse *et al.*, "Explaining freezing of gait in Parkinson's disease: Motor and cognitive determinants," *Mov. Disord.*, vol. **27**, no. 13, pp. 1644–1651, (2012)
14. L. Coughlin and J. Templeton, "Hip fractures in patients with Parkinson's disease," *Clin. Orthop. Relat. Res.*, vol. **148**, pp. 192–195, (1980)
15. A. Hosseinzadeh, M. Khalili, B. Sedighi, S. Iranpour, and A. A. Haghdoost, "Parkinson's disease and risk of hip fracture: systematic review and meta-analysis," *Acta Neurol. Belg.*, vol. **118**, no. 2, pp. 201–210, (2018)
16. N. Giladi, H. Shabtai, E. S. Simon, S. Biran, J. Tal, and A. D. Korczyn, "Construction of freezing of gait questionnaire for patients with Parkinsonism," *Park. Relat. Disord.*, vol. **6**, no. 3, pp. 165–170, (2000)
17. N. Giladi *et al.*, "Validation of the Freezing of Gait Questionnaire in patients with Parkinson's disease," *Mov. Disord.*, vol. **24**, no. 5, pp. 655–661, (2009)
18. S. Vercruysse, M. Gilat, J. M. Shine, E. Heremans, S. Lewis, and A. Nieuwboer, "Freezing beyond gait in Parkinson's disease: A review of current neurobehavioral

evidence," *Neurosci. Biobehav. Rev.*, vol. **43**, pp. 213–227, (2014)
19. E. Matar, J. M. Shine, S. L. Naismith, and S. J. G. Lewis, "Using virtual reality to explore the role of conflict resolution and environmental salience in Freezing of Gait in Parkinson's disease," *Park. Relat. Disord.*, vol. **19**, no. 11, pp. 937–942, (2013)
20. J. Nantel, J. C. McDonald, S. Tan, and H. Bronte-Stewart, "Deficits in visuospatial processing contribute to quantitative measures of freezing of gait in Parkinson's disease," *Neuroscience*, vol. **221**, no. 2012, pp. 151–156, (2012)
21. J. M. Shine *et al.*, "Freezing of gait in Parkinson's disease is associated with functional decoupling between the cognitive control network and the basal ganglia," *Brain*, vol. **136**, no. 12, pp. 3671–3681, (2013)
22. S. Vercruysse *et al.*, "Abnormalities and cue dependence of rhythmical upper-limb movements in Parkinson patients with freezing of gait," *Neurorehabil. Neural Repair*, vol. **26**, no. 6, pp. 636–645, (2012)
23. Q. J. Almeida, L. R. Wishart, and T. D. Lee, "Disruptive influences of a cued voluntary shift on coordinated movement in Parkinson's disease," *Neuropsychologia*, vol. **41**, no. 4, pp. 442–452, (2003)
24. A. Nieuwboer, S. Vercruysse, P. Feys, O. Levin, J. Spildooren, and S. Swinnen, "Upper limb movement interruptions are correlated to freezing of gait in Parkinson's disease," *Eur. J. Neurosci.*, vol. **29**, no. 7, pp. 1422–1430, (2009)
25. S. Vercruysse *et al.*, "The neural correlates of upper limb motor blocks in Parkinson's disease and their relation to freezing of gait," *Cereb. Cortex*, vol. **24**, no. 12, pp. 3154–3166, (2014)
26. A. J. Williams, D. S. Peterson, M. Ionno, K. A. Pickett, and G. M. Earhart, "Upper extremity freezing and Dyscoordination in Parkinson's disease: Effects of amplitude and cadence manipulations," *Parkinsons. Dis.*, vol. **2013**, (2013)
27. E. E. Tripoliti *et al.*, "Automatic detection of freezing of gait events in patients with Parkinson's disease," *Comput. Methods Programs Biomed.*, vol. **110,** no. 1, pp. 12–26, (2013)
28. B. T. Cole, S. H. Roy, and S. H. Nawab, "Detecting freezing-of-gait during unscripted and unconstrained activity," *Proc. Annu. Int. Conf. IEEE Eng. Med. Biol. Soc. EMBS*, pp. 5649–5652, (2011)
29. S. Rezvanian and T. E. Lockhart, "Towards real-time detection of freezing of gait using wavelet transform on wireless accelerometer data," *Sensors (Switzerland)*, vol. **16**, no. 4, (2016)
30. J. F. Hafer, S. G. Provenzano, K. L. Kern, C. E. Agresta, J. A. Grant, and R. F. Zernicke, "Measuring markers of aging and knee osteoarthritis gait using inertial measurement units," *J. Biomech.*, vol. **99**, p. 109567, (2020)
31. H. Cantú, J. N. Côté, and J. Nantel, "A new method based on quiet stance baseline is more effective in identifying freezing in Parkinson's disease," *PLoS One*, vol. **13**, no. 11, pp. 1–14, (2018)
32. J. Nantel, C. de Solages, and H. Bronte-Stewart, "Repetitive stepping in place identifies and measures freezing episodes in subjects with Parkinson's disease," *Gait Posture*, vol. **34**, no. 3, pp. 329–333, (2011)
33. J. D. Schaafsma, Y. Balash, T. Gurevich, A. L. Bartels, J. M. Hausdorff, and N. Giladi, "Characterization of freezing of gait subtypes and the response of each to levodopa in Parkinson's disease," *Eur. J. Neurol.*, vol. **10**, no. 4, pp. 391–398, (2003)

Assistive Technology for Patient with Congenital Foot Deformity

Eugenia Muñoz Garza [1], *Héctor Gerardo* Carvajal Cortés [2], *Braulio* Domínguez Godoy [3], and *Hiram Alejandro* Cantú Campos [4]

[1]Departamento de Ingeniería Biomédica, Vicerrectoría Ciencias de la Salud, Universidad de Monterrey, San Pedro Garza García, México, eugenia.munoz@udem.edu
[2]Departamento de Ingeniería Biomédica, Vicerrectoría Ciencias de la Salud, Universidad de Monterrey, San Pedro Garza García, México, hector.carvajal@udem.edu
[3]Escuela de Arte y Diseño, Vicerrectoría de Arte, Arquitectura y Diseño, Universidad de Monterrey, San Pedro Garza García, México, braulio.dominguez@udem.edu
[4]Departamento de Ingeniería Biomédica, Vicerrectoría Ciencias de la Salud, Universidad de Monterrey, San Pedro Garza García, México, hiram.cantu@udem.edu

Abstract. An assistive technology (AT) is any item, equipment or product used to increase, maintain or improve the functional capabilities of people with disabilities. The aim of this study was to design and develop two ATs in order to assist the needs of a male student from Universidad de Monterrey experiencing gait dysfunction and pain due to a congenital foot deformity preventing him from normal performance. These ATs included personalized orthopedic insoles to improve the participant's posture and stability as well as two ankle-foot orthosis (AFO) to reduce the pain he presented. In order to design the orthopedic insoles, it was necessary to scan the participant's feet; this was achieved using the photogrammetry technique. For the design of the AFOs, anthropometric measurements of the lower limbs were taken in order to modify a predefined 3D human model and obtain a digital model of the lower limbs. Both devices were manufactured using 3D printing technology. In order to analyze the participant's progress and validate the effectiveness of the ATs, we developed a methodology for movement analysis based on the marker-less motion capture system Kinect 2. Data obtained was imported into Matlab in order to calculate lower limb joint angles and compare gait before and after using the ATs. Significant improvement was seen in the participant's gait after two weeks of using the ATs. Moreover, we were able to demonstrate that the use of orthopedic insoles improved participant's posture based on the correct alignment (180°) of the heel with the ankle. We believe these posture improvements could further impact on participant's gait performance. Therefore, we expect a significant improvement on participant's gait after constant use of both ATs developed.

1. Introduction

According to 2014 data from the INEGI, 7.2 millions of Mexicans (6% of Mexico's total population) suffer from some type of disability. The most reported among the population with a 64.1% was the motor disability [1]. According to the World Health Organization, more than one billion people with disabilities in the world need an assistive technology. An assistive technology is any device used by a person who has some type of disability to improve their functional capacity [2]. However, only 10% of the population has access to them. It is expected that by 2050 more than 2000 million people will require one or more assistive technology [3]. In this study, it was proposed to carry out an evaluation of a patient experiencing gait dysfunction and pain due to a congenital foot deformity in order to select the most appropriate assistive technology that best suits his needs.

2. Methodology

The methodology that was followed for this project was divided into three main phases: the development of assistive technology, the development of a methodology for a motion analysis system and the validation of the assistive technology.

2.1 Development of assistive technology

The process of the development of assistive technology was divided into advice and evaluation by health experts, design of assistive technology which consists of design of orthopedic insoles and ankle-foot orthosis and finally, the fabrication of both ATs using the 3D printing technology.

2.1.1 Advice and evaluation by health experts

Expert advice was critical for our project. By means of x-rays physicians diagnosed the patient with a congenital foot deformity known as plano-valgus foot. Moreover, based on patient's pain experience in his heel when he first gets up in the morning and starts walking, physicians also diagnosed the condition of plantar fasciitis. Based on the health experts diagnosis and advice, it was decided to develop two assistive technologies. The first one, a pair of orthopedic insoles to improve the participant's posture and stability, the second, a pair of ankle-foot orthosis to treat the plantar fasciitis condition.

2.1.2 Design of orthopedic insoles

For the design of the orthopedic insoles for plano-valgus foot, four steps were followed. These steps included: obtaining the feet molds, the scanning, the use of specialized software and finally the material selection. To obtain the molds of the patient's feet a series of steps were followed. An alginate mixture was made to cover the patient's feet and afterwards, a plaster mixture was poured into the alginate mold and once it dried, we proceeded to unmold it. The final product obtained was a plaster replica of both patient's feet. After obtaining the molds, the scanning of the plantar surface of the patient was done. For this a technique known as photogrammetry was used, which allows to create 3D models through multiple photographs taken from different angles [4].

Once the images were captured, they were imported into a specialized software called Agisoft Metashape (Agisoft LLC, St. Petersburg, Russia). In this program, the images taken were aligned which allowed us to observe the camera path followed around the object of interest. With this information the creation of a dense point cloud could be achieved and allowed the construction of a mesh which is a high-resolution 3D model where all the points of the dense cloud are connected [5].

After obtaining the scan of the patient's' feet, a software called Rhino 3D (Robert McNeel & Associates, Miami, USA) was used with the LutraCAD plugin (LutraCAD B.V., Veghel, Nederland), a specialized software for the design of orthopedic insoles. The software automatically generated the contour around each feet (Fig. 1a) and the program allowed us to manually adjust this contour to exactly fit the surface of the feet (Fig. 1b).

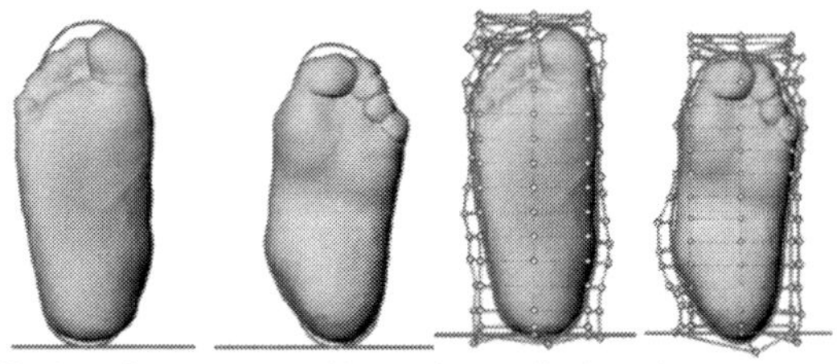

Fig. 1. a) Orthopedic insoles contour b) Orthopedic insoles contour adjusted

And finally, to be able to carry out the manufacturing process, the selection of materials had to be done. For this purpose, a comparative table (Table 1) of different materials was made, evaluating hardness, deformation, flexibility and durability [6]. For the material of the orthopedic insoles it was necessary a flexible material for greater comfort of the patient, as well as a minimum deformation to maintain the geometry of the plantar surface. Also, since the orthopedic insoles would be of daily use it was required a high durability to avoid the wearing out of these. Taking this into consideration, the best option to use was the thermoplastic polyurethane filament also known as TPU since it met all the necessary requirements.

Table 1. Comparative table of 3D printing filaments.

	PLA	TPU/TPE	PETG
Hardness	High	Medium	High
Deformation	Minimum	Minimum	Minimum
Flexibility	Low	Very high	Medium
Durability	Medium	Very high	High

2.1.3 Design of ankle-foot orthosis

An orthosis is a device external to the human body that serves to modify both functional and structural aspects. For the design of the ankle-foot orthosis different steps were followed including: taking measurements of the patients' lower limbs, generating the 3D model, the use of specialized software and finally the selection of material. Anthropometric measurements taken included the diameter of the knee, calf and ankle as well as the height between the knee and the ankle for both the right and left lower limbs. These measurements were necessary so that when designing the ankle-foot orthosis it could be adapted as best as possible to the geometry of the patient's lower limbs. Once the measurements were taken, a 3D model of human being was generated using a software called Makehuman. This software is parameterized and allowed us to modify measurements at specific points, such as the ones taken in our study and previously described.

The 3D model obtained was then exported to a specialized software called Blender (Blender Foundation, Amsterdam, Nederland). It was decided to cut the model to only have the lower limbs since those were the ones of our interest. This model of the lower limbs was our base model to be able to design the ankle foot orthosis around it. A plugin called dual mesh was applied to the structure to give an aspect of mesh-shaped cells. One of the benefits of using this plugin was that less material was required therefore the orthosis would be lighter.

Finally, it was necessary to select the material of the orthosis and for this the same comparative table (Table 1) as the one for the orthopedic insoles was used. A material with high hardness was required since it was sought that the orthosis could maintain the foot in a specific position. It also had to have a minimum deformation to maintain the design structure. Considering these specifications, the polylactic acid filament material also known as PLA was selected. The PLA, besides being cheap and easy to get, can be biodegradable.

2.1.4 3D printing

Once the final designs of each assistive technology were obtained, the manufacturing process was carried out using the 3D printing technology. The final product of the orthopedic insoles for plano-valgus foot using the blue TPU filament can be observed in Fig. 2a. The final result of the ankle-foot orthosis using the PLA filament can be observed in Fig. 2b.

Fig. 2. a) Orthopedic insoles b)Ankle-foot orthosis

2.2 Development of methodology for a motion analysis system

The gait is the pattern of a person's manner of walking. It is a series of alternating and rhythmic limb and trunk movements [7] that is divided into two phases. The first one is called stance phase and begins once the heel of the reference leg meets the ground. This phase constitutes approximately 60% of the gait. The second phase is called swing phase and begins when the leg is raised and oscillates in the air preparing for its next contact with the ground. This phase constitutes approximately 40% of the gait [8].

Gait analysis is the study of the movement of the human body that allows the identification of gait characteristics of each individual and based on these it could be diagnosed any pathology or dysfunction of the lower extremities that can be treated by specialists [9]. Currently, there are various technologies available on the market to be able to carry out a gait analysis. Existing technologies allow the use of a technique known as motion capture (MoCap) which consists of recording the movements of a human and digitize them [10]. Different systems are identified in the literature that are used to capture the movement of the human body, including the optical and non-optical systems. The optical systems are divided into those in which markers are used and those marker-less [11]. For this project a marker-less optical sensor, the Kinect 2.0 sensor, was used. The data obtained by the depth camera is processed to generate the position of each joint and store them in coordinates (x, y, z).

After understanding gait, motion capture, and gait analysis the development of the methodology for a motion analysis system could be done. This phase was divided into three different stages which included: motion capture, data processing and gait analysis. For the motion capture, a software called IPIsoft (Michael Nikonov, Moscow, Russia) was used; this included two different programs. IPIRecorder was used to record the patient's gait using the Kinect Sensor. Once this recording was obtained, it was analyzed using the IPImocap studio program with the biomech plugin. To begin recording, the initial position of the subject had to be in T-pose so that the software could recognize the human body as observed on Fig. 3. The sensor was placed 3.8 meters apart from the patient in order to allow him to walk a distance of 2.3 meters without leaving the sensor's range of vision. It is worth mentioning that this protocol was also performed by a sex and age-matched control presenting no alteration in his gait. For both participants, patient and control, a complete cycle including stance and swing phases were recorded in order to compare and observe differences among the two participants.

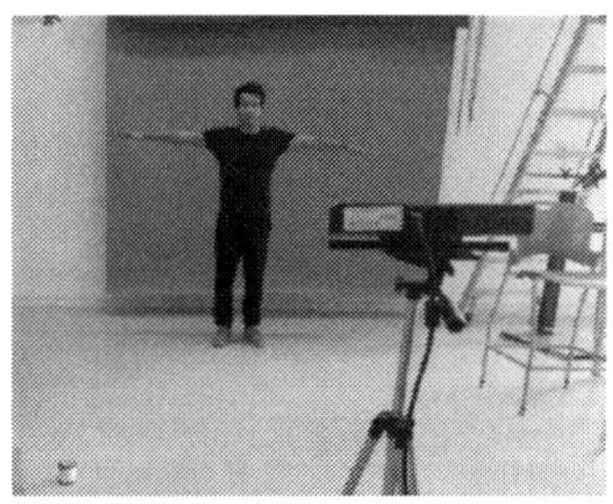

Fig. 3. Kinect set-up

Once the motion capture was done, the recording was exported to the IPImocap Studio software where the processing of the acquired data took place. In the software, two models were generated: the patient's motion model and our base model. This second one had to be adjusted to the patient's model. The biomech plugin was used to select the desired joints that were going to be analyzed. For our project we only focused on the joints of the lower limbs which included knees and feet angles. Afterwards, we exported the data in .mat format; this was a matrix of the position coordinates of the selected joints. This matrix was used in Matlab 2018b (MathWorks, Massachusetts, USA) to carry on the gait analysis.

Once having the imported data matrix in Matlab 2018b (MathWorks, Massachusetts, USA) containing position coordinates in the space (x, y, z) of the selected bones, the angles between different segments were calculated. In Matlab 2018b (MathWorks, Massachusetts, USA), a programming code was developed so that it would be able to automatically calculate the angles between segments. First, the vectors representing the segments between two points were obtained, using the following formula:

$$A = [x_1 \ y_1 \ z_1]$$
$$B = [x_2 \ y_2 \ z_2]$$
$$C = [x_3 \ y_3 \ z_3]$$
$$D = [x_4 \ y_4 \ z_4]$$

$$\overrightarrow{AB} = < x_2 - x_1 \ y_2 - y_1 \ z_2 - z_1 >$$
$$\overrightarrow{CB} = < x_2 - x_3 \ y_2 - y_3 \ z_2 - z_3 >$$

$$\overrightarrow{BC} = < x_3 - x_2 \ y_3 - y_2 \ z_3 - z_2 >$$
$$\overrightarrow{DC} = < x_3 - x_4 \ y_3 - y_4 \ z_3 - z_4 >$$

For the gait analysis it was necessary to calculate the angle of the knee and the foot, that's why we had to create different segments. We used vectors to represent the segments; the vectors created were AB representing the thigh, BC representing the leg and CD representing the foot as observed in Fig 4.

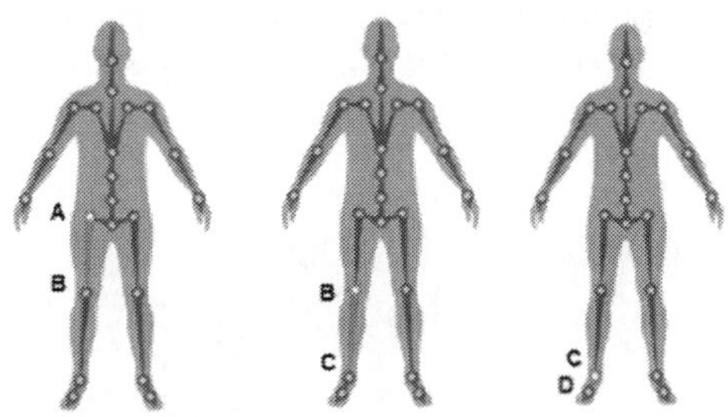

Fig. 4. Body segments

Once these vectors were calculated we could obtain the angles between the vectors. We obtained two different angles: theta representing angle between thigh and leg (Fig 5a), and phi representing angle between leg and foot (Figure 5b).

$$\|\overrightarrow{AB}\| = \sqrt{(x_2 - x_1)^2 + (y_2 - y_1)^2 + (z_2 - z_1)^2} \qquad \|\overrightarrow{BC}\| = \sqrt{(x_3 - x_2)^2 + (y_3 - y_2)^2 + (z_3 - z_2)^2}$$
$$\|\overrightarrow{CB}\| = \sqrt{(x_2 - x_3)^2 + (y_2 - y_3)^2 + (z_2 - z_3)^2} \qquad \|\overrightarrow{DC}\| = \sqrt{(x_3 - x_4)^2 + (y_3 - y_4)^2 + (z_3 - z_4)^2}$$
$$\theta = \cos^{-1}\left(\frac{\overrightarrow{AB} \cdot \overrightarrow{CB}}{(\|\overrightarrow{AB}\|)(\|\overrightarrow{CB}\|)}\right) \qquad \Phi = \cos^{-1}\left(\frac{\overrightarrow{BC} \cdot \overrightarrow{DC}}{(\|\overrightarrow{BC}\|)(\|\overrightarrow{DC}\|)}\right)$$

Fig. 5. a) Angle between thigh and leg b) Angle between leg and foot.

Once all the angles were calculated, they were saved in a struct to be able to graph them in MATLAB where the angles between the thigh-leg and leg-sole of the foot were compared for a normal and an abnormal gait.

2.3 Validation of assistive technology

For the validation through segment alignment with respect to the orthopedic insoles we had to observe the angle variation before and after the use of insoles. The initial position of the patient's feet without insoles caused its plantar surface to be turned outwards, away from the mid-plane of the body. We used Kinovea (Joan Charmant, Bordeaux, France) to mark the reference points. What was sought was to approach the desired value that was 180 degrees indicating a correct alignment and indeed we can observe (Fig 6) the angle decreased from 198 to 192 on the left foot and from 191 to 183 on the right foot both approaching 180. Making the comparison we concluded that the orthopedic insoles were effective since they allowed better alignment of the heel with the ankle of the patient's feet.

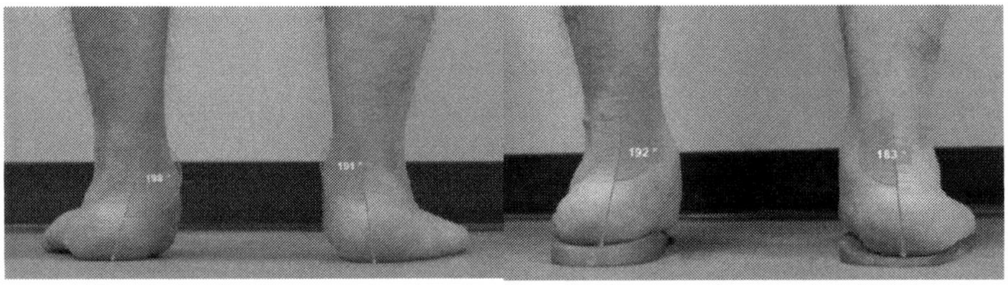

Fig. 6. Angles between heel and ankle a)Without using insoles b)Using insoles

For the validation of the ankle foot orthosis we observed the angle variation before and after the use of it. When the patient was not using the orthosis there was an angle of 129 degrees (Fig 7a). There was a lot of tension in the thick connective tissue causing plantar fasciitis therefore pain on the plantar surface. What was sought was to decrease this angle. On the other hand, the angle obtained when using the orthosis decreased to 118 degrees (Fig 7b) which proved its effectiveness. It is concluded that the use of assistive technology corrected the foot drop around 11 °.

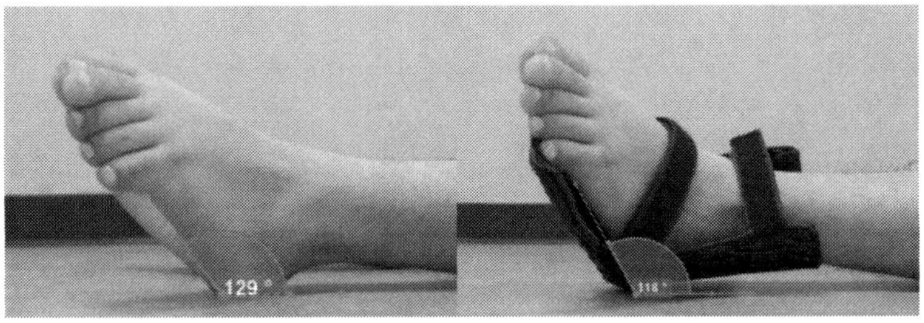

Fig. 7. Angle a)Without using AFO b)Using AFO

3. Results

For the validation of the assistive technology through gait analysis we used the software Matlab 2018b (MathWorks, Massachusetts, USA). Here we developed a programming code to calculate the angles of the knee and feet during the different gait phases. First, we had to analyze our control gait which was our reference. This was a gait of a patient who had no alterations on his feet. This reference helped us to compare it against the patient's gait and clearly observe the differences among them. The code developed allowed us to visualize a window with two graphs and an animation. In the graphs we observe the flexion angle of the knees and the feet of both legs. The animation represents the patient walking. Also, in the graphs we can observe on the x-axis, where the frames per second are located, the division between stance (blue) and swing phases (red) of the patient's gait. In Fig 8 in the upper left graph showing the knee and foot angles during different phases of the walk we observe two lines of data; the blue line refers to the angle of the right knee while the green line refers to the angle of the right foot the same with the upper right graph showing data from left knee and foot.

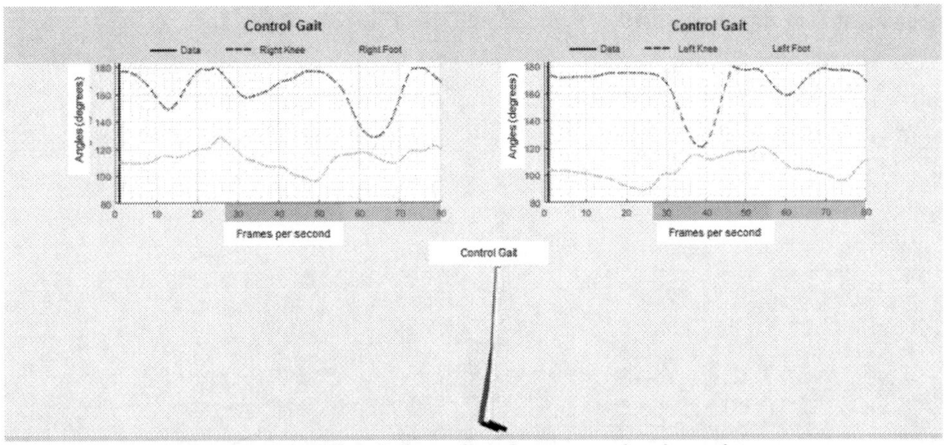

Fig. 8. Matlab window showing normal gait angles.

After analyzing our control gait, we proceeded to analyze the progress of the patient's gait through the weeks. Comparing control gait against patients gait week 0 (Fig 9) we found that the patient had very little flexion on his knees due to his condition. Another difference that we could observe were the frames per second; in our control gait we have 80 frames per second while in the patient's gait week 0 we have 45 frames per second meaning that the patient finishes a complete gait cycle in half the time of the gait control, this occurs since the patient does not have sufficient stability and therefore his steps are shorter.

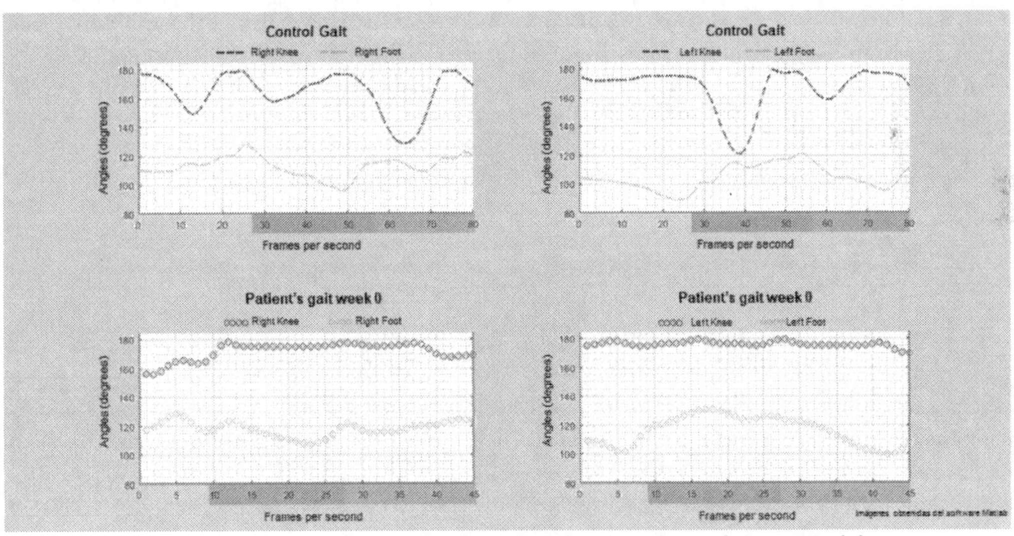

Fig. 9. Comparison control gait and patient's gait week 0 on Matlab.

Once the patient started using the orthopedic insoles, we evaluated his progress one week after and compared it to the results obtained in week 0 (Fig 10). The patient's knee flexion angle went from 160 degrees in week 0 to 180 degrees in week 1, which means the right knee is fully extended while standing before walking. Moreover, a second difference found was that his left knee begins to have more flexion angles. Finally, the frames per second differ from week 0 to week 1, longer in week 1, which means that the patient started to feel more stable and to take longer steps. Afterwards, the patient's gait was evaluated after two weeks using the orthopedic insoles and compared it to the results from week 1. Among the differences one of the most notable were the angles of flexion of the knee on both legs.

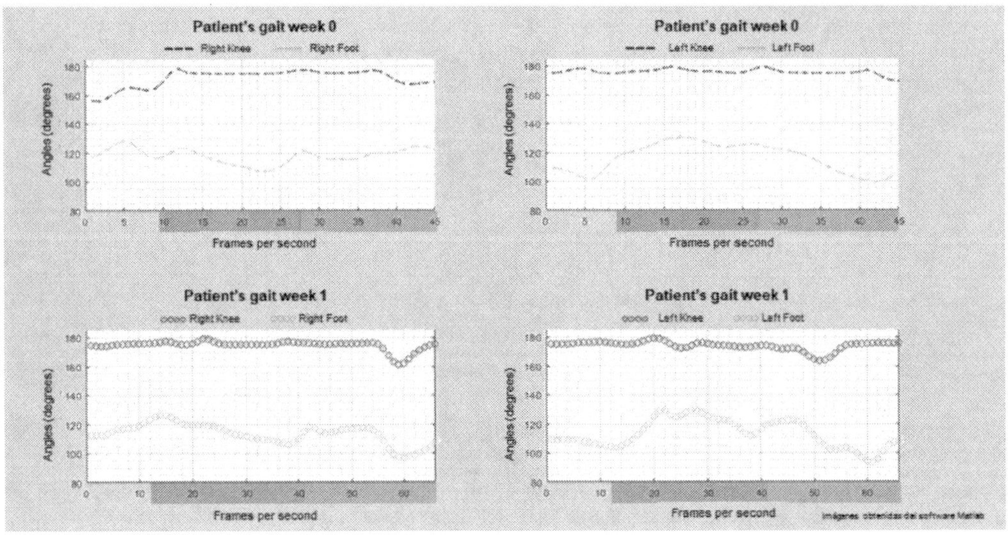

Fig. 10. Comparison patient's gait week 0 and week 1 on Matlab.

Because our methodology was extensive, we were just able to evaluate two weeks after the patient started using the orthopedic insoles. That's why for the last step of our analysis we decided to compare our control gait with the patient's gait week 2 (Fig. 11). In both gaits we observe a flexion angle of the right knee at the beginning of the gait which is a positive result. Similarly, there is an angle of flexion in the right knee at the moment that the swing phase begins, both in the control gait and in the patient's gait. Also, we observe an angle of flexion in the left knee during the stance phase in both gaits. All these results were obtained from the motion analysis system and based on these results we could conclude that the orthopedic insoles were showing positive changes in the patient's gait.

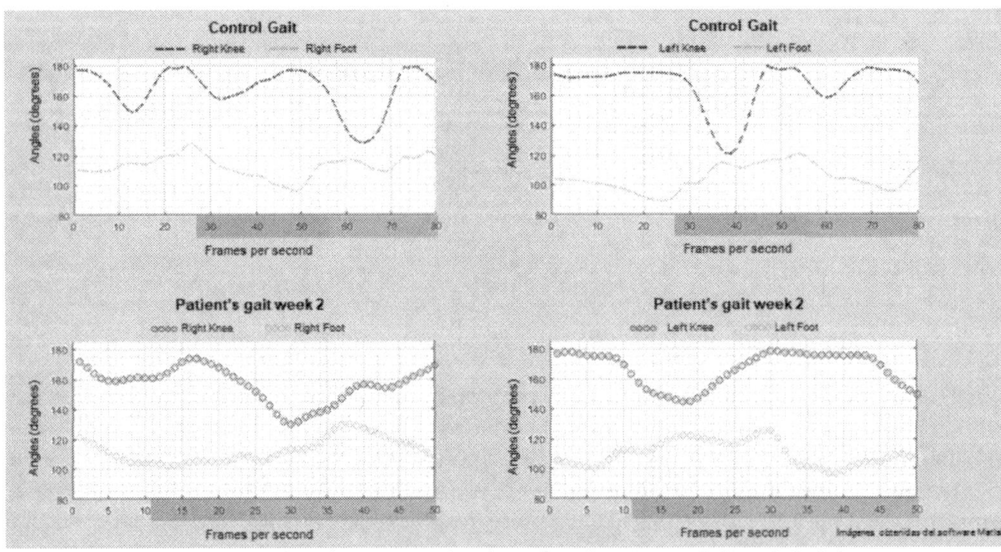

Fig. 11. Comparison control gait and patient's week 2 on Matlab.

4. Conclusion

The expectations of the project developed in its essential parts were met: the 3D design of the assistive technology and the development of the methodology for the motion analysis system. For the assistive technologies, adjustments should be considered in the future since both functional and structural changes will occur and therefore insoles will need modifications to adapt correctly to the new needs of the patient's foot. The development of the methodology for the analysis of movement in this case was used to acquire the angles of the joints of the lower limbs. However, the developed methodology can be used to acquire angles of any joint of the human body and to validate different assistive technologies apart from those designed in this project.

5. References

[1] Instituto Nacional de Estadística y Geografía (México). La discapacidad en México, datos al 2014. Obtenido el 1 de Noviembre, 2019 de http://coespo.qroo.gob.mx/Descargas/doc/DISCAPACITADOS/ENADID 2014.pdf
[2] Assistive Technology Industry Association. (n.d.). What is AT? Retrieved April 1, 2020, from https://www.atia.org/at-resources/what-is-at/
[3] Organización Mundial de la Salud. (2018, Mayo 18). Tecnología de asistencia. Obtenido el 15 de Julio, 2019 de https://www.who.int/es/news-room/fact-sheets/detail/assistive-technology
[4]3D Collective. (2018, April 17). Guia de Fotogrametría. Retrieved from https://3dcollective.es/fotogrametria/
[5]Agisoft. (2019). Agisoft Metashape User Manual . Retrieved from https://www.agisoft.com/pdf/metashape-pro_1_5_en.pdf
[6]All 3DP. (2020, March 11). 2020 3D Printer Filament Buyer's Guide. Retrieved April 1, 2020, from https://all3dp.com/1/3d-printer-filament-types-3d-printing-3d-filament/
[7]Osorio, J. H., & Valencia, M. H. (2013, Mayo 7). *Bases para el entendimiento del proceso de la marcha humana*[PDF]. Caldas, Colombia.
[8] Acosta, P. (n.d.). Biomecánica de la marcha . Retrieved from https://fisiointegracion.files.wordpress.com/2010/05/biomecanica-marcha.pdf
[9] Sumba , C., Cuenca, M. del C., & Delgado , K. M. (2013). Diseño e implementación de un sistema para el análisis de movimiento humano usando sensores Kinect, 1–102.
[10] L. L. Gómez Echeverry, A. M. Jaramillo Henao, M. A. Ruiz Molina, S. M. Velásquez Restrepo, C. A. Páramo Velásquez, G. J. Silva Bolívar, "Human motion capture and analysis systems: a systematic review", Prospectiva, Vol 16, N° 2, 24-34, 2018.
[11] Shen, A.W., & Ting, T. (2014). Marker-less motion capture for biomechanical analysis using the Kinect sensor.

AUTHOR INDEX

EDP Sciences – Web of Conferences
17, Avenue du Hoggar
Parc d'Activité de Courtabouf
BP 112
F-91944 Les Ulis Cedex A
France

ISBN 978-1-7138-1067-4

CURRAN ASSOCIATES INC.
proceedings.com